TEACHER EDUCATION YEARBOOK XXVI
Building upon Inspirations and Aspirations with Hope, Courage, and Strength

TEACHER EDUCATION YEARBOOK XXVI
Building upon Inspirations and Aspirations with Hope, Courage, and Strength

Teacher Educators' Commitment to Today's Teachers and Tomorrow's Leaders

Volume 2: Tomorrow's Leaders in Classrooms and Schools

Edited by
Nancy P. Gallavan and LeAnn G. Putney

ROWMAN & LITTLEFIELD
Lanham • Boulder • New York • London

Published by Rowman & Littlefield
An imprint of The Rowman & Littlefield Publishing Group, Inc.
4501 Forbes Boulevard, Suite 200, Lanham, Maryland 20706
www.rowman.com

6 Tinworth Street, London SE11 5AL, United Kingdom

Copyright © 2019 by Association of Teacher Educators

All rights reserved. No part of this book may be reproduced in any form or by any electronic or mechanical means, including information storage and retrieval systems, without written permission from the publisher, except by a reviewer who may quote passages in a review.

British Library Cataloguing in Publication Information Available

Library of Congress Cataloging-in-Publication Data

ISBN: 978-1-4758-4831-1 (pbk. : alk. paper)
ISBN: 978-1-4758-4832-8 (electronic)

∞™ The paper used in this publication meets the minimum requirements of American National Standard for Information Sciences—Permanence of Paper for Printed Library Materials, ANSI/NISO Z39.48-1992.

Printed in the United States of America

Contents

Foreword to ATE Yearbook XXVI ix
Karen Embry-Jenlink

Introduction xiii
LeAnn G. Putney and Nancy P. Gallavan

SECTION I: INVESTIGATING FACTORS OF HOPE, STRENGTH, AND COURAGE THAT IMPACT THE INSPIRATIONS AND ASPIRATIONS OF TEACHERS AND TEACHING 1

INTRODUCTION 3

1 College Students' Perceptions of the Characteristics of Effective Teachers in Higher Education: The Students' Voices 7
 Leona M. Johnson

2 What Teacher Candidates Believe about Teaching and Learning 25
 Nancy Caukin

3 Reinforcing MAT Course Goals during Internship Experiences via Gallavan's Seven Essential Elements 43
 Nancy P. Gallavan and Jennifer P. Merritt

4 Collaboration: A Skill that Must Be Explicitly Taught 63
 Heather K. Dillard

5 Field Experiences with Children of Trauma: Supporting Emotionally and Psychologically Injured Children (EPICs): Value Beyond Institutional Measure 81
 Jayne M. Leh

6	Inspiring Teachers across the Professional Continuum through Collaborative Coaching and Lesson Study *Jennifer M. Suh and Kim Dockery*	99
7	Strengthening Culturally Responsive Teaching through Existing Professional Development School Partnerships *Emily Reeves, Angela Malone Cartwright, and Daphney L. Curry*	119
8	Teacher Candidates' Courage in Developing Cultural Capacity through an Indigenous Cocurricular Community Service-Learning Program *Glenda L. Black and Mair Greenfield*	135

EXTENSION QUESTIONS FOR REFLECTION AND CONVERSATION — 157

SECTION II: EXAMINING FACTORS OF HOPE, STRENGTH, AND COURAGE THAT IMPACT THE INSPIRATIONS AND ASPIRATIONS FOR LEADERS AND LEADING — 161

INTRODUCTION — 163

9	Preparing the Leaders/Teachers of Tomorrow by Improving the Well-Being of Teachers Today *Denise Demers*	167
10	"I Need Collaboration Too!": Exploring the Nature of Collaboration between a Literacy Coach and University Teacher Collaborator *Grace Kang*	185
11	Charter School Special Educators: Expressions of Hope, Courage, and Strength *Sarah Irvine Belson*	203
12	Preparing Elementary School Mathematics Specialists: Aspirations for a University Endorsement Program *Susan Swars Auslander, Stephanie Z. Smith, and Marvin E. Smith*	223
13	Fighting for Hope and Inspiration: Developing Reflective Spaces for Leaders in Elementary School Mathematics *Ryan Flessner, Courtney Flessner, Katherine Reed, and Susan Adamson*	241

14	The Impact of Privatized Funding in Education and a Proposal for Reform *Todd Cherner and Catherine M. Scott*	257
15	Urban Teacher Collective Efficacy through Facilitative Leadership: An Illustrative Dialogue *Shelley Nordick, Suzanne H. Jones, LeAnn G. Putney, and Connie L. Malin*	277
16	Are You a Hope Buster or a Hope Muster? *Angela Webster*	299

EXTENSION QUESTIONS FOR REFLECTION AND CONVERSATION — **315**

Afterword — 319

References — 323

About the Contributors — 325

Foreword to ATE Yearbook XXVI

REIMAGINING EDUCATOR PREPARATION WITHIN A DEMOCRACY

Since the first ATE Yearbook was published in 1924, ATE Yearbooks have served as repositories of scholarly inquiry and discourse focused on issues in teacher education significant to ATE members (Patterson, McGeoch, & Olsen, 1990). As repositories, Yearbooks reflect contemporary issues specific to the time period during which they were published. Nearly a century later, evolving from a collection of conference papers, the ATE Yearbook XXVI is premised upon a "triadic definition of scholarship: the production of knowledge, the interpretation and synthesis of knowledge, and the application of knowledge" (ATE, 2014).

As ATE president 2017–2018, it is my pleasure to introduce the ATE Yearbook XXVI, *Building upon inspirations and aspirations with hope, courage, and strength: Teacher educators' commitment to today's teachers and tomorrow's leaders*, which resonates closely with the theme of the 2018 ATE annual meeting, "Reimagining educator preparation within a democracy: Teacher educators as public intellectuals." Today, now more than ever, teacher educators are confronted with increasing challenges of accountability and accreditation imposed by unrealistic federal mandates. These mandates support the increased corporatization of education and offer educator preparation as a commodity to generate revenue for other entities (Cochran-Smith, 2017). This neoliberal ideology is undemocratic; it does not promote educator preparation, policy, and practice for the common good (Embry-Jenlink, 2017).

To reclaim and restore the democratic ideal for education, Dewey (1916) stated in *Democracy and Education* that ". . . the conception of education as a social process and function has no definite meaning until we define the kind of society we have in mind" (p. 97). In other words, Dewey posited that we, as teacher educators, must first conceive of the society we want before we can design the educational system that we need. To restore the democratic ideal in education, first we must engage in a social reimagining of what it means to live and work together in a democratic society. Then we must rearticulate the relationship of educator preparation to the function of education within a democracy. To reimagine educator preparation within a democracy, we must be willing to accept the mantle of social, political, and moral responsibility to all of us who are involved on the front lines of teacher preparation, including teacher education faculty in colleges, universities, and P-16 classroom educators at clinical field sites.

Acting as public intellectuals, we must go beyond focusing exclusively on accreditation-focused accountability frameworks to design new and alternative pedagogies for preparing the next generation of educators for democracy. Our programs must be *reimagined* as systems of educator preparation that will prepare and support teachers who will be successful in preparing their future students for the realities of living and working within a democracy. Our teacher candidates must not only be fully equipped with the skills to engage in civil discourse, they must be prepared to serve as agents of a democracy in preparing their students for civic engagement and democratic cooperation among diverse populations in a global society.

Yearbook XXVI is an inspiring collection of research chapters and narrative stories, which highlight the aspirations, dreams, and motivations of teacher educators who are committed to quality educator preparation and professional development for teachers and educational leaders. Their collective inquiry questions political agendas and practices, many of which inhibit democratic educator preparation. The authors showcase innovation in research through collaborative spaces of community-based inquiry among communities of practice. Their research reports speak to the aspirations of teacher educators who seek to transform educator preparation in ways to meet the needs of a changing society. The authors further demonstrate creative and forward-thinking strategies which focus on hope, strength, and courage as the means to evolve educator preparation programs in ways that promote practices that are responsive, inclusive, and foster teacher voice and resilience.

The publication of Yearbooks XXV and XXVI are two volumes with research related to the same theme focused on hope, strength, and courage. These two interconnected volumes of research also are the first ATE Yearbooks issued solely in digital format as an e-book. E-books are a sign of a change of the times toward disseminating knowledge through digital media that can be archived and accessed instantly and anywhere through the Internet. As e-books, ATE Yearbooks XXV and XXVI offer a synthesis and interpretation of knowledge that is highly accessible and global.

Building upon inspirations and aspirations with hope, courage, and strength: Teacher Educators' Commitment to Today's Teachers and Tomorrow's Leaders will provide motivation and goals—both the will and the ways—for teacher educators who, acting as public intellectuals, seek to inform P-20 educational practice and policy-making through public discourse, scholarly inquiry, and participatory action in educational settings. This collective body of research provides encouraging lessons for restoring the democratic ideal in education by continually questioning and evolving educator preparation in a democracy to address the needs of an ever-changing and global society.

Karen Embry-Jenlink
Stephen F. Austin State University
ATE President (2017–2018)

Introduction
LeAnn G. Putney and Nancy P. Gallavan

The Association of Teacher Educators' (ATE) Teacher Education Yearbook XXVI is a second volume dedicated to building upon inspirations and aspirations with hope, courage, and strength relative to teacher educators' commitment to today's teachers and tomorrow's leaders. While the first volume, Yearbook XXV, presented chapters focused on teacher candidates and educator preparation programs, this second volume is focused on educational leadership in classrooms and schools. These chapters take us beyond the university classroom that involves preparing teacher and administrator candidates and moves us into seeing preK-12 classrooms and schools taking educational theory into practice.

With this two-volume series, our intention was to examine the constructs of hope, courage, and strength as three valuable attributes that accompany educators' commitment to building upon inspirations and aspirations. We recognized that hope signifies expectations and desires for particular outcomes to occur. Several of our chapters examine the construct of hope, not only as expectation and desire but also as a course of action for teachers to take to assist their students in achieving course outcomes. With the attribute of courage, our classroom and school leaders are able to face educational situations boldly; with strength, they can progress through those situations and maintain balance while also moving their students forward in academic and personal goal attainment.

With this second volume, we proceed to examine what works in educational settings through positive and transformative leadership on the part of teachers, support staff, students, and administrators. We adhere to the assertion from Hoy and Tarter (2011) that

> educational research can play a much more important role in improving schools if we begin to study what is good about schools, what works, and what is attractive . . . to document what kind of schools produce students who flourish, what

work settings support the greatest satisfaction among administrators and teachers, what educational policies result in the strongest civic engagement, and how teachers' and students' lives can be most fulfilling. (p. 429)

This volume illustrates how today's education professionals must draw upon their goals, exercising persistence and exerting resilience to respond to the ongoing onslaught of school improvement, curriculum standards, and increased attention to standardized testing. Most educators in preK-12 classrooms and schools as well as educators and administrators in university teacher preparation programs are excited to be educators, engaged in their work, and eager to advance their effectiveness as a lifelong career dedicated to teaching, learning, and schooling. Both persistence (endurance) and resilience (elasticity) equip and empower educators of all ages and stages to face each new day's challenges and facilitate possible changes.

The traditional definition of persistence indicates that an individual "carries on" and determinedly continues an action in spite of opposition. In classrooms and schools, persistence is evident (Johnson & Birkeland, 2003; Ladd, 2011; Leech & Haug, 2015; Wheatley, 2002) and the disposition of *planned persistence* (Shirrell & Reininger, 2017) contributes greatly to both the educator's perceptions of and realities associated with the school working conditions, that is, school philosophies and practices promoting collegial collaboration, decision-making, and professional support.

Likewise, the more traditional definition of resilience would suggest that one is able to "bounce back" to the original shape after confronting adversity of some sort. A newer examination of resilience has produced the concept of *dynamic resilience* that appears to apply suitably to classrooms and schools as evidenced by the chapters in this volume. Dynamic resilience (Hoy & Tarter, 2011; Sutcliffe & Vogus, 2003) refers to the ability of continuously developing strategies that promote coping with adversity, or in this case, the next wave of educational reforms.

As we consider in this volume our educational practice at the classroom and school-wide levels, the authors of these chapters examine how teachers, staff, and administrators can continually gauge their educational contexts in order to adequately assess performance of themselves and the students they encounter. As Hoy and Tarter (2011) further suggest, "Just as resilience plays an important part in student learning, it is also a key at the organizational level to confront difficulties in a positive way" (p. 439). Their call for using a positive perspective brings together the best of what scholars have been examining in terms of building teacher efficacy (Tschannen-Moran, Woolfolk-Hoy, & Hoy, 1998), school-wide collective efficacy (Goddard, Hoy & Woolfolk-Hoy, 2004), collective classroom efficacy (Putney & Broughton, 2011), as well as building trust among teachers, students, and family members as a means of improving our academic accountability and culture (Forsyth, Adams, & Hoy, 2011; Goddard, Tschannen-Moran, & Hoy, 2001; Smith, Hoy, & Sweetland, 2001).

As you will come to realize, the sixteen chapters in this volume, ATE Yearbook XXVI, relay the research findings and/or theoretical perspectives from thirty authors who provided us with their sense of educational trust, efficacy, and accountability through development of hope, courage, and strength manifested through resilience and persistence in their educational contexts. The sixteen chapters are divided into two sections. Section I includes eight chapters related to Inspirations and Aspirations for Teachers and Teaching. This section delves into a range of topics from beliefs about effective teaching at both the K-12 and university levels, to teacher intern and supervisor efficacy, teaching collaboration, supporting children who have experienced trauma, to culturally responsive teaching and engaging in building cultural capital through service-learning projects. Taken together these topics shine a light on effective teachers and teaching that bolsters collaboration and efficacy among educational participants.

Section II provides eight chapters related to Inspirations and Aspirations for Leaders and Leading. The authors of the chapters in this section describe various features in relation to leadership attributes of administrators, teachers, and support staff in various configurations in their educational settings. These constructs range from improving the well-being of teachers, to improving collaboration between university and K-12 school literacy coaches, and improving reflection among math elementary teachers and specialists. The topics also include funding reform efforts and also schools, charter schools for special needs students, as well as teachers becoming hope musters and a principal's role in engaging teachers, noninstructional licensed faculty, and support staff in a Professional Learning Community (PLC) to improve teacher and student efficacy.

We welcome you to experience these authors' journeys into educational trust, efficacy, and accountability through development of hope, resilience, and persistence. This movement toward a positive examination of schools is in line with the way that Seligman and Csikszentmihalyi (2000) describe positive psychology as a way of studying education. They note that this positive view of schools "explains valued subjective experience: well-being, contentment, and satisfaction in the past; flow and happiness in the present; hope and optimism for the future" (p. 5). ATE Yearbook XXVI affords you the opportunity to travel with us on this journey of reframing education in a positive light to ensure hope and optimism in our own educational spaces.

Section I

INVESTIGATING FACTORS OF HOPE, STRENGTH, AND COURAGE THAT IMPACT THE INSPIRATIONS AND ASPIRATIONS OF TEACHERS AND TEACHING

Introduction

Nancy P. Gallavan and LeAnn G. Putney

The eight chapters selected for Section I address a multitude of issues related to the presence and power of hope, strength, and courage and their impact on the inspirations and aspirations of teachers and their teaching. Frequently, teacher candidates have been dreaming about becoming classroom teachers for many years since their lives intersected with a caring and competent teacher and/or coach. As future teacher candidates, preK-12th grade and university students began examining the world through the lens of being an effective teacher, growing increasingly motivated to know their content, to make their classrooms inviting and exciting, and to reach every student. Teacher educators build upon their candidates' dreams to establish the disposition of persistence in collaborating positively and productively with their students, students' families, their colleagues, and their administrators. Moreover, teacher educators promote the concepts, skills, and dispositions of operating as a team with benefits to critical thinking, decision-making, and problem solving.

Through these processes, teacher candidates and classroom teachers gain insights into their efficacy and agency, frequently initiating lifelong careers of commitment and transformation that guide and support their professional development. By inspiring a sense of persistence or endurance in their teacher candidates and classroom teachers, teacher educators also are aspiring to instill a sense of resilience or elasticity to remain objective, maintain composure, seek help, weigh possibilities, make decisions, accept outcomes, and acknowledge change. Change is neither quick nor easy, yet often change results in positive and productive transformation. Mezirow writes that transformation in the context of adult learning constitutes "a dramatic fundamental change in the way we see ourselves and the world in which we live" (1994, p. 318). The eight chapters in Section I contribute to understanding and facilitating transformation in teacher candidates, classroom teachers, and teacher educators.

This book opens with chapter 1, written by Leona M. Johnson from Hampton University, titled "College Students' Perceptions of the Characteristics of Effective Teachers in Higher Education: The Students' Voice." The author delves into university students' perceptions of the characteristics of effective and ineffective teachers in face-to-face instruction. Participants in this study prioritized identified passion, organization, respect, patience, adaptability, creativity, and humor as the characteristics of effective teachers. Conversely, participants in this study identified actions and attitudes associated with being condescending, discouraging, boring, close-minded, and un-relatable as primary characteristics of ineffective teachers. As teacher candidates interact with their teachers in higher education, they experience various models of effective and ineffective teaching that influence their own preparation, practices, and professionalism.

Chapter 2, titled "What Teacher Candidates Believe about Teaching and Learning," authored by Nancy Caukin from Middle Tennessee State University provides an extensive list of teacher candidates' belief statements categorized into meaningful themes to guide and support teacher educators in their university courses and field experiences. Generating a total of 365 statements, identified themes in descending order of frequency included teacher-centered beliefs, student-centered beliefs, instruction-centered beliefs, classroom-centered beliefs, learning-centered beliefs, and content-centered beliefs. However, the author noted that no belief statements relating to social and emotional learning as well as multicultural education were reported by teacher candidates demonstrating the need for continued persistence and resilience for teacher educators.

"Reinforcing MAT Course Goals during Internship Experiences via Gallavan's Seven Essential Elements," is the title of chapter 3 co-authored by Nancy P. Gallavan and Jennifer P. Merritt from the University of Central Arkansas. This chapter describes seven expectations of interns aligned with the teacher evaluation form adopted by the state department of education and the goals of the classroom assessment course (taught by one of the coauthors) and the interactions with interns stemming from observations and discussions. From their research, the coauthors identify the roles of readiness, receptiveness, and responsiveness in ways that benefit both interns and supervisors to enhance efficacy and advance agency as part of interns' transformative learning.

Heather K. Dillard from Middle Tennessee State University is the author of chapter 4, titled "Collaboration: A Skill That Must Be Explicitly Taught." A timely and worthwhile topic, the author of this chapter considers the critical components of collaboration and communication through a qualitative study conducted with two middle level teacher candidates. The case study emphasized the candidates' real-life context and in-depth understanding from two years' of data. The results of this study show the benefits of professional learning communities and the development of norms on the candidates' focus on learning, collaboration, and results.

Chapter 5, titled "Field Experiences with Children of Trauma: Supporting Emotional and Psychologically Injured Children (EPICS)—Value beyond Institutional Measure," authored by Jayne M. Leh from The Pennsylvania State University Berks campus offers insights to a credit-free service-learning experience with undergraduate teacher candidates following a community disaster. Using field notes and surveys, the researcher dedicated three years to collecting data, the results show that service learning that is rigorous and reflective to promote candidates' comfort, confidence, competence, and commitment related to both personal growth and professional development.

"Inspiring Teachers across the Professional Continuum through Collaborative Coaching and Lesson Study," coauthored by Jennifer M. Suh from George Mason University and Kim Dockery, an educational consultant, demonstrates in chapter 6 that all teachers (i.e., teacher candidates, classroom teachers, mathematics coaches, and resource specialists) are strengthened and inspired by one another. Research conducted at a Professional Development School (PDS) during a Teacher Leader Institute and Lesson Study served as the catalyst for the construction of collaborative coaching.

Chapter 7, titled "Strengthening Culturally Responsive Teaching through Existing Professional Development School Partnerships," is coauthored by Emily Reeves, Angela Malone Cartwright, and Daphne L. Curry from Midwestern State University. This chapter examines the need for teacher candidates to experience transformational learning associated with cultural privilege prior to beginning their work with students in classrooms and schools. From their research the authors found that preparing culturally responsive teachers and teaching includes guided purposeful reflections, structured mentor interviews, and intentional instruction with small groups of students to encounter multiple perspectives throughout a semester.

Section I closes with chapter 8, coauthored by Glenda L. Black from Nipissing University, and Mair Greenfield, from the Rumie Institute. Their chapter, "Teacher Candidates' Courage in Developing Cultural Capacity through an Indigenous Cocurricular Community Service-Learning Program," advances the conversation focused on service learning, particularly related to building relationships and enhancing benefits for community youth and enhanced partnerships.

Chapter 1

College Students' Perceptions of the Characteristics of Effective Teachers in Higher Education

The Students' Voices

Leona M. Johnson

ABSTRACT

This study explored students' perceptions of the characteristics of effective and ineffective teachers in face-to-face classroom instruction. It also investigated the interpersonal attributes relative to characteristics that teachers share professionally. The goal of this study was to define effective and ineffective teaching in the classroom and to better understand what effective teacher characteristics look like in the classroom from the students' perspective. This mixed methods study employed multiple focus groups and a follow-on survey with African American undergraduate college students at a Historically Black University in the Mid-Atlantic region of the United States. One of the common threads in the research on teacher characteristics was that the knowledge of the teacher was important in the classroom. Caring and respect for students was another common thread which is in line with the literature on the importance of a caring teacher. The characteristics of ineffective teachers were also identified and defined. Findings from this study have pedagogical implications for teachers', administrators', and college students' perceptions.

KEY WORDS

Effective Teachers in Higher Education; Teacher Knowledge; Teacher Care

ACKNOWLEDGMENTS

I wish to acknowledge the student research assistants who led the focus groups: Janae Gamble, Kristina Horton, Justin Preddie, Marques Rhodeman, Mariah Robinson, and Mykea Young.

This study explored university students' perceptions of the characteristics of effective and ineffective teachers in face-to-face classroom instruction. It also investigated the interpersonal attributes relative to characteristics that teachers share professionally. The purpose of this study was to explore students' perceptions of the characteristics of effective teachers relative to face-to-face instruction. A secondary purpose of the study was to ascertain the interpersonal attributes of effective teachers and better understand what effective teaching looks like in face-to-face classroom instruction. The study also sought to better understand the characteristics and impact of ineffective teachers.

BACKGROUND OF THE STUDY

The idea of asking students to provide feedback on the quality of teaching that they encounter during their academic career is not new. Teaching is being seen as increasingly more important to the research goals of higher education. However, interest is growing in assessing students' perceptions of instruction in higher education (Delaney, Johnson, Johnson, & Tresian, 2010). Institutions of higher learning across the nation are responding to political, economic, social, and technological pressures to be more responsive to students' needs and are becoming increasingly more concerned about how well students are prepared to assume societal roles (George Mason University Article, n.d).

LITERATURE REVIEW

Effective Teaching

While effective teachers work hard to create a challenging and nurturing environment for their students, effective teaching seems to have less to do with knowledge and skills than with their attitude toward students, subject, and the work (Orlando, 2013). Stronge (2007) classified teachers as being effective by both their backgrounds and their personalities. Background wise, effective teachers were determined by their verbal ability, educational coursework, teacher certification, content of knowledge, and teaching experience.

Relative to personality, teachers were considered effective if they cared about their students, were fair and respectful, interacted with students socially, promoted enthusiasm, and motivated learning. Additional aspects were related to their attitudes toward teaching, and their use of the role of reflective practice. As teachers we need to be responsive to the needs and feelings of our students. The relationship of teacher and student giving and receiving care is a continuous one (Thompson, Greer, & Greer, 2004). Noddings (2001) connected caring in teachers to those teachers who are prepared and organized, and posits that caring is instrumental in the actions of teachers that students remember best.

In a more current study, Delaney et al. (2010) confirmed that instructors who are effective teachers are respectful of students, knowledgeable, approachable, engaging, communicative, organized, responsive, professional, and humorous. Tang, Chou, and Chiang (2005) suggested that teachers' attitudes toward students, rather than their professional abilities, is the crucial difference between ineffective and effective teachers. Improving the student-teacher relationship is important, and has both positive and long-lasting implications for students' academic and social development. On one hand, solely improving students' relationships with their teachers will not produce gains in achievement. On the other hand, those students who have close, positive, and supportive relationships with their teachers will attain higher levels of achievement than those students with more conflict in their relationships (Rimm-Kaufman & Sandilos, 2016).

The Top Two Attributes

Detick (2011) identified the top two attributes (out of thirty-five) of teaching behaviors as enthusiasm and respect for the students. Additionally, the Memorial University of Newfoundland (2008) study (as cited in Delaney, Johnson, Johnson, & Tresian, 2010) confirmed that being respectful of students and being knowledgeable were the top two characteristics that were essential for effective teaching from the student's perspective. Feldman (1976) found that characteristics such as stimulation of interest, clarity, and understandableness; knowledge of subject matter; preparation for and organization of the course; and enthusiasm for the subject matter and for teaching were consistently associated with superior college teachers or teachers (as determined in a variety of ways).

The Top Five Characteristics

Allan, Clark, and Jopling (2009) confirmed that the top five statements describing effective teachers the most positively were: having excellent knowledge of the subject, including group activities, encouraging discussion, being approachable, and starting sessions on time, while the Stevens and Adams (1981) study found that the top five traits of effective teachers were: making tests related to course materials, having clear expectations, producing fair tests, the instructor was well prepared, and the professor emphasized understanding the concepts.

Out of twelve characteristics, the Colker (2008) study noted passion, perseverance, willingness to take risks, pragmatism, and patience as the top five features of an effective teacher. Passion means having a strong drive; perseverance was described as the willingness to fight for one's beliefs; taking risks means "not settling for a 'no' answer when 'yes' will improve the quality of a child's education." Pragmatism was described as "understanding that temporarily settling for small wins would eventually lead to goals being accomplished"; patience was defined as knowing that every student learns at a different pace.

Thompson et al. (2004) noted that the top five characteristics of an effective teacher (out of twelve) were fairness, positive attitude, preparedness, personal touch, and sense of humor. Kunjufu (2002) verifies that the main characteristics of an effective teacher are enthusiasm, speaking clearly, understandably, and calmly, listening to students and apologizing when in error, never intimidating or embarrassing students, and using student questions as a course of discovering confusion.

Walls, Nardi, Von Minden, and Hoffman (2002) offered five major categories in which the effectiveness of a teacher could be determined: emotional environment, teacher skills, teacher motivation, student participation, and rules and grades. Under the category of emotional environment, teachers were deemed effective if they were warm, friendly, and caring. In the category of teacher skills, teachers were seen as effective if they were organized, prepared, and clear. Under teacher motivation, effective teachers were described as caring about learning and teaching. In the category of student participation, effective teachers were those who incorporated activities that engaged the students in "authentic learning, interactive learning, and discussion." Lastly, under rules and grades, teachers were effective if they had little difficulty managing their classroom and their care about student accomplishment set the tone for fair rules and grading.

In summary, the most offered characteristics included caring, respect for students, and the knowledge of the teacher. One of the common threads in the research on teacher characteristics was that the knowledge of the teacher was important in the classroom. Caring and respect for students was another common thread that is in line with the literature on the importance of a caring teacher.

RESEARCH HYPOTHESES AND RESEARCH QUESTIONS

1. What are the characteristics of "effective" teachers from the students' perspective in face-to-face instruction, including interpersonal attributes?
2. What are the characteristics of "ineffective" teachers from the students' perspective in face-to-face classroom instruction, including interpersonal attributes?
3. What characteristics can be effectively fostered in the classroom from the students' perspective in face-to-face classroom instruction?
4. How do effective and ineffective teachers impact the educational experience of students?

METHOD

The study used a mixed method approach. The first study employed three focus groups with undergraduate college students at a Historically Black University in the Mid-Atlantic region of the United States to obtain qualitative data. The follow-on study sought to prioritize the top five characteristics using quantitative data. Information from the focus groups afforded the researcher the opportunity to explore the characteristics from a group dynamics perspective while information from the follow-on study provided the researcher more conclusive information on teacher characteristics.

Participants from the focus groups were recruited using a flyer which was circulated on campus. The groups were audiotaped in order to record the participants' responses. The research assistants took notes as well on the questions that were asked. The questions were discussed in groups.

The students discussed perceptions of the characteristics of effective and ineffective teachers, the impact of effective and ineffective teachers on the overall educational experience of students, and how effective teacher characteristics could be fostered in a classroom setting. Demographic information was collected from the students prior to the initiation of the meeting including race, gender, major, grade point average, and classification.

The participants were asked a series of questions that caused them to think critically about what they believed to be the five important characteristics of both an effective and ineffective teacher. The first question asked participants to think of five characteristics that they felt defined an effective teacher. Next, the participants were asked to explain how these characteristics could be fostered in the classroom. After explaining how they would like to see these characteristics fostered in the classroom the participants were asked how this

Table 1.1 Focus Group Demographics

Focus Group	# of Participants	Gender	Classification
#1	4	female=3 male=1	sophomore=1 junior=3
#2	8	female=5 male=3	varied
#3	6	female=5 male=1	first year=2 sophomore=2 junior=2
#4	18	female=13 male=5	varied

would better their educational experience. Our next question asked the students to provide a list of characteristics that would make a teacher ineffective. Finally students were asked how ineffective teachers affected their overall learning experience (table 1.1).

TABLE 1 THE SURVEY OF THE CHARACTERISTICS OF EFFECTIVE TEACHERS FROM THE STUDENTS' PERSPECTIVE IN HIGHER EDUCATION: THE STUDENTS' VOICE

Instructions:

This questionnaire is designed to collect your perceptions about teaching in higher education. All responses will be treated anonymously. The questionnaire will take you less than 5 minutes.

Demographics.

1. Please circle the correct choice. Male or Female

2. Ethnicity: African American _____ Latino American _____ Asian American _____ Other Ethnicity _____(Please write in your ethnicity)

3. Classification: Please check the appropriate classification.

    Freshman _____ Sophomore _____ Junior _____ Senior _____

4. What is your Major? _____

5. Please circle your current GPA: 4.00–3.50 _____ 3.49–3.00_____ 2.99 and below _____

Part Two: Please respond to the following questions.
I. What do you feel are the characteristics of an "effective" teacher? Please prioritize them from one to five, with one being the top priority.
  1. _____
  2. _____
  3. _____
  4. _____
  5. _____
II. Please discuss how you would like to see "any one" of the above "effective" teacher characteristics fostered in the classroom. Please provide at least one example.
III. In general, what do you feel are the characteristics of *"ineffective"* teachers?
IV. What impact do the characteristics of *"effective"* teachers have on your educational experience in the classroom?
V. In general, what do you perceive are the characteristics of *"ineffective"* teachers? Please briefly explain your definition of each characteristic.
VI. What impact do the characteristics of *"ineffective"* teachers" have on your educational experience in the classroom?

Follow-On Study Fall 2015 Semester

A follow-on study was held with thirty-one undergraduate students in a psychology course to ascertain student perceptions of the characteristics of effective and ineffective teachers, the impact of effective and ineffective teachers on the overall educational experience of students and how effective teacher characteristics could be fostered in a classroom setting. Demographic information was also collected from the students including race, gender, major, grade point average, and classification.

RESULTS

Qualitative Analysis-Focus Groups

A qualitative analysis confirmed that some of the most important characteristics of effective teachers include having passion and knowledge of the subject matter, having confidence, being organized, and understanding, displaying enthusiasm, being encouraging and creative, and having respect for students. The use of technology and examples that students can relate to, hands-on learning to engage the student, classroom control and structure, the use of various vehicles—for example, videos, field trips, and so on to augment PowerPoint presentations—and learning styles were additional considerations to foster effective teaching. Students identified various characteristics of ineffective teachers that can impact their educational experience. One of the focus groups concluded that "whether teachers know it or not-they can greatly impact a student's self-esteem and self-worth."

Focus Group #1

This qualitative research included a sample of four African American students. Three students were female and one was male. Three students were juniors and one student was a sophomore. The GPA of the students varied. Various majors were represented including psychology.

Effective Teachers

The participants were asked a series of questions that caused them to think critically about what they believed to be five important characteristics of both an effective and ineffective teacher. After listing a number of potential characteristics, the list of characteristics was condensed to being passionate, encouraging, creative, relatable, and patient in that order. They defined passion as having a love for teaching and the subject matter. Encouragement was defined as being able to help students succeed and being enthusiastic about getting students to perform well. Being relatable was described as being able to communicate with teachers about professional and personal endeavors. "Being relatable makes teachers easier to talk to." Finally, patience was described as working with students when they did not understand the material.

Next, the participants were asked to explain how these characteristics could be fostered in the classroom. The playful suggestion was made "to get new teachers," however, the students seriously suggested getting better equipments like whiteboards or smart boards that help enhance interaction. More videos instead of just plain PowerPoint presentations were also suggested as ways to help the teacher be more effective. The idea that African American students learn better through movement and visual modalities also was mentioned by participants, who suggested that teachers "should try to find some way to incorporate movement and visual modalities into their daily lesson plans."

After explaining how they would like to see these characteristics fostered in the classroom the participants were asked how this would better their educational experience. All of the participants agreed that their grades would improve and they would attend class more often. The participants also stated that it would make students want to engage more with their teacher and the class. The students' expectations of themselves would also rise because they would not want to disappoint their teacher by receiving unsatisfactory grades in the class.

Ineffective Teachers

Our next question asked the students to provide a list of characteristics that would make a teacher ineffective. They came up with a list of fifteen characteristics. Of the fifteen characteristics, the following top five choices were selected: being condescending, discouraging, boring, close-minded, and un-relatable. Condescending was described as talking down to the students, and teachers who do not like to be questioned about the material that they are teaching. The participants said that a discouraging teacher was one who has little to no faith in the ability of the student, and teachers who encourage students to withdraw from a class instead of offering ways to help the student improve. A boring teacher has no enthusiasm when teaching, and the class consists of constant note taking. A close-minded teacher is one who is not open to suggestions in relation to their teaching styles, and the class strictly follows the rubric. Finally an un-relatable teacher is a teacher whose topics discussed in class do not match the course material. The participants stated that when they have an un-relatable teacher they have a hard time relating the course material to real-life experiences. They also described un-relatable teachers as one who is unapproachable outside of the classroom.

Finally we asked the students how ineffective teachers affect their educational experience. The participants agreed that when they have teachers who have the characteristics they stated as ineffective, it makes them not want to go to class or to do the class work. One participant stated that they were influenced to change their major because they had an ineffective teacher. Another stated that ineffective teachers can negatively influence a student's grades because the student will not want to study for their class and will only do the bare minimum in order to pass the class; they will not have the motivation needed to succeed.

Focus Group #2

This qualitative research included a sample of eight African American undergraduate students. Five students were female and the remaining three students were male. The classification of the students varied from freshman to senior. The participants included various majors, including psychology majors.

The students discussed their perspectives on the characteristics of an effective and ineffective teacher, and how those qualities can be implemented in the classroom. The first task required the participants to distinguish all of the characteristics that seemed to be effective in a teacher. Once this was complete, students were required to agree upon the five most noteworthy characteristics, and place them in order from highest standing to lowest.

Effective Teachers

The results confirmed that students were able to come to a mutual agreement on the characteristics of an effective and ineffective teacher. The five most important attributes of an effective teacher, in priority order, were knowledge of the subject, confidence in teaching ability, organization, understanding, and having enthusiasm in the classroom. Other notable characteristics included discipline, caring, flexibility, open mindedness, positive reinforcement, and empathy.

A significant element that contributes to the environment of the classroom is the discipline and personality of the instructor. Students perceived that they were more likely to enjoy and perform well in a class that is soundly structured and controlled. It was stated that an effective teacher can make classes more enjoyable and influence students to work more diligently. Being an effective teacher helps students to understand a difficult lesson more easily. Teachers who seem shy, timid, and submissive to students are typically taken advantage of. A lack of respect emanates from the class and they normally become frustrated with the teacher's incapability to teach efficiently.

Ineffective Teachers

The characteristics of an ineffective teacher were the complete opposite of the ones for an effective teacher. These characteristics included not having knowledge of the subject matter, not being confident, disorganized, having a lack of understanding, and not being enthusiastic in the classroom. The participants unanimously agreed that those teachers who assigned "busy work" were seen as highly ineffective. One student explained how her professor would assign certain chapters to groups of students. Each group had to acquire information on their assigned chapter and prepare a presentation to display to the class. This method of teaching makes students only focus on acquiring the information to present instead of emphasizing learning and comprehending the material.

Another example of busy work was described as a teacher assigning students to write a twenty-page-long essay, accompanied with a bibliography. The teacher then solely graded the bibliography. It was concluded that even though a teacher may be ineffective, students still desire a respectable grade. However, students are not as likely driven and passionate to take the obligatory steps that are necessary to achieve these desirable grades. One male student from the group perceived that an ineffective teacher has never been the cause for his intentionally being absent from class.

As far as the implementation of effective characteristics in the classroom, one student gave examples of how confidence could be portrayed. Being able to lecture students without being dependent on the textbook shows a high quality of confidence, as well as knowledge of the subject matter. Moreover, being able to give examples that students can relate to and be able to elaborate on can be highly beneficial.

The participants perceived that most teachers do not take learning styles into consideration. The majority of the group confirmed that they were visual learners. The other two students perceived that they learn more efficiently through hands-on activities along with visual learning. Even though they were aware of their preferred learning style, it was agreed that it is not the teacher's responsibility to adjust to the learning styles of the class. This absence of responsibility does not make the teacher ineffective. Students indicated they would adjust to the professor's teaching method.

Unexpected findings included a disagreement between males and females on the importance of having a more organized teacher versus having a more understanding teacher. It appeared that the males of the group preferred a more understanding teacher, whereas the females believed that having organization was more imperative. Students perceived that they were more likely to enjoy and perform well in a class that was soundly structured and controlled. We expected that students would be fonder of a relaxed class that was lacking in discipline so that students could act freely, however this did not prove to be the case.

Focus Group #3

This qualitative research included a sample of six African American undergraduate students; five students were female and one student was male. This focus group consisted of three sophomores, one junior, and two first year students. The academic majors represented included print journalism, broadcast journalism, psychology, political science, five-year MBA, and nursing majors.

Effective Teachers

When asked to identify the characteristics of an effective teacher, all of the participants agreed that effective teachers had a good sense of humor; made the student feel important; demonstrated passion for the subject in their role as an instructor; were organized and knowledgeable, patient, not too lenient, respectful, humble, relatable, creative, and adaptable.

The group listed the perceived characteristics in order of priority: (1) passion; (2) organization; (3) respect; (4) patience; (5) adaptability; (6) creativity; (7) humor. When discussing how these "effective" characteristics could be fostered in the classroom setting, the group unanimously agreed that the use of modern technology in the classroom was extremely important.

They gave examples such as the use of multimedia presentations, showing of videos, skits, and in-class experiments. A sophomore broadcast journalism major stated that these activities were highly interactive and forced the students to engage with one another and the teacher. They perceived that the use of visual illustrations and physical demonstrations would make complex concepts easier to understand and improve class performance.

The group also felt that effective teachers prepared students for the "real world." A sophomore print journalism major said that effective teachers left students with "food for thought" and challenged students to make real changes. The group agreed that teachers should get students "hyped up" about learning but also "keep it real." Another student stated that effective teachers do not "sugarcoat" the truth and help to foster leadership skills in their students. The entire group agreed that occasional sarcasm and rudeness was important for helping students develop a tough skin.

Additional examples of fostering effective characteristics in the classroom included the use of field trips as incentives. The group agreed that impromptu field trips would give students something to look forward to, while the change of scenery also would refresh their mind and allow for greater concentration. A sophomore print journalism major stated that it was important for effective teachers to create experiences divorced from the strict classroom setting. Another participant also advocated the integration of games into the lecture as a way of keeping students attentive and increasing retention of coursework. Another participant also suggested student-led textbook reading sessions as one method for keeping students' attention.

As a group the students described organization and respect as essential characteristics of the effective teacher. A junior nursing major stated that teachers should have an outline prior to the beginning of the semester and stick to it as closely as possible. They also perceived that effective teachers were able to quickly adjust their schedule to accommodate any unforeseen setbacks, were punctual, and avoided detaining students past their allotted time. They allowed students to ask questions and engage in discussion on the subject matter but restricted unnecessary digressions. Effective teachers also treated college students as young adults, not children, were aware of the challenges of being a student, and were realistic in their expectations.

All of the participants agreed on the positive impacts of an "effective" teacher on their overall educational experience. They stated that effective teachers could alter a student's negative perception of an entire course. The students generally left class, not only with a good grade, but also with a genuine interest in the coursework. Effective teachers make learning and retaining the information easier, reduce student stress, create a comfortable classroom environment, and remove fear of failure. A junior nursing major stated that effective teachers help students foster a passion for class as well as for the student's future profession. Effective teachers also are positive role models and sources of inspiration. They encourage students through their teaching to strive for excellence. A sophomore print journalism major described the impact of effective teachers saying, "Learning doesn't feel like learning." Another participant agreed that classes with these teachers are challenging, but not stressful.

Ineffective Teachers

When asked to identify the characteristics of an ineffective teacher, all of the participants agreed that age could be a potential factor, especially if the teacher "lived in the past" and refused to integrate technology into their pedagogy. Ineffective teachers were also frequently described as un-relatable, disrespectful, lacking humility, unwilling to accept feedback or correction, get caught up in degree "labels," and are unable to speak in layman's terms. The group also stated that these teachers frequently "put down" students or made students "feel stupid" if they struggled to grasp a concept. The group also noted that ineffective teachers place all the responsibility and blame on their students as opposed to asking for feedback. They are also likely to place value on a "high failure rate" than on a "high passing rate" in their courses.

A sophomore print journalism major felt that inconsistency was also a characteristic of ineffective teachers. The group agreed that teachers needed to establish a healthy medium between friendly and authoritative. It was generally felt that if students are allowed to become too comfortable in the class, they are less likely to follow instructions, which destabilizes the classroom dynamic. Teachers must always establish clear boundaries and expectations from the beginning to avoid confusion. Both students and teachers must be aware of their specific roles.

Members of the group also emphasized that ineffective teachers were most commonly un-relatable and disrespectful. A sophomore broadcast journalism major mentioned that some teachers are too caught up in their degrees and forget that students have yet to reach the same academic level. They speak using complex and confusing jargons that most students cannot understand. Ineffective teachers also broadcast poor grades to the entire class as opposed to discussing the grade with the student privately. It was felt that this tactic only served to embarrass targeted students and would further discourage them from studying the coursework.

When questioned as to how an ineffective teacher impacts their experience in the classroom, the participants perceived that it stifles growth. Students are not motivated to attend class or learn the subject matter, and as a result attendance and performance declines. The group also felt that ineffective teaching could potentially dissuade students from pursuing subjects they genuinely enjoy and in the most extreme cases, lead to a student changing majors as a result of the experience.

The participants also felt that too much leniency led to an overall decline in their coursework and grades. All members of the group expressed the opinion that if students were "spoon-fed" at the high school or undergraduate level, it would retard their academic progress in the future. Teachers should refrain from offering too many extra credit opportunities or incentives because in the absence of these reinforcers, a student may not develop the internal motivation necessary to survive a more challenging course. A male freshman political science major stated that the habit of "passing along" students only cripples their academic development by exacerbating deficiencies in specific subject areas. The group agreed that students sometime felt discouraged because they viewed themselves as relatively unprepared in comparison to their peers.

The group also evaluated the impact that insensitive or overly harsh teachers can have on students. It was felt that these teachers discourage students from attending the class or completing the course. One freshman MBA major stated that teachers must be mindful that their students are "only human," and should take into account the myriad effects of additional classes and responsibilities. Another group member shared the experience of witnessing a student reduced to tears by an overly critical teacher. The participants concluded that because some students are very sensitive, teachers need to be more aware of how they correct or criticize students. The general consensus was that whether they know it or not, teachers greatly impact a student's self-esteem and feelings of self-worth.

Fall 2015 Follow-on Study

This study included thirty-one undergraduate African American students; thirty students were female and one student was male. All of the students were Senior Psychology majors. The GPA of the students ranged from 2.99 and to below 4.00.

Effective Teachers

The participants were asked to list the five important characteristics of an effective teacher. The top five characteristics out of twenty-five characteristics in priority order included knowledge, effective communication, understanding, caring, and relating to students. Participants were asked to explain how these characteristics could be fostered in the classroom. For example, relative to communication, suggestions included teachers effectively communicating due dates, test times, and assignments as well as having clarity in explaining paper and assignment expectations. Relative to upcoming assignments was a perception that this could be announced in class; relating information to students could be accomplished through visual and verbal aids.

Another common thread in the characteristics of effective teachers was accessibility to students, including being available for office hours. If students asked specific questions it was important so that they might comprehend the information. The use of various teaching modalities and technology as well as consideration of student learning styles was also important. Students confirmed that effective teachers: "encourage me and push me to want to learn; make me want to go to class and look forward to class; affect my comprehension and retention of the material; allow me to hold myself to a higher standard; make me take responsibility and interest in my own learning; help me develop a new research area or topic; assist in my academic success; and make me want to build a relationship with the teacher."

Ineffective Teachers

The following top five characteristics out of twenty-five were considered characteristics of ineffective teachers: lack of passion, uncaring, inconstant reaching, non-accessibility for students, and disorganization. The impact of ineffective teachers on the students' educational experiences was just the opposite of effective teachers as stated in the focus groups as well. This study also confirmed that ineffective teachers do not encourage students to learn and that they will not have the motivation needed to succeed, or attend class.

DISCUSSION

This study has significant implications for the way that teachers deliver information and the impact of teaching methodology on the academic achievement of undergraduate students. Effective teaching is critical in student learning. What we can garner from the students' voice can provide guidance in developing curriculum as teachers are being prepared to enter the teaching environment. By understanding classrooms from the perspectives of students, educators can secure the students' voice in areas that directly affect them in the classroom. The students' voice can also be considered when working toward the enhancement of curriculum instruction, pedagogy, and student retention. The findings from both studies augmented the research on teacher characteristics at Historically Black Colleges and Universities. Most importantly, findings from the studies extended the research on how effective teacher characteristics can be fostered in the classroom. Information from the students' perspectives can also shed light on what directly affects the student in their educational experience.

CONCLUSION

One of the common threads in the research on teacher characteristics was that the knowledge of the teacher was important in the classroom. Caring and respect for students was another common thread, which is in line with the literature on the importance of a caring teacher. Students gave examples of what these characteristics looked like in the classroom. Students perceived that the consideration of learning styles was also very important to students in the classroom, including the use of multiple modalities and visual learning. Participants were asked to explain how these characteristics could be fostered in the classroom. Effective communication was given as one example that effective teaching can be seen in the classroom. This included effectively communicating due dates, test times, and assignments, as well as ensuring clarity in explaining paper and assignment expectations.

The characteristics of ineffective teachers were also identified and defined. Some of the conclusions relative to ineffective and effective teachers were that effective teachers "assist in the students' academic success and incentivize them to work harder" while ineffective teachers do not motivate students to learn and may impact class attendance. The general consensus was that whether teachers know it or not, they greatly impact a student's academic success as well as self-esteem and self-worth.

Effective teaching is critical for student learning. It will be important for educators to understand better undergraduate students' perceptions of the characteristics of effective teachers to maximize academic achievement. By understanding classrooms from students' perspectives, educators can secure the students' voice in areas that directly affect them in the classroom. The students' voice can also be considered when working toward the enhancement of curriculum instruction, pedagogy, and student retention.

REFERENCES

Allan, J., Clarke, K., & Jopling, M. (2009). Effective teaching in higher education: Perceptions of first year undergraduate students. *International Journal of Teaching and Learning, 21*(3), 362–372.

Colker, L. (2008). Twelve characteristics of effective early childhood teachers. *Young Children, 63*(2). Retrieved from http://www.naeyc.org/files/yc/file/200803/BTJ_Colker.pdf.

Delaney, J., Johnson, A., Johnson, T., & Tresian, D. (2010). Students' perceptions of effective teaching in higher education. 26th Annual Conference on Distance Teaching and Learning; University of Wisconsin, Madison, WI.

Detick, G. (2011). Student perceptions of effective teaching. Retrieved from http://gdetrick.org/education/effectiveteaching-student-perceptions/.

Feldman, K. A. (1976). The superior college teacher from the students' view. *Research in Higher Education, 5*(3), 243–288.

George Mason University. (n.d.). Teaching strategies. Retrieved fromhttp://www.gmu.edu/resources/facstaff/part-time/strategy.html.

Noddings, N. (2001). The care tradition: Beyond 'add women and stir.' *Theory into Practice, 40*(1), 29–34.

Orlando, M. (January 14, 2013). Nine characteristics of a great teacher. *Faculty Focus*. Retrieved from https://www.facultyfocus.com/articles/philosophy-of-teaching/nine-characteristics-of-a-great-teacher/.

Rimm-Kaufman, S., & Sandilos, L. (2016). Improving student's relationships with teachers to provide essential support for learning. *American Psychological Association*. Retrieved from www.apa.org/education/k2/relationships.aspx.

Stevens, G. E., & Adams, S. (1981). Student perceptions of effective teaching behaviors. *Development in Business Simulation and Experiential Exercises, 8*(1981), 133–136.

Stronge, J. H. (2007). *Qualities of effective teachers* (2nd ed.). Alexandria, VA: Association for Supervision and Curriculum Development.

Tang, F., Chou, S. M., & Chiang, H. H. (2005). Students' perceptions of effective and ineffective clinical instructors. *Journal of Nursing Education, 44*(4), 187–192.

Thompson, S., Greer, J., & Greer, B. (2004). Highly qualified for successful teaching: Characteristics every teacher should possess. Retrieved from http://www.lingofest.com/resources/Characteristics%20of%20good%20teachers.pdf.

Walls, R., Nardi, A., Von Minden, A., & Hoffman, N. (2002). The characteristics of effective and ineffective teachers. *Teacher Education Quarterly, 29*(1). Retrieved from http://www.teqjournal.org/backvols/2002/29_1/w02_walls_na rdi.pdf.

Chapter 2

What Teacher Candidates Believe about Teaching and Learning

Nancy Caukin

ABSTRACT

Teachers' beliefs about teaching and learning impact their choices in the classroom and their students' classroom experiences (Muijs & Reynolds, 2011; Pajares, 1992). While many teacher's beliefs begin earlier in life, teacher preparation programs can have an impact on teacher candidates' beliefs (Doyle, 1997; Hancock & Gallard, 2004; Lasley, 1980). This study sought to examine teacher candidates' beliefs about teaching and learning after completing their penultimate semester of their teacher preparation program at a large public university in the southeast United States. A total of 38 teacher candidates participated in this study providing a total of 365 "I Believe" statements. Themes identified from the coding included teacher-centered beliefs (ninety-three), student-centered beliefs (eighty-seven), instruction-centered beliefs (seventy-seven), classroom-centered beliefs (forty-nine), learning-centered beliefs (forty-six), and content-centered beliefs (thirteen). Explanation of each theme and examples of the teacher candidates' belief statements are aligned with InTASC standards and implications for teacher preparation programs.

KEY WORDS

Teacher Candidate Beliefs; Teacher Preparation; Residency Programs

Much scholarship has been published about the importance of teachers' beliefs associated with teaching and learning (Hancock & Gallard, 2004; Muijs & Reynolds, 2011; Pajares, 1992; Wall, 2016). Researchers have documented teachers' beliefs about students, effective teaching, and optimal learning, the importance of teachers' choices and behaviors in the classroom, and the consequential impact on student achievement (Muijs & Reynolds, 2011; Pajares, 1992). Teachers' beliefs can also impact teachers' expectations of their students that can result in extra time and additional attention given to some students that promote a self-fulfilling prophecy or denied other students in a defeating self-fulfilling prophecy (Rosenthal, 1994).

While beliefs about teaching and learning are initiated as early as K-12 students, beliefs continue to develop as university students progress through the education system and become teacher candidates (Kagan, 1992; Pajares, 1992; Wall, 2016). Personal experiences as K-16 students are only one factor that influences teacher candidates' beliefs; teacher education programs also play a role in developing teacher candidates' beliefs about teaching and learning (Doyle, 1997; Hancock & Gallard, 2004; Lasley, 1980). Field experiences during teacher preparation are particularly important parts of the teacher preparation program that impact teacher candidates' beliefs and behaviors (Wall, 2016). Doyle (1997) discovered that linking the learning in the university classroom to candidates' field experiences helped strengthen the connections candidates were making between the two parts of their teacher preparation programs. Specifically, by coupling theory to practice, a trend of beliefs was seen moving from teaching as telling to teaching as facilitating. Also, learning as receiving to learning as a process (Doyle, 1997).

PURPOSE AND CONTEXT OF THE STUDY

Lasley (1980) suggests that teacher candidates should write and defend individual sets of belief statements about the "nature of teachers, teacher education, and the classroom" (p. 40). This insightful suggestion established the purpose of this study, which was to examine teacher candidates' beliefs about teaching and learning. This study was conducted toward the end of their teacher preparation program by examining their "I Believe" statements.

The participants in this study were education minors (majoring in a specific field of study such as English, history, math, physical education, etc.) known as teacher candidates (specifically, candidates) completing the first semester of their senior year. They were enrolled in Residency I, a university course that includes one three-hour seminar each week and one to two days a week in a local public school. Residency I precedes Residency II, aka traditional student teaching. In their field placement during Residency I, candidates are assigned to a mentor teacher in whose class they learn the context of the students and of the course; plan standards-based lessons; and teach a week-long learning segment that they assess and reflect. Besides having a mentor teacher in whose class they observe and teach, candidates also observe many different subjects and grade levels during their semester-long field placement, which allows them to see many different teaching and classroom management styles. During their observations, candidates keep journals that focus on the intricacies of teaching and learning. Each week candidates are provided observation prompts taken from the state adopted evaluation model that candidates focus on, as well as their own general observations, which might include teaching strategies, classroom environment, school culture, and the many different interactions occurring.

Since schools are a complex landscape (Kagan, 1992), professors for this course have chosen to utilize Problem-Based Learning (PBL) in an effort to better prepare candidates for the physical, social, emotional, and political complexity of schools. PBL is utilized during the seminar portion of Residency I as a means to make connections between educational theory and this multifaceted landscape of school. The PBL method emphasizes "knowing *and* doing" through the identification and diagnosis of a problem or problems and exploration of possible solutions (Bridges & Hallinger, 1997). Through the PBL process, candidates bridge theory and practice in order to make connections between what they are encountering in their field placement and what they are learning in seminar (Hmelo-Silver, 2004).

THEORETICAL FRAMEWORK

The theoretical perspectives that inform Residency I include situated cognition (Brown, Collins, & Duguid, 1989), social constructivism (McMahon, 1997), and adult learning (Knowles, 1984). During Residency I, candidates are placed in both a university setting as well as in K-12 public school classrooms. In these contexts, which are social, cultural, and physical settings, candidates, who are adult learners, construct knowledge by connecting what they know and have experienced to what they are currently experiencing and learning. Utilizing the lens of Hancock and Gallard (2004), candidates come to teacher preparation with beliefs about teaching and learning and those beliefs are continuing to be informed by their experiences in Residency I.

RESEARCH QUESTIONS

Candidates in the secondary licensure path in this study were enrolled in their penultimate semester of their bachelors program in the teacher preparation program at a large public university in the southeast United States. This study sought to determine their beliefs about teaching and learning at this point in their preparation. The research question that guided this study was: What is the nature of the beliefs about teaching and learning of Residency I teacher candidates?

METHOD

This qualitative study was an inquiry into practice via a scholarship of teaching and learning (SoTL). Teaching is scholarship; it is worthy of reflection, analysis, and making public (Boyer, 1990). The SoTL involves inquiry into teaching and learning using the scholarly lens of research- and evidence-based methods (Bender & Gray, 1999; Chick, n.d.; Smith, 2016). This SoTL study was used to analyze teacher candidates' stated beliefs near the end of their teacher preparation program. Themes were identified in order to reflect on the teacher preparation program and in particular the Residency I course. Candidates throughout the semester created a list of "I Believe" statements, which explained why they believe what they believe, and what actions they plan to take because of their beliefs.

Participants

The thirty-eight participants in this study were enrolled at a large public university in the southeast United States. All participants were secondary education minors and were enrolled in one of two sections of Residency I during the fall 2016. Of the participants, twenty-one were females and seventeen were males. The distribution of participants into their specific majors was as follows: Agriculture—3, Art—3, English—5, Family & Consumer Science—1, Government—1, Health & Wellness—1, History—2, Math—6, Music—8, Physical Education—6, Science—1, and Spanish—1.

Data Collection and Analysis

Each participant created "I Believe" statements and submitted them to the digital learning management system for Residency I. Afterwards participants were provided with an explanation of the Institutional Review Board (IRB)-approved protocol to study their beliefs, then they were invited to participate. The professors explained that while the "I Believe" statements were required for the class, using them for research purposes was not required and that there would be no penalty for not participating. Questions were asked and answered and informed consents were distributed, completed, and collected. Thirty-eight out of forty-two (90%) of the Residency I teacher candidates chose to participate in this study.

The candidates' "I Believe" statements were assessed for the first time for their progress in the course during the fall semester, and then the statements were assessed a second time for the study during the following spring semester. In the spring semester data analysis, all belief statements were read through for a general analysis; then they were read through with particular attention to reoccurring words and phrases. A total of 117 different codes were identified. These codes were analyzed for similarities and differences and placed into thirteen categories. These categories were further analyzed and placed into six themes. The six themes that emerged were teacher-centered beliefs, student-centered beliefs, instruction-centered beliefs, learning-centered beliefs, classroom-centered beliefs, and content-centered beliefs. After the six themes were identified, each teacher candidate's "I Believe" statements were read again and placed into one of the six themes. The belief statements in each theme were reread for accuracy of placement and moved into a better fitting theme when appropriate. All belief statements were placed into a theme. After all themes were deemed as containing the appropriate belief statements, each theme was broken down into subthemes.

RESULTS

A total of 365 belief statements were analyzed. They were placed into six themes and further broken down into multiple subthemes. Table 2.1 shows the results of the number of belief statements in each theme and subtheme and the percentages of themes relative to each other.

Teacher-Centered Beliefs

At the beginning of the coding process, the Teacher-Centered Beliefs theme became apparent. This theme began with by far the most belief statements. However, as the analysis continued, similarities and differences became clearer, and many of the initially categorized beliefs were placed in different categories. From a total of 365 belief statements, 93 or 25% were categories as Teacher-Centered Beliefs. The identified subthemes include What Teachers Do, Teacher as Self, Teacher Community, and Teaching as the Most Important Job.

What Teachers Can Do?

The largest subtheme from the Teacher-Centered Beliefs was What Teachers Can Do?, with sixty-one belief statements. This subtheme contains statements regarding the roles and actions teachers should take with students. Box 2.1 shows the categories contained in the What Teachers Do subtheme.

Table 2.1 Theme Number (N), Subtheme Numbers (n), and Percentages

Themes	N	n	%
Teacher-Centered	93		25.5
What Teachers Can Do		61	
Teacher as Self		14	
Teacher Community		12	
Teaching Most Important Job		6	
Student-Centered	87		23.8
Positive Relationships		30	
All Students Can Learn		23	
Students are Priority		21	
What Students Do or Are		9	
Other		4	
Instruction-Centered	77		21.1
Pedagogies		38	
Differentiated Instruction		24	
Assessment		10	
Equity		2	
Other		3	
Classroom-Centered	49		13.4
Structure		15	
Classroom Management (CM)		12	
Both Structure & CM		4	
Safe Place		9	
Other		1	
Learning-Centered	46		12.6
Ways to Learn		12	
Meaningful Learning		10	
Learning is Fun		9	
Students Learn Differently		5	
Learning is Lifelong		3	
Teacher as Learner		2	
Other		2	
Content-Centered	13		3.6
Music Ed is Important		8	
Career and Technical Available		2	
Reading and Writing are Important		2	
Physical Education is Important		1	

The belief statements in this subtheme convey confidence (be a role model, have high expectations, okay to make mistakes); humanity (embrace diversity, treat students equitably, be an encourager, teach character); professionalism (be professional, use data, be prepared, have clear expectations, set goals, communicate); and engagement (engage students, be a facilitator, challenge students, learn from students, promote a growth mindset, work hard, reflect). Examples of belief statements from the What Teachers Can Do subtheme

BOX 2.1 WHAT TEACHERS CAN DO? CATEGORIES

What Teachers Can Do

Be role models	Be prepared	Learn from students
Have high expectations	Be flexible	Be professional
Teach character	Be a facilitator	Set goals
Treat students equitably	Promote a growth mindset	Reflect
Be an encourager	Challenge students	Communicate
Use data	Make mistakes	Embrace diversity
Engage students	Have clear expectations	Work hard

included, "I believe an effective teacher needs to be flexible, embrace change, and reflect on teaching" and "There is one student who looks up to you so you always need to be positive, honest, empathetic, excited, respectful, and eager to learn." Many essential characteristics of effective teachers are displayed in these "I believe" statements.

Teacher as Self

The subtheme Teacher as Self contains 14 belief statements relating information pertaining to the care and needs of themselves as teachers. Examples included the need to manage stress; asking for help when needed; having an open mind; being happy; continuing learning; belief that teacher candidates can accomplish anything; and being humble. An example of a belief statement from the subtheme Teacher as Self includes, "I believe in order to manage stress; I am going to have to find an outlet or hobby that releases my stress." Another example is, "I believe in asking for help when I need it."

Teacher Community

The subtheme of Teacher Community includes twelve belief statements. The focus is on the importance of collaboration not isolation. Belief statements in this subtheme include not working alone; leveraging resources; partnerships between teachers, students, and parents; connections with teachers in other disciplines; and the value and importance of being a part of a strong Professional Learning Community (PLC). An example of the Teacher Community subtheme belief is, "[I believe] that participating in PLCs will only assist me with growing as a teacher and a leader in my content area." Another example is, "I believe that teachers should work together to build a community of success for their students."

Teaching as the Most Important Job

This subtheme has six belief statements indicating how important teaching is. Three of the six belief statements specifically declare that teaching is the most important job in the world. Other belief statements asserted that teachers are the foundation of society and that teaching is the most challenging and rewarding career that exists. One belief statement affirmed that teaching is the greatest service that a person can do.

Student-Centered Beliefs

Of the 365 belief statements, 87 or 23.8% were categorized in the theme of Student-Centered Beliefs. The subthemes in this theme include the importance of positive relationships, all students can learn, students are priority, what students do or are, and then an unspecific group of Other.

Positive Relationships

The importance of establishing a positive relationship with students was a common belief among candidates. A total of thirty of the eighty-eight belief statements revolve around positive relationships. Teacher candidates emphasize the power of positive relationships to truly make a difference in students' lives. Many candidates feel that students want to connect to their teachers on a personal level. The candidates expressed the imperative to sincerely respect and care about students, not only from an educational standpoint, but on a deeply personal level as well. A few of the candidates reported, "Students don't care what you know until they know that you care." Compassion and tough love were also discussed. Some candidates commented on the belief that positive relationships with students can impact the students' attitude, behavior, and achievement. The idea of reciprocal learning, that is, students learning from teachers and teachers learning from students can help build those relationships, was also mentioned. Passion for students, teaching, and learning was identified as a critical component for teachers to embody. One candidate wrote, "I believe that forming a positive relationship with students brings out the best in them." Another candidate wrote, "Positive relationships foster positive learning experiences."

All Students Can Learn

The subtheme of All Students Can Learn was also prevalent among candidates, receiving twenty-three belief statements. The overarching theme conveys that even though students have had different experiences and have different abilities and interests, they all can learn. Therefore, teachers need to have high expectations of their students' learning. Candidates indicate that teachers need to challenge their students to reach higher levels and the students will rise to meet those expectations. Also noted is the need to begin with what students already know; take their prior knowledge into account, and meet them where they are. Accessibility and equity were identified as important for students to have the opportunity to learn. The belief that students want to learn and deserve to know that they have the potential to accomplish great things was also reported. Also mentioned was the belief that it is important to inform students that it is acceptable—even good—to make mistakes and the value of learning from those mistakes. An example of a quote from this subtheme is, "I believe students will rise to expectations when given responsibilities that are perceived as valuable." Another example is, "I believe that students can accomplish anything; some just hide it and need more practice and/or more work (no matter their background)."

Students Do or Are

What Students Do or Are is a subtheme that captures the nature of students. Nine belief statements reflected what students can do or the nature of students. Examples of concepts concerning what students do include being involved in extracurricular activities and professional organizations. Regarding the nature of students, statements centered on the notion that students are innately good, have something to contribute, and are drawn to vibrant and energetic programs. One example of a belief statement from this subtheme is, "[I believe] that students are naturally curious." These ideas provide insight into candidates' beliefs about the nature of students.

Within the theme of Student-Centered Beliefs were four statements that did not neatly fit into any of the subthemes. These statements included the belief that students should attend to precision; students should be taught early and often; a small success is still a success; and the importance of celebrating student success. While these statements are beliefs that warrant acknowledgment, they were considered under the category of Other.

Instruction-Centered Beliefs

Instruction-Centered Beliefs included 77 of the 365 or 21.1% of the belief statements and were organized into the subthemes of Pedagogies, Differentiating Instruction, Assessment, Equity, and Other. These belief statements focused on the specifics of instructional strategies and their value as well as how to engage and motivate students; help students to persevere; and assisting students in reaching higher levels of learning.

Pedagogies

A total of thirty-eight of the seventy-seven belief statements focused on different pedagogical practices. The categories under this subtheme were Technology, Critical Thinking/Questioning/Problem-Solving, Cooperative/Collaborative Learning, Fostering Creativity, Discovery/Inquiry Learning, Discourse, Reflection, and Teachable Moments.

The use of technology as a pedagogical tool and the value of using technology appropriately was certainly a highlight with twelve out of thirty-eight beliefs related to technology. Beliefs included the value in using technology to enhance learning, to engage students, to assist in classroom management, improve lessons, and to make a teacher's job easier. The belief that there is a right way and a wrong way to use technology was also mentioned.

The importance of teaching Critical Thinking/Questioning/Problem-Solving was another set of beliefs identified. Nine of the thirty-eight beliefs included statements regarding one or more of the three. Examples include the value of using probing questions to promote critical thinking and as a way to help focus student on the objectives and concepts. Another category is the importance of building students' curiosity and critical thinking skills as being more important than knowing the answers. The use of productive struggle to foster problem solving and perseverance was another stated belief. Mathematics majors had several specific belief statements regarding the importance of critical thinking, questioning, and problem solving to developing conceptual understanding and meaningful learning in mathematics. Another category included was the importance of group work. It was stated that cooperative/collaborative learning is believed to foster positive relationships between students; helps students implement problem-solving strategies; and increases higher levels of thinking. Some teacher candidates believe that students work more effectively in groups.

The importance of Discovery/Inquiry Learning as a way to employ scientific practices and interact with the concepts in order to construct knowledge was another stated belief. Teachers should be facilitators of inquiry for learning rather than a disseminator of information was also mentioned. Several teacher candidates identified creativity as something that should be cultivated in students and that students might need to be "pushed" to think creatively. One candidate reported that a classroom environment which cultivates creativity is one where students learn "effective problem-solving skills." Also noted was that teachable moments are all around, including mistakes made, and teachers need to utilize those moments. Discourse and reflection as important pedagogical practices were also mentioned.

Differentiated Instruction

Twenty-four belief statements related to the idea of differentiating instruction. Many belief statements were specific in using the terms differentiated instruction or differentiation, while other statements were implicit in their belief statement. For example, one candidate wrote explicitly, "Differentiation is about accommodating the needs of all students." An implicit example is, "In order for teaching to be effective, teachers must structure their instruction around the current and preexisting understandings that their students have." This belief was stated by one teacher candidate that differentiating instruction has the potential to reach students on many levels, including academically, socially, and behaviorally. Some belief statements mentioned specific strategies such as modeling, incorporating multiple representations, using knowledge of students' hobbies and interests in creating lessons, using a variety of methods, using visuals, using manipulatives, employing multimodal instruction, and the use of student choice in an effort to meet the varied needs of students.

Assessment

Assessment was discussed in ten belief statements. Candidates specifically mentioned preassessments, formative assessments, and summative assessments as all being critical for driving quality instruction. Comments emphasized that assessments should be used to not only inform teaching, but they are useful to inform learning as well. Fair assessments, a variety of assessments, and constructive feedback were all noted as being important for student learning. One example of an assessment belief is, "I believe assessment should be continuous to track student progress." Another example is, "I believe that giving informal feedback to students regarding their academic progress is essential to the learning process."

Equity

Only two belief statements addressed equity. One candidate stated that mathematics should be equitable and accessible to all students. The other candidate indicated that equal opportunity was more important than equality. Three belief statements did not readily fit into another category and were deemed "Other." One candidate indicated that bell work should be connected to the lesson plan; another candidate stated that practicing meditation and mindfulness could help students prepare for learning; and the third candidate submitted a belief about the "unGoogleable" curriculum.

Classroom-Centered Beliefs

In this study 49 of the 365 or 13.4% of the statements were Classroom-Centered Beliefs. The subthemes identified in this theme were Structure, Classroom Management, Structure and Classroom Management combined, Safe Place, and Other.

Structure, Classroom Management, and Both

A total of fifteen of the forty-nine statements mentioned or implied structure (not counting those belief statements that mentioned both structure and classroom management together). The subthemes of structure and classroom management could have been combined; however structure can exist without classroom management, so these two statements were categorized separately. Structure beliefs included not only the word "structure" but also words like organized, balance of autocratic and democratic classroom, procedures, routines, and consistency.

Classroom management beliefs included statements about how classroom management impacts learning, respect, and behaviors as well as how the classroom environment can impact behaviors. Teacher proximity affecting classroom management was mentioned, and one candidate stated that classroom management should be proactive rather than reactive. One candidate stated the belief that the best classroom management is to keep students engaged. Another candidate stated that discipline is important. Yet other candidates conveyed that positive reinforcement is better than negative reinforcement, patience is needed for a peaceful classroom, and students thrive on a well-managed classroom. Belief statements that were identified as both Structured and Classroom Management had a duality about them that included many of the same concepts within this theme. An example of a belief statement that was placed in the Structure and Classroom subtheme is, "I believe that staying organized is an important classroom management skill and displays a level of professionalism that is important to model to students and creates a stronger learning environment."

Safe Place

A total of nine belief statements reflected the importance of having a safe place for students. These statements included students feeling safe and secure; the classroom being a safe place both physically and emotionally; and the teacher being the creator of a safe classroom where respect is displayed and students are unafraid to make mistakes. An example of a belief statement expressing the need for a safe place is, "I believe that teachers should work to cultivate a classroom environment where students feel safe, respected, and are not afraid to make mistakes."

Positive Environment

Eight belief statements focused on a positive environment. Belief statements in this subtheme highlighted the importance of a positive environment for learning. Included were statements about how enjoyable a positive environment can be. Also included were statements about developing trust, vulnerability, and honesty. One teacher candidate simply wrote, "Positive

Classroom environments are essential to students learning." Another teacher candidate wrote, "A successful class is an enjoyable class." One statement was unspecified. This belief statement involved the impact of temperature on student learning.

Learning-Centered Beliefs

A total of forty-six Learning-Centered Belief statements (12.6%) were reported. These belief statements were placed in the following subthemes: Ways to Learn, Meaningful Learning, Learning is Fun, Students Learn Differently, Learning is Lifelong, Teacher as Learner, and Other.

Ways to Learn

Ways to Learn contained twelve of the forty-six belief statements. Most of these statements were single ideas of ways students learn. Examples include learning using real-world contexts, learning just as much from peers as from the teacher; learning from informal feedback; building procedural fluency from conceptual understanding; using scaffolding to learn new concepts; using procedures and routines to be sure students are learning; learning a growth mindset; students learn better with peers, and learning using competition. An example of a belief statement in the Ways to Learn subtheme is, "I believe that all students, regardless of ability, learn better together." Another example is, "Students must understand they are part of the learning process, not passive recipients of information."

Meaningful Learning

Ten Meaningful Learning belief statements were noted. Several teacher candidates simply stated that learning should be meaningful. Other candidates wrote statements like learning should be personal, relatable, and hands-on. One teacher candidate said that learning should be student and culture-centered to be meaningful. Another stated that incorporating current events helps to make learning meaningful. An example of a Meaningful Learning belief statement is, "I believe hands on learning and real-world experience is the best way to prepare our students for postsecondary education and the work force." Another example is, "I believe that each lesson should have a significant and positive impact on student learning."

Learning Is Fun

Nine teacher candidates stated that learning is, can be, should be, or should contain elements of fun. One teacher candidate indicated that students learn more when they experience "enjoyment, autonomy, and personal satisfaction." Another stated that students learn more when the teacher makes learning fun. One teacher candidate wrote, "Students learn better when they are interested/having fun." Another teacher candidate wrote, "I believe that learning and teaching should be fun."

Students Learn Differently

Five belief statements related to students learning differently. Some statements focused on students being unique, other statements addressed the need for students to learn at their own pace, and other statements attended to students approaching learning based on their personal experiences. An example of a belief statement from this subtheme is, "Students learn at different rates, but all students learn."

Parent Involvement

Three statements focused on the need for parent involvement in student learning. One indicated that parent involvement creates a better learning environment, another stated that parent involvement is essential for students' academic progress, and the third voiced that parents should be involved in their student's success.

Teacher as Learner

Two teacher candidates wrote belief statements about the teacher as the learner. One stated that the teacher learns more than the students and the second indicated that teachers should never stop learning and should learn from their students.

Two unspecified belief statements remained. One indicated that the one working the hardest is learning the most. The second statement indicated the importance of standardized tests, but the inability of those tests to measure all of the students' achievements.

Content-Centered Beliefs

Only 13 or 3.6% of all 365 statements were Content-Centered Beliefs. The subthemes identified were: Music Education Is Important, Career and Technical Education Should Be Available, Reading and Writing Are Important, and Physical Education Is Important.

The belief statements revolving around music education include the value of music to enhance learning in other subject areas; music is important to educating the whole child; all teachers should use music in their instruction; the value of music to improve social skills; that music education makes better leaders; and music helps students to express their emotions.

One belief statement indicated that physical education is the most important content area in education. Two belief statements suggested that Career and Technical Education should be available to all students and should be an integral part of any school. One belief statement specified that reading is the foundation to learning. Another belief statement indicated that writing is a "fundamental and practical skill."

CONCLUSION

Residency I teacher candidate beliefs reflect a manifold view of teaching and learning. When thinking about the teacher candidates' experiences in Residency I, their beliefs mirror what many of our speakers during coursework discussed, what they learned in the PBL scenarios, and what they observed and experienced in their field placement. This interaction and intersection of fieldwork and coursework is critical for preparing teacher candidates to *know* like teachers, *act* like teachers, and *feel* like teachers (Wall, 2016).

We had nine speakers who presented topics such as the importance of professionalism; what differentiating instruction looks like; how a PLC should work; working with English language learners; all kinds of assessments; technology in the classroom; experiences of new teachers; state tests/value added model/teacher observation; and culture and climate in schools. Many teacher candidates wrote belief statements reflecting what was presented by the speakers.

The PBLs tackled topics such as response to intervention and instruction (RTI^2), individual education plans, learning environments, classroom management, PLCs, student-teacher relationships, growth verse fixed mindset, mentors, teaching strategies, academic language, effective feedback, and teacher observations. Many belief statements focused precisely on many of these topics.

Ideally teacher candidates' engagement with the speakers and PBL events were reinforced by what they were seeing and experiencing in the field. Certainly connections between theory and practice that were articulated reflect the teacher candidates' intentions of engaging in praxis related to what was learned (Wall, 2016).

While not explicitly taught during Residency I, but intentionally embedded in the course, were the InTASC Standards for Model Teaching. Parts of the InTASC standards are also reflected in many instances in the teacher candidates' belief statements. For example, Standard #1: Learner Development and Standard #2: Learning Differences are reflected in teacher candidates' beliefs that students come with many different needs and learn at different rates, therefore it is the teacher's responsibility to meet the needs of the students while having high expectations of their learning. Standard #3: Learning Environments is mirrored in the teacher candidates' beliefs that positive, safe, and engaging classrooms are necessary for learning. Standard #5: Application of Content Knowledge was apparent in teacher candidates' beliefs, in particular the beliefs that learning should be reflective of real-world problems, promote critical thinking, foster creativity, and allow for collaborative learning. Standard #6: Assessment is evident in the teacher candidates' belief statements in so far as they articulate the need for multiple methods of assessment to track student progress over time and the use of that information to drive instruction. Standard #7: Planning was addressed in the need to plan and prepare for meaningful learning experiences. Standard #8: Instructional Strategies were evident in the belief statements. For example, differentiating instruction based on the students' needs, interest, and abilities were addressed as well as the use of specific pedagogies for student learning. Standard #9: Professional Learning and Ethical Practice was addressed, in particular the professional learning piece, when beliefs referred to the teacher as a learner and how learning never stops. Standard #10: Leadership and Collaboration was reflected in the teacher candidates' beliefs when discussing the importance of teacher community, collaboration, and involvement in a PLC. Leadership was referenced in relation to being engaged in a PLC. While most of the InTASC standards were evident in the belief statements, they could be deemed as representing a basic level in this format and indicative of novice teachers.

Whereas the researcher detected a sense of gratification that the teacher candidates' beliefs are reflective of the intention of the course through the standards and curriculum, the researchers also noted areas to consider. For example, the lack of reference to social and emotional learning and multicultural education is an indication that the program may need to incorporate more guidance and support in these areas explicitly (Elias et al., 2002).

Teacher-Centered Beliefs contained the most belief statements (25.5%). While teacher educators want teacher candidates to think beyond and outside of themselves as teachers, Kagan (1992) points out that a sense of inward focus is to be expected of novice teachers, in fact a strong sense of self as a teacher is important for establishing personal identity as a teacher.

Also, Learning-Centered Beliefs were represented in a smaller percentage (12.6%) compared to Teacher-Centered Beliefs (25.5%), Student-Centered Beliefs (23.8%), and Instruction-Centered Beliefs (21.1%). This could be suggestive that the program and the course (Residency I) may need to emphasize focusing on learning more than teaching.

Teacher preparation programs should take the opportunity to explore their teacher candidates' beliefs in order to have a better understanding of what they believe (Kagan, 1992; Lasley, 1980). Beliefs could be collected early and tracked as they encounter more experiences aand move through the program (Minor et al., 2002; Wall, 2016). This can be used to inform future instruction (Kagan, 1992). Looking at teacher candidates' beliefs is similar to looking into a mirror and seeing a reflection of this teacher preparation program.

REFERENCES

Bender, E., & Gray, D. (1999). The scholarship of teaching. *Research and Creative Activity, 22*(1). Retrieved from http://www.indiana.edu/%7Ercapub/v22n1/p03.html.

Boyer, E. (1990). *Scholarship reconsidered.* Lawrenceville, NJ: Princeton University Press. ED326149. Retrieved from https://eric.ed.gov/?id=ED326149.

Bridges, E. M., & Hallinger, P. (1997). Using problem-based learning to prepare educational leaders. *Peabody Journal of Education, 172*(2), 131–146.

Brown, J. S., Collins, A., & Duguid, P. (1989). Situated cognition and the culture of learning. *Educational Researcher, 18*(1), 32–41.

Chick, N. (n.d.). *A scholarly approach to teaching. A guide from the Vanderbilt University center for teaching.* Retrieved from https://my.vanderbilt.edu/sotl/understanding-sotl/a-scholarly-approach-to-teaching/.

Doyle, M. (1997). Preservice teachers' beliefs about teaching and learning. *College Student Journal, 31*(4), 519–532.

Elias, M., Zins, J., Weissberg, R., Frey, K., Greenberg, M., Hayes, N., Kessler, R., Schwab-Stone, M., & Shriver, T. (1997). *Social and emotional learning: Guidelines for educators.* Alexandria, VA: Association of Supervision and Curriculum Development.

Hancock, E., & Gallard, A. (2004). Preservice science teachers' beliefs about teaching and learning: The influence of K-12 field experiences. *Journal of Science Teacher Education, 15*(4), 281–291.

Hmelo-Silver, C. E. (2004). Problem-based learning: What and how do students learn? *Educational Psychology Review, 16*, 235–266.

Kagan, D. (1992). Professional growth among preservice and beginning teachers. *Review of Educational Research, 62*(2), 129–169.

Knowles, M. (1984). *Andragogy in action.* San Francisco, CA: Jossey-Bass.

Lasley, T. (1980). Preservice teacher beliefs about teaching. *Journal of Teacher Education, 31*(4), 38–41.

McMahon, M. (1997). *Social constructivism and the World Wide Web.* Retrieved from http://www.ascilite.org/conferences/perth97/papers/Mcmahon/Mcmahon.html.

Minor, L., Onwuegbozie, A., Witcher, A., & James, T. (2002). Preservice teachers' educational beliefs and their perceptions of characteristics of effective teachers. *Journal of Educational Research, 96*(2), 116–127.

Muijs, D., & Reynolds, D. (2011). *Effective teaching: Evidence and practice.* Thousand Oaks, CA: SAGE.

Pajares, M. F. (1992). Teachers' beliefs and educational research: Cleaning up a messy construct. *Review of Educational Research, 62*(3), 307–332.

Rosenthal, R. (1994). Interpersonal expectancy effects: A 30 year perspective. *Current Directions in Psychological Sciences, 3*(6), 176–179.

Smith, K. (2016). *What is the scholarship of teaching and learning (SoTL)?* University of Florida Faculty Center for Teaching and Learning. Retrieved from http://www.fctl.ucf.edu/ResearchAndScholarship/SoTL/.

Wall, C. R. G. (2016). From student to teacher: Changes in preservice teacher educational beliefs through-out the learning-to-teach journey. *Teacher Development, 20*(3), 364–379.

Chapter 3

Reinforcing MAT Course Goals during Internship Experiences via Gallavan's Seven Essential Elements

Nancy P. Gallavan and Jennifer P. Merritt

ABSTRACT

In their accreditation standards, CAEP (the Council for the Accreditation of Educator Preparation, 2013) states that educator preparation programs (EPPs) should provide high-quality field experiences connecting concepts with practices. However, many teacher educators who serve as supervisors during the culminating internship field experience recognize that teacher candidate interns tend to be challenged, if not overwhelmed, by the extensive number, expansive scope, and equal importance of criteria they are expected to demonstrate quickly, comprehensively, and proficiently. Prompted by these concerns, research was conducted at one mid-south mid-sized university with MAT teacher candidate interns to identify a more manageable, measurable, and meaningful approach for guiding and supporting interns to document their "effectiveness and positive impact on all students' learning and development" (CAEP, 2013, para 2.3). The professor of the MAT Classroom Assessment course who also served as an internship supervisor developed *Gallavan's Seven Essential Elements for Facilitation of Effective Learning Experiences* rubric based on selected competencies from the state teacher evaluation criteria aligned with the goals of the Classroom Assessment course. Data collected during two fifteen-week internships revealed that interns benefit when they demonstrate their readiness to teach, their receptiveness to feedback, and their responsiveness to expectations. These three aspects of influence advance teacher self-efficacy for interns as they embark upon their careers as PK-12 teachers facilitating effective learning experiences.

KEY WORDS

Readiness to Teach; Receptiveness to Feedback; Responsiveness to Expectations

INTRODUCTION

CAEP-accredited educator preparation programs (EPPs) at U.S. institutions of higher education, that is universities and colleges, offer a variety of teacher preparation programs designed specifically for both undergraduate and graduate students that incorporate a sequence of program courses and field experiences (Council for the Accreditation of Educator Preparation (CAEP), 2013). In addition to CAEP accreditation standards, teacher preparation programs tend to be aligned with the state's expectations and the teachers' evaluation criteria. Further, teacher education faculty establish their program purposes and course goals to showcase their institutions' conceptual framework for candidates to delve into the concepts and practices related to all expectations included in the teacher preparation program.

Faculty in teacher preparation programs focus on content and pedagogical knowledge; as program faculty, they map their curricular content, distribute their instructional strategies, and coordinate their key assessments for their teacher candidates to understand and demonstrate course goals, that is, knowledge, skills, and dispositions, throughout their sequence of courses. Faculty presume that their program purposes and course goals will be integrated appropriately during the candidates' field experiences known as practicum and internship.

However, the successful transfer of program purposes and course goals may not be fully understood or demonstrated by some teacher candidates; likewise, program purposes and course goals may not be clearly communicated or promoted by the field experience supervisors, particularly during the culminating field experience called internship. "Unfortunately, neither decades of research nor volumes of policy documents on quality teaching and teacher education have yielded a definitive way to make those patterns consistent across contexts with different students, teachers, subject matter, and curricula, among other characteristics" (Wang, Linn, Spaulding, Klecka, & Odell, 2011, p. 331).

The authors bring their experiences as teacher preparation program faculty who teach courses and supervise field experiences. Their interns, that is, teacher candidates completing internship, tend to be challenged, perhaps overwhelmed, by the extensive number, expansive scope, and equal importance of criteria they are expected to demonstrate quickly, comprehensively, and proficiently as they advance through their final internship semester. Prompted by these concerns, this research study was conducted to identify a more manageable, measurable, and meaningful approach for guiding and supporting interns. Our intentions are to help interns transfer learning gleaned specifically from their Classroom Assessment course to increase their "effectiveness and positive impact on all students' learning and development" (CAEP, 2013, para 2.3) and to enhance their self-efficacy evident in their PK-12 teaching, learning, and schooling.

RELEVANT LITERATURE

In 2010, when most U.S. university and college teacher preparation programs were accredited by NCATE: the National Council for the Accreditation of Teacher Education, a blue ribbon panel issued a report that called for *Turning the Education of Teachers Upside Down* (NCATE, 2010, pp. 2–4). The major transformation required "a shift in the emphasis of teacher education programs *from* an emphasis on course work *to using evidence-based knowledge* to inform practice so it effectively addresses students' needs" (NCATE, 2010, p. 4).

Subsequent research findings published in *Reforming Teacher Preparation: The Critical Clinical Component* (American Association of Colleges for Teacher Education (AACTE), 2010), *Transforming Teacher Education through Clinical Practice* (National Council for Accreditation of Teacher Education (NCATE), 2010), and *Our Responsibility, Our Promise* (Council of Chief State School Officers (CCSSO), 2012) reinforced the importance of high-quality field experiences integrated into teacher preparation programs to produce effective teachers (Walker, 2008; Welsh & Schaffer, 2017).

More precisely, research focused on high-quality teacher education program purposes and course goals, showed that activities and outcomes matter (Wayne & Youngs, 2003). Activities and outcomes must be designed and delivered to equip and empower teacher candidates to be attentive to and accountable for the teaching, learning, and schooling (Gallavan & Maiden, in press). Ultimately, classroom teachers are responsible for increasing engagement and achievement of all PK-12 learners (Cochran-Smith & Fries, 2009) and must take ownership of their professionalism. Consequently, teacher preparation program faculty develop field experience expectations and evidence-gathering methods to ensure authentic documentation of PK-12 learner growth; activities and outcomes introduced, practiced, and mastered throughout their teacher preparation program courses must contribute to the enhancement of teacher self-efficacy.

High-Quality Field Experiences

In 2013, NCATE was reorganized into CAEP, the Council for the Accreditation of Educator Preparation (CAEP, 2013), with updated standards released in 2016 (CAEP, 2016). CAEP Standard 2 addresses Clinical Partnerships and Practice emphasizing that clinical experiences should offer "sufficient depth, breadth, diversity, coherence, and duration to ensure that candidates demonstrate their developing effectiveness and positive impact on all students' learning and development" (CAEP, 2013, para 2.3). This description of high-quality field experiences relies on the fulfillment of CAEP Standard 1: Content and Pedagogical Knowledge facilitated by teacher preparation program faculty during teacher preparation program courses and by supervisors during field experiences, particularly the culminating internship.

The purpose of high-quality field experiences is for teacher candidates to integrate the course goals, activities, and outcomes into their PK-12 classroom teaching, learning, and schooling. Research investigating high-quality field experiences indicates that the majority of teacher interns experience decreased anxiety, increased confidence, and enhanced self-efficacy (Singh, 2017) with proper preparation, specific direction, and continuous assistance. However, when Grisham et al. (2014) examined if teacher candidate interns are learning the concepts and practices they are taught about literacy education at ten teacher preparation programs located across the United States, the researchers discovered that interns expressed only a fair level of congruence or 70% of the program and course goals. Notably, some of the items that these interns found most congruent between program courses and internship related to the knowledge, skills, and dispositions interns had absorbed as PK-12 students themselves and not from their teacher preparation programs.

In 2016, Brabeck et al. assessed the assessments of teacher preparation programs stating, "teacher preparation programs have both a desire and a responsibility to demonstrate, with affirmative evidence, that teacher education makes a difference in PreK–12 student learning" (p. 160). Brabeck et al. reviewed a 2012 report titled *Assessing and Evaluating Teacher Preparation Programs* published by a task force comprised of members of the American Psychological Association's Education Directorate with support from the Council for the Accreditation of Educator Preparation (CAEP). This task force was charged with developing a practical, user-friendly resource based on the psychological science of program assessment.

Reviewing this publication, Brabeck et al. (2016) concluded that "the report emphasizes basic assessment principles and recommendations. First, student learning is recognized as the most critical outcome of effective teaching and should be integrated into teacher preparation programs' fidelity assurance; programs need such evidence both to assure the public and to improve their programs" (2016, p. 161). Second, assessments must be used "appropriately in the service of improving learning outcomes" (p. 162).

Third, "using multiple sources of data (multiple measures) will result in better quality data for making valid inferences" (Brabeck et al., p. 162). Fourth, "quality program evaluation (can be achieved) by providing training for institutions and individuals that will permit programs to acquire the capacity needed to make changes in a timely manner." And, fifth, "faculty and administrators, state policy makers, and accrediting bodies must all take responsibility for addressing the merits of programs" (Brabeck et al., 2016, p. 162). These five conclusions reinforce the need for the following:

> Teacher education faculty members [need] to work in partnership with school districts and states to invest time and resources in the development of systems that allow them to demonstrate with confidence that candidates completing their programs are making substantive contributions as new teachers to the learning outcomes of all of the students that they teach. (Brabeck et al., 2016, p. 165)

Effective Teacher Preparation Courses

Concomitantly, teacher preparation program faculty must ensure that their coursework offers concepts, vocabulary, and practices that produce effective teachers (Smith, Stapleton, Cuthrell, Brinkley, & Covington, 2016), that is, professionals attentive to and accountable for the teaching, learning, and schooling. Therefore, courses should follow the FEAT Model (Gallavan, n.d.). FEAT Model courses are founded on theory and research, engage candidates in significant activities, advance learning via developmentally appropriate outcomes, and transfer learning from courses to classrooms emphasizing practical and professional pedagogy. (Moreover, a slightly modified FEAT Model provides a practical frame for teacher candidates to use their own classrooms substituting theory with standards and professional pedagogy with useful application in the real world.) Coursework must integrate with well-organized, closely supervised field experiences (Darling-Hammond, Hammerness, Grossman, Rust, & Shulman, 2005; Zeichner, 2010; Zeichner & Conklin, 2005). And ideally, teacher preparation program course faculty should serve as internship supervisors to strengthen the coursework-candidate-classroom connection.

Interns' Concerns

Although much research has been published related to effective teacher preparation internships and interns as prospective teachers, little research has been published related to the interns' three concerns to fulfill the expectations of internship as university students. As internship supervisors, the authors of this research study have held many conversations regarding the extensive number of expectations that must be prioritized, the expansive scope of the expectations that must be itemized, and the equal importance of the expectations that must be contextualized. This research study focused on these three concerns in relationship to one course, Classroom Assessment, in an attempt to provide a tool for facilitating effective learning experiences that are manageable, measurable, and meaningful.

RESEARCH

In one mid-south mid-sized four-year university, the college of education offers a nationally recognized Master of Arts in Teaching degree for students who have earned an undergraduate degree and want to become PK-12 classroom teachers. This MAT program was designed for teacher candidates to earn their masters degrees while employed as classroom teachers, especially in geographical areas of the state where qualified classroom teachers are needed. Teacher candidates complete a sequence of courses in face-to-face, online, and hybrid formats and two field experiences. The first field experience, called Practicum, may be completed at any time during the program prior to internship; the second field experience, called internship, may be completed only after all other courses have been completed.

Practicum, usually conducted early in the MAT program, entails observing and teaching in a classroom for a specified number of hours throughout the semester coupled with submitting reflections related to identified outcomes. Internship, conducted as the culmination of the MAT Program, entails teaching a classroom for a semester, approximately fifteen weeks, coupled with submitting various assignments documenting the intern's progress and proficiency. Three observations conducted by the university supervisor ensure accountability during internship. During the MAT internship, interns are evaluated by their supervisors; supervisors include both full-time and part-time university teacher preparation program faculty, some of whom teach courses in the MAT program.

Background

In this research study, the first author, a MAT teacher preparation program faculty who also supervises interns, reviewed the overarching goals of the course that she originated and has taught in the MAT program for ten years. The course, Classroom Assessment, is taught online and features four purposes: "to increase *awareness* of attitudes, purposes, and cycle of assessment; to expand *acquisition* of concepts, vocabulary, and practices associated with assessment; to develop *applications* of various practices for effective assessments; and to communicate *appreciation* of the processes for increasing learners' achievements and enhancing self-efficacy with positive and productive assessments and accountability" (Gallavan, 2018, class notes). The course is considered ambitious yet achievable; students' comments on the course evaluation overwhelmingly report that (1) this course is one of the most important courses in the MAT program, (2) the content examines assessment concepts and practices that tend to be previously unknown to candidates in their PK-12 student experiences and their MAT PK-12 practicum experiences; and (3) the instructor models the assessment practices exactly as PK-12 teachers should use them in their classrooms.

In addition to teaching the Classroom Assessment course, the first author supervises MAT interns every semester. Likewise, the second author, a graduate of this MAT program, supervises MAT interns most semesters. MAT supervisors use the state Teacher Excellence and Support System (TESS) Formative Evaluation/Self-Assessment Form (Arkansas Department of Education, 2017) to evaluate interns. Built on the research of Danielson (2011), TESS consists of four domains: (1) Planning and Preparation; (2) Classroom Environment; (3) Instruction; and (4) Professional Responsibilities. Each of the four domains is subdivided into five or six competencies. The TESS rubric uses the four rating categories: "Distinguished," "Proficient," "Basic," and "Unsatisfactory." All four domains and twenty-one competencies are introduced, analyzed, and practiced during the MAT program courses.

Purpose of This Research Study

All four domains and twenty-one competencies are evaluated during the three classroom observations conducted in internship. However, no standardized guidelines have been established for supervisors' use of the TESS rubric; therefore, the coauthors of this research study, both internship supervisors, focused on ways to prioritize, itemize, and contextualize the TESS domains and competencies to improve interns' awareness, acquisition, application, and appreciation to improve their teaching, learning, and schooling. Additionally, the first author realized that the concepts, vocabulary, and practices of the Classroom Assessment course taught by the first author were not fully developed in interns' lesson plans or clearly evident during the classroom observations. Consequently, two steps were taken.

Step One

The first author, who also teaches the Classroom Assessment course, designed an assignment for the course for the teacher candidates to identify developmentally appropriate assessments for six TESS competencies related to assessment. Drawing from another Classroom Assessment course assignment, the Impact on Student Learning Project, teacher candidates detailed the specific evidence that classroom teachers would provide to earn a score of "Proficient" and the special evidence that the corresponding students would provide for the teacher to earn a score of "Proficient." The TESS form includes scores on a range of points from 1.00–4.00 labeled "Distinguished," "Proficient," "Basic," and "Unsatisfactory."

The six TESS competencies with descriptions (categorized within the four domains) for which the teacher candidates provided teacher and student evidence are shown in table 3.1.

TABLE 3.1 SIX TESS COMPETENCIES FEATURED IN CLASSROOM ASSESSMENTS

Domain	Competency and Criteria
1: Planning & Preparation	1F: Designing Student Assessments Congruence with outcomes; Criteria & standards; Formative Assessments; Use for planning
2: Classroom Environment	(no applicable components)
3: Instruction	3A: Communicating with Students Expectations for learning; Directions & procedures; Explanations of content; Use of oral & written language 3B: Using Questioning & Discussion Techniques Quality of questions; Discussion techniques; Student participation 3D: Using Assessment in Instruction Assessment criteria; Monitoring of student learning; Feedback to students; Student self-assessment
4: Professional Responsibilities	4A: Reflecting on Teaching Accuracy; Use in future teaching 4B: Maintaining Accurate Record Student completion of assignments; Student progress in learning; Non-instructional records

Step Two

Next, the first author constructed a rubric featuring seven critical features of a lesson plan for the supervisor and interns to use during classroom observations in internship as shown in table 3.2. Coordinated with the Classroom Assessment course assignment identifying specific evidence of assessment practices related to TESS, *Gallavan's Seven Essential Elements for Facilitating an Effective Learning Experience* rubric identifies seven parts of a lesson plan that need to be detailed in the written plan, prepared in advance of class, and evident in the taught lesson plan. The rubric includes the number, title, abbreviation, description, and recommended time to be allotted to completing each element. The rubric also includes scores for each element with a range of +, ✓, and –, and space for both supervisor comments and intern comments.

TABLE 3.2 GALLAVAN'S SEVEN ESSENTIAL ELEMENTS FOR FACILITATING AN EFFECTIVE LEARNING EXPERIENCE

# Title	Abbreviation	Time
Description		Score + ✓ –
Comments	+ = Proficient; ✓ = Adequate; – = Unsatisfactory	

All seven essential elements should be detailed in the written lesson plan, prepared in advance of class, and evident in the facilitated learning experience.

# Title	Abbreviation	Time
1 **Preassessment**	PRE	8–10 min
Teacher administers a written or an electronic preassessment independently and in compliance with each student's IEP. Preassessment data are used during lesson.		**Score: + ✓ –**
Supervisor Comment:		
Intern Comment:		
2 **Objective**	OBJ	3 min
Teacher displays and/or distributes at least one written objective aligned with standards that is read aloud and discussed briefly to confirm comprehension.		**Score: + ✓ –**
Supervisor Comment:		
Intern Comment:		
3 **Student Selection System**	SSS	ongoing
Teacher uses a written or electronic system for selecting students to participate ensuring that every student is called on to speak or participate during every lesson. The SSS may allow for space to record assessment data.		**Score: + ✓–**
Supervisor Comment:		
Intern Comment:		

#	Title	Abbreviation	Time
	Description		Score + ✓ −
	Comments	+ = Proficient; ✓ = Adequate; − = Unsatisfactory	
4	**Written Instruction/Expectations/Self-Assessment**	WISEA	ongoing
	Teacher distributes prepared written instructions guiding the lesson with clearly stated expectations related to outcomes, specifically participation and productivity accompanied by a self-assessment checklist or rubric that includes space for student and teacher comments.		**Score: + ✓ −**
	Supervisor Comment:		
	Intern Comment:		
5	**Formative Assessment/Practice-Guided & Independent FAPGI**		ongoing
	Teacher monitors and measures progress using a checklist or rubric during guided practice while the teacher is facilitating instruction and during independent practice while students are completing outcomes ensuring that a written score is recorded for every student.		**Score: + ✓ −**
	Supervisor Comment:		
	Intern Comment:		
6	**Closure**	CLOS	10 mins
	Teacher facilitates a group conversation or activity reviewing the objectives and outcomes of the day's learning experience ensuring that all students contribute to the closure.		**Score: + ✓ −**
	Supervisor Comment:		
	Intern Comment:		
7	**Postassessment**	POST	8–10 mins
	Teacher administers the same written or an electronic preassessment as the postassessment with the same five to ten items that every student completes independently and/or in compliance with each student's IEP. Postassessment are used to prepare for the next lesson.		**Score: + ✓ −**
	Supervisor Comment:		
	Intern Comment:		

Therefore, this research study was conducted to investigate MAT interns' transfer of learning from the Classroom Assessment course to their internship classroom observations. The research study was framed by two research questions:

1. What is the level of proficiency demonstrated by teacher preparation interns in applying seven essential elements of classroom assessment in their facilitation of effective learning experiences?
2. What is the range of comments communicated by teacher preparation interns associated with observation feedback?

Data Collection

The first author implemented the new Classroom Assessment assignment for two years, a total of three semesters per year, including the summer semester, allowing time for the majority of MAT teacher candidates to complete the course. Then, during the third year the first author, in the role as internship supervisor, began using the *Seven Essential Elements* rubric while conducting the three classroom observations.

During each of two semesters of one academic year, four interns participated in this research study for a total of eight interns. The group of interns was described as four female interns and four male interns; six Caucasian interns and two Hispanic interns; one elementary school, four middle school, and three high school interns. All interns were teaching as the teacher of record in classrooms that matched their areas of licensure.

Data collection followed the sequence shown in table 3.3. Notably, the *Seven Essential Elements* rubric was not shared with the interns prior to conducting Observation 1. Just as the rubric begins with a preassessment, Observation 1 was conducted as a preassessment. Then, following Observation 1, the rubric was shared with interns and described in detail; individual feedback was given to each intern. Again, this procedure parallels the *Seven Essential Elements* of the rubric by establishing the objective, providing a written copy of the instructions with expectations and self-assessment, noting the use of the rubric as a formative assessment during the observation. Feedback provided closure and postassessment.

Prior to conducting Observation 2, the rubric was emphasized to the interns both as a group and individually. Following Observation 2, feedback was given to each intern with comments related to changes (positive and negative). Then, prior to Observation 3, the series of seven essential elements was repeated again. Throughout all data collection, the first author communicated frequently with the interns via email and telephone to ensure that all interns

TABLE 3.3 DATA COLLECTION SEQUENCE

Observation 1:	Conduct and score Observation 1 prior to sharing the *Seven Essential*
	Elements rubric with interns using the *Seven Essential Elements* rubric
Post Observation 1	Introduce the *Seven Essential Elements* rubric and conduct a thorough
Group Email:	group conversation to ensure comprehensive understanding
Post Observation 1	Provide individual feedback emphasizing strengths and weaknesses from
Individual Email:	Observation 1. Encourage each intern to ask questions and seek assistance
Pre Observation 2	Remind interns to be attentive to the *Seven Essential Elements* rubric as
Group Email:	they detail their written lesson plans, prepare their documents before teaching the observed class, and rehearse for Observation 2
Observation 2:	Score Observation 2 using the *Seven Essential Elements* rubric
Post Observation 2	Provide individual feedback emphasizing strengths and weaknesses from
Individual Email:	Observation 2 noting changes from Observation 1
Post Observation 2	Summarize the changes in written lesson plan preparation and facilitated
Group Email:	learning experience between Observation 1 and Observation 2
Pre Observation 3	Again, encourage interns to be attentive to the *Seven Essential Elements*
Group Email:	rubric as they detail their written lesson plans, prepare their documents before teaching the observed class, and rehearsing for Observation 3
Pre Observation 3	Provide individual guidance and support related to the elements on the
Individual Email:	*Seven Essential Elements* rubric that the intern did not demonstrate proficiently in the written lesson plan or facilitated learning experience
Observation 3:	Score Observation 3 using the *Seven Essential Elements* rubric
Post Observation 3	Provide individual feedback emphasizing strengths and weaknesses from
Individual Email:	Observation 3 including feedback related to the intern's willingness to listen to feedback, read the comments, and change the written lesson plan and/or facilitation of the learning experience to enhance effectiveness
Post Observation 3	Summarize the importance of and usefulness for the *Seven Essential*
Group Email:	*Elements* specifically to increase to increase student engagement and achievement in relationship to the TESS competencies

understood the significance of the *Seven Essential Elements* rubric for their observations specifically and their pedagogy in general.

Data Summary Tool

The *Seven Essential Elements* rubric was completed for each of the eight interns' three observations. Likewise, a Summary Data Tool was used to record each intern's scores and comments for all three observations as shown in table 3.4. A Sample Summary Data Tool is shown in table 3.5.

TABLE 3.4 DATA SUMMARY TOOL—INDIVIDUAL INTERNS

Intern:							
Observation 1 Scores S Comments I Comments	PRE	OBJ	SSS	WISEA	FAGIP	CLO	POST
Observation 2 Scores S Comments I Comments	PRE	OBJ	SSS	WISEA	FAGIP	CLO	POST
Observation 3 Scores S Comments I Comments	PRE	OBJ	SSS	WISEA	FAGIP	CLO	POST

TABLE 3.5 SAMPLE DATA SUMMARY TOOL—INDIVIDUAL INTERNS

Intern: A							
Observation 1 Scores	PRE –	OBJ ✓	SSS –	WISEA –	FAGIP –	CLO ✓	POST –
S Comments: *OBJ and CLO evident; other elements need S instruction*							
I Comments: *will give PRE & POST & develop WISEA; hesitant re: SSS & FAGIP*							
Observation 2 Scores	PRE ✓	OBJ +	SSS –	WISEA ✓	FAGIP –	CLO ✓	POST ✓
S Comments: *OBJ better, PRE, POST, WISEA, CLO evident; missing SSS & FAGIP*							
I Comments: *agrees with PRE, POST, WISEA, & CLO; still against SSS and FAGIP*							
Observation 3 Scores	PRE +	OBJ +	SSS ✓	WISEA ✓	FAGIP ✓	CLO +	POST +
S Comments: *PRE, POST, & CLO better; used FAGIP; used FABGIP for SSS*							
I Comments: *agrees with PRE, POST & FAGIP to record scores and collect data*							

Findings

Data from each interns' Summary Data Tool were recorded on the findings from the eight interns as shown in table 3.6.

TABLE 3.6 FINDINGS FROM THE EIGHT INTERNS

Observation 1		PRE	OBJ	SSS	WISEA	FAGIP	CLO	POST
Scores	+	0	2	0	0	0	1	0
	✓	0	3	1	0	0	3	3
	−	8	3	7	8	8	4	5

Findings: *provide details related to 7EE and connect with TESS and Classroom Assessment activities; check comprehension with each intern*

Observation 2		PRE	OBJ	SSS	WISEA	FAGIP	CLO	POST
Scores	+	1	3	2	1	1	3	1
	✓	6	5	4	5	4	5	7
	−	1	0	2	2	3	0	0

Findings: *emphasize the benefits of the 7EE as part of TESS and the upcoming Impact on Student Learning Project; share strengths, weaknesses, and changes with each intern; note resistance*

Observation 3		PRE	OBJ	SSS	WISEA	FAGIP	CLO	POST
Scores	+	4	5	3	4	3	4	4
	✓	4	3	4	4	4	4	4
	−	0	0	1	0	1	0	0

Findings: *changes continue to improve; emphasize value of the 7EE to professional practice; relate to Impact on Student Learning Project; communicate with the one resistant intern*

Three Aspects Influencing Interns' Competencies

The scores and comments from the three observations recorded on the table 3.6 reveal three critical aspects influencing the interns' proficiency to facilitate effective learning experiences. The first aspect encompasses readiness to teach as noted by the scores. The data clearly show that the interns were not ready to demonstrate proficiency with the *Seven Essential Elements* rubric during Observation 1. Their readiness to teach improved when provided the *Seven Essential Elements* rubric and details as a group accompanied by guidance and support as an individual. Their readiness exhibited additional improvement with feedback from Observations 1 and 2 in preparation for Observation 3.

The second aspect entails receptiveness to feedback as noted by the comments. The comments indicate that the interns demonstrated a range of openness and willingness to integrate the seven essential elements into their written lesson plans and facilitated learning experiences. Levels of receptiveness to feedback expressed as agreement and acceptance increased while levels of resistance decreased. Interns who produced more comprehensive and complete Impact on Student Learning Projects exhibited greater receptiveness to the guidance and support offered by the supervisor. Levels of receptiveness to feedback expressed as reluctance and resistance increased by interns who shared they needed to integrate some elements.

The third aspect embodies responsiveness to expectations as noted by a combination of scores and comments. Interns who increased their scores from − to ✓ to + visibly internalized and initiated responsibility for and ownership of the seven essential elements as integral to their core of the teaching, learning, and schooling: teacher self-efficacy.

DISCUSSION

Scoring the eight interns' observations using the *Seven Essential Elements* rubric equipped the interns with an approach to integrate their Classroom Assessment goals, activities, and outcomes with their internship. Providing immediate feedback empowered the interns to make immediate modification to the teaching, learning, and schooling. Their increased attention to and accountability for the teaching, learning, and schooling enabled the interns to enhance their self-efficacy shown as Gallavan's Triad of Teacher Self-Efficacy in figure 3.1. Documenting their learners' engagement and achievement while assessing their own effectiveness using the *Seven Essential Elements* rubric, the interns increased their awareness, acquisition, application,

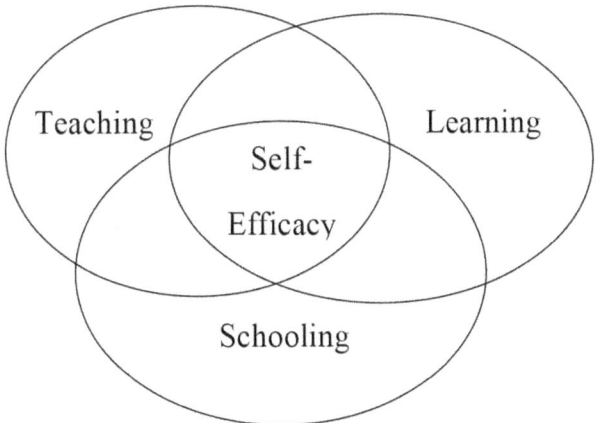

Figure 3.1 Gallavan's Triad of Teacher Self-Efficacy.

and appreciation of the concepts, vocabulary, and practices of their Classroom Assessment course.

Simultaneously, interns could relate the seven essential elements to TESS, the state teacher evaluation criteria. Given the advanced concepts, vocabulary, and practices associated with classroom assessments, the rubric provided the interns with a tool that helped them to make the expectations of internship more manageable, measurable, and meaningful as a university student.

Zeichner (2005) contended that teacher education program field experience supervisors needed additional preparation; they could not simply transfer their own classroom teaching experiences as the basis for mentoring interns, especially if they did not teach courses in the teacher preparation program. Dangel and Tanguay (2014) advanced this contention and proposed that a critical aspect in ensuring high-quality field experiences during teacher preparation programs relates to the field supervisors. Supervisors are more effective when they operate within a framework of useful strategies that provide "professional development that supports and strengthens supervision."

From the authors' findings, we conclude that not only would field experience supervisors benefit from additional preparation, research needs to be conducted investigating the concerns of interns as well as the concerns of supervisors related specifically to the extensive number, expansive scope, and equal importance of the expectations. Although the published research addresses most other aspects of teacher preparation coursework and field experiences, little research addresses the concerns of interns as university students attempting to prioritize, itemize, and contextualize the expectations.

RECOMMENDATIONS

Therefore, from this research study, the authors offer three recommendations:

1. All teacher preparation program faculty should also supervise their program's teacher candidates during internship to increase faculty awareness of interns' acquisition and application of course goals and activities into their classroom practices. Faculty, supervisors, and interns benefit when interns are cognizant of their readiness to teach. This recommendation offers hope for teachers to be competent in increasing learner engagement and achievement.
2. All teacher preparation program faculty should align program purposes and course goals with the state expectations and teacher evaluation criteria integrated into internship expectations. Faculty, supervisors, and interns benefit when interns are adept in their receptiveness to feedback. This

recommendation offers courage for teachers to be accessible in advancing teacher growth, pedagogical modifications, and professional development.
3. All teacher preparation program faculty should assess and analyze their teaching, learning, and schooling honestly and holistically. Faculty, supervisors, and interns benefit when interns are professional in their responsiveness to expectations. This recommendation offers strength for teachers to be persistent in pursuing insights and inspirations via models and mentors to sustain career success and satisfaction.

CONCLUSION

The Carnegie Corporation of New York report (2006), *Teachers for a New Era: Transforming Teacher Education*, concluded, "Our investment in teachers has many objectives but one singular overriding aim. It is to improve student learning growth in schools in the United States, and thus improve the life chances of our citizens" (p. 9). As means to this end, teacher preparation programs must focus on their teacher candidates, university courses, and field experiences given that teachers' abilities are the most crucial contributors to students' learning (Darling-Hammond, 2006). We advocate that these aspirations pertain to both PK-12 classroom teachers as well as higher education faculty in all iterations of teacher preparation programs (Zeichner, 2013). Therefore, the pedagogical preparation, practical application, and professional development of teacher candidates in their journeys in becoming and advancing their proficiencies as classroom teachers facilitating effective learning experiences is critical to schools, classrooms, students, and communities.

REFERENCES

American Association of Colleges for Teacher Education (AACTE). (2010). *Reforming teacher preparation: The critical clinical component*. Washington, DC: Author.

Arkansas Department of Education (ADE). (2017). *Teacher expectation and support system* (TESS). Retrieved from http://www.arkansased.gov/divisions/educator%20effectiveness/educator-support-development/teacher-support-and-development/teacher-excellence-and-support-system-tess.

Brabeck, M. M., Dwyer, C. A., Geisinger, K. F., Marx, R. W., Noell, G. H., Pianta, R. C., Subotnik, R. F., & Worrell, F. C. (2016). Assessing the assessments of teacher preparation. *Theory into Practice, 55*(2), 160–167.

Carnegie Corporation of New York. (2006). *Teachers for a new era: Transforming teacher education*. New York, NY: Author. Retrieved from https://www.carnegie.org/media/filer_public/6e/05/6e055df3-8558-4916-8237-0542696e5ce5/ccny_grantee_2006_teachers.pdf.

Cochran-Smith, M., & Fries, K. (2009). Researching teacher education in changing times. In M. Cochran-Smith & K. Zeichner (Eds.), *Studying teacher education: The report of the AERA Panel on Teaching and Teacher Education* (pp. 69–107). Washington, DC: American Educational Research Association (AERA).

Council for the Accreditation of Educator Preparation (CAEP). (2013). *Final CAEP accreditation standards.* Retrieved from http://caepnet.org/accreditation/final-standards/.

Council for the Accreditation of Educator Preparation (CAEP). (2016). *CAEP accreditation handbook: Version 3.* Retrieved from http://caepnet.org/~/media/CAEP%20Accreditation%20Handbook_March%202016.pdf?la=en.

Council of Chief State School Officers (CCSSO). (2012). *Our responsibility, our promise: Transforming educator preparation and entry into the profession.* Washington, DC: Author.

Dangel, J. R., & Tanguay, C. (2014). "Don't leave us out there alone": A framework for supporting supervisors. *Action in Teacher Education, 36*(3), 3–19.

Danielson, C. (2011). *Enhancing professional practice: A framework for teaching* (2nd ed.). Alexandria, VA: Association for Supervision and Curriculum Development (ASCD).

Darling-Hammond, L. (2006). Constructing 21st-century teacher education. *Journal of Teacher Education, 57*(3), 300–314.

Darling-Hammond, L., Hammerness, K., Grossman, P., Rust, F., & Shulman, L. (2005). The design of teacher education programs. In L. Darling-Hammond, J. Bransford, P. LePage, K. Hammerness, & H. Duffy (Eds.), *Preparing teachers for a changing world. What teachers should learn and be able to do* (pp. 390–441). San Francisco, CA: Jossey-Bass.

Gallavan, N. P. (n.d.). FEAT model. Teaching in Higher Education, course notes.

Gallavan, N. P., & Maiden, S. (in press). Organizing and facilitating online teaching, learning, and schooling via effective classroom assessments. In B. Eisenbach & P. Greathouse (Eds.), *The online classroom: Resources for effective middle level virtual education.* Charlotte, NC: Information Age Publications.

Grisham, D. L., Yoder, K. K., Smetana, L., Dobler, E., Wolsey, T. D., Lenski, S. J., Young, J., Chambers, S. S., Scales, R. Q., Wold, L. S., Ganske, K., & Scales, W. D. (2014). Are teacher candidates learning what they are taught: Declarative literacy learning in ten teacher preparation programs. *Teacher Education & Practice, 27*(1), 168–189.

National Council for the Accreditation of Teacher Education (NCATE). (2010). *Transforming teacher education through clinical practice: A national strategy to prepare effective teachers. Report of the blue ribbon on clinical preparation and partnerships for improved student learning.* Washington, DC: Author.

Singh, D. K. (2017). Role of clinical practice in teacher preparations: Perceptions of elementary teacher candidates. *Education, 138*(2), 179–189.

Smith, J. J., Stapleton, J. N., Cuthrell, K. C., Brinkley, J., & Covington, V. M. (2016). Improving the internship model; Instructional coaches for teacher candidates. *Teacher Education and Practice, 29*(2), 344–358.

Walker, R. J. (2008). Twelve characteristics of an effective teacher: A longitudinal, qualitative, quasi-research study of in-service and pre-service teachers' opinions. *Educational Horizons, 87*(1), 61–68.

Wang, J., Lin, E., Spalding, E., Klecka, C., & Odell, S. (2011). Quality teaching and teacher education: A kaleidoscope of notions. *Journal of Teacher Education, 62*(4), 331–338.

Wayne, A. J., & Youngs, P. (2003). Teacher characteristics and student achievements gains: A review. *Review of Educational Research, 73*(1), 89–122.

Welsh, K. A., & Schaffer, C. (2017). Developing the effective teaching skills of teacher candidates during field experiences. *Educational Forum, 81*(3), 301–321.

Zeichner, K. (2005). Becoming a teacher educator. *Teacher and Teacher Education, 21*(2005), 117–124.

Zeichner, K. (2010). Rethinking the connections between campus courses and field experiences in college- and university-based teacher education. *Journal of Teacher Education, 61*(1–2), 89–99.

Zeichner, K. (2013). Two visions of teaching and teacher education for the 21st century. In X. Xhu & K. Zeichner (Eds.), *Preparing teachers for the 21st century* (pp. 3–20). Heidelberg: Springer.

Zeichner, K., & Conklin, H. (2005). Teacher education programs. In M. Cochran-Smith & K. Zeichner (Eds.), *Studying teacher education* (pp. 645–735). New York, NY: Routledge.

Chapter 4

Collaboration

A Skill that Must Be Explicitly Taught

Heather K. Dillard

ABSTRACT

Collaboration has become an essential skill in the 21st-century workplace (Morel, 2014). Major companies such as Google have touted the need for collaboration to create significant impacts on all aspects of their industry (Lafargue, 2015). The National Education Association (NEA) (n.d.) has listed collaboration and its companion skill of communication as two of the four critical components that must be taught in schools for students to become competitive in the global marketplace. If teachers need to teach students how to become proficient communicators and collaborators, then they too need to master these skills. Therefore, the onus is on colleges of education to provide proper training in collaboration skills. This study examines two teachers as they experience their first two years as educators and interact in professional learning communities. These two teachers had been participants in a previous study that followed them throughout their student teaching and first year of teaching. When the teachers became members of the same PLC team for the second year of teaching, the researcher continued the study with these two members alone. This chapter examines the experiences and opinions of the two participants throughout the thirty months of their participation in the study. Additionally, implications for teacher education programs will be discussed.

KEY WORDS

Professional Learning Communities; Collaboration; Teacher Preparation

BACKGROUND

Course Work

In the spring of 2013, the Educational Leadership Department at Middle Tennessee State University was charged with creating a new course, titled Residency I, which was first offered in the fall semester of 2013. This course was to become the mandated course for teacher candidates to take during the semester prior to student teaching, now titled Residency II. In creating the course, professors placed two central components into the curriculum, Problem-Based Learning (PBL) and Professional Learning Communities (PLC). All coursework was to be delivered in a PBL format as candidates interacted as a PLC to complete much of their work.

The two components created a perfect symbiotic relationship. Working collaboratively in PLC teams of six to eight, candidates were faced with various problems for which each team member would need to research information to bring back to the group to solve the problem. One of the first PBLs discussed the various components of PLCs. As the candidates interacted with the PBL event, each individual researched various aspects of PLCs, observed PLC meetings in a local K-12 school, and began forming norms by which the team would operate when they met collaboratively. These norms were modeled after the National Staff Development Council's procedures (Richardson, 1999). From this point forward in the semester, all team meetings with the candidates were dubbed PLC meetings, much of their work was completed collaboratively, and each group was required to work within their stated norms.

In addition to researching these topics, the candidates completed fieldwork in local K-12 schools two days per week for the duration of the semester. In their schools and classrooms, candidates interviewed teachers on the PBL topics as well as observed and assisted teachers working in a typical school day including attended PLC meetings. Also, while in the field, candidates were required to meet together for one class period to discuss their research findings and to complete various tasks for the Residency I class.

Furthermore, the candidates were required to attend a weekly seminar course that was team taught by a group of three professors. Each professor had a group of six to ten candidates that had been placed in a different school in the same district. Each PLC team of candidates was able to share their experiences with one another, allowing them to gain an awareness of some of the unique differences that occurred in each of the schools. Not only did the candidates observe PLCs in the school system, they also interacted as a PLC and were taught by a group of professors who were also following the PLC model. The professors met weekly to discuss various topics, organize fieldwork placements, create common assessments, discuss student data, and plan seminar lessons.

Original Study

In the spring of 2014, the researcher began a longitudinal study of former candidates as they progressed through Residency II and their first year of teaching. Three questions were formulated as the main objective for this qualitative study: (1) What is the relationship between a novice teacher's training in PLCs and the teacher's ability to be a member of a PLC? (2) What specific experiences in the PLC training helped prepare novice teachers to be a member of a PLC? (3) What specific experiences were not present in the PLC training that could have better prepared novice teachers to be a member of a PLC?

Findings from this study revealed that training candidates in the concept of PLCs was beneficial to new teachers (Dillard, 2016). Not only did the novice teachers recognize the need to collaborate with their colleagues and work interdependently for the benefit of all students, they were willing to develop these practices in schools that did not require the teachers to work collaboratively. This comfort level with the collaborative practices required in a PLC was attributed to the immersion process of training that the participants received in their Residency I course (Dillard, 2016).

While many of the experiences of the eighteenth-month study were positive for the ten participants, there were struggles for which these new teachers did not feel prepared. These struggles mainly centered around philosophical and personality conflicts between the PLC team members. The participants felt strongly that they had a greater understanding of the purpose and responsibility of the PLC meetings and did not comprehend why the work was not more student focused (Dillard, 2016). Additionally, as new teachers, the participants struggled with dominant personalities that controlled the meetings and became hesitant to interject at times. It was concluded that teacher candidates would benefit from deeper concentration on establishing and monitoring group norms when interacting in the Residency I course (Dillard, 2016). During the final interviews with the participants, it was discovered that two of the participants were going to be teaching in the same PLC team during the following school year. The researcher requested and was granted permission to continue the study with these two participants for the duration of the next school year.

Participants

The participants for this study included two 8th-grade social studies teachers in their second year of teaching. Harper (pseudonym to protect anonymity), a Caucasian female in her late twenties, had taught 7th-grade English during her first year of teaching. Having a middle school endorsement, she was able to teach outside of her main content area of social studies for which she held a bachelor's degree. Mason (pseudonym to protect anonymity), an African American male also in his late twenties, had taught 8th-grade social studies during his first year of teaching. He, too, had earned a bachelor's degree in social studies. When the two members of Mason's team took jobs in another school, Harper and a newly hired first year teacher were placed together as the 8th-grade PLC team at Floyd Middle School (FMS) (pseudonym employed to protect the anonymity of the subjects) for the 2015–2016 school year.

During their time in the Residency I course, both Harper and Mason were members of the same PLC team. This team was taught by the researcher and ironically placed at FMS for their two day per week fieldwork placements. Both candidates had attracted the eye of the head principal and were hired after they completed Residency II.

First Year Experiences

Both Harper and Mason were hired during the summer of 2014 by FMS. They entered the school year with excitement about teaching and for the opportunity to work in a PLC group. Before the school year began, Harper stated that she "look[ed] forward to attempting to lead and participate in PLC meetings in my first year, hoping that they are used correctly." During her student teaching, Harper recognized that not all teachers took their PLC meetings seriously. She noted attending meetings that were "filled with gossip and sports talk and not relevant to student achievement." Additionally, she noticed that some teachers did not get along with one another. These experiences caused her to be aware of the possibility of unprofessional practices in PLCs, yet she remained hopeful for a positive experience.

Mason also expressed similar comments before the school year began. During his student teaching, Mason noticed that "some teachers are more aggressive while other are more passive, and some teachers have an attitude that screams 'I don't care.'" Nevertheless, his attitude toward the PLC process maintained that PLCs were "beneficial as long as each teacher brings something to the table, is willing to compromise, and open for suggestions."

As the first year progressed both Harper and Mason indicated they were struggling with their PLC teams. Harper's first few journal entries contained statements of "I feel as though we (she and another first year teacher on the team) are still student teachers because we are told what to do instead of asked for insight"; "I am scared to share my ideas as they are often shut down and I feel inadequate"; "I feel as though I have to prove myself to my team every day." Mason's early journal entries stated, "I do not feel like an equal partner . . . one person does typically dominate the group"; "the work environment . . . can get political and cold-hearted." Sensing that the two teachers might benefit from opportunities to describe their experiences together, the researcher scheduled time to interview both Harper and Mason together in December. Initially, the intention was to conduct all interviews independently. However, since Harper and Mason had worked on the same PLC team in Residency I, the researcher determined that both would feel comfortable doing the interviews collectively. In this interview, both Harper and Mason explained that teachers at FMS were very stressed by the state report card scores from the previous year. Harper and Mason felt that this pressure could be attributing to the way veteran teachers approached new teachers. Mason stated that he was learning to express himself in the meetings, and Harper stated she was trying not to take things personally when dominant personalities were opposed to her.

One item that was repeatedly discussed in the interviews was the topic of norms. Both Harper and Mason indicated that they assumed group norms would be followed closely. The process of establishing the norms in their department meetings was discussed and both teachers stated it was an item on the agenda in their first meeting of the year. However, Harper stated, "It is just a sheet of paper we were forced to create." Mason followed with, "It is kind of like words on a sheet of paper and your actions don't follow." While both expressed that norms were important, what was more important was to establish some type of consequence for not following them rather than allowing it to become "the norm of not following the norms." As the interview came to a close, Mason re-emphasized the need for norms. He stated, "I believe it would be very beneficial at the beginning of every PLC to state your group norms, to make sure people understand . . . and hold each other accountable." With Harper nodding in agreement, Mason went on to say, "I think it is the only way we are actually going to get to having functional PLCs."

Although Mason had given in to the idea that he would have to complete much of his work in isolation, Harper had found an ally in the other new teacher on her team. The two of them had begun meeting informally after the PLC meetings. They were developing lessons and tests together, analyzing data, and sharing students to remediate and enrich learning based on the test data. These encounters had helped to lessen the frustration she was feeling in her team and further given her hope for the PLC process.

As the year progressed, the teachers' journal entries indicated that little progress had been made for either PLC team. Harper expressed a feeling of the veterans "babysitting" her. At meetings she stated that she was "interrogated" about her lesson plans and told to change them. She stated that at these meetings she felt anxious and "scared they will tell me I can't do something . . . and I have to change everything." She was also frustrated that data were not discussed in meetings. Mason stated that his group was "dysfunctional" because one voice, dominating the group, made it difficult to plan. He stated they were "only a group on paper" but that they were not a good fit. Although he desired to "work more closely and lessen the work load," he did not believe the group could work through their disagreements to do so.

In the final interview, conducted during the last week of school, Mason and Harper decided to participate in another group interview. By this time, they were aware that they would be teaching together in the next school year. As they spoke about their experience from the first year, there was an air of excitement about working together next year. Both teachers expressed that very few improvements had been made in their PLC teams; rather both teachers had learned how to operate within the customs that had been established.

Expectations for the Second Year

As Harper and Mason were discussing their first year experiences, they expressed much hope for the opportunity to collaborate together during their second year. Both teachers agreed that the group dynamic would be totally different from what they had previously experienced due to their laid back and positive personalities. Harper stated, "I think we will be like siblings together . . . able to have fun but also get our stuff done . . . it is going to be awesome." Mason agreed, stating, "It is really going to change things for next year. We worked together over the past couple of years . . . the other member will see how well we work together and . . . get on board." Harper went on to explain that their common understanding of PLCs and the fact that they are open to admit their weaknesses with one another would help them to be "focused on what a PLC should be" causing them to "keep each other on track."

Additionally, both Harper and Mason discussed areas in which they had grown during their first year and how they would utilize that in the upcoming school year. Leadership was one area for which both agreed they wanted to be more vocal. Mason admitted that his laid back, "go with the flow," personality had led him to be uncomfortable being vocal in meetings. In the past, he feared hurting someone's feelings but agreed that in the upcoming school year he would "speak up and say what needs to be said." Harper also admitted to having a desire to lead the PLC meetings but never gaining the opportunity in her first year. She expressed, "I would love for when we are doing the PLC meeting, whoever is doing the minutes to be the leader of that PLC just to make sure" that the agenda is covered.

Harper had experienced great success in her informal PLC meetings with the other new teacher in her PLC group. By the end of the school year they were meeting daily to create assessments, analyze data, create lesson plans as well as remediation and enrichment activities requiring them to swap students. Harper explained that these positive experiences had caused her to become open to try new activities that previously she would not have tried. Additionally, it helped her to understand how to best utilize the Guaranteed Learning Sheets utilized by FMS. As Harper discussed wanting to "make sure that we do this in the new PLC meetings," Mason agreed that it would help them "see trends with students" which would help with remediation and enrichment. Both agreed that the key lay in making sure everyone kept their data sheets updated and came prepared to discuss them in the meetings. This, they agreed, would need to become a norm in the next school year.

Regarding the norms, Mason stated that he had not figured out a way to hold one another accountable to maintaining the norms. However, he did not seem to think this would be an issue in the upcoming school year stating, "I know Harper is going to come in and follow the norms. I am going to follow the norms" so therefore next year should be "way more effective." Secondly, "we know each other, so I think we are going to naturally hold each other accountable . . . I think we are going to feel comfortable with voicing that and holding each other accountable with staying on task and on time." These two items of staying on task and on time had been of particular contention for both Harper and Mason's PLC groups over the past year.

METHODOLOGY

Design

This qualitative case study was a continuation of a previous study conducted by the researcher. In an attempt to discover shared behavior patterns (Gay, Mills, & Airasian, 2006), this case study focused upon one specific group within their real-life context (Yin, 2003). This design was appropriate since the researcher sought an in-depth understanding (Yin, 2006).

Data

The data utilized for this study included five interviews for both participants, twelve journal entries for both participants, and one survey each. Interviews occurred at the conclusion of student teaching, at midyear during their first and second year of teaching, and at the conclusion of years one and two. These interviews were held separately for the second year of the study. Participants submitted three journal entries per semester of both the first and second school year. Additionally, one survey was conducted a month before the final interview in order to assist the researcher in formulating the content of the interview. The Trust on Our Team Survey (Appendix A) by Graham and Ferriter (2010) contains sixteen items that ask individuals to consider the degree to which the individual agrees with the statement and the level of importance placed on the statement. This table is located at https://www.solutiontree.com/free-resources/plcatwork/bplc. Questions include items regarding colleagues' willingness to share, to be welcomed in their classroom, intentions with themselves and students, level of honesty and competence, trustworthiness, ability to make meaningful contributions, and so on.

Data Analysis

The researcher recorded and transcribed all interviews into seventy-two single spaced pages. Utilizing the constant comparative method, (Glasser & Strauss, 1967) initial coding resulted in 271 codes. The 53 pages of double spaced journal entries were coded with 218 initial codes. All 489 codes discussed 92 different categories. These categories were compared to one another and later unified into nine themes, consisting of: administration, collaboration, communication, differences, environment, needed improvements, relationships, sharing, and training.

Survey data for each of the sixteen items on the Trust on Our Team Survey were compared between Harper and Mason's responses. First, the researcher compared how both participants agreed, disagreed, or were neutral on an item. Second, the importance of the item was compared to see if both participants viewed the item as very important, somewhat important, or not important.

FINDINGS

Research Question 1

Research Question 1 posed: What is the relationship between a novice teacher's training in PLCs and his/her ability to be a member of a PLC? Findings from the second year of this study confirmed findings from the first year that training in PLCs helped the novice teachers to maintain a high level of comfort with the PLC process. Both Harper and Mason held a deep appreciation for the potential advantages of working collaboratively for the benefit of their students. They created common formative assessments, both formal assessments where the school required data to be submitted and informal weekly quizzes. Mason explained he loved this opportunity to take a collective look at how the students were doing each week. Even though the school did not require the common weekly quizzes, Mason stated that "if you are going to assess you might as well do it commonly so you can . . . get a more rounded picture" of how the students are doing.

Harper stated that this team was "more focused on data" than her previous team. She described the process of data analysis after a quiz as they attempted to look for patterns with the students and the individual standards to "try to figure out what the underlying cause is behind" the students' scores. Additionally, by the middle of the first semester, the team had added a second meeting most weeks to focus more specifically on lesson plans. This meeting was not mandated by the school's administration, rather the group felt it was important to "make sure we are all on the same page for the week," stated Harper.

Research Question 2

Research Question 2 posed: What specific experiences in the PLC training helped prepare novice teachers to be a member of a PLC? This research question did not surface in the second year study perhaps because the participants were so far removed from their training in Residency I. The first year findings indicated that "all of the participants felt extremely comfortable with their training on professional learning communities" (Dillard, 2016) and attributed that comfortability to the immersion process. During Mason's second interview at the midpoint of his first year of teaching, he stated, "We had a great mentor and a leader to teach us how PLCs were supposed to go and a great program to teach us how PLCs are really supposed to function. We had people come in and talk to us about PLCs. We really received that training." He also stated that the training caused PLCs to become "a natural atmosphere."

Harper made similar statements about her training in Residency I. When asked what additional items could have been added to her training she stated, "there was plenty of training and observations in PLCs" indicating that she did not have a suggestion of how to improve it. She also mentioned the use of norms in the training as beneficial because "we reminded each other of the norms throughout the course."

Research Question 3

Research Question 3 posed: What specific experiences were not present in the PLC training that could have better prepared novice teachers to be a member of a PLC? The second year study produced significant findings with this particular research question, especially since the participants had received the same training on PLCs and were team members in the same Residency I PLC team. Three areas of weakness were discovered including (1) how to communicate honestly without hurting feelings, (2) how to complete the norming process, and (3) the main focus of PLC meetings.

Honest Communication

Throughout the second year it appeared that Harper and Mason were struggling to communicate. On the same day that Harper would express feeling that no one was listening to her or ever using her ideas, Mason was stating that she had great ideas that he often used. It seemed the two had different perspectives on several topics. Harper had expressed a lot of frustration throughout the year regarding Mason's level of participation. Harper viewed his responses to her requests for information as vague while Mason stated he was "sharing his insight." However, Mason did express that he needed to share more with Harper after winter break. Harper desired a level of sharing that Mason was not providing, yet she did not seem to be able to express with him her desire for more depth.

In the final interview, Mason stated that the trust on their team had "eroded" over the course of the year and expressed "a need for communication" as the root of the problem. Mason had become aware of Harper's frustration with him by someone who was not on their team. He was bothered by the fact that Harper had spoken with someone else rather than with him. Earlier in the year, Harper had expressed that she had a nonconfrontational personality and was fearful of bring up issues of frustration. Although she had hinted at her feelings, she had never outright stated how she was frustrated by her teammates. By midyear, she feared that because she had waited so long to express her feelings, her team members might not take it as "I am drowning, I need your help" but rather feel as if she was attacking them.

A further frustration emerged in the need for leadership in the PLC team. While Harper voiced that she had taken on a leadership role, she stated that it was because "no one else will do it" and seemed to think work would not be accomplished otherwise. Whereas Harper viewed a leader as the person to keep the team on task and hold one another accountable, she would have preferred if Mason would be the leader but did not know if he wanted to do it. Ironically, throughout the year, Mason voiced that he felt a need to become "more vocal and provide more of a leadership role" since he had "a year's worth of experience in the content." By the close of the school year, Mason's frustration with Harper further developed in this area. He sensed that Harper was "trying to set herself up as the leader" but he felt in a PLC team no one should be "the leader" because they all had an equal role.

Throughout the year, the team was missing several opportunities to learn from one another, yet both seemed to desire this type of interaction. Unfortunately, the lack of communication caused both Mason and Harper to go into self-preservation mode. Harper had begun sharing her ideas with other teachers in different schools across the state. By hearing how the strategies worked in a different classroom she felt she was able to learn and grow. She enjoyed the opportunity to ask "Did it work in your class? and How did you do it different than I did?" Conversely, Mason determined that he "had to do for self" and did not "reach out" to his team members. He stated that he needed "to make sure things get done and I am doing it" yet he acknowledged that it would "make things easier on each other" if they would work together more.

Norms

In their first year of teaching both Harper and Mason stressed the need for creating norms and holding one another accountable to them. Both were bothered by the fact that their team members did not take norms seriously. Mason suggested that norms should be revisited at the beginning of every meeting to remind the members of their agreed upon commitments to one another. However, in their second year, the topic of norms was not stressed by the team. During the midyear interview, both Harper and Mason were asked to describe the process by which the team established norms. Mason explained that FMS did not require the teams to create norms this year and therefore, since they "did not have to" submit them to the administration, they did not write them down. Harper stated that during the first PLC meeting the topic of norms was brought up and the three members agreed upon the norms. Yet, when both Harper and Mason were asked to list their team norms, they did not list the same norms. Mason stated there were three norms: (1) Be on time, (2) Be prepared, and (3) Come ready to contribute to the group. Harper also stated there were three norms. She listed: (1) Team meetings begin at 1:25 every Friday, (2) Have your data ready for data meetings, and (3) Don't take anything personal.

Throughout the second year, the topic of norms was brought up repeatedly by both Harper and Mason as it had been in the first year. By the end of the second year, both felt that the norms needed to be addressed in the upcoming year. This revelation had been stated at the conclusion of year one, yet the two seemed to lack an understanding of how to properly address the norms.

Mason felt the need to be more specific in stating the norms and to read aloud the norms at the beginning of each PLC meeting. Harper also stated a need to go over the norms in each meeting and to enforce them. Additionally, both teachers wanted to add norms for the upcoming year. Harper wanted to add a norm that required each member to "bring something constructive for everyone to each meeting." Throughout the year, Harper had indicated that she was doing most of the work and felt that her two teammates were not giving her enough in return. Since Mason had taught the subject previously, Harper expected that he would be more forthcoming with materials. In her October journal entry she wrote, "I feel as though I do the majority of the work . . . I share out ideas all the time . . . then I ask for ideas from the other members. . . . Mason does not share any PowerPoints or resources of what he is doing." To combat this problem, Harper set up a OneDrive folder for the group to share their documents. Her November journal entry stated that she had added ten to fifteen items to the folder and Mason had not added any items. This action was very frustrating for Harper as she felt teaching "could be so much easier" if her team members "were willing to work with" her.

Interestingly, Mason acknowledged that "as the year progressed we started doing stuff on our own, not sharing materials and lesson ideas." When asked why this occurred, Mason acknowledged he thought it was due to their different teaching styles. He stated that "when you share and you know that person is not going to use it then it is" pointless to share.

Mason desired to add two new norms in the next school year. First, he wanted to add a norm regarding communication. He desired to see more honest communication between the members. When he realized that Harper had spoken with someone else about her frustrations with him he did not take it very well. "I feel like I am a very approachable person that you can come and talk to about anything." By speaking to someone outside of the group, he felt that it "broke the trust a little bit." Additionally, Mason wanted to add a norm to critique one another's work. He felt that often work was divided among the group for the sake of completing tasks to meet deadlines. He stated, "If I make something, I want someone to go in behind me . . . to critique me . . . I love critiquing because I make mistakes all the time. I feel we should have had that as a process of our PLC to make each other better."

However, Harper stated that it felt as if the team was "looking to each other for someone to lead" the PLC meetings. Since the first PLC meeting had been held in her classroom, it became the norm to always meet in her classroom. Consequently, her computer and overhead projector was utilized to display the minutes and other documents used in the meetings. As a result, Harper felt she had "become a little bit of the leader" and was "making sure that [the work] was done right." During the previous school year, Harper had indicated that the person who took the minutes was viewed as the leader in her PLCs. Therefore, taking on this task in the second year, further added to the norm, in her opinion, that she was viewed as the leader.

Focus of PLC Meetings

During the first year of the study, both Harper and Mason felt they knew more about the PLC process than their teammates. Yet when they worked together in the second year, it became obvious that they needed a refresher on the main purpose of PLC meetings. This outcome could have been a result of working for a year in teams that were not following the PLC procedures properly. The DuFour, DuFour, and Eaker (2008) model of PLCs establishes four primary questions as the focus of the work for PLC teams. These questions ask teams to consider: (1) What do we want the students to learn? (2) How will we know that the students have learned the information? (3) What will we do if students have not learned the information? and (4) What will we do if students have learned the information? To do this work, PLC teams must focus on "The Three Big Ideas" of a PLC that include (1) Focus on Learning, (2) Collaborative Culture, and (3) Focus on Results (DuFour et al., 2008). The Three Big Ideas require teams to establish the guaranteed and viable curriculum that all teachers on the team will teach, to create common formative assessments that all teachers will give to their students, to analyze the data from the assessments, and to develop a plan to provide both remediation and enrichment on a student by student, skill by skill basis (Eaker & Keating, 2015).

Both Harper and Mason recognized a need to collectively create common assessments and then analyze the data from the assessments. They were not, however, using that data to inform their next decisions regarding the students' needs for remediation or enrichment and their opinion appeared to vary about the nature of the data discussions. Mason stated, "The conversations as far as talking about the data and how we can improve . . . didn't really happen as much as I feel like it should." He went on to explain, "we have our data there, but we do not really break it down . . . we just kind of look at the numbers and say ok" but we are not asking why "your kids are at 70% and mine are at 56% . . . we don't talk about 'what did you do in that unit that I did not do.'"

Harper's interpretation of data meetings differed in that these meetings were the ones she most appreciated. She enjoyed the fact that "everyone contributed . . . and I learned from that." She stated that the team looked at groups of students and how they performed on each standard and then discussed how they taught the lessons. She gave an example, "I am seeing that lecturing the Civil War did not work but activities for the Civil War works. So I am learning how to change things for next year." According to Harper, the problem was in what to do when the team did not have data to discuss.

Harper was discouraged that "non-data days" were often little more than checking to see that the team was all on the same page regarding the topic they were currently teaching. When reminded of the four PLC questions in her final interview, Harper seemed to be encouraged about how to proceed in the upcoming school year. She stated, "I think those questions should be added to the minutes." She went on to state that the current form, created by the school to fill out as teams met, was equivalent to a check list of boxes. She stated that if the minutes consisted of an area to record data from common assessments and the four PLC questions then the nature of the meetings would improve.

Ironically, both Harper and Mason expressed a desire to have more common components in their classrooms. Mason articulated a desire to actually have "common everything" in an effort to "really see where our kids struggle." Although the team had been making common quizzes, which was not mandated by the school, the teachers were not putting in the "extra effort to pull data from the quizzes" according to Harper. However, both Harper and Mason acknowledged that if they were analyzing more data than they could create common bell work assignments that could be used as remediation and/or enrichment. This process would give them a third set of data to discuss.

Survey Data

After reading eleven of the twelve journal entries for the participants and conducting four of the five interviews, the researcher decided to survey Harper and Mason on their level of trust with one another. This information was utilized in helping to form some of the final interview questions. Both Harper and Mason had the exact same responses to the extent that they agreed or disagreed with nine of the sixteen statements. Their responses matched on eight of sixteen statements regarding the importance of the statement. Both teachers agreed that the other teacher was honest; competent and capable; unafraid to share; had good intentions with their interactions with both students and one another; and felt welcome in one another's classroom before, during, and after school. Both teachers also acknowledged that they were not pulling in the same direction nor were they celebrating the personal and professional successes of one another.

Three areas of major differences were acknowledged in the survey data. Mason stated that he agreed with the statements of "My colleagues willingly share their materials, resources, and ideas with me"; "I know that I can count on my colleagues"; and "I believe that I can learn from my colleagues." For each of these three statements, Harper reported that she disagreed. Both teachers stated that they saw these three items as either very important or somewhat important. When questioned during the final interview about her responses to these three items, Harper stated that she knew she could learn from Mason if he was willing to share with her. Because he had not been more willing to share during the school year, she felt that she could not count on him.

CONCLUSIONS AND RECOMMENDATIONS

First, as witnessed in the first year study, "providing training on Professional Learning Communities is very beneficial to new teachers" (Dillard, 2016, p. 18). Such training causes new teachers to recognize "the need for working interdependently to help further the learning of all students" (Dillard, 2016, p. 18). While the first year study recommended "teacher-training programs require teacher candidates to work collaboratively utilizing PLC characteristics when possible" (Dillard, 2016, p. 18), the second year study reveals a need for an even more concerted effort in establishing PLC practices. When teacher candidates are working interdependently with other teacher candidates, they should be reminded of the Three Big Ideas of PLCs (DuFour, DuFour, Eaker, Many, & Mattos, 2016). Teachers should be asked to consider if the work they are currently doing is addressing a focus on learning, collaborative culture, and/or results.

Further, whenever possible, these collaborative groups should be asked to address the four questions of a PLC. This goal can be accomplished by allowing teacher candidates to co-plan units, teach a lesson or lessons, and then discuss the findings collaboratively. Even on a mini-lesson, teacher candidates can collect data and discuss them with their peers to develop future plans that consider every K-12 student, student by student and skill by skill (Eaker & Keating, 2015). Whether or not the teacher candidates are allowed to teach the entire unit is not as important as learning to work collaboratively in designing future lessons based on student data. Until teachers begin to "act in accordance with the tenets of a professional learning community [they cannot] begin to understand them at a deeper level" (Eaker, DuFour, & DuFour, 2002, p. 79).

Second, the need for developing norms cannot be overstated. While this study continues to agree that "teacher candidates should create norms for their collaborative groups and hold one another accountable to the norms," (Dillard, 2016, pp. 18–19) the norming process needs to be carefully considered. Although "instructors should take a minimal role in the creation of norms and oversight for holding students accountable to those norms," (Dillard, 2016, p. 19) it is imperative that instructors are very direct in explaining the importance of the norming process. PLC literature addresses the opportunity for teachers to build norms with their students in the classroom (DuFour et al., 2008). These same concepts could be utilized in the higher education classroom with teacher candidates.

By using norms in the classroom, professors are establishing collective commitments of each member of the class (DuFour et al., 2008). Rather than creating a list of student rules, this process addresses "the collective commitments students can make to one another to promote positive relationships, academic success, and a sense of community" (DuFour et al., 2008, p. 287). Further, "the collaborative process of developing norms is more important than the actual list of norms . . . and every student in the class should be engaged in making those commitments" (DuFour et al., 2008, p. 287).

Once these norms are established, professors should review the norms at the beginning and end of every class period for the first few months (DuFour et al., 2008). Then teacher candidates should "engage in a written or verbal reflection of how well he or she feels the class is living up to the norms, and then ask each student to report on his or her own observance of the norms" (DuFour et al., 2008, p. 288). Not only does this process reinforce the value of the norms, it helps the teacher candidates to "become more adept at monitoring their own behavior and applying gentle peer pressure if others are violating classroom norms" (DuFour et al., 2008, p. 288).

Additionally, teams should be encouraged to develop team roles to be used during meetings as one of the group norms. Utilizing this concept helps meetings "run smoother when everyone is clear about what his or her contributions . . . should look like" (Graham & Ferriter, 2010, p. 114). These roles should not remain static for the duration of the semester, rather they should be changed in each meeting to allow each member to hold various roles. Examples of team roles might include the leader, scribe, timekeeper, and devil's advocate.

By adding concerted opportunities for teacher candidates to work collaboratively in developing plans with their peers and concentrated efforts in the norming process, teacher candidates will be given great opportunities to have honest communication with their colleagues. Learning to hold difficult conversations in the higher education classroom would be a great benefit to new teachers entering the field. Holding conversations has the potential to facilitate in the development of trust that has been identified as the first of the five most common team dysfunctions (Lencioni, 2002). As school leaders know, it is much more important for PLC team members to trust one another than it is for them to like one another (Mattos, DuFour, DuFour, Eaker, & Many, 2016).

REFERENCES

Dillard, H. (2016). Preservice training in professional learning communities benefits novice teachers. *Transformative Dialogues: Teaching & Learning Journal*, 9(2), 1–13.

DuFour, R., DuFour, R., & Eaker, R. (2008). *Revisiting professional learning communities at work: New insights for improving schools*. Bloomington, IN: Solution Tree.

DuFour, R., DuFour, R., Eaker, R., Many, T., & Mattos, M. (2016). *Learning by doing: A handbook for professional learning communities at work* (3rd ed.). Bloomington, IN: Solution Tree Press.

Eaker, R., DuFour, R., & DuFour, R. (2002). *Getting started: Reculturing schools to become professional learning communities.* Bloomington, IN: Solution Tree Press.

Eaker, R., & Keating, J. (2015). *Kid by kid, skill by skill.* Bloomington, IN: Solution Tree Press.

Gay, L., Mills, G., & Airasian, P. (2006). *Educational research: Competencies for analysis and applications* (8th ed.). Upper Saddle River, NJ: Pearson.

Glasser, B., & Strauss, A. (1967). *The discovery of grounded theory: Strategies for qualitative research.* Chicago, IL: Aldine.

Graham, P., & Ferriter, W. (2010). *Building a professional learning community at work: A guide to the first year.* Bloomington, IN: Solution Tree Press.

Lagargue, V. (2015). *Working better together: A study of collaboration and innovation in the workplace.* Retrieved from https://storage.googleapis.com/gfw-touched-accounts-pdfs/Collaboration%20Study%20-%20June%202015.pdf.

Lencioni, P. (2002). *The five dysfunctions of a team. A leadership fable.* San Francisco, CA: Jossey Bass Publishers.

Mattos, M., DuFour, R., DuFour, R., Eaker, R., & Many, T. (2016). *Concise answers to frequently asked questions about professional learning communities at work.* Bloomington, IN: Solution Tree Press.

Morel, N. (2014). *Collaboration: An essential skill for the 21st century.* Lipscomb University. Retrieved from http://www.lipscomb.edu/education/blog/education/2014/4/17/collaboration-an-essential-skill-for-the-21st-century.

National Education Association (NEA). (n.d.). *Preparing 21st century students for a global society: An educator's guide to the "Four Cs."* Retrieved from http://www.nea.org/assets/docs/A-Guide-to-Four-Cs.pdf.

Richardson, J. (1999). *Norms put the "Golden Rule" into practice for groups.* Oxford, OH: National Staff Development Council.

Yin, R. (2003). *Case study research: Design and methods* (3rd ed.). Thousand Oaks, CA: Sage Publications.

Yin, R. (2006). Case study methods. In J. Green, G. Camilli, & P. Elmore (Eds.), *Handbook of complementary methods in education research* (pp. 111–121). Mahway, NJ: Lawrence Erlbaum Associates.

Chapter 5

Field Experiences with Children of Trauma

Supporting Emotionally and Psychologically Injured Children (EPICs): Value Beyond Institutional Measure

Jayne M. Leh

ABSTRACT

The perceived benefits to undergraduate participants and the sustainability of a credit-free field experience with emotionally and psychologically injured children (EPICs) whose primary trauma was a community disaster were examined. Data were collected from teams of undergraduates primarily majoring in education and applied psychology who volunteered for the Camp Noah National Service Program across three years. Results indicated increased participation due to reenrollment and self-perceived personal and professional benefits as a result of supporting EPICs. The findings suggest the sustainability of an undergraduate team experience to support EPICs without course credit contingencies and the multifaceted value of this community disaster response program when used as a service-learning experience. Implications regarding the value of such experiences to aid in participants' vocational decision-making process are discussed.

KEY WORDS

Teacher Candidates; Field Experiences; Childhood Trauma

INTRODUCTION

The discussion regarding teacher preparation to support diverse learners in the U.S. classrooms continues to be a topic of extreme importance (e.g., Burkart & Thompson, 2014; Cushner, 2012). Novice teachers are frequently placed in classrooms with high populations of minority children, yet report feelings of discomfort with their placement (Case & Hemmings, 2005; Skepple, 2014). The classroom should promote a sense of comfort and belonging; however, teachers who are unable to engage comfortably with their students may inadvertently promote problem behavior, and a sense among some, of alienation, inadequacy, and poor self-esteem (Durlak, Weissberg, Dymnicki, Taylor, & Schellinger, 2011; Schonfeld et al., 2015).

Unfortunately, many of these children may not receive the support they require because many teachers experience great difficulty in identifying and understanding characteristics of children with internalizing disorders (e.g., anxiety, poor self-esteem, isolation, rejection, self-hate) (Anthony et al., 2005; Headley & Campbell, 2013). As such, many children are overlooked for services (Gresham, 2007; Sleeter, 2001). Identification is extremely important because mental health-related issues such as internalizing disorders may be associated with childhood trauma, suicide, delinquency, behavior issues, and lower academic achievement (Armsworth & Holaday, 1993; Walker, Nishioka, Zeller, Severson, & Feil, 2000) and children who are overlooked for treatment are at a greater risk to develop posttraumatic stress symptoms (Goenjian et al., 2005; Layne et al., 2014). Moreover, 13% of school-aged children suffer with mental health-related issues (Centers for Disease Control and Prevention [CDC], 2013), indicating a sense of urgency in terms of training teacher candidates to identify and intervene with children suffering from emotional and psychological issues.

In fact, the mosaic of classroom diversity is complicated and deserves greater focus in terms of teacher training (Marsh, 2016) to support the emotional and psychological wellness of children. To do this, teachers need to feel comfortable with the diverse populations that they teach to understand their needs. Therefore, field experiences in authentic learning environments with children of diversity may increase a teacher's comfort level and provide training in identifying EPICs, and should be considered essential in teacher-training programs (Author, 2016; Marsh, 2016). Community disasters (e.g., school shootings, hurricanes, flooding, tornadoes), and the trauma associated with such experiences may have damaging effects on a child's mental health (e.g., Giannopoulou et al., 2006). As such, attending to these children in the context of a service-learning experience may be valuable in terms of a learning opportunity for undergraduates interested in supporting school-aged children.

Through service-learning experiences, students engage in organized activities within a community in the context of clearly defined learning objectives, which are usually associated with credit-bearing courses (Bringle & Hatcher, 2009). As students address real-world problems in an authentic environment, engage in reflective activities and inquiry-based practices, the experience helps to crystalize the curricular content; consequently, learning becomes meaningful (Schenck & Cruickshank, 2015). Experiences can be tailored to specific areas of study (see Celio, Durlak, & Dymnicki, 2011 for a review), and benefits have been noted in areas of cultural awareness, diversity (Desrochers, 2006; Goldberg & Coufal, 2009), critical thinking, problem solving (e.g., Dardig, 2004), and citizenship (Bringle & Hatcher, 1996).

Supporting children who have been traumatized by community disasters can be viewed as a valuable service-learning opportunity, especially for university students as they prepare for careers in education, criminal justice, special education, child development, psychology, and social work. In fact, working with traumatized children in a community setting may appeal broadly to many disciplines in terms of student interest. Effective programs for childhood trauma victims that focus on building resiliency and coping skills report decreases in fear and anxiety (e.g., Camp Noah) (see Zotti, Graham, Whitt, Anand, & Replogle, 2006). Unfortunately, such programs are rare and usually offered in the summer, thus limiting undergraduate participation if taken for course credit.

Many universities generously engage in service to the community, recognizing that learning is at the center of the service-learning concept; however, the rewards of serving may be too narrowly focused and firmly lodged in fulfilling academic requirements. Although a body of literature supports service-learning across numerous disciplines and reports on the results of longitudinal service-learning programs (e.g., Brail, 2013; Jones, Blinkhorn, Schumann, & Reddy, 2014), the rewards and sustainability of a university service-learning program *without* academic grade association reveal a dearth of investigations (e.g., Beehr, LeGro, Porter, Bowling, & Swader, 2010).

According to Selznick's (1992) social participation theory, volunteerism with tangible rewards is largely driven by a cost-benefit mindset (i.e., external motivation), and when associated with course credit, the contractual aspect may compel students to volunteer, thus taking away free choice. Volunteerism without tangible rewards, however, is driven by intrinsic satisfaction, which results in stronger commitment, and greater personal and professional impact (Beehr et al., 2010); yet placement without critical reflection is insufficient for growth to take place in areas such as diversity (Desrochers, 2006). In fact, because service learning is rooted in civic engagement with the intent of learning to serve (Annette, 2003), volunteerism without credit may be better suited to the true notion of service learning. However, few investigations are longitudinal in nature; even fewer are void of course credit (e.g., Brail, 2013; Jones et al., 2014), and sustained programs where students volunteer in the context of a faculty-guided educational experience are difficult to locate in the research literature. Therefore, the sustainability of such a model in terms of enrollment is grossly unclear.

In the context of the Camp Noah National Service Program, this three-year study investigated the sustainability of a noncredit-bearing service-learning experience in terms of enrollment and the influence of the experience on students' perceptions both personally and professionally. The Camp Noah program description is presented first. Next, the study objectives are presented according to the project year, followed by an overall description of the project methods and project findings according to each year. Benefits to children were not evaluated.

CAMP NOAH PROGRAM DESCRIPTION

Camp Noah is a national program that responds to children in communities impacted by disasters, both natural and human-made, and offers an opportunity for children to process feelings of fear, loss, and pain through various activities in a nurturing environment. Volunteer teams help children to process their disaster experience while building trusting relationships through creative activities and play along with fostering coping and resiliency skills. The program seeks to empower children by helping them to recognize their personal value, inner strength, and to develop a sense of belonging in family and community (Zotti et al., 2006).

The program began in 1997 in response to flooding in the Red River Valley in North Dakota. The Minnesota-based operation connects teams of eighteen to twenty volunteers with sites expressing support in the aftermath of a community disaster and who can commit to hosting the weeklong day camp in their community. Any child from the immediate community between the ages of kindergarten and 6th grade is welcome to register, with registration usually capping between fifty-five and seventy children.

STUDY OBJECTIVES

To determine the sustainability of this credit-free experience, reenrollment data were collected over three years. Year I was exploratory in nature and piloted a team of university students and examined the perceived benefits to participants as a result of the experience with EPICs, which was further investigated in Years II and III. Data collection consisted of field notes and open-ended post-camp surveys in Years I and II; Year III employed pre- and post-camp assessments to determine participants' motivation for serving EPICs and how perceived personal and professional benefits of serving may have changed as a result of the experience.

METHOD

Participants

Each year for three years, undergraduate students from a university in the northeastern U. S. volunteered for the Camp Noah National Service Program to work with EPICs. No monetary compensation or university course credit was offered. Undergraduate volunteers completed applications, signed forms of consent to participate in the study, were trained (see Training), passed security clearance investigations (e.g., child abuse, criminal history), and were dispatched for one week during the summer. Some students participated multiple years and were resampled.

Parents of children enrolled in Camp Noah were required to sign waiver and consent forms in order to attend camp each year; however, no data were collected from children. As such, outcomes of children were not examined in this study; only undergraduate student outcomes were evaluated. Methodology, team demographics, destination, and circumstances of the childhood trauma varied each year (see table 5.1). The same two university staff volunteered each year to accompany the students.

Year I Participant Demographics

To pilot an undergraduate team, a total of eleven students volunteered from the applied psychology (36.3%, $n = 4$) and education (63.6%, $n = 7$) programs. Students were between nineteen and twenty-two years of age.

Table 5.1 Participant and Camp Demographics According to Year

		Participants	Camp Demographics		
Year	Objective	N	Children N	Location	Disaster Type
I	Student team pilot	11	35	Pennsylvania	Storm flooding
II	Perceived benefits	24	57	Connecticut	School shooting
III	Changes in perceived benefits	29	90	Maryland	Hurricane

Note: Students N = total number of university student participants; Children N = number of children enrolled at the camp each year.

Year II Participant Demographics

In Year II, twenty-four students volunteered from the applied psychology (54%, $n = 13$), education (37.5%, $n = 9$), and speech pathology (CSD) (8.3%, $n = 2$) disciplines. Students were between nineteen and twenty-three years of age; three students had participated in Year I and were resampled.

Year III Participant Demographics

In Year III, thirty-three students volunteered and served the week; however, four students did not complete post-camp surveys, resulting in twenty-nine participants with viable data. Students volunteered from the education (44.8%, $n = 13$), applied psychology (51.7%, $n = 15$), and science (3.4%, $n = 1$) disciplines. Students were between eighteen to twenty-three years of age; sixteen students who participated previously were resampled.

Training

All participants in all years attended mandatory team trainings consisting of one eight-hour professional development workshop and one four-hour mandatory team-building workshop three months preceding the experience. The professional development workshop addressed childhood trauma (e.g., childhood developmental responses), team expectations, stages of community disaster and recovery, the therapeutic approach of Camp Noah, program objectives, and the Camp Noah curriculum. To foster a sense of community, participants were grouped into pairs to form teaching and activity teams during the team-building workshop and reviewed the curriculum that they would use to teach the children.

Curriculum and Logistics

Participants chose from either a teaching or activity role as their main service capacity and had the option to also volunteer for minor service roles in puppetry or skits. Each teaching team consisted of a leader, an aide, and a helper. Activity teams (e.g., art, music, recreation) consisted of a leader and a helper. The participants self-selected their roles, teammates, and preferred grade levels whenever possible. Participants majoring in education and applied psychology were paired together to create cross-disciplinary classroom teaching teams. In Year III, at least one member in each team had previous experience with Camp Noah.

Participants followed the five-day Camp Noah curriculum using music, art, storytelling, and reflection to help children identify and talk about their feelings of fear, loss, anger, and anxiety. Large and small group activities (e.g., parachute games, puppet shows, painting, skits, journaling) offered participants opportunities to work with children to understand their needs. Children arrived each morning between 8:30 and 9:00. Participants led the children in a large group activity time of song and a daily skit. Small group class time began at 9:30 as participants in teaching teams used the curriculum to explain the daily theme, facilitate open discussions, and guide small group activities using play dough, games, and songs to help children express their emotions.

Teaching teams guided the children to reflect on daily lesson themes using journal prompts to help children process their feelings (e.g., "How did you feel when . . .?"). Journal responses remained confidential among the team. However concerns noted in the journals (e.g., hopelessness, guilt, extreme sadness, etc.) were discussed during debriefings with the mental health professionals provided by the Camp Noah program. Lessons focused on daily themes designed to foster resilience, by acknowledging that crises occur in life and fear is a natural response; yet no one is alone in their suffering.

The theme for day 1 was designed to establish the child's identity within a larger community and foster a sense of empowerment, belonging, and support by teaching that each child is a unique individual. Day 2 focused on preparedness to reduce anxiety. Handmade donated quilts were distributed for children to use during the week when they felt the need for warmth and comfort and were taken home at the end of the week as a memento. Preparedness packs with items for use in a disaster were distributed, and teachers discussed the usefulness of the items in preparation for emergencies (e.g., flashlights, batteries, bottled water, phone numbers).

Day 3 addressed the disaster and acknowledged that children have feelings of loss associated with the disaster. The curriculum developers anticipated that children would individually begin sharing their stories on day 3; therefore, the focus also included the importance of locating safe places and anticipating better days. Teaching teams explained that disasters bring change and guided children to identify changes in their lives that occurred as a result of the disaster, which may be associated with great emotion. Therefore, participants were instructed to anticipate this and prepare to call on the support of the on-site mental health specialists that were provided by the Camp Noah administration, if needed.

The theme of day 4 acknowledged the survivor in each child and encouraged reflection on gifts, talents, and feelings of thankfulness. Day 5 focused on the future and revisited each child's gifts and talents as a means to encourage the development of hopes and dreams for their future. Participants organized a talent show as a way to showcase each child. Families were invited to celebrate the final day and the future of the community in the recovery process.

Participants who were on activity teams led the children in outdoor recreation, music, and craft. The participants taught the children games to foster teamwork, uplifting songs, and led them in creating artwork while encouraging cooperation, communication, and self-reflection on the daily theme. For example, they interacted with children as they worked to create a mural of a garden where each child's hope for the future was a seed that turned into a flower.

Participants had lunch with the children at the site allowing for an opportunity of joking and storytelling. Afternoon activities varied each day (e.g., police or fire station visit, scavenger hunt, water games, movie, talent show) and participants guided children through activity stations, talking and listening as they participated in the activities with the children. Before dismissal at 3:00, participants put on a puppet show and led the children in songs that reflected the theme of the day. After dismissal, all team members gathered for a debriefing session.

Team Debriefings

Katula and Threnhauser (1999) stress the importance of explicitly guiding students to process experiences appropriately to ensure that learning takes place; therefore, mandatory team debriefings took place at the close of each day. Meetings encouraged reflection on targeted aspects of the day to help facilitate participant learning (Seaman & Rheingold, 2013), and to nurture the emotional and psychological health of the team. The team discussed successful moments and issues that required attention (e.g., crowded classrooms, behavior issues). To inform participant's future interactions with children, participants problem-solved, reflected on causes of problem behavior, and discussed viable solutions (Thompson, Windschitl, & Braaten, 2013). Debriefing sessions concluded by acknowledging the team's dedication in supporting EPICs and an overview of the next day. Debriefings lasted between sixty and ninety minutes. Mental health professionals assigned by the Camp Noah administration attended debriefings.

Data Collection and Analysis

Data collection consisted of field notes and surveys.

Field Notes

Field notes were collected by the author and recorded as (1) observations of interactions between participants and children during twenty-minute blocks of time that were sampled throughout the day and (2) the verbal content of the debriefing sessions (e.g., discussions, participants' perceptions, and analyses). Both structured and unstructured activities were observed, including small group (e.g., formal teaching sessions, craft, stories) and large group sessions (e.g., puppet shows, games, lunch) to determine the receptivity between children and undergraduate students. Interactions were later rated according to type (physical, verbal) and tone (i.e., ease of interaction: not comfortable, comfortable, extremely comfortable), and duration and frequency and then summarized.

Surveys

Researcher-designed post-camp surveys were designed to evaluate participants' perceptions of personal benefits (perceived confidence, self-perception in value of serving), professional benefits (identifying characteristics of EPICs, strategies to support EPICs, vocational direction), and willingness to serve again. A more extensive researcher-designed pre-camp survey was added in Year III to assess changes to participants' perceived personal and professional benefits as a result of the experience.

The pre-camp survey was administered Sunday evening before camp began on Monday morning. Post-camp surveys were administered on the last day of camp immediately after the debriefing session. Open-ended survey items were evaluated by creating categories to classify themes of common responses, and then tallied according to the frequency that participants mentioned each category. Students often responded extensively and addressed multiple categories in their short answer responses; therefore, although surveys from twenty-nine participants were viable for comparison, many items reflect greater than twenty-nine responses.

RESULTS

Overall Results

Regarding the sustainability of this credit-free service-learning experience, the results indicated that over three years, fifty-one different students volunteered and volunteerism increased 200% from Year I to Year III (eleven students in Year I, to thirty-three students in Year III). Of the fifty-one volunteers, fifteen students (29.4%) returned at least one time and one student (2%) returned two times (31.4% of all volunteers reenrolled). Three students from Year I (27.3%) returned for another experience and fifteen students from Year II (62.5%) returned in Year III. In Year III, 48.5% of the thirty-three participants were returning volunteers and over all three years, all participants indicated a willingness to serve again, with one exception who responded "maybe" (98%, $n = 51$). Taken together, these data suggest the sustainability of this non-credit-bearing service-learning experience in terms of student enrollment, sustained student interest, and attractiveness of the experience.

Field Notes: Results of Years I, II, III

Observations

The observation data from Years I, II, and III revealed that interactions were playful and extremely comfortable (e.g., children hung on participants, teased them, attempted to play hide-and-seek, wrestle, and race during unstructured times) and affectionately verbal (e.g., "you're awesome," "I love you"). Interactions were extremely frequent (students rarely had sixty seconds without child interaction) and began on day one (e.g., children began sharing their trauma stories without provocation).

Although the curriculum prepares children during the first two days of camp to begin sharing their stories of trauma by day 3, results indicated that children began sharing emotions and stories on day one. This possibly attests to the development of the noted comfort level that was present very early between the participants and children. These results suggest that the undergraduate students, curriculum, and environment facilitated an extreme and immediate level of comfort for the childhood trauma victims, which is important for children in terms of processing their grief given the relatively short nature of the one-week camp (Sullivan & Simonson, 2016).

In addition, reciprocity was noted during interactions as participants played with one another and the children. For example, participants dumped buckets of water on themselves as children watched and laughed, perhaps as a way to engage the children in play without jeopardizing the comfort level that they already established. This suggests that participants found satisfaction as volunteers, which reflects previous findings (Beehr et al., 2010).

Debriefings

The debriefing data from Years I, II, and III revealed that discussions mainly focused on behavior concerns but moved from discussing externalizing behaviors to discussing internalizing behaviors throughout the week. On days 1 and 2, student discussions primarily focused on logistics of the day (e.g., more time allocated for small groups) and how to manage externalizing behavior issues (e.g., running, fighting). On days 3, 4, and 5, student discussions primarily focused on internalizing behaviors (anxiety and fear articulated by children verbally, physically, and through artwork) and referenced the child's story of disaster.

The exception was in Year II, where participants responded to a school shooting. Participants framed externalizing behavior as early as day one as a concern for potential traumatization as a result of the shooting and discussed behaviors in relationship to the trauma, perhaps because of the obvious and serious nature of the reported source of trauma. This shift in Years I and

III perhaps suggests an increased understanding of childhood behaviors as a result of the pre-camp training, the insight that the experience offered, and the value of debriefing to process service-learning experiences (Seaman & Rheingold, 2013).

Survey Results

Years I and II

Survey data from Years I and II indicated that participants valued the rich, authentic learning environment, the strength they sensed in serving a university team, and the value of the multiple scenarios that children presented. For example, participant #6 noted the real-life setting requiring her to "think on [her] feet as a real professional would" and stated the "great value [of the experience] in working as part of a team in an academically supervised field experience."

Participants reported perceived increases in personal strength and professional direction as a result of the experience and stated the benefits of engaging with the children in a therapeutic environment, which offered an opportunity to develop relationships. For example, Participant #8 stated "I made a connection with many children and made a real difference in many children's lives. They didn't want to leave me, it made me feel like I was someone important to them."

Participants frequently reported the professional value of the experience. For example, Participant #4 stated "This experience helped me learn how to reach troubled children and made me realize that I want to—and can do this as a career." Another participant reported, "Although it's hard, it is worth it to know how you changed children's lives." Still another stated that "developing relationships with children in such a short time—supporting and uplifting them to make them feel important and helping children find their own strength to overcome and heal was so rewarding." Because Year III investigated if changes to perceived personal and professional benefits were evident as a result of serving, these data were examined separately and are reported next.

Year III

The survey results suggested several perceived personal and professional benefits. First, participants at pre-camp most frequently indicated they would gain knowledge, spread happiness, listen, and care (e.g., "Listen to children and keep them company"). At post-camp, responses reflected a deeper understanding of children and the importance of establishing a relationship. For example, Participant #6489 at pre-camp responded, "I will be a listening ear. I will love them, make them laugh and be there to listen when they need someone" The same student at post-camp stated, "I gave them [the children] the love they desperately needed. I was there to help them through challenges, talk to them about the importance of helping others and their home lives, which felt wonderful."

Interestingly, these reports of great personal reward conflict with some research that indicates participants had mixed emotions after serving (Carson & Domangue, 2013). This may suggest that self-selection into the program by volunteering allowed for matching the type of service to the student's interests (rather than a course-mandated service component). For example, participants overwhelmingly reported that they saw themselves as role models, suggesting they took pride in their role and felt comfortable in their capacity. The self-perceived image as a role model was reported so frequently that this response category reflected 72% of the item responses at post-camp when asked how participants believed they helped the children most. For example, Participant #8789 at pre-camp stated, "I will be someone who will listen" and at post-camp the participant stated, "I was someone who listened and solved the problem with words, not violence."

Second, results also indicated increases in perceptions of professional identity and clarity in terms of serving diverse populations as a profession and perceived gains in interpersonal skills through the team nature of the experience. For example, when asked about professional benefits, at pre-camp Participant #5479 stated, "I will get classroom leadership experience with the team" and at post-camp stated, "It helped me to be able to get kids to listen, and gain some serious practice with classroom management." Participant #8939 at pre-camp stated, "I will better understand how children deal with traumatic experiences." At post-camp the same participant stated, "The emotional part showed me how hard it can be to be a teacher, and to never give up even during difficult situations. I learned that I picked the right profession because the experience made me sure of who I want to be!"

The explicitness of the descriptions suggests that participants' skills in serving were crystalized, and participants began to envision themselves in a professional light as a teacher, school psychologist, counselor, social worker, and so on. These findings support preliminary findings by Hamre et al. (2012) that asserted the value of carefully crafted instructional environments where teacher candidates can practice teacher-child interactions as a means to develop effective instructional practices, to foster more meaningful encounters.

Finally, results of survey item #10 indicated no changes to perceived confidence from pre-camp to post-camp as measured using a 5-point Likert scale (1 = not at all confident, 3 = neutral, 5 = extremely confident). Participants remained highly confident in their ability to substantially help EPICs (pre-camp mean = 4.16; post-camp mean = 4.10). Because participants reported the benefits at pre-camp and post-camp of a university team that offered them a sense of strength as a united family in serving a community in need, this may be related to the unchanged levels of confidence. Taken together, these results may suggest that the dynamics of serving on a university team offered a perceived sense of strength and "family support," coupled with the faculty guidance, observations, and debriefings resulting in high levels of confidence.

DISCUSSION

Some service-learning investigations have reported participants' displeasure with the forced nature of serving, the time commitment, the rigor of the experience, and the placement, leading researchers to question the role of choice to create meaningful experiences (Beehr et al., 2010; Pedersen, Meyer, & Hargrave, 2015). The rigor of this credit-free volunteer program was extensive in terms of trainings, travel to remote locations, and physical and emotional dedication. Despite this, participants overwhelmingly perceived the experience to be positive and an opportunity to discover their own personal strengths and professional value.

Volunteerism increased from Year I to Year III by 200%. Participants reported no displeasure with the experience or placement, and 98% of the fifty-one volunteers indicated a willingness to serve again. As such, the credit-free nature of the experience was not a hindrance to the sustainability in terms of student enrollment; rather, consistent with internal theories of motivation (Ryan & Deci, 2000), great satisfaction reported by participants led them to reenroll. Kirschner, Sweller, and Clark's (2006) work illuminates the importance of instructional guidance to support and integrate learning; as such, without institutional backing to support faculty involvement, the program's sustainability overall could be jeopardized.

The carefully designed program in terms of training, faculty guidance, and team debriefings, to support participants, may have created an environment where extreme comfort was established between children and university students as early as day one. Participants indicated that they perceived themselves to belong to something greater because of their role with the university team. They framed the team as "a united family." The perceived "family" afforded participants a sense of empowerment in supporting EPICs. Participant #4770 in Year III stated, "Children tend to look up to college-aged individuals, and as a university team we united and worked as a team to benefit these poor kids as best as possible." This was also reflected in the very high levels of perceived confidence that remained unchanged from pre-camp to post-camp in participant's ability to make a difference in the children's lives in Year III.

Limitations

Caution in generalization of findings is suggested in light of the following limitations. First, the evolving nature of the program necessitated slight variability in data collection tools and evaluation procedures each year. For example, the changing sample size, team configuration, various disaster circumstances, and emotional climate of each camp varied, which may have influenced responses. However, qualitative findings seem to suggest the overall strength of the research methods in terms of processing the experience (e.g., integrating prior learning through training and interaction with EPICs, debriefings to encourage reflection, team problem solving, and faculty guidance) (Schenck & Cruickshank, 2015).

Second, the various components to the program and participant individuality were not parceled out, and differences between returning and first-time participants were not examined, making it difficult to determine specific aspects that may have been responsible for the results reported. As such, the various aspects of the program, participant individuality, sample size, and sample of convenience present a limitation in generalization and should be investigated using a broader representation of students across universities.

Third, the benefits to the children were not evaluated. Observational field notes indicated that children interacted openly and comfortably with university students. In fact, many children began sharing their trauma stories on the first day of camp, rather than day 3. This was surprising given anecdotal historic accounts from Camp Noah administrators, curriculum developers, and activity logs from hundreds of camps, which may suggest unprecedented value in a team of university students. Specifically, if a greater level of comfort is possible with university students compared to traditional adult teams, children may begin processing their trauma sooner resulting in increased healing rates.

A clear understanding of the benefits to children is extremely important in order to determine both the benefits to children and to ensure that compounded trauma is avoided (Jaycox et al., 2010). Finally, because service learning is typically linked to course credit and an institutional grade, the absence of stress associated with assessments toward a final grade may have offered a more comfortable experience for the participants in comparison to credit-bearing courses and should be investigated.

CONCLUSIONS AND IMPLICATIONS

These results suggest the value of field experiences to develop confidence and skills when interacting with children of trauma. However, experiences must be rigorous and reflective if the experience is to be educationally meaningful (Thompson, Windschitl, & Braaten, 2013; Seaman & Rheingold, 2013). In addition, some experts in the field have called for further investigations into the elements that support novice teachers' commitment to teaching and sense of efficacy (Kelly & Northrop, 2015). As such, follow up is important after students obtain their first teaching placement to determine the beneficial effects of the service-learning experience in terms of students' perceived confidence and comfort when working with children of trauma.

Gage, Larson, Sugai, and Chafouleas (2016) report the importance of promoting a school climate that evokes comfort and acceptance when considering children from diverse populations (e.g., EPICs). This study sheds light on one method to establish that comfort and the value of similar experiences as a potential tool to empower teacher candidates to facilitate comfort with diverse populations, including EPICs. Sullivan and Simonson (2016) recently concluded that the current body of research is extremely limited in terms of serving children of trauma in school-based settings. Given the unique connection reported here in terms of establishing comfortable interactions between child and university student, more efficient therapeutic outcomes might therefore be possible with regards to time spent facilitating healing and should be investigated.

REFERENCES

Annette, J. (2003). Service-learning internationally: Developing a global civil society. In S. Billig & J. Eyler (Eds.), *Deconstructing service-learning: Research exploring context, participation, and impacts* (pp. 241–249). Greenwich, CN: Information Age.

Anthony, B. J., Anthony, L. G., Morrel, T. M., & Acosta, M. (2005). Evidence for social and behavior problems in low-income, urban preschoolers: Effects of site, classroom, and teacher. *Journal of Youth and Adolescence, 34*(1), 31–39.

Armsworth, M. W., & Holaday, M. (1993). The effects of psychological trauma on children and adolescents. *Journal of Counseling and Development, 71*(4), 49–56.

Beehr, T. A., LeGro, K., Porter, K., Bowling, N. A., & Swader, W. M. (2010). Required volunteers: Community volunteerism among students in college classes. *Teaching of Psychology, 37*(4), 276–280.

Brail, S. (2013). Experiencing the city: Urban studies students and service learning. *Journal of Geography in Higher Education, 37*(2), 241–256.

Bringle, R. G., & Hatcher, J. A. (1996). Implementing service learning in higher education. *The Journal of Higher Education, 67*(2), 221–239.

Bringle, R. G., & Hatcher, J. A. (2009, fall). Innovative practices in service-learning and curricular engagement. *New Directions for Higher Education, 147*, 37–46.

Burkart, K. I., & Thompson, C. J. (2014). Intercultural mindedness: Teachers left behind. *Florida Association of Teacher Educators Journal, 1*(14), 1–14.

Carson, R. L., & Domangue, E. A. (2013). The emotional component of service-learning. *Journal of Experiential Education, 36*(2), 139–154.

Case, K., & Hemmings, A. (2005). Distancing strategies: White women preservice teachers an antiracist curriculum. *Urban Education, 40,* 606–626.

Celio, C. I., Durlak, J., & Dymnicki, A. (2011). A meta-analysis of the impact of service-learning on students. *Journal of Experiential Education, 34*(2), 164–181.

Centers for Disease Control and Prevention. (2013). Trends in the prevalence of behaviors that contribute to violence national YRBS: 1991–2013 Retrieved from https://www.cdc.gov/healthyyouth/data/yrbs/pdf/trends/2015_us_violence_trend_yrbs.pdf.

Cushner, K. (2012). Planting seeds for peace: Are they growing in the right direction? *International Journal of Intercultural Relations, 36*(2), 161–168.

Dardig, J. C. (2004). Urban connections: A course linking college students to the community. *College Teaching, 52*(1), 25–30.

Desrochers, C. (2006). Educating preservice teachers for diversity: Perspectives on the possibilities and limitations of service learning. *The Journal of Educational Thought, 40*(3), 263–279.

Durlak, J. A., Weissberg, R. P., Dymnicki, A. B., Taylor, R. D., & Schellinger, K. B. (2011). The impact of enhancing students' social and emotional learning: A meta-analysis of school-based universal interventions. *Child Development, 82*(1), 405–432.

Gage, N. A., Larson, A., Sugai, G., & Chafouleas, S. M. (2016). Student perceptions of school climate as predictors of office discipline referrals. *American Educational Research Journal, 53*(3), 492–515.

Giannopoulou, I., Strouthos, M., Smith, P., Dikaiakou, A., Galanopoulou, V., & Yule, W. (2006). Post traumatic stress reactions of children and adolescents exposed to the Athens 1999 earthquake. *European Psychiatry, 21*(3), 160–166.

Goenjian, A. K., Walling, D., Steinberg, A. M., Karayan, I., Najarian, L. M., & Pynoos, R. (2005). A prospective study of posttraumatic stress and depressive reactions among treated and untreated adolescents 5 years after a catastrophic disaster. *The American Journal of Psychiatry, 162*(12), 2302–2308.

Goldberg, L. R., & Coufal, K. L. (2009). Reflections on service-learning, critical thinking, and cultural competence. *Journal of College Teaching and Learning, 6*(6), 39–49.

Gresham, F. M. (2007). Response to intervention and emotional and behavioral disorders. *Assessment for Effective Intervention, 32*(4), 214–222.

Hamre, B. K., Pianta, R. C., Burchinal, M., Field, S., LoCasale-Crouch, J., Downer, J. T., . . . Scott-Little, C. (2012). A course on effective teacher-child interactions: Effects on teacher beliefs, knowledge, and observed practice. *American Educational Research Journal, 49*(1), 88–123.

Headley, C., & Campbell, M. A. (2013). Teachers' knowledge of anxiety and identification of excessive anxiety in children. *Australian Journal of Teacher Education, 38*(5), 48–66.

Jaycox, L. H., Cohen, J. A., Mannarino, A. P., Walker, D. W., Langley, A. K., Gegenheimer, K. L., . . . Schonlau, M. (2010). Children's mental health care following Hurricane Katrina: A field trial of trauma-focused psychotherapies. *Journal of Traumatic Stress, 23*(2), 223–231.

Jones, K., Blinkhorn, L. M., Schumann, S. A., & Reddy, S. T. (2014). Promoting sustainable community service in the 4th year of medical school: A longitudinal service-learning elective. *Teaching and Learning in Medicine, 26*(3), 296–303.

Katula, R. A., & Threnhauser, E. (1999). Experiential education in the undergraduate curriculum. *Communication Education, 48*(3), 238–255.

Kelly, S., & Northrop, L. (2015). Early career outcomes for the "Best and the Brightest": Selectivity, satisfaction, and attrition in the Beginning Teacher Longitudinal Survey. *American Educational Research Journal, 52*(4), 624–656.

Kirschner, P. A., Sweller, J., & Clark, R. E. (2006). Why minimal guidance during instruction does not work: An analysis of the failure of constructivist, discovery, problem-based, experiential, and inquiry-based teaching. *Educational Psychologist, 41*(2), 75–86.

Layne, C. M., Greeson, J. K. P., Ostrowski, S. A., Kim, S., Reading, S., Vivrette, R. L., . . . Pynoos, R. S. (2014). Cumulative trauma exposure and high risk behavior in adolescence: Findings from the National Child Traumatic Stress Network Core Data Set. *Psychological Trauma: Theory, Research, Practice, and Policy, 6*(1), S40–S49.

Marsh, R. J. (2016). Identifying students with mental health issues: A guide for classroom teachers. *Intervention in School and Clinic, 51*(5), 318–322.

Pedersen, P. J., Meyer, J. M., & Hargrave, M. (2015). Learn global; serve local: Student outcomes from a community-based learning pedagogy. *Journal of Experiential Education, 38*(2), 189–206.

Ryan, R. M., & Deci, E. L. (2000). Self-determination theory and the facilitation of intrinsic motivation, social development, and well-being. *American Psychologist, 55*, 68–78.

Schenck, J., & Cruickshank, J. (2015). Evolving Kolb: Experiential education in the age of neuroscience. *Journal of Experiential Education, 38*(1), 73–95.

Schonfeld, D. J., Adams, R. E., Fredstrom, B. K., Weissberg, R. P., Gilman, R., Voyce, C., Tomlin, R., & Speese-Linehan, D. (2015). Cluster-randomized trial demonstrating impact on academic achievement of elementary social-emotional learning. *School Psychology Quarterly, 30*(3), 406–420.

Seaman, J., & Rheingold, A. (2013). Circle talks as situated experiential learning: Context, identity, and knowledgeability in "learning from reflection." *Journal of Experiential Education, 36*(2), 155–174.

Selznick, P. (1992). *The moral commonwealth: Social theory and the promise of community.* Berkley, CA: University of California Press.

Skepple, R. G. (2014). Preparing culturally responsive pre-service teachers for culturally diverse classrooms. *Kentucky Journal of Excellence in College Teaching and Learning, 12,* Article 6.

Sleeter, C. E. (2001). Preparing teachers for culturally diverse schools: Research and the overwhelming presence of Whiteness. *Journal of Teacher Education, 52*(2), 94–106.

Sullivan, A. L., & Simonson, G. R. (2016). A systematic review of school-based social-emotional interventions for refugee and war-traumatized youth. *Review of Educational Research, 86*(2), 503–530.

Thompson, J., Windschitl, M., & Braaten, M. (2013). Developing a theory of ambitious early-career teacher practice. *American Educational Research Journal, 50*(3), 574–615.

Walker, H. M., Nishioka, V. M., Zeller, R., Severson, H. H., & Feil, E. G. (2000). Causal factors and potential solutions for the persistent under-identification of students having emotional or behavioral disorders in the context of schooling. *Assessment for Effective Intervention, 26*(1), 29–39.

Zotti, M. E., Graham, J., Whitt, A. L., Anand, S., & Replogle, W. H. (2006). Evaluation of a multistate faith-based program for children affected by natural disaster. *Public Health Nursing, 23*(5), 400–409.

Chapter 6

Inspiring Teachers across the Professional Continuum through Collaborative Coaching and Lesson Study

Jennifer M. Suh and Kim Dockery

ABSTRACT

This case study highlights how educators along the professional continuum (teacher candidates, classroom teachers, mathematics coaches, and resource specialists) gained strength and inspiration from one another through collaborative coaching at a professional development school that implemented a Teacher Leadership Institute and Lesson Study (Lewis, 2002; Lewis, Perry, Hurd, & O'Connell, 2006). We share specific design decisions made around the professional learning model of the Teacher Leadership Institute and Lesson Study that provided opportunities for educators to engage in collaborative coaching. Lesson Study (Fernandez & Yoshida, 2004; Lewis, Perry, & Hurd, 2004; Stigler & Hiebert, 1999) is a model of professional learning that offers situated learning through collaborative planning, teaching, observing, and debriefing that affords opportunities for teachers to reflect individually and collectively. In addition, it offers what we define as collaborative coaching, a support network of professionals working together to enrich each educator along the professional continuum by sharing the educator's individual expertise and strengths. It contrasts with the traditional one-on-one mentoring model where the experienced teacher is seen as the mentor and the novice or prospective teacher is the mentee. Instead, collaborative coaching allows each educator to leverage strength and expertise to learn from one another and take advantage of the mutual exchange. In this way, educators are able to inspire one another and strengthen their professional practice.

KEY WORDS

Collaborative Coaching; Lesson Study; Teacher Leadership

INTRODUCTION: SCHOOL, A PLACE FOR TEACHERS TO LEARN TOGETHER

Situated learning is a model of learning (Lave & Wenger, 1990) where learning that takes place is in the same context in which it is applied. Research has shown that situating professional learning in schools and classroom contexts are more effective than learning that occurs in non-situated professional learning communities (Putnam & Borko, 2000). The situated learning also takes place through participating in a community of practice. Lave and Wenger (1990) also coined the term legitimate peripheral participation (LPP), which describes how newcomers become experienced members and eventually old timers of a community of practice.

In LPP, newcomers become members of a community by participating in professional activities with the community members. Through peripheral activities, novices become acquainted with the tasks, vocabulary, and organizing principles of the community. In schools, professional learning communities are very much communities of practice and have emerged as one approach for job-embedded professional learning. In these professional learning communities, teachers have the opportunity to collaborate with the end goal of improving their teaching practices as well as promote continuous school improvement.

Lesson Study, which originated from Japan, came into vogue as a teacher-led professional development model because it empowers teachers and provides a collaborative structure, much like the professional learning communities for developing reflection for critical dialogue about pedagogical content knowledge among teachers (Lewis, 2002; Stigler & Hiebert, 1999). In Japan, teacher candidates frequently conduct Lesson Study as part of their student teaching:

> They will prepare a study lesson in collaboration with their university-based mentors and the teacher with whom they have been assigned to work at their school site. They will then teach the lesson in this school, and all the teachers in the building, the university mentors, and other student teachers will come observe. (Fernandez, 2002, p. 395)

Collective inquiry in teaching and learning is supported as a highly effective component of professional development for teachers (Chazan et al., 1998; Fernandez & Yoshida, 2004; Roth & Tobin, 2004). When teacher candidates and classroom teachers participate in a Lesson Study Cycle of collaboratively planning a research lesson, teaching and observing the lesson, reflecting on and revising the lesson, and repeating the cycle, all members of the group benefit from the professional inquiry (Fernandez & Yoshida, 2004; Suh & Parker, 2010).

Lesson Study involves many of the practice-based skills for teaching, including establishing lesson objectives, evaluating instructional materials, determining how to assess student understanding, reviewing one's understanding of mathematical concepts, and situating an instructional experience in the curriculum. All these tasks provide opportunity for individual and collective reflection on content and pedagogy and have the potential to deepen a teacher's pedagogical content knowledge.

However, teacher candidates have limited experience in planning lessons and are not adept at performing the task or anticipating students' responses. Experienced classroom teachers have the experience base to know what to anticipate of students and the common misconceptions that occur during lessons. Benefits of collaborating on planning lessons with novice and experienced teachers include exposure to multiple perspectives and new ideas that result from sharing experiences and expertise.

Developing reflective practice is one of the key dispositions that teacher educators encourage and is one of the key characteristics of effective career educators. Multiple opportunities for reflection are needed to build teachers' capacity for critical reflection. In our teacher education program, we use this model at our Professional Development Schools, where our teacher candidates become enculturated into this professional practice by working with clinical faculty, who are also experienced teachers, to teach and participated in collective reflection of the teaching and the learning process.

Professional Development Schools (PDS) are innovative institutions formed through partnerships between professional education programs and P–12 schools (NCATE, 2000). The design of the PDS lends itself to providing an ideal environment for Instructional Rounds and Lesson Study with the necessary infrastructure to capitalize on the professional development of teachers at all levels, experienced and novice. The fundamental design principle of PDS sites is one in which school and university partners together emphasize improving teacher education, the professional development of practicing teachers, and student learning (Castle, Fox, & Fuhrman, 2009; NCATE, 2010; Zeichner & Conklin, 2008).

Collaborative Coaching to Build Collective Knowledge

Transforming practice requires a transformation of beliefs and new experiences that are valued by the individual or group. In transformative leadership,

The collective action that transforming leadership generates empowers those who participate in the process. There is hope, there is optimism, there is energy. In essence, transforming leadership is leadership that facilitates the redefinition of people's mission a vision, a renewal of their commitment, and the restructuring of their systems for goal accomplishment. (Roberts, 1985, p. 2014)

Transformational leadership requires teachers and administrators to undergo a paradigm shift and have direct experiences related to this new paradigm. Shifting the leadership paradigm from a hierarchical structure to one of distributed leadership builds the belief that "everyone has the right, responsibility and capability to work as a leader" (Lambert, 2003, p. 43). By distributing leadership, different teachers rise to the level of instructional leadership which leads to a community of leaders that then evolves into facilitative leadership. The fact that facilitative leadership is also known as participative leadership, shared leadership, and distributed leadership emphasizes the collective ability of the school to adapt, solve problems, and improve performance (Leithwood, 1992). Smylie and Brownlee-Conyers (1992) found that teacher participation in school-based decision-making was positively related to instructional improvement and student academic outcomes. They found that in productive participative school settings, frequent, regular, and inclusive teacher participation and shared leadership existed between principals and teachers; decision-making was more collaborative and consensus-driven; decisions seemed "co-constructed." Focus included school mission, curriculum and instruction, staff development; leadership was shared between principal and teachers, both took initiatives, and both assumed responsibility.

Related to the collective shared leadership is the research literature on team coaching and how it alleviates some of the resistance to change that coaches encounter when working with a team of teachers. Miller and Stuart (2013, p. 292) state, "Thinking about coaching as "team work" can circumvent many of the issues (related to fear of change) by diffusing much of the threat around change and allowing teachers to think creatively about their work with others."

Collaborative coaching has been in vogue in the business world as documented in books like the *Leadership Team Coaching in Practice: Developing High Performing Teams* (Hawkins, 2014) where the author discusses the key elements of high-performing teams. Such key elements include "Co-creating: the team being more effective in how they collectively work together to cocreate generative thinking and action, which is greater than the sum of their individual efforts" (Hawkins, 2014, p. 8). Heffernan (2013, p. 373) who states, "Innovative institutions and organizations thrive not because they pick and breed superstars but because they cherish, nurture and support the vast range of talents, personalities and skills that true creativity requires."

School-based Lesson Study and professional learning communities provide opportunity for educators not only to cocreate but allow educators to bring together all their expertise and strength that add up their collective knowledge. Collective knowledge yields more than the sum of their individual knowledge which in turn enhances one's individual instructional practice but also provides opportunities for school teams to develop collective teaching efficacy. Goddard, Hoy, and Woolfolk-Hoy (2000) identified two elements important to the development of collective teaching efficacy: (a) teachers' involvement in the analysis of the teaching task and (b) the assessment of teaching competence (peer observations). Collective efficacy is strongly related to student achievement in schools. The link occurs because a strong sense of group capability establishes expectations (cultural norms) for success that encourages organizational members to work resiliently toward desired ends (Bandura, 1993; Goddard et al., 2000).

Teachers need time to understand new concepts, learn new skills, develop new attitudes, research, discuss, reflect, assess, try new approaches and integrate them into their practice; and time to plan their own professional development (Cambone, 1995; Corcoran, 1995). Donahoe (1993) suggests that such set-aside "collective staff time" is particularly important when significant school improvement plans are underway. In addition, professional development must foster a culture of sharing and providing sustained support for teachers (i.e., knowledge networks) (Barab, Makinster, Moore, & Cunningham, 2001, p. 74). Sustained support can occur through collaborative planning and implementation, engaging teachers in opportunities that promote continuous inquiry and improvement that is relevant and appropriate to local sites (Northwest Regional Educational Laboratory [NWREL], 1998). Another aspect of support is to facilitate joint construction of knowledge through conversation and other forms of collaborative analysis and interpretation (Cochran-Smith & Lytle, 2001, p. 53).

THE CONTEXT

This study took place at a PDS where the school district had implemented a leadership institute for teachers in early August. This PDS provided a lab setting for new and developing teachers to observe, practice, and refine new skills before they assume classroom responsibilities. The lab, called the Teacher Leadership Institute (TLI), was designed with the intention of rethinking the teacher work year and teachers' professional responsibilities. Well-noted in professional development research is the challenge of time. Switching to effective professional development, the most significant cost item for districts will be purchasing time for teachers to spend in professional learning communities and with coaches (Gulamhussein, 2013). The National Education Commission on Time and Learning (2005) stated that a design flaw in the United States remains with amount of time provided teachers for professional development,

> Unyielding and relentless, the time available in a uniform six-hour day and a 180 day year is the unacknowledged design flaw in American education. By relying on time as the metric for organization and curriculum, we have built a learning enterprise on a foundation of sand. (National Education Commission on Time and Learning, 2005, p. 6)

Studies have shown how, compared to other countries against which our students' performance is gauged, U.S. teachers have less time to plan, collaborate, and perform research National Education Commission on Time and Learning, 2005). Flexible time would allow teachers to interact professionally, observe one another's teaching, and experience productive professional development. To address the challenge of meeting the demands of today's schools, the school district invited schools to submit Teacher Leadership Development grant proposals. Within the proposal, schools could utilize four different contract lengths of 203, 208, 218, and the traditional 194 days to create the time necessary to do the work of a learning organization. Of the 204 schools in the district, more than 80 schools submitted proposals, and 25 schools were selected to pilot the Teacher Leadership Development grants. The research presented here relates one school's experiences.

Westlawn Elementary: A Cluster II Lab School

As a diverse Title I school in Fairfax County, Virginia, school staff had worked diligently to develop as a professional learning community (PLC). Shared vision, mission, and values with an intense focus on instructional practice by collaborative teams, coupled with a culture of inquiry fostered by a PDS partnership with a local university, fueled the questions that began the "visioning." What if all teachers began the year with the cultural understanding of the school and school community? What if the teachers, that is, new, developing, and expert, started on the first day with the common language and common practices that supported high student achievement? What if best practices were common practices? What if the culture of reflection was visible as teachers modeled, coached, and mentored each other?

Westlawn Elementary: A Cluster II Lab School is the vision of redistributing time and compensation for teachers to create a successful learning organization. To design a professional learning environment where teacher leaders and teacher learners can codevelop in multiple ways, the PDS principal and the university mathematics educator worked together to design the TLI with the summer lab school and the follow-up Lesson Study during the academic year.

By placing teacher candidates called interns at this stage of their preparation in the August lab setting, the university mathematics educator, who was also the university supervisor for the interns, was able to work with educators across the professional continuum in Lesson Study. This involvement included teacher candidate interns, classroom teachers, the mathematics specialist, and resource teachers who service the diverse student population. This case study documents the design and implementation of the professional activities and report on the outcome of this project.

Design Framework for the Professional Development

Based on research on effective leadership and motivating educators in professional development, the researchers developed the framework called T.I.M.E. for Excellence, which included four main elements that guided our TLI and Lesson Study initiatives:

T = Teacher-led Professional Development by in-school experts;
I = Inquiry into Teaching and Learning through Lesson Study;
M = Mentoring and Modeling Best Practices; and
E = Experiential Learning for Teachers through summer PD Lab.

1. Teacher-led Professional Development by In-School Experts

The teacher-led professional development during the summer was the cornerstone of the leadership institute because it afforded the opportunities to grow teacher leaders and establish a common vision for the school shared by all teachers. The specific goals for the TLI were to focus on: increasing pedagogical content knowledge, increasing ability to observe and assess students, building stronger collegial networks, connecting daily practice to long-term goals, increasing motivation and teacher efficacy.

The teacher-led professional development began with careful attention to what classroom teachers already knew (i.e., their current conceptions of subject area, of teaching, and of learning) through an instructional inventory survey. Using information from the inventory survey, teacher leaders designed workshop modules for new and developing teachers. These modules included components critical to the culture of the school through Payne's Framework for Understanding Poverty (Payne, 2005); Rath's StrengthFinders (Rath, 2007); and Cooperative Learning (Kagan & Kagan, 2009; Slavin, 1995) and components critical to the instructional practices of the school through the use of Classroom Observation Rubrics (Danielson, 2006, 2007); Reading and Writing Workshop (Fountas & Pinnell, 2001); and Five Strands of Mathematical Proficiency (National Research Council (NRC), 2001).

2. Inquiry into Teaching and Learning through Lesson Study

The desire for school-wide reflection from the TLI led to grade-level Lesson Study during the academic year, which magnified the shared mission, vision, and values. Lesson Study, a form of teacher-led professional development model became the structure for teachers to continue to develop as leaders throughout the academic year as they focused on problem solving together as professionals and inquiry into teaching and learning.

Lesson Study (Lewis, 2002) and the professional learning communities model (DuFour, 2004) provided opportunities for new and experienced teachers to engage in professional shared learning. While working collaboratively with the grade-level teams, these mentors capitalized on the shared expertise among a group of teachers: new and experienced teachers, special educators, and ESOL teachers. This mutual exchange of ideas and instructional strategies among different teachers helped create a sustainable teacher-led PLC.

3. Mentoring and Modeling Best Practices

It was important that teachers participating in the TLI saw their colleagues as teacher leaders, who had subject area and instructional expertise, and that administrators believed in shared leadership and aligning teacher leadership with professional learning. Not only did these teacher leaders help their colleagues refine their craft before the school year began but continuously gave them confidence and coached them in their teaching throughout the school year.

4. Experiential Learning for Teachers through Summer PD Lab School

The TLI had a focus on "Experiential Learning for Teachers." For our TLI, we transformed the existing Community-Based Summer School into a lab school to form the perfect laboratory for observation and real-life practice of strategies imperative to school achievement. We shifted the lab school to August so that we could provide a preparation time where students remembered, practiced, and became familiar with the routines and structures of school so that students also got a jump-start into their academic year. The range of programs offered through the lab school provided training opportunities in best practice strategies in areas such as reading and writing workshop, math conceptual understanding, and differentiation for learners in settings from intervention to enrichment.

RESEARCH QUESTIONS

1. How did the TLI with the Instructional Rounds and Lesson Study allow for teachers along the professional continuum to collaboratively coach, inspire educators, renew, and motivate them to pursue deeper understanding about their craft?
2. How are the inspirations and aspirations from different members along the professional continuum similar and different?

METHOD

A case study is bounded by a system usually by time, place, context, and/or some activity (Creswell, 2003; Miles & Huberman, 1994; Stake, 1995; Yin, 1989). This case study was bounded around the educators at the PDS site that participated in the TLI and Lesson Study. The TLI summer institute and lab school took place in the first three weeks of August. For the summer institute, 36 teachers were on an extended 208-day contract (16 were new and preservice teachers and 20 were summer lab school teachers) and 2 teachers were on 218-day contracts.

For three weeks in the summer, teacher leaders provided training in best practice strategies in areas such as reading and writing workshop, mathematics, and differentiation for diverse learners. In addition, teacher learners were given opportunities to observe and reflect on those teaching practices in action in a summer lab classroom. Academic year focus to support learning that involved reflection and refining of instructional practice continued throughout the school year with Lesson Study and professional conversations.

Semi-structured interviews, observations, lesson study debriefs, and reflective journals were used to document the experience of participants as they went through the TLI and the Lesson Study. The PDS site was a Title One school with diverse ethnicity of students, including Hispanic 51.88%; Asian (Vietnamese) 24.88%; White 14.89%; Other 5.89%; Black 2.45%; Subgroups Poverty 55.16%; Limited English Prof. 51.88%; ESOL 41.57%; and Special Education 16.20%.

RESULT

Impact of Teacher Leadership and Lesson Study: T.I.M.E. for Developing Collective Competencies and Strengths

The beauty of the teacher-led professional development was that the teacher leaders—who had intimate knowledge of the school culture, community, students, and family—were able to prescribe the appropriate instructional strategies that had proven to be effective in targeting the special population of students they served. Without this intimate knowledge, outside consultants or experts cannot really affect change in teachers' practice to the magnitude that effective teacher leaders from one's own school may affect. By empowering teachers to lead other teachers, a sense of *collective competencies and strengths* grew among the faculty. These teachers collectively believed that this school had what it takes to get children to learn. They believed every child can learn and felt well prepared to teach the subjects they were assigned to teach. If they did not feel adequately prepared for a particular content, they knew who the skillful teachers were with differing expertise who would help them succeed. Together they believed that the teachers in this school had the skills needed to produce meaningful student learning. This collective competencies and strengths empowered the teachers in this school as evidenced by these teacher responses.

The lab school concept deepens the school vision of spreading best practice strategies in a systematic way. This time ensures the existing school practices are deepened and explicitly taught to new staff so that the culture is self-sustaining and can weather any change in personnel. It also ensures that we are not a school with pockets of excellence but that all practices that are shared across classrooms and across programs. Response from a teacher leader

Our new teachers "hit the ground running" in September. They have developed a knowledge of the school culture and practice and have seen it in action in the summer school classrooms. They have had time to both observe and often teach lessons that directly relate to the best practices embedded in the school— both academic and managerial, such as Kagan Structures (Kagan & Kagan, 2009). *New teachers are given the tools they need to begin the school year with more confidence in both the curriculum and the culture of the school.* Response from a teacher leader

The summer institute enabled new and continuing teachers the opportunity to take classes at their school. The institute also gave teachers the opportunity to explore their leadership skills by sharing their knowledge by doing turn around training. Teachers' focus group interviews revealed evidence that mutual learning was evident among the professionals along the continuum.

It gave teachers the opportunity to work collaboratively with other teachers without the stress and time constraint of the school year. It also allowed new teachers to learn about the school culture and network with other teachers. Response from a teacher participant

Students are exposed to a "feed it forward" model and begin the year ahead of the game. Teachers (new & experienced) are given a chance to

model and practice their craft, as well as, try new methods and strategies out for the first time. We can learn from one another. Response from a teacher participant

Developing Aspirations for Their Professionalism through Experiential Learning and Collaborative Coaching

During the Summer PDS lab school, teachers were observing, learning, and refining assessment and instruction with teacher leaders. They were able to note, question, and analyze in a true school setting. In the afternoon, teachers shared observations and reflections. Coaches provided new learning that could be observed or attempted by teachers the following days in summer school. This provided opportunity to refine and practice teaching behaviors immediately, making best practices common practices. In addition, teacher candidates became part of the learning cadre at the lab school and supported the teaching of students during the summer session.

Through teacher-led professional development, teachers observed how high-performing colleagues (teacher leaders) demonstrated mastery experiences through modeling. The collaborative coaching approach allowed for teachers to consult, observe colleagues, and engage in professional activities, which deepened critical questioning, reflection, and allowed the refinement of their craft. The success of teacher leadership depends largely on the cooperation and interaction between teacher leaders and their colleagues and the support from their administrators (Moller & Pankake, 2006). The designed professional activities allowed for colleagues to develop collaborative mutual learning relationships that capitalized on teachers' strengths; and identified the teacher experts in the school who could be sought out during the instructional year. One of the teacher leader voiced how she viewed a shift in her role as an educator of just students, to now an educator for her students and colleagues.

When I began my teaching career, I viewed my job as being completely focused on the students in my classroom. Now I feel like about 50% of my work is focused on the specific students in my classroom. The other 50% is on improving my own skills, and those of my colleagues in our professional learning community. Response from teacher leader

Working with a Team of Professionals along the Continuum

While working collaboratively with the grade-level teams, we capitalized on the shared expertise among a group of teachers: new and experienced teachers, special educators and ESOL teachers by giving them a forum to share what they gained from working with each other. This mutual exchange of ideas and instructional strategies among different teachers helped create a sustainable teacher-led PLC.

> *Working in a collaborative team helps with ideas of what's worked in other classrooms. It also brings to the forefront challenges that may not have been considered before. Having a colleague helped me because she was my support system. I am not very good at math but working with her, I was able to think outside the box for solutions and she encouraged my thinking. This offered me the opportunity to reflect on how else I could solve a problem.* Response from a classroom teacher

Teacher Candidates Learn from Working with a Colleague to Instill the PLC

One of the important outcomes of the professional development model was that teacher candidates were able to witness and be a part of a PLC. Today, the teaching profession is no longer a profession of isolation but a profession that encourages collaboration. Providing teacher candidates with this collaborative network early in their career sets them up for the dispositions needed to be a team player. Some of their comments revealed the impactful knowledge of co-planning and co-teaching with their fellow preservice colleagues. Other comments referenced the knowledge gained from the feedback from the experienced teachers and clinical faculty.

> *I learned a lot about working cooperatively through this and the center activity assignment. My group members and I would often have very different ideas about what we should do and how our lesson and activity should go. It was important for all of us to be patient with one another and respect each other's opinions. It was a valuable experience for us as future teachers because teaching is not a solo career; we will be working to plan with a team more often than we will be planning on our own. It is important to have these experiences working with different teachers to get the practice.* Response from a teacher candidate
>
> *It was good to hear feedback from the site facilitator because it helped my understanding of the importance of directions, timeliness, and use of math vocabulary. Every lesson needs reflection and this lesson was a blast to work on with such a supportive group of students, teachers, and colleagues.* Response from a teacher candidate

Voices from the Novice Teachers

In addition to impacting teacher candidates, the professional development model provided novice teachers and teachers new to the school to learn about the school culture, school norms for instructional practice as well as the special population of diverse students that they would be teaching in the upcoming year.

> *It was really nice working with a small-school based team because I was able to bounce ideas off of every member. As a first year teacher, I was able to learn from each teacher and how they would approach this problem and how much guidance to give my students. I am very grateful for the opportunity.* Response from a novice teacher

For a teacher who had experience but transferred to the new school, the professional development model allowed time for her to meet the school specialists and get to know colleagues that she could go to for specific needs.

> *Being new to the school and content area, the team helped build a resource base. I started the year knowing people I could go to get help. The coach offers insights and presents questions to explore other options. Having a team of different teachers provided a variety of strategies that have been used, not necessarily done by others. By discussing how they use them, it helps us to implement a strategy new to us/me.* Response from a teacher new to the school

Voices from the Experienced Teachers

The learning was not only for the new and prospective teacher but the collaboration and coaching allowed for even experienced teachers to gain from the mutual exchange. Often times, they commented on the novel teaching approaches or the latest technology tools that the new teachers shared with them or commented on the enthusiasm and energy that the new teachers brought to the team. In exchange, the experienced teachers had a deep practice-based knowledge of how students learn and respond to specific concepts and lessons that the new or prospective teachers did not have.

> *It was nice to have colleagues who are new to the profession share their enthusiasm and novel ways of teaching like using new technology tools. With my experiences, I was able to offer the knowledge I have gained about how students from the past responded to problems like these and their common misconceptions.* Response from an experienced teacher

Voices from the Coaches

Finally, the voices from the coaches revealed that the professional development learning model allowed for them to learn more about how to motivate and lead adult learners. Many of the coaches and resource specialists were once classroom teachers who were skillful at teaching elementary students. Most of them had transitioned to the leadership position or coaches' role due to their aspirations to work with teachers but this institute and Lesson Study provided a time and space for them to really work with adult learners and unpack how they learn and understand what motivates their professional learning.

> *It helped me as the coach to gain more insight into my teachers and their thinking about kids thinking about mathematics. How some of their expectations of the solutions were different than the actual solutions. The students surprised them with abilities they did not think the students were capable of demonstrating.* Response from a coach
> *Teachers not used to teaching using groups and more open-ended tasks saw the difference in how students reacted. Comments about being surprised about way students participated was very telling to me. Much of the information I gleaned about student and teacher learning was based on conversations with the teachers. It was encouraging to take form the conversations that they noticed certain things important to moving the student thinking about math forward.* Response from a coach

CONCLUSIONS

Through this case study, we noticed an unanticipated outcome, which was how quickly teacher learners evolved into teacher leaders necessitating a reconceptualization of our project design to include teacher leadership for all educators along the professional continuum. Many of the teacher learners became teacher leaders at this PDS site. Some of the novice teachers aspired to be clinical faculty in following years. This aspiration to become a clinical faculty came about because they worked with teacher leaders who were clinical faculty and saw themselves serving in these roles for the teacher candidates in the PDS program.

The TLI had many of the critical features of effective professional development practices. For example, the institute was experiential and collaborative, involving a sharing of knowledge among educators; connected to and derived from teachers' work with their students as well as to examinations of subject matter and teaching methods; sustained and intensive, supported by modeling, coaching, and problem solving around specific problems of practice; connected to other aspects of school change; and a model in which teachers confront research and theory directly, are regularly engaged in evaluating their practice, and use their colleagues for mutual assistance (Darling-Hammond & McLaughlin, 1995; Garet, Birman, Porter, Desimone, & Herman, 1999; Hirsh, 2009; Yoon, Duncan, Lee, Scarloss, & Shapley, 2007).

In conclusion, we learned that inspiration and strength for educators came from within their own colleagues, educators along the professional continuum (see figure 6.1).

Inspiring Teachers across the Professional Continuum 113

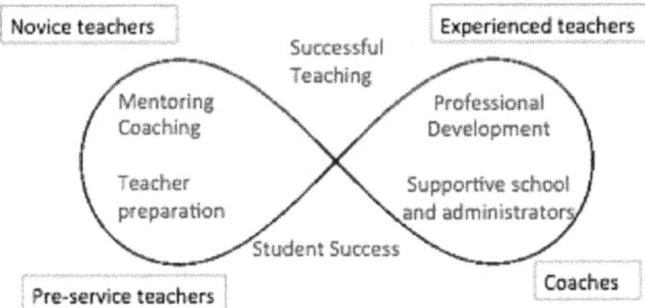

Figure 6.1 Sources of Inspirations.

The diagram with the infinity sign represents the continuous professional learning that educators along the professional continuum take part in to renew their strength and inspiration. The teacher candidates learn through settings like the PDSs, where trained clinical faculty support their learning. Novice teachers gain inspiration from coaches and experienced mentors who support them through the induction years, while experienced teachers gain renewed inspiration through professional development activities like content institutes or working with a teacher intern. Coaches gain their inspiration from a supportive school culture with administrators who are their advocates and from teachers who appreciate the support they provide.

Through the numerous Instructional Rounds and Lesson Study debriefs, it was evident that these collective individuals gained experiences, epiphanies, inspirations, and strength from their colleagues. Through the support of colleagues but also the evidence from having student success in teaching and learning, teachers adopted research-based practices. In addition, the collaborative coaching allowed for a greater yield in the collective knowledge. They all knew that an in-school expert was among them to guide and support them with the important topics related to teaching and learning.

Members within this professional continuum also identified with other educators' experiences. For example, individuals who were on the experienced end of the professional continuum identified with the teacher candidates and novice teachers, as they all were once in their roles. Having been in their roles, the experienced teachers were knowledgeable and provided hope, courage, and strength to the teacher candidates and novice teachers. Teachers along the professional continuum voiced the mutual exchange of professional learning that was respected among the new and experienced teachers.

The experienced teachers felt rejuvenated as they exchanged novel teaching ideas and the chance to observe other teachers infuse reform practices, which made them rethink their traditional teaching approaches. Meanwhile, the teacher candidates and novice teachers who were not be as familiar with the ways students responded to tasks, benefited greatly from the experienced teachers and coaches who banked on their experiences to anticipate how students would respond to a task or misconceptions that may arise when teaching a challenging concept. Finally, the mathematics specialists who had specialized knowledge about the content and pedagogy inspired their teachers to be at the top of their game by learning more about teaching mathematics and understanding more about how students learn.

We began this project thinking that teacher leaders would provide a network of support and resources for our teacher learners. While the principal spent planning days with the teacher leaders, she became a mentor to these teachers expanding their awareness of leadership roles. As a result, teachers gained confidence in leading their colleagues and began to inquire about methods for engaging adult learners. This was evidenced by the principal's trust in these teacher leaders, which encouraged leadership competence and confidence.

Teacher learners gained knowledge from the experienced teachers and coaches, but also had ways to share their knowledge of most current research-based practices that they were learning from the university. These relationships deepened as the year progressed and infused throughout the culture of the school. They moved beyond the TLI participants and impacted all staff members as the school became a network of hubs and nodes of communication of expertise (Reeves, 2006).

A hallmark of these professional relationships were the "on-the run" conversations that occurred hourly throughout the school: teachers passing in the hallway stopped to discuss professional practice, teachers in the lunchroom reflected on a lesson taught, or teachers in the copy room conferred to analyze individual student achievement. Providing the extra time for professional learning and establishing this collaborative structure and continuous professional learning created the school's sense of shared leadership and ownership of the school's success focused on students' achievement. Looking forward, we are committed to furthering this collaborative culture and enhancement of professional practice while growing the leadership capacity at our PDS.

REFERENCES

Bandura, A. (1993). Perceived self-efficacy in cognitive development and functioning. *Educational Psychologist, 28*(2), 117–148.

Barab, S. A., Makinster, J. G., Moore, J. A., & Cunningham, D. J. (2001). Designing and building an on-line community: The struggle to support sociability in the inquiry learning forum. *Educational Technology Research and Development, 49*(4), 71–96.

Cambone, J. (1995). Time for teachers in school restructuring. *Teachers College Record, 96*(3), 512–543.

Castle, S., Fox, R. K., & Fuhrman, C. (2009). Does professional development school preparation make a difference?: A comparison of three teacher candidate studies. *School-University Partnerships, 3*(2), 58–68.

Chazan, D., Ben-Chaim, D., Gormas, J., Schnepp, M., Lehman, M., Bethell, S. C., & Neurither, S. (1998). Shared teaching assignments in the service of mathematics reform: Situated professional development. *Teaching and Teacher Education, 14*(7), 687–702.

Cochran-Smith, M., & Lytle, S. L. (2001). Beyond certainty: Taking an inquiry stance on Practice. In A. Lieberman & L. Miller (Eds.), *Teachers caught in the action: Professional development that matters* (pp. 45–58). New York, NY: Teachers College Press.

Corcoran, T. C. (1995). *Transforming professional development for teachers: A guide for state policymakers.* Washington, DC: National Governors' Association.

Creswell, J. (2003). *Research design: Qualitative, quantitative and mixed methods approaches* (2nd ed.). Thousand Oaks, CA: SAGE Publications.

Danielson, C. (2007). *Enhancing professional practice: A framework for teaching.* Alexandria, VA: Association for Supervision and Curriculum Development.

Danielson, C. (2006). *Teacher leadership that strengthens professional practice.* Alexandria, VA: Association for Supervision and Curriculum Development.

Donahoe, T. (1993). Finding the way: Structure, time, and culture in school improvement. *Phi Delta Kappan, 75*(4), 298–305.

DuFour, R. (2004). Schools as learning communities. *Educational Leadership, 61*(8), 6–11.

Fernandez, C. (2002). Learning from Japanese approaches to professional development: The case of lesson study. *Journal of Teacher Education, 53*(5), 393-405.

Fernandez, C., & Yoshida, M. (2004). *Lesson study: A case of a Japanese approach to improving instruction through school-based teacher development.* Mahwah, NJ: Lawrence Erlbaum.

Fountas, I. C., & Pinnell, G. S. (2001). *Guiding readers and writers grades 3–6: Teaching comprehension, genre, and content literacy.* Portsmouth, NH: Heinemann.

Garet, M. S., Birman, B. F., Porter, A. C., Desimone, L., & Herman, J. (1999). *Designing effective professional development: Lessons from the Eisenhower program [and] technical appendices.* Washington, DC: U.S. Department of Education.

Goddard, R. D., Hoy, W. K., & Woolfolk Hoy, A. (2000). Collective teacher efficacy: Its meaning, measure, and impact on student achievement. *American Educational Research Journal, 37*(2), 479–507.

Gulamhussein, A. (2013). *Teaching the teachers effective professional development in an era of high stakes accountability.* Alexandria, VA: Center for Public Education.

Hawkins, P. (Ed.). (2014). *Leadership team coaching in practice: Developing high-performing teams.* London ; Philadelphia, PA: Kogan Page.

Heffernan, M. (2014). *A bigger prize: How we can do better than the competition.* New York, NY: Public Affairs.

Hirsh, S. (2009). New definition. *Journal of Staff Development, 30*(4), 11–16.

Kagan, S., & Kagan, M. (2009). *Kagan cooperative learning.* San Clemente, CA: Kagan Publishing.

Lambert, L. (2003). *Leadership capacity for lasting school improvement.* Alexandria, VA: Association of Supervision and Curriculum Development.

Lave, J., & Wenger, E. (1990). *Situated learning: Legitimate peripheral participation.* Cambridge, UK: Cambridge University Press.

Leithwood, K. (1992). The move toward transformational leadership. *Educational Leadership, 49*(5), 8–12.

Lewis, C. (2002). *Lesson study: A handbook of teacher-led instructional change.* Hillsdale, NJ: Research for Better Schools.

Lewis, C., Perry, R., & Hurd, J. (2004). A deeper look at lesson study. *Educational Leadership, 61*(5), 18–22.

Lewis, C., Perry, R., Hurd, J., & O'Connell, P. (2006). Lesson study comes of age in North America. *Phi Delta Kappan, 88*(4), 273–281.

Miles, M. B., & Huberman, A. M. (1994). *Qualitative data analysis* (2nd ed.). Thousand Oaks, CA: Sage Publications.

Miller, S., & Stewart, A. (2013). Literacy learning through team coaching. *The Reading Teacher, 67*(4), 290–298. doi: 10.1002/trtr.1219.

Moller, G., & Pankake, A. (2006). *Lead with me: A principal's guide to teacher leadership.* Larchmont, NY: Eye on Education.

National Education Commission on Time and Learning [NECTL]. (2005). *Prisoners of time.* Washington, DC: Author.

National Council for the Accreditation of Teacher Education (NCATE). (2000). *Standards for professional development schools.* Washington, DC: NCATE.

National Council for the Accreditation of Teacher Education (NCATE). (2010). *Transforming teacher education through clinical practice: A National Strategy to prepare effective teachers.* Report of the Blue Ribbon Panel on Clinical Preparation and Partnerships for Improved Student Learning. Washington, DC: NCATE.

National Research Council (NRC). (2001). *Adding it up: Helping children learn mathematics.* Washington, DC: National Academy Press.

Northwest Regional Educational Laboratory (NWREL). (1998). *High-quality professional development.* Retrieved from http://www.nwrel.org/request/june98/article 11.html.

Payne, R. K. (2005). *A framework for understanding poverty.* Highlands, TX: aha! Process, Inc.

Putnam, R. T., & Borko, H. (2000). What do new views of knowledge and thinking have to say about research on teacher learning? *Educational Researcher, 29*(1), 4–15.

Rath, T. (2007). *Strengths finder 2.0.* New York, NY: Gallup Press.

Reeves, D. (2006). Hub, bridges, and networks. *Education Leadership, 63*(8). Alexandria, VA: Association for Supervision and Curriculum Development.

Roberts, N. (1985). Transforming leadership. A process of collective action. *Human Relations, 38*(11), 1023–1046.

Roth, W. M., & Tobin, K. (2004). Coteaching: From praxis to theory. *Teachers and Teaching: Theory and Practice, 10*(2), 161–180.

Smylie, M. A., & Brownlee-Conyers, J. (1992). Teacher leaders and their principals: Exploring the development of new working relationships. *Educational Administration Quarterly, 28*(2), 150–184.

Slavin, R. E. (1995). *Cooperative learning: Theory, research, and practice* (2nd ed.). Boston, MA: Allyn and Bacon.

Stake, R. E. (1995). *The art of case study research*. Thousand Oaks, CA: Sage Publications.

Stigler, J. W., & Hiebert, J. (1999). *The teaching gap; Best ideas from the world's teachers for improving education in the classroom*. New York, NY: Free Press.

Suh, J. M., & Parker, J. (2010). Developing reflective practitioners through Lesson Study with pre-service and in-service teachers. *AMTE monograph. VII. Mathematics Teaching: Putting Research into Practice at All Levels. Associations of Mathematics Teacher Educators*, 125–140.

Yin, R. K. (1989). *Case study research: Design and methods* (2nd ed.). Newbury Park, CA: Sage Publications.

Yoon, K. S., Duncan, T., Lee, S. W. Y., Scarloss, B., & Shapley, K. (2007). *Reviewing the evidence on how teacher professional development affects student achievement* (Issues & Answers Report, REL 2007–No. 033). Available at http://ies.ed.gov/ncee/edlabs/regions/southwest/pdf/REL _2007033.pdf.

Zeichner, K., & Conklin, H. G. (2008). Teacher education programs as sites for teacher preparation. In M. Cochran-Smith, S. Feiman-Nemser, D. J. McIntyre, & K. E. Demers (Eds.), *Handbook of research on teacher education: Enduring questions in changing contexts* (3rd ed., pp. 269–289). New York, NY: Routledge.

Chapter 7

Strengthening Culturally Responsive Teaching through Existing Professional Development School Partnerships

Emily Reeves, Angela Malone Cartwright,
and Daphney L. Curry

ABSTRACT

Our ability to coexist in a diverse society is largely learned in public schooling. Before teacher candidates can lead their classes in transformational learning, especially candidates whose privilege is yet to be acknowledged, teacher candidates must first experience transformational learning. Grounded in a strong multicultural framework and diverse placements for interns, rich clinical experiences are deliberately designed to produce culturally responsive teachers. Concrete examples of these efforts include guided reflection, structured interviews, and discussions with mentor teachers, small group reading instruction, and assignments that encourage interns to think through the different perspectives that K-12 students may have in the professional development school setting. Preparing culturally responsive teachers cannot be one lesson each semester but must be an intentional, systematic, and continuous experience contextualized in rich and transformative activities that better prepares teachers to serve a constantly changing and diverse population.

KEY WORDS

Teacher Candidates; Culturally Responsive; Professional Development Schools

INTRODUCTION

Our ability to coexist in a diverse society is largely learned in public schooling. Karp (1995) asserted that "public school is where students are taught what society thinks of itself" (p. 33), and Mazza (2009) argued that "school is where student should learn about tolerance and pluralism, which are great aspects of the diversity of the United States" (p. 343). Demographics of public schools, in which students of color now make up the majority of the student body (Maxwell, 2014; Sleeter, Neal, & Kumashiro, 2014) while the teaching force continues to be mostly white (Subedi, 2006), highlight the continuing significance of their argument. The demographics also indicate that many teacher candidates will need significant education if they are to be prepared for the challenging task of interrogating dominant assumptions and creating space for voices of difference (Butin, 2007; Cochran-Smith, 2004; Marshall, 2006).

Conklin (2008), drawing on McDonald and Zeichner's contribution to the *Handbook of Social Justice in Education*, refers to the issue as the demographic imperative, described as "the convergent challenges of an increasingly diverse student population; teachers whose lived experiences differ markedly from those of their students; and the gap in educational opportunities and outcomes" that characterizes public education in the United States (p. 655). Because classroom practices, such as curriculum design, materials selection, and pedagogical decisions, are influenced by personal beliefs and important commitments (Villegas, 2007), teacher educators, as well as classroom practitioners, must reflect on their epistemologies so that public education can be a site for cultural exchange, as opposed to cultural indoctrination (Cymrot, 2002). The dominance of hegemony is sustained by its invisibility. When dominance is made visible, it must be confronted (Applebaum, 2004; Crocco, 2010; Freire, 1970; Mura, 1999; Young, 2011). Public education institutions are frequently the location of confrontations about dominance and diversity because they are the "agents of child socialization and enculturation, where children assimilate a culture's core values, traditions, and authority structures" (Faiman-Silva, 2002, p. 189). Public schools are often the first site of introduction to systemic structures of unfettered privilege.

The only element that can disrupt the delivery of privilege is a change to the structures that maintain inequalities (Leonardo, 2004). The necessity of systemic change is based in the systemic nature of true domination, which is codified through time. "It does not form out of random acts of hatred, although these are condemnable, but rather out of patterned and enduring treatment of social groups" (Leonardo, 2004, p. 139; see also Mura, 1999; Young, 2011). Systemic change is rather difficult to engineer, as the dominant group would have to willingly give up its unfair access to material privilege. For even the most sympathetic dominant listener, the "message [of the necessity of systemic change] produces psychological dissonance between [the] desire for . . . justice and her inability to accept radical change" (Leonardo, 2004, p. 143; see also Ellsworth, 1989; Williams, 1997; Young, 2011). Because of the consequences of acknowledging the legitimacy of oppressed groups' claims, many members of dominant groups cling to the discredited idea of colorblindness, arguing the purity of meritocracy (Williams, 1997; Young, 2011).

Teacher Candidates and Transformative Learning

Before teacher candidates, especially candidates whose privilege is yet to be acknowledged, can lead their classes in transformational learning, they must first experience transformational learning. Transformational learning occurs when a new awareness changes the way individuals perceive themselves, others, and the world around them (Cole, 2011). Marshall (2006) suggests that teacher education programs include explicit discussions regarding identity, culture, and these construct intersect with the schooling process, as well as experiential learning in the communities where teacher candidates will serve. Eck (2007) utilizes an assignment that encourages university students to interrogate their own assumptions and beliefs, while Blumenfeld (2006) suggests utilizing the theory of constructivism in order to deconstruct assumptions and replace them with more inclusive perspectives. However, teacher preparation programs are increasingly focusing on preparing candidates for the standardized classroom while failing to engage them in the ongoing dialogue about the role of the classroom in society (Butin & Schutz, 2013). Multicultural education courses are rarely required coursework unless mandated by the state, and when multicultural education courses are required, they are rarely presented in ways that encourage teacher candidates to move outside of their comfort zones (Butin, 2007).

Multicultural education is a "hopeful and idealistic" result of the turbulent decades of the Civil Rights Movement (Bennett, 2001, p. 171). Bennett's description is supported by the focus of early multicultural education scholarship on the cultural and academic needs of minority students in newly desegregated schools. A strong argument can be made regarding earlier historical roots of multicultural education, such as late 19th- and early 20th-century African American studies and the Intergroup Education Movement (Banks, 1996; Hytten & Bettez, 2011; Ladson-Billings & Tate, 1995). However, Bennett's (2001) focus on the later date purposely privileges the conscious efforts of mid-century scholars, educators, and activists to utilize public education as a tool to encourage multiculturalism instead of homogeny. Bennett's (2001) description of the shift from assimilation to pluralism models is a useful illustration of the intentional shift in the purpose of public education. Regardless, the initial issues-based scholarship born of desegregation gave way to broader conceptual frameworks in the 1970s (Bennett, 2001). Focus began to shift from preparing students, teachers, and communities for their new experiences, interactions, and expectations; scholars were now beginning to considering larger issues of equity. Born out of a concern for difference and equality, and evolving organically over time, the field of multicultural education has come to include a variety philosophies and pedagogies.

At its core, multicultural education seeks to create multicultural competence in individuals (Bennett, 2001). This journey requires a reconciliation with the self (Banks, 1996) that requires individuals in all groups to see past their own perspectives. Indeed, one of the key concepts of multicultural competence is the ability to see past one's own positioning to "the 'whole picture'"; thus, multicultural competence is, in some ways, "a way of looking at the world" and interacting with others (Case, 1993, p. 318). Without these crucial components in their undergraduate education as teacher candidates, it is unlikely that classroom teachers will see among their goals the "responsibility for building classroom communities that confront controversy and take responsibility for creating a better community, one that values diversity and human integrity and fights inhumanity" (Santora, 1995, pp. 21–22).

Neutrality is arguably nonexistent as all perspectives are limited by positionality. Positionality, which asserts that social factors used to define people are relative, determines the knowledges and experiences that will be privileged in a society (Banks, 1996; see also Carlisle, Jackson, & George, 2006; Greene, 1995; Holland, Lachicotte, Skinner, & Cain, 1998; Quin, 2009). Understanding the influence of positionality and privilege is imperative for teacher candidates to be provided meaningful exposure to multiple narratives and perspectives so that they can develop a stance of acceptance. Quin (2009) eloquently described the distinction in the researcher's discussion of having a position versus taking a stance. Quinn argues that position refers to the way in which one sees the world, a location that can still be passive. Conversely, stance is described as an active engagement, reminiscent of roots in the terminology "fighting stance" (Quin, 2009, p. 117; see also Nieto, 2000).

As Bennett (1993) explains, acceptance is reached when "difference is both acknowledged and respected," without value judgment, "as a necessary and preferable human condition" (pp. 47–48). As opposed to the common practice of avoidance, educators should embrace their potential role as molders of public perception (Subedi, 2006). Educators can play a large role in promoting pluralism, which "takes the reality of difference as its starting point," and does not attempt to "erase difference, nor to smooth out differences under a universalizing canopy, but rather to discover ways of living, connecting, relating, arguing, and disagreeing in a society of differences" (Eck, 2007, p. 745).

Culturally Responsive Teaching

The classroom, whether P-12 or higher education, is an opportune site for the development of a multicultural identity, as classrooms are locations of diversity convergence. If students are encouraged to acknowledge and consider diverse perspectives and experiences in positive and constructive ways, then they can work through the stages of resistance toward acceptance (Bennett, 1993). This process can be quite difficult for individuals, especially students, who are forced to confront their own dominance for the first time; it can be a significant challenge to their sense of identities. However, individuals begin to value certain traits based on their membership in social groups (Reynolds & Prior, 2006), so creating a space in which multicultural competence is valued is crucial for its development. The social influence on individual values creates a dynamic where an intensely personal quest is made public. Students arrive in the classroom with a personalized store of potential selves but will nurture and develop only those that receive praise or acknowledgment (Thoits & Virshup, 1997). Given a choice, most students will not choose identities that lead to social exclusion. The traits individuals use to create their identities are the ones they perceive as having value (Reynolds & Prior, 2006). The critical factor is determining which characteristics are valued, and educators, both P-12 and higher education, have a responsibility to create spaces and provide experiences where multicultural competence is valued and encouraged.

Professional Development Schools: A Lasting Legacy

State University (SU) (not the actual name) is a public, state-funded liberal arts university located in a semi-urban city in the south central part of the United States. The West College of Education (WCOE) is one of five professional colleges at SU. In 1997, West COE embarked on a collaborative venture with local and regional schools to create a field-based teacher education program using the professional development school (PDS) model (National Association of Professional Development Schools, 2008). The purpose of the original agreement was to establish a field-based teacher education program that fostered the following goals: cognitive/reflective-based approach to learning; emphasis of skills, knowledge, and dispositions that reflect best practices; integrate technology to promote active learning environments; provide professional development to both university and public school faculty (West College of Education, 1997). Over the past two decades, WCOE has improved and expanded its collaborative partnerships to include approximately fifty preK-12th-grade campuses and eight designated PDSs. The COE considers collaboration with its PDS partners a vital component of its teacher preparation program. Collaboration with its school and community partners is ongoing and occurs in the design, implementation, and evaluation of every clinical experience. WCOE maintains a collaborative relationship with several independent school districts in the area. School and community stakeholders participate and reflect on field-based program effectiveness through advisory councils, teacher education committees, and shared professional development.

PDSs: Linking Professional Learning and Schools

Increasingly diverse school populations (U.S. Bureau of Census, 2012) require university-based educator preparation programs (EPPs) to rethink how they prepare their teacher candidates. The PDS model has the potential to change both individuals and society through challenging, supportive, hands-on environments in the context of rich and diverse clinical experiences. The mission of WCOE is to prepare skilled and reflective practitioners through the use of best practice. The WCOE conceptual framework (2013) emphasizes the following knowledge, skills, and dispositions for their initial teacher candidates and professional graduate programs as related to culturally diverse field experiences, professional learning, and collaboration:

- Differentiated Learning—an understanding of individual differences, cultures, and communities;
- Planning—planning instruction that meets and supports individual needs through best practice and rigorous standards for learning;
- Professional Learning Opportunities and Ethics—ongoing professional learning and continuous evaluation and reflection of practice; stressing the effects their actions have on students, educational colleagues, and families;
- Collaboration and Leadership Responsibilities—the ongoing leadership and collaboration responsibilities of educational professionals; stressing learner growth and advancement of the profession;
- Evaluation/Assessment—the role assessment plays in professional growth and student learning; stressing teacher and learner decision-making
- Development of the Learner—individual learner growth and development; stressing individual variance across cognitive, linguistic, social, emotional, cultural, and physical development;
- Knowledge of Content—pedagogy that make content learning accessible and meaningful for all learners;
- Instructional Strategies—implementation of a variety of instructional strategies (best practice) that encourages all learners to connect with content in meaningful ways; stressing how to build and apply knowledge and skills in meaningful ways.

Initial teacher candidates participate in a variety of clinical experiences in surrounding school districts under the mentorship of WCOE faculty and public school teacher mentors. WCOE faculty have established strong relationships with several designated PDSs in the area. PDSs are specifically selected because of the rich clinical opportunities and experiences inherent in ethnically diverse student populations. Linda Darling-Hammond's (2006) review of EPPs emphasizes the benefits of rich clinical experiences that link schools and university-based faculty and course work within the PDS framework. PDSs allow the WCOE to provide a living laboratory for teacher candidates to practice and improve their pedagogical skills. Within the PDS model, teacher candidates complete a series of clinical experiences in field-based professional block methods courses prior to clinical teaching. These experiences provide intense, cohesive, and diverse opportunities for candidates to practice the knowledge, skills, and dispositions of culturally responsive teaching. The WCOE PDS framework uses a 50/50 model comprised of 50% methods course work and 50% field experience. The 50/50 models allows WCOE teacher candidates to apply the content-related knowledge, skills, and dispositions they learn in their professional methods courses in an actual classroom setting. All WCOE methods courses are taught on-site with PDSs providing classrooms for WCOE methods faculty and students to use for coursework.

The WCOE and PDS districts work together to provide technology equipped classrooms for WCOE faculty and students. WCOE resources such as iPads, laptop computers, interactive whiteboards, and projectors are shared with PDS partners. Professional learning is a reciprocal process between the WCOE and our PDS partners. WCOE faculty and PDS faculty provide professional learning through workshops, professional development, technology demonstrations, and professional conferences. Public school classroom placement decisions are a collaborative process among school administrators, WCOE methods faculty, and classroom teachers. Within the PDS framework, WCOE teacher candidates plan, implement, evaluate, and reflect on their teaching. PDS classroom teacher mentors and WCOE methods faculty conference with teacher candidates after each lesson delivery to give them feedback on their teaching.

The PDS framework also allows teacher candidates many opportunities to observe their WCOE methods faculty and classroom teacher mentors modeling of instructional planning, lesson delivery, and assessment of student learning. WCOE teacher candidates are also afforded opportunities to participate in parent conferences, professional development, PDS campus committees, curriculum and grade-level planning, professional learning communities, and related community-school events under the guidance of their classroom teacher mentor.

PDS Challenges: Overcoming Obstacles

As population demographics change, schools must adjust their pedagogy to meet the needs of their students. Unfortunately, ethnic diversity among teachers is not keeping pace with current school population demographics in the United States (National Center for Educational Statistics, 2015). Teacher candidates are often unprepared to meet the needs of children from cultures different from their own (Sleeter, 2001). Many researchers have studied the impact teachers have on overall student learning (Darling-Hammond & Youngs, 2002; Goe, 2007) with differing results and perspectives. Related research investigating teacher preparation programs and new teacher professional development suggests a positive impact on student achievement (Darling-Hammond, 2000; Hill, Rowan, & Ball, 2005). Although teacher preparation and professional development may have a positive impact on diverse student performance, implementation does not come without challenges.

For example, forming a strong PDS that is mutually beneficial to both teacher candidates and mentor teachers begins with building strong relationships. These relationships are built on a commitment to both teacher preparation and ongoing professional development. With current time constraints because of demanding schedules and distance between PDS schools and the university, the commitment must be strong enough to make scheduling a top priority. When relationships are strong between the university, K-12 school administration, and mentor teachers, the commitment and scheduling becomes more manageable. When the relationship is not strong and PDS is not a priority, basic scheduling can be problematic. Another aspect of PDS that is a challenge is communication. When trying to facilitate timely communication between and among the K-12 mentor teachers, teacher candidates, university faculty, and school administrators all efforts must be made to make sure that everyone is aware of schedules and duties. Email cannot be relied on and university faculty must make the extra effort to talk with K-12 administrators, mentor teachers, and teacher candidates on a regular basis.

Other PDS challenges are balancing the shared work load between K-12 mentor teachers and university faculty when evaluating teacher candidates. Mentors are not paid for their service but receive professional development and extra help in the classroom. For most mentors this is a positive experience however, occasionally there are mentors who either do not complete the required evaluations or feel overwhelmed by the process and decide not to mentor in the future. With this in mind, it is important for the university faculty member to be supportive and communicate on a regular basis with mentor teachers so they are aware of issues as they occur. Finally, consistency between mentors in how they evaluate interns is not always ideal. To be proactive, active discussion of the evaluation process is encouraged among seasoned mentors, new mentor teachers, and university faculty. Although there are several challenges that successful PDS must address, being aware of the challenges and actively working to negate problems that arise is part of the success.

Partnerships that Work: Rich Clinical Experiences

In keeping with its mission, WCOE strengthens culturally responsive teaching (CRT) through existing PDS partnerships. WCOE is dedicated to integrating diversity into the culture and professional learning of its teacher preparation program. WCOE PDS relationships are strengthened through continuous monitoring and close relationships with WCOE professional block methods faculty and assigned clinical experience liaisons. Currently, the WCOE has PDS partnerships with two local school districts. These districts provide eight designated PDS sites: four elementary schools, one middle school, and two high schools. As part of their initial teacher preparation all EC-6 teacher candidates participate in two professional methods block courses in the following content areas: math, science, social studies, and English language arts. Pseudonyms have been used to protect the privacy of the PDSs. For the purpose of this article, only the elementary PDSs will be discussed. WCOE has established PDS partnerships with four elementary schools: Adams, Holt, Lincoln, and Reagan Elementary. Holt and Lincoln Elementary are relatively new PDS partners. Adams, Lincoln, and Regan Elementary are located in a small neighboring community near a military base. Lincoln Elementary is located on a military base and has approximately 300 students. Lincoln and Adams Elementary provide a unique clinical experience because the majority of students are from military families. Although, predominately white, the military population of Lincoln, Holt, and Reagan Elementary allow WCOE teacher candidates to work with students from many different parts of the United States and abroad. For example, Lincoln Elementary currently has a student population that includes thirty-one Arabic students, five German students, three Japanese students, four Dutch students, and four Danish students. This provides great opportunity to not only work with culturally diverse students but also language diversity. Holt Elementary is an ethnically diverse school with approximately 340 students (National Center for Educational Statistics, 2013b). Holt Elementary is a Title I school with the majority of students receiving free or reduced lunch. Holt Elementary gives WCOE teacher candidates opportunities to work with students from many different ethnic and racial backgrounds.

Theory Translated into Clinically Rich Practices

Grounded in a strong multicultural framework and diverse placements for interns, rich clinical experiences are deliberately designed to produce culturally responsive teachers. Concrete examples of these efforts include guided reflection, structured interviews, and discussions with mentor teachers, small group reading instruction, and assignments that encourage interns to think through the different perspectives that K-12 students may have. Teaching Tolerance (n.d.), a website that is a project of The Southern Poverty Law Center, is an excellent resource for principals, professors, mentor teachers, and interns. The website offers videos, lessons, and many other resources for promoting culturally responsive instruction. Teaching Tolerance is one of many resources used in the PDS to specifically address multicultural framework and CRT.

As a way to begin each semester and help interns actively think about their own perspective, they are asked to complete the Reflection: What is your FRAME? (Teaching Tolerance, n.d.) activity. This guided reflection pushes interns to really think about where they are coming from and what their own biases may be before entering the field. Initially, interns write down aspects of their own FRAME. This includes their background such as where they grew up, their own cultural norms, socioeconomic class, language, and so on. Next, students are asked to think about their FRAME in a specific way relating to the students they may have. Directly from the Teaching Tolerance activity:

- F—Figure out the facts: Not just what is apparent to you, but all the facts. Seek more information, ask questions, and listen.
- R—Reflect on reality: Is it my reality or their reality? Am I looking at this through my FRAME or trying to see it through their FRAME?
- A—Acknowledge and challenge assumptions: Think about your expectations and whether they are appropriate. Are you making assumptions based on your FRAME?
- M—Maintain an open mind: Just because someone else's FRAME differs from yours doesn't make them wrong. What can you learn from them? What can they learn from you? What do you have in common?
- E—Expand your experiences: Explore, expose yourself, and encounter differences; expand your comfort zone; increase your cultural competence. (Teaching Tolerance, n.d.)

Starting each semester with a reflective attitude about cultural differences provides a consistent framework for the entire semester and helps better equip interns to work with students in a meaningful, relevant way. Although this is a good start, reflection throughout each semester is critical to maintaining the conversation about CRT and how CRT impacts instruction and student performance. Developing culturally responsive teachers must be ongoing and not limited to one class or assignment. Linking the idea of CRT to immediate experiences strengthens the process opposed to occasional or isolated discussions. For many interns, this is a transformative process because they know the catch phrases and personal ideas but are not as secure in execution.

In addition to reflection and classroom discussions, conversations between teacher mentors and interns are also a critical part of developing culturally responsive teachers. These conversations are facilitated using the Common Beliefs Survey (Teaching Tolerance, n.d.). The survey provides both a Likert scale and an area for mentors and interns to elaborate on why they feel the way they do. For example, one questions is "I don't think of my students in terms of their race or ethnicity. I am color blind when it comes to my teaching" (Teaching Tolerance Common Beliefs Survey, n.d.). Procedurally, interns take the survey toward the beginning of the semester and then use the same survey to interview their mentor teacher. Having students take the survey and think about their own responses before interviewing their mentor provides a platform for deeper reflection. After the interviews, a whole class discussion and open reflection takes place between interns and the professor. This discussion becomes ongoing as it is referred back to throughout the rest of the semester. As interns become more and more comfortable talking about diversity and issues that arise in the classroom, they begin to share their own experiences and work through issues as a group. This type of conversation drives the transformative process of becoming culturally responsive teachers.

Reflective conversations also characterize interns' evaluations of curricular materials and instructional activities. In Social Studies Methods, interns apply their developing cultural competency when discussing learning activities for the Culture TEKS in their grade bands. After identifying TEKS that are supported by the activity suggestions found in the Social Studies Methods textbook, interns then analyze the portrayal of nondominant cultures in the activities and evaluate their appropriateness for classroom instruction. It is important to note that the activities are not all culturally sensitive, nor do they all portray nondominant cultures appropriately. Interns must apply not only the multicultural competency skills they've developed, but also take into consideration the multicultural awareness of their students when evaluating the activities and articulating their decisions.

The evidence that this is truly a rich and transformative process and not a mandatory and almost robotic reflection is to see and hear student who suddenly realize that they do actually have biases and start to think about how being aware of their own biases enables them to better serve their own students. For example, it is common for interns to "agree strongly" with the question about seeing their students through a color blind lens; however, when students also "agree strongly" that "Students of different races and ethnicities often have different learning styles and good teachers will match their instruction to these learning styles" (Teaching Tolerance Common Beliefs Survey, n.d.), the wheels start to turn. How can a teacher be color blind but also responsive to learning styles based on different races and ethnicities? And, is it a good idea to assume that a student has a specific learning style based on their race or ethnicity? These discussions provide a fantastic basis for an ongoing rich discussion throughout the semester while students actively plan and teach lessons while completing internships prior to starting student teaching.

The Lincoln Elementary PDS is structured in a way that allows interns to work with students each morning from 8:00 to 8:30 in small groups. This opportunity allows interns to work with students who are having language and in some cases, a hard time with cultural adjustment to American public school. During the morning small groups, interns work as tutors and mentors. Interns also work with individuals if a mentor has one specific student that needs individual attention. The relationship building that comes from this thirty-minute block is valuable to both the intern and the student. As reported by the principal in multiple conversations about the process, "This time is invaluable."

Culturally responsive expectations are a consistent component throughout the PDSs. Interns and student teachers must include accommodations in each lesson plan, actively participate in discussions, and actively engage with students and mentor teachers. After each formally observed lesson, interns and student teachers conference about how the lesson was implemented and what may be modified in the future. Strengths are highlighted and reflection is used to decide on an action plan to address weaknesses in future lessons. Through this systematic process, evidence of higher quality teaching can be found in the intern's portfolio that is maintained as an ongoing assessment of each intern's efforts in lesson planning, teaching, and reflection.

CONCLUSION

Training culturally responsive teachers cannot be one lesson each semester but must be systematic and continuous. Stepping back, this looks much like a quality lesson plan. Reflection: What is your FRAME? (Teaching Tolerance, n.d) acts as a preassessment and the interviews, discussions, lesson planning, and conferences act as an ongoing lesson. Finally, students are asked to revisit their initial Common Beliefs Survey and discuss any changes in their thinking throughout the semester. This is truly a rich and transformative piece that better prepares teachers to serve a continually more diverse population.

REFERENCES

Applebaum, B. (2004). Social justice education, moral agency, and the subject of resistance. *Educational Theory, 54*(1), 59–72. doi: 10.1111/j.0013-2004.2004.00003.x.

Ayers, W., Quinn, T, & Stovall, B. (2009). Social justice teacher education. In M. McDonald & K. Zeichner (Authors), *Handbook of social justice in education* (pp. 595–610). New York: Routledge.

Banks, J. A. (1996). *Multicultural education, transformative knowledge, and action.* New York, NY: Teachers College Press.

Bennett, C. (2001). Genres of research in multicultural education. *American Educational Research Journal, 71*(2), 171–217. doi: 10.3102/00346543071002171.

Bennett, M. J. (1993). *Education for the intercultural experience.* Yarmouth, ME: Intercultural Press.

Blumenfeld, W. J. (2006). Christian privilege and the promotion of "secular" and not-so "secular" mainline Christianity in public schooling and in the larger society. *Equity & Excellence in Education, 39*(2), 195–210. doi: 10.1080/10665680600788024.

Butin, D. W. (2007). Dark times indeed: NCATE, social justice, and the marginalization of multicultural foundations. *Journal of Educational Controversy, 2*(2). Retrieved from http://www.wce.wwu.edu/Resources/CEP/eJournal/v002n002/a003.shtml.

Butin, D. W., & Schutz, A. (2013). Beyond dependency: Strategies for saving foundations. *Critical Questions in Education, 4*(2), 60–71.

Carlisle, L. R., Jackson, B. W., & George, A. (2006). Principles of social justice education: The social justice education in schools project. *Equity & Excellence in Education, 39*, 55–64.

Case, R. (1993). Key elements of a global perspective. *Social Education, 57*(6), 318–325.

Cochran-Smith, M. (2004). *Walking the road: Race, diversity, and social justice in teacher education.* New York, NY: Teachers College Press.

Cole, S. (2011). Situating children in the discourse of spirituality. In N. N. Wane, E. L. Manyimo, & E. J. Ritskes (Eds.), *Spirituality, education & society: An integrated approach* (pp. 1–14). Rotterdam, Netherlands: Sense.

Conklin, H. G. (2008). Modeling compassion in critical, justice-oriented teacher education. *Harvard Educational Review, 78*(4), 652–674.

Crocco, M. S. (2010). [How] Do we teach about women of the world in teacher education? In B. Subedi (Ed.), *Critical global perspectives: Rethinking knowledge about global societies* (pp. 19–38). Charlotte, NC: Information Age.

Cymrot, T. Z. (2002). Chapter two: What is diversity? In L. Darling-Hammond, J. French, & S. P. Garcia-Lopez, *Learning to teach for social justice* (pp. 1–7). New York, NY: Teachers College Press.

Darling-Hammond, L. (2000). Teacher quality and student achievement: A review of state policy evidence. *Education Policy Analysis Archives, 8*(1), 1–44.

Darling-Hammond, L. (2006). *Developing learning-centered schools for students and teachers.* Thousand Oaks, CA: SAGE.

Darling-Hammond, L., & Youngs, P. (2002). Defining 'highly qualified' teachers: What does scientifically-based research actually tell us? *Educational Researcher, 31*(9), 13–25.

Darling-Hammond, L. (2006). *Developing learning-centered schools for students and teachers.* Thousand Oaks, CA: SAGE.

Eck, D. L. (2007). Prospects for pluralism: Voice and vision in the study of religion. *Journal of the Academy of American Religion, 75*(4), 743–776.

Ellsworth, E. (1989). Why doesn't this feel empowering? Working through the repressive mythis of critical pedagogy. *Harvard Educational Review, 59*(3), 297–325.

Faiman-Silva, S. (2002). Students and a "Culture of resistance" in provincetown's schools. *Anthropology & Education Quarterly, 33*(2), 189–212.

Freire, P. (1970). *Cultural action for freedom.* Cambridge, MA: Harvard Educational Review.

Goe, L. (2007). *The link between teacher quality and student outcomes: A research synthesis.* Washington, DC: National Comprehensive Center for Teacher Quality.

Greene, M. (1995). *Releasing the imagination: Essays on education, the arts, and social change.* San Francisco, CA: Jossey-Bass.

Hill, H. C., Rowan, B., & Ball, D. L. (2005). Effects of teachers' mathematical knowledge for teaching on student achievement. *American Educational Research Journal, 42*(2), 371–406.

Holland, D., Lachicotte, E., Skinner, D., & Cain, C. (1998). Identity in practice. In D. Holland, E. Lachicotte, D. Skinner, & C. Cain (Eds.), *Identity and agency in cultural worlds* (pp. 270–288). Cambridge, MA: Harvard University Press.

Hytten, K., & Bettez, S. C. (2011). Understanding education for social justice. *Educational Foundations, 25*(1/2), 7–24.

Karp, S. (1995). Trouble over the rainbow. In D. Levine, R. Lowe, B. Peterson, & R. Tenorio (Eds.), *Rethinking schools: An agenda for change* (pp. 23–36). New York, NY: The New Press.

Ladson-Billings, G., & Tate, W. F. (1995). Toward a critical race theory of education. *Teachers College Record, 97*(1), 47–68.

Leonardo, Z. (2004). The color of supremacy: Beyond the discourse of 'white privilege.' *Educational Philosophy and Theory, 36*(2), 137–152.

Marshall, J. M. (2006). Nothing new under the sun: A historical overview of religion in U.S. schools. *Equity & Excellence in Education, 39*(3), 181–194. doi: 0.1080/10665680600792737.

Maxwell, L. A. (2014). U.S. schools become 'majority minority.' *Education Week, 34*(1), 1–15.

Mazza, O. (2009). The right to wear headscarves and other religious symbols in French, Turkish, and American schools: How the government draws a veil on free expressions of faith. *Journal of Catholic Legal Studies, 48*(2), 303–343.

Mura, D. (1999). Explaining racism to my daughter. In T. Ben Jelloun's (Ed.), *Racism explained to my daughter* (pp. 93–137). New York, NY: The New Press.

National Association of Professional Development Schools: 9 Essentials. (April 12, 2008). Retrieved March 14, 2017, from https://napds.org/nine-essentials/

National Center for Educational Statistics. (2013b). *Characteristics of public and private elementary and secondary schools in the United States: Results from the 2011–2012 schools and staffing survey.* Retrieved from https://nces.ed.gov/pubsearch/pubsinfo.asp?pubid=2013312.

National Center for Educational Statistics. (2015). *Racial/ethnic enrollment in public schools.* Retrieved from http://nces.ed.gov/programs/coe/indicator_cge.asp.

Nieto, S. (2000). Placing equity front and center: Some thoughts on transforming teacher education for a new century. *Journal of Teacher Education, 51*(3), 180–187.

Quin, J. (2009). Growing social justice educators: A pedagogical framework for social justice education. *Intercultural Education, 20*(2), 109–125.

Reynolds, F., & Prior, S. (2006). The role of art-making in identity maintenance: Case studies of people living with cancer. *European Journal of Cancer Care, 15*(4), 333–341.

Santora, E. D. (1995). *The drama of dominance and diversity: A multicultural curriculum framework for secondary social studies/language arts core.* Retrieved from https://archive.org/stream/ERIC_ED387379/ERIC_ED387379_djvu.txt.

Sleeter, C. E. (2001). Preparing teachers for culturally diverse schools: Research and the overwhelming process of whiteness. *Journal of Teacher Education, 52*(2), 94–106.

Sleeter, C. E., Neal, L. I., & Kumashiro, K. K. (Eds.). (2014). *Diversifying the teacher workforce: Preparing and retaining highly effective teachers.* New York, NY: Routledge.

Southern Poverty Law Center. (n.d.). *Teaching tolerance.* http://www.tolerance.org.

Subedi, B. (2006). Pre-service teachers' beliefs and practices: Religion and religious diversity. *Equity & Excellence in Education, 39*(3), 227–238. doi: 10.1080/10665680600788495.

Thoits, P. A., & Virshup, L. K. (1997). Me's and we's: Forms and functions of social identities. In R. D. Ashmore (Ed.), *Self and identity: Fundamental issues* (pp. 5–130). New York, NY: Oxford University Press.

U.S. Bureau of Census. (2012). *U.S population projections: 2014–2060.* Retrieved from https://www.census.gov/population/projections/data/national/2014.html.

Villegas, A. M. (2007). Dispositions in teacher education: A look at social justice. *Journal of Teacher Education, 58*(5), 370–380. doi: 10.1177/0022487107308419.

West College of Education (WCOE). (1997). *West College of Education professional development school agreement.* Retrieved from http://www.mwsu.edu/Assets/documents/academics/education/ncate/Exhibit-Room-Indecies/indexstandard3.pdf.

West College of Education (WCOE). (2013). *West College of Education conceptual framework.* Retrieved from http://www.mwsu.edu/Assets/documents/academics/education/ncate/Exhibit-Room-Indecies/indexstandard3.pdf.

Williams, P. J. (1997). *Seeing a colour-blind future: The paradox of race.* London, UK: Virago Press.

Young, E. Y. (2011). The four personae of racism: Educators' (mis)understanding of individual vs. systemic racism. *Urban Education, 46*(6), 1433–1460.

Chapter 8

Teacher Candidates' Courage in Developing Cultural Capacity through an Indigenous Cocurricular Community Service-Learning Program

Glenda L. Black and Mair Greenfield

ABSTRACT

Service learning is a teaching methodology that incorporates academic learning in the classroom with community service—volunteering. The purpose of this study was to explore the impact of a community service-learning initiative on the teacher candidates and the Indigenous community they service. Using a case study design, data were collected from sixty-five teacher candidates in the form of anticipatory and post-BCSL (Biidaaban Community Service-Learning) reflections and eleven individual semi-structured interviews with a former faculty facilitator, a First Nations Education Director, a First Nations community coordinator, and eight former teacher candidates. The discussion related to the research question on the effects and impact of participating in the BCSL settled into five main categories: (a) building relationships between the teacher candidates and the Indigenous children and youth, (b) enhancing professional skills, (c) developing professional confidence, (d) developing different levels of cultural competence, and (e) enhancing benefits for community youth and enhanced partnerships.

KEY WORDS

Community Service Learning; Indigenous; Teacher Education; Cultural Competence

The goals of teacher preparation programs are to develop and inspire teacher candidates' professional and personal capacity to meet the diverse needs of the 21st-century learners. Teacher preparation programs (TPP) are experiencing global, political, financial, and technological pressures. To confront these issues, faculty in the TPPs are challenged to create and implement innovative curricula and increase learning opportunities. Participating in a service-learning program provides a unique opportunity for teacher candidates to show initiative and step out of their comfort zones to develop cultural understanding by working directly with community members and their children and youth (Harrison, 2013). Using service learning as the connector to the community, teacher candidates can be empowered to be agents for positive social change.

For the past few decades, service learning has become a valuable part of postsecondary programs in the United States. However, little information is known about the different service-learning approaches and its implications in Canadian universities (Chambers, 2009). Using service learning as a pedagogy to develop teacher candidates' cultural competency has become an important component in the academic curricula (Keen & Hall, 2009) for TPP to address the cultural reality of Canadian classrooms. The potential of cocurricular service-learning has not been fully unwrapped in the literature (Keen & Hall, 2009; Vogelgesang, 2004).

Canada's population "continues to be more racially diverse as current immigration and Canadian birth patterns change the face of the population" (Ryan, Pollock, & Antonelli, 2009, p. 592) and is reflected in the student demographic of Canadian K-12 classrooms. In particular, "The Aboriginal population increased by 232,385 people, or 20.1% between 2006 and 2011, compared with 5.2% for the non-Aboriginal population" (Statistics Canada, 2011, p. 4). In Canada, the term "Aboriginal" is a general term defined in the *Constitution Act, 1982*, to describe three groups of people who have unique heritages, languages, cultural practices, and spiritual beliefs. These three groups include the Métis, Inuit, and Indian. Métis people have a distinctive history and identity that link both First Nation and European ancestry. Inuit people are Aboriginal groups who have inhabited northern regions of Canada, including Nunavut, Northwest Territories, Northern Quebec, and Northern Labrador. The term "Indian" is rooted in colonial legislation (the *Indian Act*, [1876], as cited in R.S.C., 1985, c. I-5), considered offensive, the term is often replaced by the general self-designation of First Nations or by specific community identification (e.g., Anishinaabe, member of Nipissing First Nation).

We and other educational researchers (Cushner & Mahon, 2009) believe teacher candidates are graduating from TPP without the necessary competencies to ensure equitable support for all students in achieving their personal and professional goals. Since the 1960s evidence of support for cross-cultural experiential learning to progress teachers' cultural perspectives has been documented (Taylor, 1969). In the 1980s, Wilson (1982) noted while an intuitive acceptance of the value of intercultural experiences is growing, "few connections have been made between the teachers' cross-cultural experience and his or her experience as a teacher in the classroom" (p. 84). Cultural competence in education is becoming a professional imperative (Diller, 2011). Diller and Moule (2005) propose culturally competent teachers have acute personal and interpersonal cultural awareness, sensitivity, knowledge, and skills.

Research on the positive effects of community service learning (CSL), for participants and the community, is substantial (Prentice, 2011; Prentice & Robinson, 2007). Service learning is a teaching methodology that incorporates community service and classroom learning. The roots of CSL are grounded in experiential education theory (Kielsmeier, 2011). Different from volunteerism, service-learning programs are structured with intentional learning objectives. In the program of study, the goal is to support literacy and numeracy with First Nation, Métis, and Inuit youth. Teacher candidates in the post-undergraduate Bachelor of Education program are invited to participate in service-learning partnerships with First Nation communities and public and reserve schools. The candidates commit to a series of orientation sessions, workshops, and a minimum of two hours per week working at one of the community partners.

As educators of future teachers it is incumbent on us to explore as many avenues as we can to support teacher candidates' learning. A strength of service learning "is it engages the students in worthwhile activity" (Eyler, 2000). Through the creation of increased learning opportunities, the goal remains to develop teacher candidates with specific skills for the teaching profession, while remaining respectful to the candidates and the learners they service. An urgent need exists for research that develops more comprehensive understandings of the effects of service learning and its impact on the teacher candidates and the community they serve.

LITERATURE REVIEW

The literature is replete with the professional benefits for university students participating in service learning, which includes validating their career choice (Fudge, Fuss, Burton, McClam, & Diambra, 2008; Simons, Hirschinger-Bank, & Kenyon, 2009). Service learning allowed university students to use the academic knowledge and skills taught on campus and apply them to real-world experiences in the community—theory to practice through enhanced understanding of their professional role (Harrison, 2013; Jenkins & Sheehey,

2009), apply their acquired skills (Chambers & Lavery, 2012; Fudge et al., 2008), develop professional confidence (Chambers & Lavery, 2012; Fudge et al., 2008; Harrison, 2013; Richards & Novak, 2010), and cultivate leadership skills (Chambers & Lavery, 2012).

After working directly in the community university students reported they developed a sense of belonging to the community (Dugan & Komives, 2010; Harrison, 2013); they promoted positive attitudes about the community (Buch & Harden, 2011; Parker et al., 2007), a desire to positively contribute to the community (Buch & Harden, 2011; Prentice & Robinson, 2007); and they fostered empathy for the K-12 students and community (Chambers & Lavery, 2012). University students spending forty hours working directly with Hispanic migrant workers (Wehling, 2008), and teacher candidates assigned to classrooms in rural Appalachia developed cultural sensitivity to the community they serviced (Harrison, 2013).

The literature on service learning notes that communities benefit by developing strong relationships and an awareness of what the university and university students can offer (Richards & Novak, 2010); "agencies receive an infusion of creativity and enthusiasm from participating youth" (Williams, 1998, p. 12); "providing unique learning experiences that focus on building citizenship, cultural diversity, community partnerships, knowledge of community resources, critical thinking skills, and respect for humankind" (Richards & Novak, 2010, p. 1). The literature is especially robust in the areas of implementing service learning, the service-learning connection with academic courses and the promotion of civic growth (Steinberg, Bringle, & Williams, 2010). However, the impact of service learning on the individuals involved is still untapped (Burr, 2001; Eyler, 2002; Steinberg et al., 2010).

THEORETICAL FRAMEWORK

Although educators Ramsay and Sigmon coined the phrase service learning in 1967 (Seitsinger, 2005), the foundation of service learning is from the experiential education theory of Dewey (1938) and more recently, Kolb (1983).

Cross-cultural Experiential Learning

Cultural Competence

Teachers in culturally diverse environments are under increasing pressure to provide a quality education that fosters the achievement of all students. Some researchers go as far as to suggest cross-cultural experiential learning should be a component of every teacher education program (Merryfield, Jarchow, & Pickert, 1997; Wilson, 1982). Cross, Bazron, Dennis, and Isaacs (1989) developed a conceptual framework for the process of cultural competence that continues to inform policy and practice in education (Dillar & Moule, 2005; NEA, 2008) and includes five elements: "(1) value diversity; (2) have capacity for cultural self-assessment; (3) be conscious of dynamics inherent in cultures; (4) have institutionalized cultural knowledge; and (5) have developed adaptations to diversity" (p. v).

Valuing diversity is accepting and respecting people from different cultural backgrounds. Cultural self-assessment is examining one's biases, beliefs, values, and professional background. Conscious of dynamics inherent in cultures is an awareness of the interactions across cultures, which may include understanding the historical experiences of the cultures. For example, Indigenous Peoples have experienced discrimination and unfair treatment from the dominant culture. It was believed that Indigenous knowledge, practice, and belief were inferior to Euro-Western understandings of the world, which led to "power and control in the hands of Europeans. It delegitimized other ways of knowing as savage, superstitious, and primitive" (Akena, 2012, p. 600). This experience led to the forced education of Indigenous Peoples in residential schools, which attempted to destroy their traditional connections and where many experienced mental, physical, and sexual abuse.

Institutionalizing cultural knowledge and diversity is designing, and implementing educational practices based on the understanding of students' culture. In Indigenous culture for example, education is described as wholistic thinking, as it involves a deep connection to place and the environment. Students need to see themselves in the curriculum. The Medicine Wheel could be used as a template about the world. It is a symbol of harmony and balance and is important in teaching values and well-being. Our meaning perspectives are often acquired uncritically, and although they provide us with direction and meanings, they also distort our thoughts and perceptions (Mezirow, 1997). For teachers to effectively work with a diverse group of students, it is imperative they first critically examine their own biases about other cultures, and understand the world through different lenses (Banks, 1994; Mwebi & Brigham, 2009).

Experiential Learning

It is appropriate to start the discussion of experiential learning with John Dewey as he is considered the grandfather of experiential learning. In *Experience and Education* (1938), Dewey espoused the philosophy that experience is necessary for learning to take place. Jacobs and Archie (2008) state that "experiential education, both as a methodology and philosophy, is well suited to potentially have a positive influence on a learner's sense of community" (p. 284). Atkinson (2009) suggests, "Regardless of how much classroom preparation, reading, philosophy, and theory a student may have, there is no substitute for experience to learn one's field of work. As an educational strategy field experience flows out of the experiential learning theory popularized by John Dewey" (p. 11).

Kolb (1983) builds on Dewey's philosophy by proposing the theory of experiential learning. The learner progresses through a cycle of four modes of learning, which takes the learner from concrete experience, and reflecting on that experience, forming new concepts or ideas based on reflection, to testing or action upon what was learned. D. A. Kolb and A. Y. Kolb's (2005) cyclical model allows the learner to construct knowledge from experiences by synthesizing their reflections and using the new learning in new applications (Kolb & Kolb, 2005). A critical factor in the experiential learning process is the reflective process on the experience to develop insights for action (Connors & Mundt, 2001; Eyler, 2009).

Service Learning

The origins of service learning in postsecondary began with work-study programs in the 1960s (Bowley & Meeropool, 2003). In the 1990s service learning gained momentum and was integrated into higher education in response to calls for reform (Driscoll, Holland, Gelmon, & Kerrigan, 1996). Service learning was purported to enhance teaching and research by bringing together students from the campus in direct contact with the community, which would provide opportunities for students to apply their skills and knowledge and further their cognitive development (Edgerton, 1995). Collaboration between universities and the communities is supported by national organizations and associations (Kezar, 1998).

Although many definitions of service learning are available, broadly understood, "Community Service-Learning (CSL) is an educational approach that integrates service in the community with intentional learning activities. Within effective CSL efforts, members of both educational institutions and community organizations work together toward outcomes that are mutually beneficial" (Canadian Alliance for Community Service-Learning, n. d.). Service learning utilizes the four processes outlined by Kolb and Kolb's (2005) model for experiential learning in the preparation, action, and reflection of the service-learning cycle (Seifer & Connors, 2007). A mutual benefit for the teacher candidate and the community partners persists. The hyphen in service learning is a vital part of the definition, as it represents equal partnership in the experience (Sigmon, 1996). This type of reciprocity sets service-learning pedagogy apart from other methods of experiential learning. Most postsecondary service-learning programs are connected to a course. Cocurricular service learning is facilitated by the university and participation is completely voluntary.

Setting Context: Biidaaban Community Service Learning

Biidaaban Community Service Learning (pronounced bee-daw-bun; BCSL) is Anishinaabemowin meaning "the point at which the light touches the earth at the break of dawn." "Biidaaban" symbolizes the beginning of a new partnership designed to enhance the lives of First Nation, Métis, and Inuit students and communities. BCSL at Nipissing University partners with local schools, not-for-profit organizations, faculty, and teacher candidates. Teacher candidates commit to volunteer a minimum of two hours per week to improve literacy and numeracy skills in Indigenous youth.

The faculty facilitators for the BCSL assign participating teacher candidates a reflection assignment, typically an anticipatory and post-BCSL reflection. To prepare for the BCSL experience, teacher candidates participate in a vigorous sixteen-hour, cultural awareness training and CSL orientation. This training also involves an orientation to ethics in Indigenous communities and such topics as duty to report, working with students at risk, behavioral concerns, and generally, dealing with different scenarios and situations. Prior to students going out into the communities, interviews are conducted to make best-fitting partnerships between the teacher candidates and the communities.

METHOD

A case study design was used in the research, which allowed us the tools to explore a complex phenomenon within its context. Miles and Huberman (1994) define case as "a phenomenon of some sort occurring in a bounded context" and the case is "in effect, your unit of analysis" (p. 25). The phenomenon we wish to explore is the BCSL program coordinated through the Office of Indigenous Initiatives at Nipissing University and its impact on the program's participants. This type of case study is explanatory in nature, as the explanations link the program's implementation with the program's effects (Yin, 2003). The purpose of this study was to explore the impact of a CSL initiative on the teacher candidates and Indigenous community they support . More specifically, the research was guided by the following research questions: What are the perceived effects of a cocurricular CSL initiative on teacher candidates and the Indigenous community they served? How does engaging in the CSL program impact teacher candidates' cultural competence?

Stake (1995) and Yin (2003, 2006) propose the case study method ensures the phenomenon is well explored and the essence of the experiences are revealed and dependent on one's perspective. Case study research permits the use of multiple data sources, which enhances the data's credibility (Yin, 2003). Through the personal narratives or stories from the participants, we were able to understand the participants' perspectives (Lather, 1992). Data, in the form of anticipatory and post-BCSL reflections were collected over three years from sixty-five teacher candidates in the Bachelor of Education program ($n=65$). Individual semi-structured interviews were conducted with a former faculty facilitator, a First Nations Education Director, a First Nations community coordinator, and eight teacher candidates who volunteered in the BCSL within the past three years ($n=11$). We integrated the interview data and reflections collected from the multiple sources, to provide a holistic understanding of the BCSL phenomenon. Our field notes as a faculty facilitator and BCSL placement officer provide context to the data.

Methods of analysis for the project included three streams of activity identified by Miles and Huberman (1994): data reduction, data display, and conclusion drawing/verification. Deriving categories and themes, then subsequently drawing conclusions with regard to the major research, proceeded primarily from the various data displays. Verification involved constant comparison of data from the various sources (interviews, reflections, field notes) to test the trustworthiness of the results (Glaser & Strauss, 1967; Handsfield, 2006).

RESULTS

While the results are based on self-perception it is a valuable indicator of relevance in providing insight into the impact of a CSL initiative on the teacher candidates and the Indigenous community they support. The results are presented in relation to the research questions. We used pseudonyms in place of all the names of the participants.

Research Question: Perceived Effects of BCSL on Teacher Candidates?

Four themes emerged from the reflections and experiences of the teacher candidates. However, it must be noted the CSL program is voluntary, which may account, in part for the positive responses from the candidates.

Apply and Enhance Professional Skills

All the teacher candidates and faculty facilitator reported the BCSL provided the candidates with the opportunity to apply and enhance their teaching practice. The discussion around professional practice is organized around the topics of theory to practice, understanding students' readiness for learning, instructional and assessment strategies, and collaboration.

Theory to Practice

Avery specifically noted he was able to apply what he was learning on campus to the classroom: "The BCSL program gives teacher candidates the opportunity to apply the theory that they are learning at the university to real-world experiences with this group of Aboriginal youth." Later in the interview he explained, "We learned about theories and models of learning in class, like constructivism. I am an example of this theory. Like the students I worked with, I need an experiential activity to construct the knowledge."

Understanding Student Readiness

Acknowledging how connected students' social and emotional well-being are to their academic achievement was a theme that threaded through all the discussions. As reflected in Drew's comments, "I went into the BCSL thinking I was just going to be working on academics and realizing that academics was the least of what some of these students needed help with." Drew explained, "I worked with one young woman who had two of her own children at home while she was still in high school." Blair explained his high school students used the opportunity to share social and emotional challenges that interfered with their learning potential, "For some of them—they would just end up talking about their life, their home life and discussing why it is hard for them and why they are not very good students. For some of them it may have been a lack of sleep." The students would go on to describe life at home, "I will not get much sleep because this and this is going on at home. And why should I bother with this stuff when it does not matter?"

The candidates discussed at length at how important it was to get to know their students and they were learning though the rich oral tradition of Indigenous knowledge sharing. Further, they became aware of how colonization and continued discrimination still affect Canadian Indigenous peoples. Personal contact with Indigenous youth allowed candidates to learn about Indigenous history and current conditions, which they would not know without their service-learning experience. As a reciprocal relationship, service-learning benefits both partners; the candidates learn about Indigenous culture and the Indigenous youth are supported academically, socially, and emotionally.

Instructional Strategies

The participants reported an enhanced instructional repertoire in their approach to students' learning. After repeated attempts to teach a middle school student a math concept without success he had "to sit back and think about my approach, because it was not helping." Avery went on to explain his learning process: "Eventually, I decided to use anchor charts and examples to look at the information and visually take in the math. This was one of those eureka/aha moments—I felt like an idiot." The candidates learned to adjust their practice to meet their students' needs. Another candidate went on to explain how reflecting on the students' learning came to realize that "teaching is more organic than that. Yes, some students will thrive off of a heavy amount of structure, but some students need the chance to explore on their own and inquire into different topics." Candidates' insights did not specifically acknowledge the difference in Western and traditional Indigenous approaches to learning. Nevertheless, they were aware of how Indigenous children learned in an environment that allowed wholistic thinking, which is different from a Western approach, described as linear thinking (Fixico, 2003).

Working directly with students in the different grade levels provided experiences they would not have on their regular assigned practicum. For example, teacher candidates in the intermediate-senior (middle to high school) program had the opportunity to work with students from JK-12. In reference to her BCSL experience working with 2nd-grade students, Taylor, an intermediate-senior teacher candidate, proclaimed, "The BCSL experience helped me realize that working with younger aged children is something I am also interested in and made me realize that I would be able to handle an elementary class. It also really opened up my creative side." Taylor went on to explain, "This placement is part of the reason why I am going to take my junior qualification over the summer."

Teamwork

Most of the teacher candidates are assigned to a partner or team in their BCSL placements. The candidates reported the challenges and the benefits of working as part of a team to deliver learning. Candidates reported in their reflections and the interviews approaches they used to deal with the teamwork challenges, which included over preparing in case someone else was not prepared to becoming more flexible to the groups dynamic. Jesse explained the BCSL prepared her for working with many teachers, which regular placements do not. In their scheduled placement the candidates are assigned one cooperating teacher for each placement. The BCSL provides the candidates with the opportunity to build a community of teachers; in Jesse's words, "In reality that is how your teaching experience is going to be. I really did foster those skills in developing community and working with other teachers—getting planned, organized, and everyone sharing in that process."

Participating in the BCSL, candidates are encouraged to follow Indigenous practices of commitment to community, which is different from their regular teaching placement where the emphasis is on individual competence and evaluation.

Relationship Building with Students

The results clearly indicate the teacher candidates' understanding and appreciate the opportunity to build relationships with students. Avery explains, "If you develop that rapport with them they are going to begin to respect and trust you and care about what you have to say to them. Then they will start to listen to you." Now a teacher in her own classroom, Jesse emphasized the value of being able to work with small groups of students: "You may have only two students, but the relationship you build with those two students really prepares you for working with a class and building super strong relationships with your own students."

Erin, another graduate in her own classroom in an Indigenous community shared how the "program opened my eyes to what education is and not just what we do in the classroom and it is not all about your lesson planning. It is about the students as people." She went on to explain some students struggle academically in school and they need to know you understand and care for them. "They have a lot of insecurities and when they don't trust you it is way to easy to act out and get kicked out of class than it is to focus on something that is difficult." Rapport building is Erin's first priority at the beginning of the year since you have to trust the person you are working with because, "you have to be vulnerable in order to work on something that is challenging."

Professional Confidence

A theme that threaded through the data was the development of teacher candidates' professional confidence. In reference to an unexpected outcome of participating in the BCSL, Reagan stated with emphasis, "Now I have a lot of confidence. Not only dealing with kids, but with my peers." The faculty facilitator shared repeatedly how the experience built confidence in our teacher candidates. She went on to explain how a teacher shared with the candidate the improvement in the academic assessment of a student she had been working with for four months. The candidate called her mom and said, "I can do this, I can be a teacher."

As a cocurricular experience, the BCSL is a voluntary experience and not connected to a specific course. Rather, candidates are able to bring together the learning from all the campus classes and previous experience to the BCSL placement. Candidates and the faculty facilitator spoke often of the opportunity to practice their teaching skills without the stress of being observed or evaluated. The faculty facilitator explained, "They liked being in schools where they were not being evaluated. They liked the fact that they were being treated more like a colleague." For some students their motive to participate is to volunteer for the improvement of the community. As Erin stated, "People are doing it for the right reason. Not for the grade or credit."

Research Question: Perceived Effects of BCSL on the Community?

From the perspective of the teacher candidates, faculty advisor, First Nation Education Director and First Nation (FN) community coordinator, the BCSL is having positive effects on the Indigenous community. As background to the BCSL initiative, the FN Education Director discussed how the Indigenous community was introduced to the initiative. She liked the idea of working in partnership with the university. She remembers presenting the BCSL idea to the education committee. Although the committee was supportive, they did question the university's motives for the program. In her explanation to the committee it was "assuring them this is not research—we are not being observed or studied. There was nothing being asked of us other than allow teacher candidates to come and participate in the program."

Consistent

As described by the FN Education Director, "When we started I thought it was a really great idea, but I had no idea how long it would last or how sustainable it was. That says something it has been going since 2008 to 2015." She remarked that the sustainability of the BCSL has positively contributed to the community. In the FN Education Director's words, "That is certainly somewhat unique in First Nations communities because so much of our funding is not sustainable. I think that's probably contributed to the comfort level of the community—having the program going on." Provisions are in place for continued partnership between the university and the FN community.

Relationships

Working in collaboration with the university is regarded by the FN Education Director as a valuable partnership. As affirmed by the FN Education Director, "I really like working in partnerships. Also, you see this accumulative good experience happening when things are sustainable. This is not the one shot deal." She went on to explain this positive FN community partnership with the university has developed a different kind of relationship and "has been good for the First Nation. Trying to move beyond those notions of the university and research. They are always studying the First Nations. There is a comfort level—at least for the people who are closely involved."

Although we did not speak directly to Indigenous children, the teacher candidates, the FN Education Director, and FN Community Coordinator consistently reported positive interactions with the parents and students in connection with the BCSL. The FN Education Director witnessed the Indigenous students' excitement when the teacher candidates were due to arrive at the library to meet with the students: "I would hear kids coming into the room and asking Jamie, are the university students coming tonight. Then hearing, yah they are here! That says a lot to see the enthusiasm and to see how excited the kids are." Jamie, the FN Community Coordinator, described the students' reactions: "Its fulfilling to see the anticipation on the kids' faces before the university students get there." She continued by explaining, "Once they are there—the children are anxious to get started on their homework because they really like the person or group they are in. It is nice to see that bond." The bond Jamie refers is between Indigenous children and the teacher candidates.

The teacher candidates consistently reported positive interactions with Indigenous students. Avery described the students' disappointment as the program came to the end: "I think that speaks a lot in itself to the positive reception of the program because our students are one of the most important evaluators." Supporting the candidates' reports were the positive interactions between the teacher candidates, parents, and students at the invitational end of the year event, "I got a lot of positive feedback from parents saying, the program gave their children something fun to look forward to and that many of them enjoyed interacting with their volunteers."

Cultural Transitioning

The Indigenous students are able to interact with university students (teacher candidates) and attend an end of year event hosted by the BCSL office and teacher candidates. Spending time on campus demystifies the university for Indigenous students. As noted by the FN Education Director, she appreciates the opportunity for Indigenous youth, some have participated in the program and the events on campus for five or six years and their presence on campus is "already doing some transition preparation for our kids going into postsecondary. The whole notion of post-secondary of the university, up on the hill and what is it all about. That it *is* [with emphasis] quite attainable."

Research Question: Impact of BCSL on Teacher Candidates' Cultural Competence

The results are organized into the cultural competence framework developed by Cross et al. (1989): value diversity, capacity for cultural self-assessment, be conscious of dynamics inherent in cultures; institutionalized and develop adaptations to diversity.

Valuing Diversity

All the teacher candidates had the opportunity to go into the FN community for the orientation and training sessions and some candidates worked directly with the Indigenous students in their own community and their own territory. Other candidates worked with Indigenous students in the public schools or Indigenous community centers. The teacher candidates consistently reported they developed respect and cultural awareness for Indigenous culture. David described his experience walking into the FN secondary school for the first time: "I experienced a culture shock. I could smell the sweet grass burning, see the colors [Medicine Wheel colors] on the wall, and hear the chanting down the hall." David continued by affirming, "Overall, with this BCSL experience, I gained considerable insight toward Aboriginal education, Aboriginal culture, Aboriginal issues, literacy skills, special education, and poverty. No other placement has such a wealth of experiences presented themselves."

Cultural Self-Assessment

The reflective component of the BCSL provided the candidates with an opportunity to examine their biases, beliefs, values, and professional background. As an example, Adrien explains the value of the reflective process, "Reflection is essential to the way in which we view the world around us. Just as reflection is important in science to explain how we see with our eyes, it is important to use reflection to see with our minds." Blair reflected on his learning about Indigenous culture, "Hearing true stories from them was huge for me. People say that they are all drunks and all alcoholics. You hear it so much that it becomes ingrained and you assume that maybe it is the case." He continued to clarify, "It is good to hear the facts and the truths, but also very sad to hear, but hopefully that can help drive some change. And it is good for that reason." Similarly, Avery reflected, "I thought the students would view their schoolwork as a waste of time. However, this wasn't the case. That was my lack of knowledge. These students enjoyed their schoolwork and actually were quite inquisitive." The candidates traced the roots of these stereotypes to not having any contact with people of Indigenous ancestry. The BCSL facilitated the connection that developed into a positive relationship between the teacher candidates and the Indigenous youth. Fostering these relationships has the potential to continue the decolonizing process.

Conscious of Dynamics Inherent within the Culture

Teacher candidates are required to participate in the intensive orientation and cultural sensitivity training before volunteering in the BCSL program. The candidates develop an awareness of the historical unfair treatment and discrimination of Indigenous peoples from the dominant culture. Through their participation in the orientation, training, and direct contact with Indigenous students they developed an understanding why a distrust of the education system by the Indigenous community due to residential schools exists. Drew's level of understanding the impact of the residential schools on Indigenous communities is clearly evident in her reflection, "I have been given a new appreciation for how families are just now catching up on where they came from and how they should be doing things; how their grandparents and great grand parents did things." Drew continued by describing how she learned life skills and her heritage from her mother, father, and grandmother and how she is passing this tradition to her son. She goes on to say, "I cannot imagine the devastation those families went through when their children were taken to a residential school. If I did not have my family teach me about my heritage and the abilities I have to be self supporting." Although most candidates did not achieve the same level of awareness as Drew, most candidates discussed their greater awareness, empathy, and respect for Indigenous heritage culture. To assist more candidates to achieve this level of awareness, which included more reflections and mandatory attendance of volunteers to debriefing sessions that are scheduled throughout the academic year. The BCSL office, faculty facilitators, and the Elder in Residence led the debriefing sessions.

Institutionalized and Develop Adaptations to Diversity

As the candidates became more comfortable at their BCSL placement the candidates were able envision new possibilities for knowledge sharing that are consistent with Indigenous culture. For example, the candidates used the Seven Grandfather teachings, modeling, and storytelling strategies. Blair shared how he used culturally appropriate resources like culturally appropriate puppets, drums, traditional wampum belts, and children and youth literature to make meaningful connections with students. As a teacher he is able to relate to them in some way or make a connection to their culture to make them feel comfortable. Now, as a classroom teacher, Drew acknowledged how the BCSL helps her work with Indigenous students, "knowing that it's really important that I incorporate Native studies into the things that we're doing and help be able to let them know that the things that have happened in the past. We can't forget everything that's happened, but we do need to work on improving it for others."

DISCUSSION

The discussion related to the research questions on the effects and impact of participating in the BCSL settled into five main categories: (a) building relationships between the teacher candidates and the Indigenous children and youth, (b) enhancing professional skills, (c) developing professional confidence, (d) developing different levels of cultural competence, and (e) enhancing benefits for community youth and enhanced partnerships. The results speak directly to the call from researchers to explore impacts of service learning on individuals and communities (Burr, 2001; Eyler, 2002; Steinberg et al., 2010).

The first research question addressed the effects of the BCSL on the participants. It can be stated unequivocally, in support of previous research, an outcome of participating in service learning is relationship building (Chambers & Lavery, 2012; Richards & Novak, 2010; Williams, 1998; Wehling, 2008). The relationship and rapport building theme was the strongest thread that ran through the results. Clearly, the teacher candidates developed positive relationships with Indigenous children and youth. Mostly, the candidates worked individually or in small groups with the Indigenous students, which facilitated the rapport building. Repeatedly teacher candidates reported their appreciation of how critical it was to develop a trusting relationship to enhance students' well-being (i.e., academically, socially, emotionally, etc.). Consistent with the literature, developing strong relationships between the university and community was evidenced in the results (Richards & Novak, 2010). Considering the historical context of distrust on the part of Indigenous community, partnering with a research institution, the university-community partnership was a unique experience, benefiting both partners. For Indigenous community, the benefits are the Indigenous students' improved literacy and numeracy skills and access to the university facilitates transitioning into postsecondary education and the university benefits from an enhanced profile serving the community.

Consistent with the literature, the opportunity to work directly with students enhanced teacher candidates' professional skills (Chambers & Lavery, 2012; Fudge et al., 2008). The BCSL program afforded teacher candidates the opportunity to practice the theory they learned on campus with small groups of students. The candidates developed a greater awareness of understanding students' readiness for learning and insight into the challenges of their future students. Although the candidates acknowledged challenges to team work, the candidates developed a professional community during their placements with the teachers they worked with and their peers, which can be applied to the realities of collaborative relationships in a school community.

Similar to previous research, the teacher candidates developed confidence in their professional abilities (Chambers & Lavery, 2012; Fudge et al., 2008;

Harrison, 2013; Richards & Novak, 2010). The nonevaluative nature of the BCSL contributed to the confidence of the teacher candidates. This cocurricular service-learning approach moves from the one course-one instructor approach to a cross-curricular approach, which allows students to build on experiences from their entire teacher education program. Removing the stress of evaluations, by cooperating teachers and faculty, the candidates repeatedly noted they had the courage and confidence to step out of their comfort zone to improve their professional skills.

The second research question addressed the impact of the BCSL on teacher candidates' cultural competency. As an explanation for cross-cultural experiential learning, the cultural competence framework developed by Cross et al. (1989) for education (as cited in Dillar & Moule, 2005; NEA, 2008) and experiential learning (Dewey, 1938; Kolb, 1983) offered valuable insight for the actions of the participants in this study. Teacher candidates reported their preference for the hands-on learning experience, which is strongly supportive of Dewey's (1938) experiential learning. The candidates were learning by doing and working directly with youth in the community, which provided them the opportunity to scaffold their learning and apply what they learned on campus to further enable Indigenous youth. Consistent with the literature (Harrison, 2013; Wehling, 2008), the teacher candidates developed cultural sensitivity to the community they served. Here, through planned, purposeful, critically analyzed, and reflected upon cocurricular cross-cultural experiential learning, the candidates developed cultural confidence. Although the depth of cultural competence ranged among the teacher candidates, all candidates developed a greater awareness and sensitivity to Indigenous students. We support the researchers who proclaim cross-cultural learning should be a component of every teacher education program (Cushner & Mahon, 2009; Diller, 2005; Diller & Moule, 2011; Merryfield et al., 1997; Wilson, 1982).

RECOMMENDATIONS

An agreement that CSL is a critical component to teacher candidates' personal and professional growth is present. Based on the findings from this study and the literature, we offer the following recommendations:

Teacher Preparation Programs

Participating in BCSL brings critical thinking and problem-solving opportunities for candidates. Reflections and consistency in placements are key structural components to the effectiveness of the BCSL program. Through their participation in the cocurricular BCSL, teacher candidates developed the courage to step outside their comfort zone to teach in a cross-cultural learning experience. The candidates repeatedly reported the value of the experience was to their personal and professional growth and to think more deeply about fairness, justice, reciprocity, and other societal issues. The candidates, who are now teachers, are using their BCSL experience to be agents of social change in their teaching practice. Consistently noted by the candidates was how important the reflections were to reflect on their actions and the goals of the program. The reflections afforded the teacher candidates the opportunity to confront their own biases and assumptions about their culture and the culture of the students they served. Consistency in placements was important to the teacher candidates and the community. For the teacher candidates, working week after week with the same student(s) was critical to developing trusting relationships. For Indigenous community, consistency in the structure of the program facilitated their participation year after year.

Universities

Service-learning programs are becoming a common feature in the postsecondary landscape. Since Canadian undergraduate students rarely attend universities outside their home province (Finnie & Qiu, 2009), their service-learning experiences are more likely to translate into improving conditions in the community for the region they are located. For a university, the benefit of a well-implemented service-learning program is the collaboration between the university and the community. The notion of gown and town in partnership of substance and value presents the university as a positive contributor to the community (Chambers, 2009). Although service learning is not a performance indicator or requirement for undergraduate degrees in Canada (CMEC, 2007), the decisions made in the university to collaborate with the community has broader societal implications. Universities have a role in social responsibility they are not just an engine for economic development. The service-learning approach and the outcomes of the relationships formed through community collaboration have the potential to influence support by policymakers. However, maintaining a quality service-learning program requires a great amount of effort on the part of all of the stakeholders.

Future Research

Findings of this research are consistent with the literature. However, this study is unique in the cocurricular cultural competence CSL. Although we reached out to candidates three years after their participation in the BCSL, the concern of the sustained impact of the service-learning experience on the teacher candidates arose (Chambers, 2009). We are in agreement more longitudinal studies are needed on the sustainability of the long-term impact

CONCLUSION

Educators in TPP use a range of pedagogies to assist teacher candidates in developing the knowledge, skills, and attitudes to become reflective educators. Methods on instruction for theories and teaching practices include lecture, class discussion, hands-on and problem-solving activities, and practical experience under the supervision of a cooperating teacher. The opportunity for additional real-life experience through cocurricular service learning has the potential to assist teacher candidates in becoming agents for positive social change by developing specific skills, knowledge, and the cultural competency necessary to meet the diverse learners needs in our elementary and secondary classrooms.

REFERENCES

Akena, F. A. (2012). Critical analysis of the production of western knowledge and its implications for indigenous knowledge and decolonization. *Journal of Black Studies, 43*(6), 599–619.

Atkinson, H. (2009). An introduction to field education in higher Christian education. *Christian Education Journal, 6*(1), 9–23.

Banks, J. (1994). *Multiethnic education: Theory and practice.* Needham Heights, MA: Allyn and Bacon.

Bowley, E., & Meeropool, J. (2003). Service-learning in higher education: Trends research and resources. *The Generator: Journal of Service Learning and Youth Leadership, 21*(3), 12–16.

Buch, K., & Harden, S. (2011). The impact of a service-learning project on student awareness of homelessness, civic attitudes, and stereotypes toward the homeless. *Journal of Higher Education Outreach and Engagement, 15*(3), 45–61.

Burr, K. L. (2001). Building for hope: Progressive service learning enhances education. *Journal of Industrial Teacher Education, 38*(4), 84–93.

Canadian Alliance for Community Service-Learning. (n.d.). *What is community service-learning?* Retrieved from http://www.communityservicelearning.ca/en/welcome_what_is.htm.

Council of Ministers of Education, Canada (CMEC). (2007). *Ministerial statement on quality assurance of degree education in Canada.* Toronto, ON. Retrieved from https://www.cicic.ca/docs/cmec/QA-Statement-2007.en.pdf.

Chambers, T. (2009). A continuum of approaches to service-learning within Canadian post-secondary education. *Canadian Journal of Higher Education, 39*(2), 77–100.

Chambers, D. J., & Lavery, S. (2012). Service-learning: A valuable component of pre-service teacher education. *Australian Journal of Teacher Education, 37*(4), 127–137.

Connors, J. J., & Mundt, J. P. (2001). Experiential education and career development events. *The Agricultural Education Magazine, 73*(6), 6–8.

Cross, T. L., Bazron, B. J., Dennis, K. W., Isaacs, M. R. (1989). *Towards a culturally competent system of care.* CASSP Technical Assistance Center, Mental Health Services. Retrieved from http://www.mhsoac.ca.gov/meetings/docs/Meetings/20 10/June/CLCC_Tab_4_Towards_Culturally_Competent_System.pdf.

Cushner, K., & Mahon, J. (2009). Developing the intercultural competence of educator and their students: Creating the blueprint. In D. K. Deardorff (Ed.), *The Sage handbook of intercultural competence* (pp. 304–320). Thousand Oaks, CA: Sage Publications, Inc.

Dewey, J. (1938). *Experience and education.* New York, NY: Kappa Delta Pi.

Diller, J. V. (2011). *Cultural competence: A primer for the human services* (4th ed.). Boston: MA: Cengage Learning.

Diller, J. V., & Moule, J. (2005). *Cultural competence: A primer for educators.* Belmont, CA: Thomas/Wadsworth.

Driscoll, A., Holland, B., Gelmon, S., & Kerrigan, S. (1996). Comprehensive case studies of impact on faculty, students, community, and institution. *Michigan Journal of Community Service, 3*(1), 72–81.

Dugan, J. P., & Komives, S. R. (2010). Influences on college students' capacities for socially responsible leadership. *Journal of College Student Development, 51*(5), 525–549.

Edgerton, R. (1995). Crossing boundaries: Pathways to productive learning and community renewal. *AAAHE Bulletin, 48*(1), 7–10.

Eyler, J. (2000). What do we most need to know about the impact of service-learning on student learning? *Michigan Journal of Community Service Learning* (Special Issue), 11–17.

Eyler, J. (2002). Stretching to meet the challenge: Improving the quality of research to improve the quality of service-learning. In S. H. Billig & A. Furco (Eds.), *Service-learning: Through a multidisciplinary lens. Advances in service-learning research series* (pp. 3–25). Greenwich, CT: Information Age.

Eyler, J. (2009). The power of experiential education. *Liberal Education, 95*(4), 24–31.

Finnie, R., & Qiu, T. (2009). *Moving through, moving on: Persistence in postsecondary education in Atlantic Canada, evidence from the PSIS* (Research Paper). Ottawa, ON: Ministry of Industry, culture, Tourism, and the Centre for Education Statistics.

Fixico, D. (2003). *The American Indian mind in a linear world: American Indian studies and traditional knowledge.* New York, NY: Routledge.

Fudge, D. L., Fuss, A., Burton, B., McClam, T., & Diambra, J. F. (2008). An analysis of a service-learning project: Students'' expectations, concerns, and reflections. *Journal of Experiential Education, 30*(3), 236–249.

Glaser, B., & Strauss, A. (1967). *The discovery of grounded theory: Strategies for qualitative research.* Chicago, IL: Aldine Publishing Company.

Handsfield, L. (2006). Being and becoming American: Triangulating habitus, field, and literacy instruction in a multilingual classroom. *Language & Literacy, 8*(3), 1–26.

Harrison, L. M. (2013). Service learning and its impact on middle level preservice teachers' learning from field experiences. *Middle Grades Research Journal, 8*(3), 2013, 23–38.

Indian Act. (1876). RSC 1985, c I-5. Retrieved from http://canlii.ca/t/52fln.

Jacobs, J., & Archie, T. (2008). Investigating sense of community in first-year college students. *Journal of Experiential Education, 30*(3), 282–285.

Jenkins, A., & Sheehey, P. (2009). Implementing service learning in special education course-work: What we learned. *Education, 129*(4), 668–682.

Keen, C., & Hall, K. (2009). Engaging with difference matters: Longitudinal student outcomes of co-curricular service-learning programs. *The Journal of Higher Education, 80*(1), 59–79.

Kezar, A. (1998). Community service learning movement. In J. A. Craig (Ed.), *Advances in Education Research* (Vol. 3, pp. 1–5). Washington, DC: National Library of Education.

Kielsmeier, J. (2011). Service-learning: The time is now. *Prevention Researcher, 18*(1), 3–7.

Kolb, D. A. (1983). *Experiential learning: Experience as the source of learning and development.* Upper Saddle River, NJ: Prentice-Hall.

Kolb, D. A., & Kolb, A. Y. (2005). Learning styles and learning spaces: Enhancing experiential learning in higher education. *Academy of Management Learning & Education, 4*(2), 193–212.

Lather, P. (1992). Critical frames in educational research: Feminist and post-structural perspectives. *Theory into Practice, 31*(2), 87–99.

Merryfield, M., Jarchow, E., & Pickert, S. (1997). *Preparing teachers to teach global perspectives.* Thousand Oaks, CA: Corwin Press.

Mezirow, J. (1997). Transformative learning: Theory to practice. *New Directions for Adults and Continuing Education, 74,* 5–12.

Miles, M. B., & Huberman, A. M. (1994). *Qualitative data analysis* (2nd ed.). Thousand Oaks, CA: Sage.

Mwebi, B. M., & Brigham, S. M. (2009). Preparing North American pre-service teachers for global perspectives: An international teaching practicum experience in Africa. *The Alberta Journal of Educational Research, 55*(3), 414–427.

Nation Education Association (NEA). (2008). *An NEA policy brief: Promoting educators' cultural competence to better service culturally diverse students.* Retrieved from http://www.nea.org/assets/docs/PB13_CulturalCompetence08.pdf.

Parker, K. L., Ackerman, B. E., & Parker, L. W. (2007). *Enhancing Christian school experiences for pre-service teachers through service-learning partnerships.* Retrieved from http://digitalcommons.liberty.edu/cpe/vol1/iss1/5.

Prentice, M. (2011). Civic engagement among community college students through service learning. *Community College Journal of Research and Practice, 35,* 842–854.

Prentice, M., & Robinson, G. (2007). *Linking service learning and civic engagement in community college students.* Washington, DC: American Association of Community Colleges.

Richards, E. A. L., & Novak, J. C. (2010). From Biloxi to Cape Town: Curricular integration of service learning. *Journal of Community Health Nursing, 27*(1), 46–50.

Ryan, J., Pollock, K., & Antonelli, F. (2009). Teacher diversity in Canada: Leaky pipelines, bottlenecks, and glass ceilings. *Canadian Journal of Education, 32*(3), 591–617.

Seifer, S. D., & Connors, K., Eds. (2007). *Faculty toolkit for service-learning in higher education.* Scotts Valley, CA: National Service-Learning Clearinghouse.

Simons, L., Hirschinger-Blank, N. B., & Kenyon, A. (2009). An evaluation of a service- learning model for criminal justice undergraduate students. *Journal of Experiential Education, 32*(1), 61–78.

Seitsinger, M. (2005). Service-learning and standards-based instruction in middle schools. *The Journal of Educational Research, 99*, 19–31.

Sigmon, R. L. (1996). The problem of definitions in service-learning. In R. L. Sigmon & colleagues (Eds.), *Journey to service-learning* (pp. 9–12). Washington, DC: The Council of Independent Colleges.

Stake, R. E. (1995). *The art of case study research.* Thousand Oaks, CA: Sage.

Steinberg, K. S., Bringle, R. G., & Williams, M. J. (2010). *Service-learning research primer.* Scott Valley, CA: National Service-learning Clearinghouse.

Statistics Canada. (2011). *Aboriginal peoples in Canada: First Nations People, Métis and Inuit: National Household Survey, 2011.* Retrieved from http://www12.statcan.gc.ca/nhs-enm/2011/as-sa/99-011-x/99-011-x2011001-eng.pdf.

Taylor, H. (1969). *The world as teacher.* New York, NY: Doubleday.

Vogelgesang, L. J. (2004). Diversity work and service-learning: Understanding campus dynamics. *Michigan Journal of Community Service Learning, 11*(2), 34–43.

Wehling, S. (2008). Cross-cultural competency through service-learning. *Journal of Community Practice, 16*(3), 293–315.

Williams, S. (1998). *Expanding teacher education through service-learning handbook.* Retrieved from http://files.eric.ed.gov/fulltext/ED432547.pdf.

Wilson, A. H. (1982). Cross-cultural experiential learning for teachers. *Theory into Practice, 21*(3), 184–192.

Yin, R. K. (2003). *Case study research: Design and methods* (3rd ed.). Thousand Oaks, CA: Sage.

Yin, R. K. (2009). *Case study research: Design and methods* (4th ed.). Thousand Oaks, CA: Sage.

Extension Questions for Reflection and Conversation

Nancy P. Gallavan and LeAnn G. Putney

The eight chapters selected for Section I share authors' research findings associated with inspirations and aspirations for teachers and teaching. The coeditors of ATE Yearbook XXVI have provided extension questions to prompt reflection and conversation for each of the chapters.

Chapter 1, authored by Leona M. Johnson from Hampton University, titled "College Students' Perceptions of the Characteristics of Effective Teachers in Higher Education: The Students' Voice," reveals important information for teacher educators to feature in their teacher preparation programs.

Extension Questions for Reflection and Conversation:

1. What are the top five characteristics of effective teachers reported in this study?
2. What the top five characteristics of ineffective teachers reported in this study?
3. What are your college students' perceptions of effective and ineffective teachers in higher education?
4. Why is it valuable for teacher educators to be aware of college students' perceptions of effective and ineffective teachers in higher education?
5. What changes might you make to your teacher preparation program and courses knowing the results of this study?

Chapter 2, titled "What Teacher Candidates Believe about Teaching and Learning," authored by Nancy Caukin from Middle Tennessee State University presents an extensive list of teacher candidates' belief statements categories into meaningful themes indicating the beliefs that candidates recognize and/or value as well as the beliefs that candidates neglect and/or disregard.

Extension Questions for Reflection and Conversation:

1. Based on the findings reported in this research, what are the five most frequently reported teacher candidates' belief statements?
2. Do you agree with these findings based on your experiences as a P-12th-grade classroom teacher and/or as a university teacher educator?
3. Why is it important for teacher educators to be aware of teacher candidates' beliefs about teaching and learning?
4. What are the influences of the teacher preparation program, instructors, courses, activities, and assignments on teacher candidates' beliefs?
5. How can you use the findings from this research to improve your program?

Coauthored by Nancy P. Gallavan and Jennifer P. Merritt from the University of Central Arkansas, chapter 3 is titled "Reinforcing MAT Course Goals during Internship Experiences via Gallavan's Seven Essential Elements." This study details Gallavan's Seven Essential Elements that the researcher selected and used to frame observations generating the need for readiness, receptiveness, and responsiveness on behalf of the intern as well as the supervisor.

Extension Questions for Reflection and Conversation:

1. What are Gallavan's Seven Essential Elements?
2. What document provides the framework for the Seven Essential Elements?
3. What course serves as the basis of the Seven Essential Elements?
4. Why did the researcher select these seven elements?
5. What are the benefits of understanding readiness, receptiveness, and responsiveness for both the intern and the supervisor?

Chapter 4 is authored by Heather K. Dillard of Middle Tennessee State University titled "Collaboration: A Skill That Must Be Explicitly Taught." Analyzing data from a two-year case study conducted with two middle level teacher candidates, the researcher identifies several important findings.

Extension Questions for Reflection and Conversation:

1. Why did the researcher spend two years collecting data?
2. Why is this study case limited to two middle level teacher candidates?
3. What is collaboration?
4. How should collaboration be taught?
5. What are the benefits of collaboration?

Chapter 5, titled "Field Experiences with Children of Trauma: Supporting Emotional and Psychologically Injured Children: Value beyond Institutional Measure," authored by Jayne M. Leh, submits insights to a three-year study of a credit-free service-learning experience with undergraduate teacher candidates following a community disaster and the dynamics perceived by both the teacher candidates and the university instructors.

Extension Questions for Reflection and Conversation:

1. What are the characteristics of effective service-learning experiences?
2. Why was the credit-free approach used for this service-learning experience?
3. Why was this particular camp helpful for the teacher candidates?
4. Why are rigor and reflection key components of service learning?
5. How could a similar service-learning experience be offered in your teacher preparation program?

Coauthored by Jenifer Suh from George Mason University and Kim Dockery, an Educational Consultant, chapter 6 is titled "Inspiring Teachers across the Professional Continuum through Collaborative Coaching and Lesson Study." The coauthors share their professional learning model of the Teacher Leadership Institute and Lesson Plan focused on situated learning promoting collaborative planning, teaching, observing, and debriefing.

Extension Questions for Reflection and Conversation:

1. What is situated learning and what are its benefits for teachers?
2. What is legitimate peripheral participation and what are its advantages for teachers?
3. What is the history of lesson study and how has lesson study been used in U.S. classrooms?
4. What do the authors mean by collaborative coaching and what are its values for teachers?
5. What did the authors discover about teacher leadership using their professional continuum?

Chapter 7, "Strengthening Culturally Responsive Teaching through Existing Professional Development School Partners," coauthored by Emily Reeves, Angela Malone Cartwright, and Daphney L. Curry from Midwestern State University, found that transformational experiences designed for teacher candidates contribute to the development of culturally responsive teachers and teaching. The transformational experiences must be intentional, systematic, continuous, and contextualized in rich and diverse activities.

Extension Questions for Reflection and Conversation:

1. What is the demographic imperative and why is it important for teacher candidates to understand?
2. What is culturally responsive teaching and why should candidates be equipped and empowered with the knowledge, skills, and dispositions associated with it?
3. What programs and practices should be included in teacher candidates' diverse field experiences?
4. What are transformative experiences and how do they occur with teacher candidates?
5. How do the authors use the FRAME activity and what is its purpose with their teacher candidates?

Chapter 8, coauthored by Glenda L. Black from Nipissing University and Mair Greenfield from The Rumie Institute, investigate "Teacher Candidates' Courage in Developing Cultural Capacity through an Indigenous Cocurricular Community Service-Learning Program." Using a case study design, data collected from sixty-five teacher candidates through anticipatory and post–Biidaaban Community Service-Learning reflections were sorted into five categories indicating the effects and of the candidates' service-learning voluntarism.

Extension Questions for Reflection and Conversation:

1. What is service-learning and how is it useful for teacher candidates?
2. Why is service-learning an important component for teaching in Canada's classrooms?
3. What is cross-cultural experiential learning and how does it apply to Canada's classrooms?
4. What is Biidaaban Community Service Learning?
5. What are the authors' recommendations resulting from their research?

The eight chapters of Section I, associated with the factors of hope, strength, and courage that impact the inspirations and aspirations of teachers and teaching, include research conducted with undergraduate and graduate university students and teacher candidates at all stages of their preparation programs. Written by authors from two countries, various types of institutions, and multiple perspectives, Section I makes visible the importance and benefits of conducting research and reporting findings for teacher educators in all capacities to read, grow, and change.

Section II

EXAMINING FACTORS OF HOPE, STRENGTH, AND COURAGE THAT IMPACT THE INSPIRATIONS AND ASPIRATIONS FOR LEADERS AND LEADING

Introduction

LeAnn G. Putney and Nancy P. Gallavan

The eight chapters selected for Section II continue the theme of examining the presence and power of hope, strength, and courage and their impact on the inspirations and aspirations of educational leaders in schools and classrooms. The collection of chapter for this section take us into classrooms and schools to examine the leadership of teachers and administrators in practicing educational theory. These authors take us into their school and community contexts to illustrate how they gauge the quality of environment for teachers and students that result in transformative and inclusive teaching.

The chapters move us through attempts at improving teacher professional focus through coaching strategies and reflective practice as well as improving collaborative efforts between teachers and specialists in content areas of literacy and math. The authors take us into the heart of reform efforts, to include issues related to privatized external granting procedures, as well as understanding charter schools as schools of choice in public education. The promotion of hope through professional development for teachers relates to promoting beliefs and habits of mind through growth mindset and facilitative leadership. Taken together, the eight chapters in Section Two contribute to understanding and facilitating transformative education as it occurs on a local level in classrooms and schools that are built on resilience and perseverance to encounter the best for our PK-12 students.

Section II opens with chapter 9, written by Denise Demers of the University of Central Arkansas, titled "Preparing the Leaders/Teachers of Tomorrow by Improving the Well-Being of Teachers Today." The author examines the causes of stress in the work-life of teachers in classrooms and calls for evidence-based strategies to assist teachers in coping with classroom stressors. Much of the stress documented for teachers comes from sources external to the classroom and can be attributed to a tension between teachers' professional goals that are not realized in their environment. Teachers must cope with seemingly ever-changing curriculum, testing routines, regulations, and standards that they must cover while attempting to maintain student engagement and achievement. Stress reduction techniques incorporated in mindfulness training may be one way to increase teacher well-being, mindfulness, and self-compassion.

Chapter 10 is titled "'I Need Collaboration Too!' Exploring the Nature of Collaboration between a Literacy Coach and University Teacher Collaborator," and is authored by Grace Kang of Illinois State University. In this chapter, Kang examines the collaborations between a literacy coach, classroom teachers, and a university teacher collaborator. Her review of literature demonstrates that working in collaboration with a coach or other colleagues has been meaningful and effective in leading to change in teacher practice. While the job of literacy coach has been shown to be beneficial, a question remains how to bolster the effectiveness of the literacy coach through collaboration with more experienced others at the university. The strong relationships among the teacher, literacy coach, and UTC worked to create a strong culture of collaboration in this building.

For chapter 11, we encounter a study by Sarah Irvine Belson from American University titled "Charter School Special Educators: Expressions of Hope, Courage, and Strength." This study is an examination of the work of special educators in public charter schools and how they work to serve students with disabilities in spite of encountering funding and curricular issues. Special education teachers' behaviors, particularly those who stay in high-needs urban schools, can defined by resilience. This case study demonstrates that the strength of urban public charter school special education teachers can be seen in their capacity to engage with colleagues, to help educate the school's administration, and to work with students who may seem resistant to making changes.

In chapter 12, three authors invite us to share their work titled, "Preparing Elementary School Mathematics Specialists: Aspirations for a University Endorsement Program." Two authors, Susan Swars Auslander and Stephanie Z. Smith are from Georgia State University, while Marvin E. Smith hails from Kennesaw State University. Their study examines the implementation of a university K-5 Master of Education program with course experiences grounded in the current literature on ways to best prepare elementary school teachers mathematically, with the hopes of prompting motivation, learning, and change.

The authors of chapter 13 promote "Fighting for Hope and Inspiration: Developing Reflective Spaces for Leaders in Elementary School Mathematics." The authors who collaborated on this piece are Ryan Flessner from Butler University, Courtney Flessner from Indiana University, Katherine Reed, from the Hinkle Creek Elementary School, and Susan Adamson, also from Butler University. Their study examines reflective work that occurred during a Math Leadership Group that was sponsored by the Indiana Partnership for Young Writers. Through the use of vignettes from one of the participants they document what mathematical leadership can look like in our current educational landscape.

In chapter 14, we encounter "The Impact of Privatized Funding in Education and a Proposal for Reform," authored by Todd Cherner of Portland State University and Catherine M. Scott of Coastal Carolina University. While affluent citizens and organizations (i.e., edu-philanthropists) help to fund public education, they may also be furthering a particular agenda through their competitive granting procedures. The authors offer an alternative, grassroots model for applying for such grants to help in further initiatives that align with public education issues.

Chapter 15 delves into "Urban Teacher Collective Efficacy through Facilitative Leadership: An Illustrative Dialogue." This chapter was authored by Shelley Nordick from Jordan School District, Suzanne H. Jones from Utah State University, LeAnn G. Putney from the University of Nevada, Las Vegas, and Connie L. Malin from Innovations International Charter School of Nevada. Building from a prior study of teacher beliefs regarding the principal's role in building teacher collective efficacy, these authors engaged a K–12 public charter school principal in conversation about her role as a facilitative leader. Insights into actions that promote school-wide efficacy from this study are illustrative and potentially transferable to other administrators and in other school settings.

Chapter 16 wraps up the yearbook with Angela Webster of the University of Central Arkansas in her study titled, "Are You a Hope Buster or Hope Muster?" In this study the author discusses the notion of hope, parallel conceptions of hope, and variances of hope in her examination of teacher practices. Her working descriptors of hope-based schools demonstrates how to build bridges through cultural understanding, cultural relevance, culturally responsive pedagogy, and engagement of familial and community assets to alleviate marginalization and disenfranchisement.

Chapter 9

Preparing the Leaders/Teachers of Tomorrow by Improving the Well-Being of Teachers Today

Denise Demers

ABSTRACT

While stress in life can be beneficial, typically stress is associated with a general disruption in the perception of a person's homeostasis (Selye, 1974) or sense of balance and well-being. Nearly 75 to 80% of the employees today consider themselves and their jobs to be stressful in some way. The American Institute of Stress (American Psychological Association [APA], 2014) rates situations related to employment as the number one cause of stress in the United States. Clearly these statistics apply to the profession of teaching. Roeser et al. (2013), among other researchers, consider teaching as one area of employment that is an emotionally challenging profession, especially for women. Women over the last century have been impacted by many changes and challenges. It is imperative that professional development focus on emotional resources to guide and support educators, particularly women educators. Many professional development courses directed at well-being or teacher effectiveness have been attempted throughout the years. The courses ranged from coaching strategies, workshops that included cognitive tactics, social support, and behavioral techniques to work and environment changes, such as redesigning tasks or creating flexible work hours with minimal effect. While each course has its place and the strategies may work on an individual basis with some teachers, recent researchers have shown the mindfulness-based interventions (MBIs) have the greatest effect on teachers' general well-being (Bayraktar & Yilmaz, 2016; Beshai, McAlpine, Wear, & Kuyken, 2015; Gould, Dariotis, Greenberg, & Mendelson, 2017; Kuyken et al., 2013).

KEY WORDS

Teaching; Stress; Mindfulness; Well-being

INTRODUCTION

According to the National Center for Educational Statistics (U.S. Department of Education, 2011), more women than men are earning all levels of postsecondary school degrees, many of whom enter fields of education. A quick look at past yearbooks or teaching logs at schools shows that the majority of K-12 teachers are female. Regardless of the explanations for the majority of female teachers in the past, the dominance remains today. Likewise, the university level is equally dominated by women instructing and guiding new teachers.

After World War II, women became more prevalent in the workforce (Goldin, 1991; Seierstad & Kirton, 2015). Shortly after the assimilation of women into the workforce, studies began to look at the work-life balance, that is, how women can work all day at a job then come home and work more. Hochschild (1989) termed the work-life balance the "second shift" in her book by the same name. Both Voydanoff (1984) and Fox and Hesse-Biber (1984) wrote similar books about the changing context of work and family roles. Comparable research continues as women remain contenders in the labor force of this nation (Fernandez, 2013; Weiner, 2003). This topic has continually maintained momentum to the present day as Hochschild and Machung (2012) advance revisions of their book on the second shift. Suffice it to say, women remain breadwinners as well as caretakers of household duties and childcare responsibilities (Bianchi, 2011; Bianchi & Milkie, 2010). The accumulation of multiple roles, with little time for self, often leads to an overload of stress (Demers, 2014). Additionally, as quoted in Allred (1892), without time to relax one's mind, the mind will lose its elasticity just as a "bow strung up all the time" (p. 472).

As women entered the workforce, many of them became teachers (Nash & Romero, 2012). Roeser et al. (2013) call teaching an emotionally challenging profession and not the only researchers to make this type of statement. Echoing Roeser et al. (2013) are Addison and Yankyera (2015); Beshai et al. (2015), who call it a "serious endemic concern" (para. 1); Jones (2016); and Naghieh, Montgomery, Bonell, Thompson, and Aber (2015), among other researchers. The same sentiment resounded in the findings of educational researchers as long as thirty years ago (Crow, 1985; Kaiser & Polyczynski, 1982). More revealing, researchers who began studying work-related stress began nearly twenty years before Crow (1985) or Kaiser and Polyczynski (1982) in the 1960s and 1970s (Jones, 2016) also found teaching to be emotionally challenging. Kugiejko (2015) found that women tend to be burned out or stressed more because of their sensitivity to emotional exhaustion. Thus, as women tend to occupy a majority of the positions in education and experience a greater sensitivity to emotional exhaustion, finding evidence-based techniques to combat stress continues to be a worthwhile endeavor.

Sources of Stress

A variety of sources in classrooms and schools account for stress in teachers. Many sources may sound current and familiar even though they stem from previous generations. Stressors include teaching unmotivated students, maintaining discipline, increasing pressures and workload, changing environments, being evaluated, dealing with colleagues, maintaining self-esteem and status, interacting with administration and management, and balancing the ambiguity of roles (Kyriacou & Sutcliffe, 1978). Blasé (1986) discussed how extra duties, additional paperwork, and multiple meetings all contribute to the stress of teachers. While many causes of stress for teachers continue, Chang (2013) brings the present back to the past showing that life may not have changed in the last thirty years as much as assumed or expected. Chang found that as educators continuously deal with students' problematic behaviors, educators tend to reach burnout quickly because of the negative emotions involved. Blasé's (1986) study showed that "student stress" was the second largest stressor, whether the stress related to fighting, bullying, vandalism, or cheating.

Published research is supplemented by the many anecdotes told to this researcher by contemporary teachers, administrators, teacher candidates, and teacher educators with whom this researcher has interacted personally and professionally (Demers, D., personal communications, 2017). Sadly, some of the teachers expressed their strong desires to quit teaching due to the changes and challenges associated with stress. To keep classroom management and administrative duties under control, educators at all levels benefit by governing their emotions (Sutton & Wheatley, 2003).

Whether from personal reasons or from professional work, stress is ubiquitous and research surrounding the phenomenon of continues to grow. Likewise, prevention and coping strategies continue to evolve. Kaiser and Polczynski (1982) state "today's educators must cope with an ever-growing number of social and environmental forces impinging on their time. Yet, the ability to cope is becoming increasingly more difficult with the resultant stress taking its toll on physical and mental well-being" (p. 127). However, if research surrounding stress and its effects on educators has been studied for so long, why is it still a problem? This chapter will highlight the need for evidence-based strategies to help teachers and teacher educators, specifically women, effectively cope with increasing stressors in life, both at work and at home.

Contextualizing the Problem of Stress

As time continues forward, stressors that affect the lives of people remain ever-present. Whether from personal reasons including, but not limited to, issues related to health, personal life, relationships, security, work, occupation, and so on stress remains a daily issue for most people. Importantly, stress and its effects are not new topics. Researchers such as Lazarus (1966), Hinkle (1973), and Selye (1974) all weighed in on the definition and parameters of change from homeostasis and the associated stress. Even nearly 100 years ago, Cannon (1935) defined stress in relation to a natural tendency to resist a change in homeostasis. Thus, the phenomenon of stress is not novel in the 20th and 21st centuries, yet stress may be becoming a greater problem and for more people. The American Psychological Association's (APA's) (2010) survey on stress in America in general shows an overstressed nation; specifically, the survey highlighted an overall dissatisfaction with an individual's employer's lack of help for the employees' balance of work and life responsibilities. Although most people in America know the detrimental effects stress can have, the APA survey also showed a universal paralyzation in an individual's efforts to make necessary changes. APA (2010) reported that 75% of adults experienced at least moderate and some high levels of stress with increases over the past year. Half of the survey participants reported that they want help managing such stress.

As a nation, stress costs American businesses in the United States as much as $300 billion per fiscal year. But the costs of stress do not stop in the United States. The plague of stress has also expanded beyond U.S. borders to become a global epidemic, which the World Health Organization (WHO) (2017) states is the "leading cause of disability, costing the global economy $1 trillion dollars annually on lost productivity" (para. 2).

Stress in Teaching

Researchers refer to teaching as an emotionally challenging profession (Roeser et al., 2013), or a "serious endemic concern" (Beshai et al., 2015, para. 1). While stress costs the nation nearly $300 billion per year, teacher turnover costs more money, increasing that figure by $7.3 billion per year (Barnes, Crowe, & Schaefer, 2007). To keep occupational turnover low, teacher burnout also must be decreased. Schools must keep classroom management and administrative duties under control. Chang (2013) considers burnout as the moment that requirements exceed a teacher's tolerance to a workload. Chang also found that educators continuously dealing with students' problematic behaviors led to burnout because of the negative emotions involved (Kugiejko, 2015). To accomplish a reduction of burnout and, therefore, teacher turnover, governing an individual's emotions is a great benefit to teachers (Sutton & Wheatley, 2003).

Another reason for teacher burnout and turnover is demoralization. Tsang and Liu (2016) define demoralization as when teachers experience negative emotional experiences that affect their well-being and quality of teaching. Clarke and Kissane (2002) define demoralization as an inability "to cope, together with associated feelings of helplessness, hopelessness, meaninglessness, subject incompetence and diminished self-esteem" (p. 733). Much of teachers' morale is determined by the teachers' perceptions of inclusion in the decision-making processes concerning their classrooms (Ingersoll, 2003; Tsang & Liu, 2016) and the impact of administration (Ingersoll, 2003; Leithwood & Beatty, 2008), both of which contribute to the high turnover rate among teachers. Although the initial goals upon entering the profession are to make a difference in students' lives, many teachers may feel demoralized and have negative feelings toward teaching (i.e., burnout) because of these identified perceptions. When teachers' work environments do not match their professional goals (Santoro, 2011), some teachers leave teaching and other teachers settle into an unmotivated resentful state of compliance.

Life is full of stressful incidents for both men and women alike. However, stressful incidents are handled differently by each gender. Likewise, personality types and coping styles differ between genders, hence predicting stress in an occupation for either men or women is difficult (Blonna, 2005). Therefore, because women tend to have a greater sensitivity to emotional exhaustion (Kugiejko, 2015), and women tend to occupy a majority of the positions in the emotional challenging field (Roeser et al., 2013) of education, this chapter focuses on the stressors women feel in their education professions, as well as techniques that work best for them.

Purpose and Research Questions

The purpose of this chapter is to highlight the growing need for evidence-based strategies to help teachers and teacher educators, particularly women educators, effectively cope with the increasing stressors they face in their roles. This research is guided by the following questions: (1) What are the stressors of teachers and teacher educators? (2) What coping strategies have been used? and (3) Which coping strategies work? The researcher hopes to paint a picture of the scope of stress in the world of education, more particularly how it affects the mental health of teachers and teacher educators.

Suggested preventions and strategies to cope with the ever-growing factors resulting in stress for this population are provided.

Research Methods

This research two methods of research. First, a review of the literature revealed strategies used to benefit teachers and administrators, including historical changes of evidence-based concepts and practices. Second, I spoke with a variety of teachers, administrators, and students about stress to identify what stressors they face and to describe the ways they handle the stressors on a daily basis. A variety of women within some aspect of the teaching profession added to the body of this research. As I compared their experiences to the experiences of women in the reviewed literature, a more complete picture of stress in a teacher's world came into view.

Subjects

Because much of this chapter is a systematic review, frequently the participants were unknown to me. However, the participants that I interviewed and spoke with range from varying levels of students in education at universities to new teachers and seasoned teachers/administrators including professionals who educate novice professional teachers and administrators at the college level. Rarely did I contact these individuals concerning their stress and stressors in their workplaces. Instead, many individuals came to me as friends sharing the hardships of life and their perceptions, particularly as women, of their jobs in education. Thus, I utilized no method of recruitment. Each individual knew of my expertise in mental health, especially for women and wanted to share their situations with me both to vent and unload as well as for guidance and support.

Findings/Discussion

As I researched the topic of this chapter, many experiences came to mind about teachers from my own past. One experience stands out related to my 6th-grade teacher, Mrs. Boston. She seemed perfect, taking the time to care about her students while pushing them forward both academically and individually. She believed in me, in who I was and who I could become someday. It was not necessarily the words she used, but merely who she was. Within her class I learned that I was capable and that I could do anything in this world. Learning became fun, something I craved. As a twelve-year-old, I never had the slightest inkling that her job may have been stressful. I knew she was a mother because she spoke of her children. However, she never spoke of the trials of teaching or the system she worked within.

As I continued to reflect on my past, I also began to think about the same type of teachers that influenced my own children. A particular 2nd-grade teacher is memorable. Not only was she able to see the inner potential of every student on a very personal level, she skillfully helped each student blossom into what the child could become. Like Mrs. Boston, my child's 2nd-grade teacher expanded my child's view of himself and the world, of lifelong learning, and of being successful in whatever my child chose to do and become.

Interestingly, the teacher was hesitant to ever share the hardships of her chosen career, until my third child was enrolled in her class and a budding friendship between us as adults had begun. Piloting a new curriculum that her state department of education was proposing was difficult. I could see the stress in her face and hear it in the tone of her voice when telling me about it. She was struggling. A teacher shortage coupled with a student overload plus the requirement to pilot a new curricular program that the teacher initially did not believe in, seemed to wear her down. Although she struggled, she kept on going, like most teachers do, but she needed me to share her stress.

As an adult and mother, I have begun to understand a smidgen of what this teacher was experiencing. However, until I became a teacher myself, empathy and understanding were incomplete. Now I teach at a university, and while it is difficult and stressful in its own regard, my situation is much different than the situations that classroom teachers face. Classroom teachers are consistently being mandated to implement new curriculum or new testing routines or a new law or new standard. Now as a university teacher and mother, many of my friends are teachers. Although the classroom teachers love what they do, much like the teachers I described, I see the strain the teachers go through with added workloads, increased number of students in their classes, additional obligatory responsibilities, and so on with only one short prep period to complete all their work. From my conversations with my teacher friends and after listening to their venting about difficulties, I realized that the overall theme was how much they love their students. My general understanding of life as a teacher was forming.

I continued to acquire glimpses into the heart and feelings of teachers. In a recent phone call with a middle school teacher who loves her job and has a great passion for teaching youth, I found her struggling with a desire to quit, to "go be a Walmart greeter" because of the pressures she is feeling. She mentioned that many of her colleagues go through similar hardships in their teaching careers. Her struggles were the result of many of her students' parents and the administrative system. Her stories parallel the research; Kaiser and Polcynski (1982) and Lipsky (1980) found similar discoveries over thirty years ago. The high student-teacher ratios and the demanding administrative behaviors such as taking attendance, performing recess duty, and grading assignments all serve as bureaucratic procedures that act as catalysts to job stress.

Another woman I spoke with is an elementary school principal. Until this past year, she has absolutely loved her job. Like any career, struggles exist but the passion prevails. But, due to administrative changes, superiors coasting to retirement not willing to rock the boat or to provide assistance, and a school board that struggles to be fair to all, this elementary school principal is looking elsewhere for a job. When I spoke with her, she said she would go anywhere; she had even toyed with the idea of going back to teaching just to leave the present situation at her school. Clearly, she is overwhelmed and overstressed much of the time.

Although both women described here were ready to quit, stress affects teachers in different ways. Likewise, two types of teachers exist: teachers who are goal-oriented and teachers who place a greater emphasis on keeping the system running in order and according to the bureaucratic processes of education (Tsang & Liu, 2016). Both types of teachers experience the struggles of teaching very differently. What stresses the goal-oriented teachers may actually be welcomed by the other teacher who emphasizes order keeping. Evidently, school districts need both types of teachers for the success of the student and education as a whole. Yet, when bureaucracy prevails, levels of stress become unacceptable because movement toward achievement is eclipsed by the level of bureaucratic interference. The balance of forces (Kaiser & Polczynski, 1982), as shown in figure 9.1, is disrupted and causes high levels of stress, particular for the achievement-oriented teachers.

Qualities of Effective Teachers

Additionally, research is replete with the ongoing debate about which qualities are most needed to create an effective teacher (Roehrig et al., 2012). Obviously, subject knowledge is at the top of the list (Shulman, 1987), but more recently, other researchers make a case for emotional resources (Jennings & Greenburg, 2009). These emotional resources are essential to effective teaching, including classroom management. Likewise, emotional experiences within a classroom can directly affect a teacher's emotional exhaustion (Keller, Chang, Becker, Goetz, & Frenzel, 2014) and are associated with student-rated instructional quality (Frenzel, Goetz, Stephens, & Jacob, 2009; Klusmann, Kunter, Voss, & Baumert, 2012). Seiz, Voss, and Kunter (2015) found that there is a significant interaction between cognitive and emotional resources. Job stress affects a multitude of aspects of the classroom and the teacher. Researchers link it to poor mental and physical health (Maldonado, 2014) and anxiety, depression, colds, asthma, chest pains, and difficulty in breathing (Pruitt & Stein, 1999).

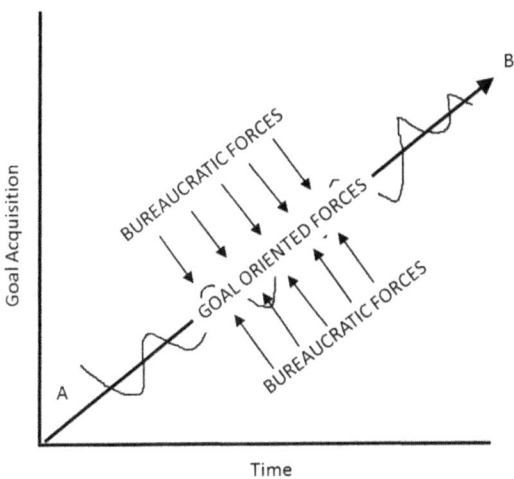

Figure 9.1 Relationship between Goal Acquisition and Time Impacting Bureaucratic Forces (Kaiser & Polczynski, 1982).

It is interesting that this same bureaucratic process seems to have grown and amplified its hold on education. In her recent venting during a telephone conversation, my friend mentioned this cause of her stress as do many other teachers with whom I interact on a daily basis. But other factors contribute to the stress of educators that have been noted in the past. In 1977, Cooper and Marshall's framework discussing the contributing factors of stress included five factors that relate to educational organizations and bureaucracy. The factors include (a) factors intrinsic to the job, (b) role in the organization, (c) relationships with organization, (d) career development, and (e) organizational structure of climate.

Furthermore, Taylor (2003) attributes stress to work overload. Some teachers seem to handle the stress and maintain control. However, some teachers do not. Factors affecting the stress levels of teachers do not seem to have changed through the years. Of the women teachers in Addison and Yankyera's 2016 study, most agree that their jobs are stressful and that "work-overload, personal development, interpersonal relations, and organizational climate" all are root causes of their stress (p. 19). Moreover, with pressures for increased accountability, unmotivated students, enormous amounts of duties and responsibilities both in and outside the classroom, minimal time to prepare and/or relax, testing pressures, an absence of administrative support, large class sizes, and concern for the general safety and well-being of their students, being among the many sources of stress for teachers, many teachers are leaving the profession (aka, experiencing teacher turnover) or reporting more physical and mental issues related to work (Blasé, 1986; Kyriacou & Sutcliffe, 1978; Richards, 2012).

Most items identified as stressors includes what Blasé (1986) describes as "organizational stress." He asserts that "student stress"—including discipline, apathy from students, low achievement or motivation, or general absences—was number two as rated by 392 elementary, middle school/junior high, and high school teachers with inadequate levels of earnings rated number one. Helms-Lorenz and Maulana (2016) concur, adding a lack of learning opportunities for beginning teachers as well as poor social organizational aspects to the stress factors. Conversely, Kugiejko (2015) adds that when discussing tensions and stressors in the education profession, the topics must also include emotional exhaustion for women and depersonalization for men.

In addition to insufficient earnings, increasing bureaucratic demands (including curricular changes), and escalating student concerns, teachers reported inadequate working conditions and unpleasant co-workers interactions as work-related byproducts contributing to their stress, tension, burnout, and emotional exhaustion. And, unfortunately, teacher stress is not localized to the United States, but prevalent in the Netherlands (Helms-Lorenz & Maulana, 2016), Poland (Kugiejko, 2015), Canada, the United Kingdom, and Israel (Meiklejohn et al., 2012), and many other countries not cited here. Work-related stress truly is a global epidemic (WHO, 2002).

Preventing and Coping with Stress

Although the causes of stress remain consistent, attention to ways of preventing and coping with stress are increasing. Over thirty years ago, Miller (1979) suggested that individuals start examining their own lifestyles, reviewing their jobs, and reflecting on their health. Efforts in earlier years were also made to decrease blood pressure, oxygen consumption, and respiration. Muscle tension known as the "relaxation response" (Benson, 1974) also was employed more recently in the widespread movement of mindfulness, which has its impetus nearly forty years ago (Kabat-Zinn, 1990).

Therefore, schools must focus on a combination of both logical knowledge and emotional resources for teachers in order to help teachers make the greatest effects upon their students, the rising generation.

Implications/Recommendations

Who focuses on just one task at a time anymore? Most people live moment to moment without much time to think in between the deluge of their work responsibilities and their extracurricular activities as evidenced by the plethora of self-help, emotional well-being, mindfulness and stress relief books being published. A quick Amazon search for mindfulness books comes up with over 170,000 items. Add mindfulness or stress relief apps and we see that over 1400 apps exist, at least through Amazon. Check your phone's app store and you may be scrolling endlessly through a superabundance of the new and trending meditation apps available, some given five stars by nearly 40,000 people. Furthermore, at the end of 2014, the American Mindfulness Research Association included more than 3000 articles (Black, 2015).

To reap the greatest benefit for the teaching profession, professional development concentrating at least in part on emotional resources is imperative. Helms-Lorenz and Maulana (2016) found a negative correlation between self-efficacy and stress. Therefore, when self-efficacy increases, stress and tension will decrease. Conversely, Yu, Wang, Zhai, Dai, and Yang (2015) found that added pressures on the job create a decrease in self-efficacy as well as an increase in being tired of working. Can and how do we halt this vicious cycle? Through focused time spent on emotional resources and on complete wellness, activity-based professional development seminars can benefit all teachers, whether novice or experienced; teacher or administrator; public, private, or university setting.

For example, Jones (2016) conducted a workshop in which 20 teachers participated in a 3.5-hour workshop with 3 core components: cognitive growth, social support, and behavior techniques. All twenty teachers remarked on how helpful it was to take a step back and do something for themselves. Moreover, social support was also shown to be an effective coping strategy particularly for the women teachers (Addison & Yankyera, 2016). However, Naghieh et al. (2015) researched four separate studies that had been conducted with more than 2000 teachers. Interventions ranging from work changes, such as redesigning tasks or work environments, to creating more flexible work schedules resulted in only minimal low-quality evidence of any significant improvement in well-being of teachers or teacher retention. Nor did the coaching support network or incentive based strategies produce compelling reasons to institute such programs permanently into the schools. Improving self-efficacy (Helms-Lorenz & Maulana, 2016) and social support (Addison & Yankyera, 2016; Jones, 2016) seem to be the best solutions suggested in recent research findings. One way to promote a greater sense of self-efficacy, or complete well-being, is through mindfulness training (Bandura, 1997; Charoensukmongkol, 2014; Soysa & Wilcomb, 2015).

Mindfulness-Based Interventions

Although workshops (Jones, 2016), social support (Addison & Yankyera, 2016), self-confidence, optimism, or coping techniques have their places as effective coping strategies for teachers experiencing stress (Bayraktar & Yilmaz, 2016), studies show that mindfulness-based interventions (MBIs) seem to have the greatest effect on teachers in general (Beshai et al., 2015;

Bayraktar & Yilmaz, 2016; Gould et al., 2017; Kuyken et al., 2013). In the last decade, Meiklejohn et al. (2012) document precursory interventions and initiatives being piloted in multiple countries including the United States, the United Kingdom, Canada, Israel, and other countries, blending mindfulness into K-12 education for the benefit of both the students as well as the teachers. Their research suggests that when adults, specifically teachers, continue a sustained regiment of mindfulness training, both attention and self-regulation are enhanced. Consequently, such enhancements promote more productive learning environments for students as well as more inviting work places for teachers. Personal mindfulness training results in greater teacher well-being and self-efficacy as well as an improved ability to manage classroom behaviors as teachers establish more supportive relationships with their students.

Therefore, professional development that highlights, at least in part, emotional resources is necessary. Although fairly new to public education, the idea of mindfulness training has been recognized for many hundreds of years (Meiklejohn et al., 2012). Kabat-Zinn, a young molecular biologist from MIT and avid student of Buddhist meditation, brought the age-old Eastern disciplines of mindfulness meditation and yoga to America, to the University of Massachusetts Medical Center to help patients with chronic pain and multitude of other ailments who were often treated with drugs, rehab, and surgery. Kabat-Zinn termed "just a little pilot on zero dollars" (Kabat-Zinn, 2003) has grown exponentially until now his approach is found in multibillion dollar corporations such as Google's "Search Inside Yourself" mindfulness training (taught by Chade-Meng Tan whose official title is Jolly Good Fellow (Bush, 2014)), universities (Swain, 2016), and even in the public schools (Meiklejohn et al., 2012).

Multiple strategies have surfaced over the years and mindfulness training has become well known throughout the world. Flook, Goldberg, Pinger, Bonus, and Davidson (2013) found that mindfulness programs provide teachers with the tools necessary to implement such techniques in their own classrooms, which, in turn, buffers the effects of stress individually as well as collectively, as shown by multiple other researchers (Lutz et al., 2008, 2009; Mañas, Franco, & Justo, 2011; Roeser et al., 2013).

Additionally, Beshai et al. (2015) found MBIs reduce stress and significantly increase teacher well-being, mindfulness, and self-compassion. Binding the training on emotional resources with professional development in teacher education offers a synergistic effect upon both cognitive and emotional stamina. With such stamina, Seiz et al. (2015) posit, "work-related stress and burnout may be lessened or even avoided" (p. 70). Thus, MBIs are influential strategies for coping with stress for teachers.

CONCLUSION

Educators face a multifaceted barrage of stress-inducing experiences on a daily basis including salaries, bureaucracies, students, environments, and colleagues impacting their well-being and lifestyles. Districts, schools, and universities have a responsibility to help with the well-being of each teacher. Teacher preparation and professional development at all levels must guide and support all teachers in their careers to teacher their students. Like Mrs. Boston for me, and countless other teachers who teach the youth of the world, guidance and support for preventing and coping with stress contributes to individuals and a world with greater strength, hope, and courage.

REFERENCES

Addison, A. K., & Yankyera, G. (2015). An investigation into how female teachers manage stress and teacher burnout: A case study of West Akim Municipality of Ghana. *Journal of Education and Practice, 6*(10), 1–24.

Allred, W. M. (1892). Recollections of the prophet Joseph Smith. *Juvenile Instructor, 27*(15), 457–489.

American Psychological Association (APA). (2014). *2104 Stress in America survey.* NY: American Institute of Stress.

Bandura, A. (1997). *Self-efficacy: The exercise of control.* New York, NY: Freeman.

Barnes, G., Crowe, E., & Schaefer, B. (2007). *The cost of teacher turnover in five school districts: A pilot study.* Washington, DC: National Commission on Teaching and America's Future. Retrieved from: http://nctaf.org/research/publications/.

Bayraktar, H. V., & Yilmaz, K. O. (2016). Examination of stress-coping methods of primary school teachers in terms of different variables. *Journal of Education and Training Studies, 4*(8), 167–179. doi:10.11114/jets.v4i8.1673.

Beshai, S., McAlpine, L., Wear, K., & Kuyken, W. (2015). A non-randomized feasibility trial assessing the efficacy of a mindfulness-based intervention for teachers to reduce stress and improve well-being. *Mindfulness,* 1–11. doi: 10.1007/s12671-015-0436-1. Retrieved from http://cedar.exeter.ac.uk/media/universityofexeter/schoolofpsychology/cedar/documents/mindfulness/Beshai_et_al._(2015)_Mindfulness_(1).pdf.

Benson, H. (July 1974). Your innate asset in combating stress. *Harvard Business Review.* Retrieved from https://hbr.org/1974/07/your-innate-asset-for-combating-stress.

Bianchi, S. M. (2011). Changing families, changing workplaces. *The Future of Children, 21*(2), 15–36.

Bianchi, S. M., & Milkie, M. A. (2010). Work and family research in the first decade of the 21st century. *Journal of Marriage and Family, 72*(3), 705–725. doi: 10.1111/j.1741-3737.2010.00726.x.

Black, D. S. (2015). Mindfulness journal publications by year, 1980–2014. Retrieved from https://goamra.org/resources/.

Blasé, J. (1986). A qualitative analysis of sources of teacher stress: Consequences for performance. *American Educational Research Journal, 23*(1), 13–40.

Blonna, R. (2005). *Coping with stress in a changing world*. New York, NY: McGraw-Hill Companies Inc.

Bush, M. (July 30, 2014). What's it like to take Google's mindfulness training? Retrieved from https://www.mindful.org/whats-it-like-to-take-googles-mindfulness-training/.

Cannon, W. B. (1935). Stresses and strains of homeostasis. *American Journal of Medical Science, 189*(1), 13–14.

Chang, M.-L. (2013). Toward a theoretical model to understand teacher emotions and teacher burnout in the context of student misbehavior: Appraisal, regulation and coping. *Motivation and Emotion, 37*(4), 799–817. doi: 10.1007/s11031-012-9335-0.

Charoensukmongkol, P. (2014). Benefits of mindfulness meditation on emotional intelligence, general self-efficacy, and perceived stress: Evidence from Thailand. *Journal of Spirituality in Mental Health, 16*(3), 171–192. doi: 10.1080/19349637.2014.925364.

Clarke, D. M., & Kissane, D. W. (2002). Demoralization: Its phenomenology and importance. *Australian and New Zealand Journal of Psychiatry, 36*(6), 733–742. Retrieved from http://www.ncbi.nlm.nih.gov/pubmed/12406115.

Cooper, C., & Marshall, J. (1977). *Understanding executive stress*. New York, NY: Petrocelli.

Crow, M. L. (1985). The female educator at midlife. *The Phi Delta Kappan, 67*(4), 281–284.

Demers, D. (2014). *"I am the captain of the ship": Mother's experiences balancing graduate education and family responsibilities* (Order No. 3642735). Available from ProQuest Dissertations & Theses Global (1609384869). Retrieved from https://search.proquest.com/docview/1609384869?accountid=10017.

Fernández, R. (2013). Cultural change as learning: The evolution of female labor force participation over a century. *The American Economic Review, 103*(1), 472–500. Retrieved from http://www.jstor.org/stable/23469650.

Flook, L., Goldberg, S. B., Pinger, L., Bonus, K., & Davidson, R. J. (2013). Mindfulness for teachers: A pilot study to assess effects on burnout, and teaching efficacy. *Mind, Brain, and Education, 7*(3), 182–195. doi: 10.1111/mbe.12026.

Fox, M. F., & Hesse-Biber, S. (1984). *Women at work*. Mountain View, CA: Mayfield Publishing Company.

Frenzel, A., Goetz, T., Stephens, E., & Jacob, B. (2009). Antecedents and effects of teachers' emotional experiences: An integrated perspective and empirical test. In P. A. Schutz & M. Zembylas (Eds.), *Advances in teacher emotions research: The impact on teachers' lives* (pp. 129–146). New York, NY: Springer.

Goldin, C. D. (1991). The role of World War II in the rise of women's employment. *The American Economic Review, 81*(4), 741–756.

Gould, L. F., Dariotis, J. K., Greenberg, M. T., & Mendelson, T. (2016). Assessing fidelity of implementation (FOI) for school-based mindfulness and yoga interventions: A systematic review. *Mindfulness, 7*(1), 5–33. doi:10.1007/s12671-015-0395-6.

Helms-Lorenz, M., & Maulana, R. (2016). Influencing the psychological well-being of beginning teachers across three years of teaching: Self-efficacy, stress causes, job tension and job discontent. *Educational Psychology, 36*(3), 569–594. doi: 10.1080/01443410.2015.1008403.

Hinkle, L. (1973). The concept of "stress" in biological sciences. *Science, Medicine, and Man, 1*(1), 31–48.

Hochschild, A. R. (1989). *The second shift: Working parents and the revolution at home.* New York, NY: Viking.

Hochschild, A. R., & Machung, A. (2012). *The second shift: Working parents and the revolution at home.* New York, NY: Penguin Books.

Ingersoll, R. M. (2003). *Who controls teachers' work? Power and accountability in America's schools.* Cambridge, MA: Harvard University Press.

Jennings, P. A., & Greenburg, M. T. (2009). The prosocial classroom: Teacher social and emotional competence in relation to student and classroom outcomes. *Review of Educational Research, 79*(1), 491–525. doi: 10.3102/0034654308325693.

Jones, L. (Spring, 2016). Finding the resilient teacher within: A workshop to address K-12 teacher wellbeing. *Educational Specialist, Paper 26.* Retrieved from http://commons.lib.jmu.edu/cgi/viewcontent.cgi?article=1020&context=edspec201019.

Kabat-Zinn, J. (1990). *Full catastrophe living: Using the wisdom of your body and mind to face stress, pain and illness.* New York, NY: Delacorte.

Kabat-Zinn, J. (2003). Mindfulness-based interventions in context: Past, present, and future. *Clinical Psychology: Science and Practice, 10*(2), 144–156.

Kaiser, J. S., & Polczynski, J. T. (1982). Educational stress: Sources, reactions, preventions. *Peabody Journal of Education, 59*(2), 127–136.

Keller, M., Chang, M.-L., Becker, E., Goetz, T., & Frenzel, G. (2014). Teachers' emotional experiences and exhaustion as predictors of emotional labor in the classroom: An experience sampling study. *Frontiers in Psychology, 5*(1442), 1–10. doi:10.3389/fpsyg.2014.01442.

Klusmann, U., Kunter, M., Voss, T., & Baumert, J. (2012). Occupational stress of beginning teachers: The effects of personality, pedagogical experience and professional competence. *Journal of Educational Psychology, 26*(4), 275–290. doi:10.1024/1010-0652/a000078.

Kugiejko, M. (2015). A professional skill set of teacher and university lecturer in relation to the causes and prevention of burnout. *Problems of Education in the 21st Century, 67*, 40–51. Retrieved from http://oaji.net/articles/2015/457-1449572275.pdf.

Kuyken, W., Weare, K., Ukoumunne, O. C., Vicary, R., Motton, N., Burnett, R., ... Huppert, F. (2013). Effectiveness of mindfulness in schools programme: Non-randomised controlled feasibility study. *The British Journal of Psychiatry, 203*(2), 126–131. doi: 10.1192/bjp.bp.113.126649.

Kyriacou, C., & Sutcliffe, J. (1978). Teacher stress: Prevalence, sources, and symptoms. *British Journal of Educational Psychology, 48*(2), 159–167.

Lazarus, R. (1966). *Psychological stress and the coping process*. New York, NY: McGraw-Hill.

Leithwood, K., & Beatty, B. (2008). *Leading with teacher emotions in mind*. Thousand Oaks: Corwin Press.

Lipsky, M. (1980). *Street level bureaucracy: Dilemmas of the individual in public services*. New York, NY: Russel Sage Foundation.

Lutz, A., Slagter, H., Dunne, J., & Davidson, R. (2008). Attention regulation and monitoring in meditation. *Trends in Cognitive Sciences, 12*(4), 163–169.

Lutz, A., Slagter, H., Rawling, N., Francis, A., Greischar, I. I., & Davidson, R. J. (2009). Mental training enhances attentional stability: Neural and behavioural evidence. *Journal of Neuroscience, 29*(42), 13418–13427.

Maldonado, M. (2014). How stress affects mental health. *World of Psychology*. Retrieved from https://psychcentral.com/blog/archives/2014/02/25/how-stress-affects-mental-health/.

Mañas, I., Franco, C., & Justo, E. M. (2011). Reducing levels of teacher stress and days of sick leave in secondary school teachers through a mindfulness training programme. *Clínica y Salud, 22*(2), 121–137.

Meiklejohn, J., Phillips, C., Freedman, M. L., Griffin, M. L., Biegel, G., Roach, A., ... Saltzman, A., (2012). Integrating mindfulness training into K-12 education: Fostering the resilience of teachers and students. *Mindfulness, 3*(4), 291–307.

Miller, S. M. (1979). Coping with impending stress: Psychophysiological and cognitive correlates of choice. *Psychophysiology, 16*(6), 572–581. doi: 10.1111/j.1469-8986.1979.tb01523.x.

Naghieh, A., Montgomery, P., Bonell, C. P., Thompson, M., & Aber, J. L. (2015). Organizational interventions for improving wellbeing and reducing work-related stress in teachers. *Cochrane Database of Systematic Reviews, 8*(4). doi: 10.1002/14651858.CD010306.pub2. Retrieved from http://onlinelibrary.wiley.com/wol1/doi/10.1002/14651858.CD010306.pub2/full.

Nash, M., & Romero, L. (2012). Citizenship for the college girl: Challenges and opportunities in higher education for women in the United States in the 1930s. *Teachers College Record, 114*(2), 22.

Pruitt, B. E., & Stein, J. J. (1999). *Health styles: Decisions for living well* (2nd ed.). Boston, MA: Allyn & Bacon.

Richards, J. (2012). Teacher stress and coping strategies: A national snapshot. *The Educational Forum, 76*(3), 299–316. doi: 10.1080/00131725.2012.682837.

Roehrig, A. D., Turner, J. E., Arrastia, M. C., Christensen, E., McElhaney, S., & Jakiel, L. M. (2012). Effective teachers and teaching: Characteristics and practices related to positive student outcomes. In K. R. Harris, S. Graham, T. Urdan, S. Graham, J. M. Royer, & M. Zeidner (Eds.), *APA educational psychology handbook, Volume 2: Individual differences and cultural and contextual factors* (pp. 501–527). Washington, DC: American Psychological Association. doi: 10.1037/13274-020.

Roeser, R. W., Schonert-Reichl, K. A., Jha, A., Cullen, M., Wallace, L., Wilensky, R., ... Harrison, J. (2013). Mindfulness training and reductions in teacher stress and burnout: Results from two randomized, waitlist-control field trials. *Journal of Educational Psychology, 105*(3), 787–804. doi:10.1037/a0032093.

Santoro, D. A. (2011). Good teaching in difficult times: Demoralization in the pursuit of good work. *American Journal of Education, 118*(1), 1–23. doi:10.1086/662010.
Santoro, D. A. (May 3, 2012). Teacher demoralization and teacher burnout: Why the distinction matters. *AJE Forum, Forum of the American Journal of Education.* Retrieved from http://www.ajeforum.com/teacher-demoralization-and-teacher-burnout-why-the-distinction-matters/.
Seierstad, C., & Kirton, G. (2015). Having it all? Women in high commitment careers and work-life balance in Norway. *Gender, Work & Organization, 22*(4), 390–404. doi:10.1111/gwao.12099.
Seiz, J., Voss, T., & Kunter, M. (2015). When knowing is not enough: The relevance of teachers' cognitive and emotional resources for classroom management. *Frontline Learning Research, 3*(1), 55–77.
Selye, H. (1974). *Stress without distress.* New York, NY: J. B. Lippincott Company.
Shulman, L. S. (1986). Those who understand: Knowledge growth in teaching. *Educational Researcher, 15*(2), 4–14. doi: 10.2307/1175860.
Shulman, L. S. (1987). Knowledge and teaching: Foundations of the new reform. *Harvard Educational Review, 57*(1), 1–22.
Soysa, C., & Wilcomb, C. (2015). Mindfulness, self-compassion, self-efficacy, and gender as predictors of depression, anxiety, stress, and well-being. *Mindfulness, 6*(2), 217–226. doi: 10.1007/s12671-013-0247-1.
Sutton, R. E., & Wheatley, K. F. (2003). Teachers' emotions and teaching: A review of literature and direction for future research. *Educational Psychology Review, 15*(4), 327–358.
Swain, H. (January 26, 2016). Mindfulness: The craze sweeping through schools is now at a university near you. *The Guardian RSS.* Retrieved from https://www.theguardian.com/education/2016/jan/26/mindfulness-craze-schools-university-near-you-cambridge.
Taylor. S. E. (2003). *Health psychology* (5th ed.). New York, NY: Pearson Education Company.
Tsang, K. K., & Liu, D. (2016). Teacher demoralization, disempowerment and school administration. *Qualitative Research in Education, 5*(2), 200–225.
U.S. Department of Education, National Center for Education Statistics. (May 2011). The Condition of Education 2011 (NCES 2011-033), Indicator 26. Retrieved from https://nces.ed.gov/pubs2011/2011033.pdf.
U.S. Department of Labor, U.S. Bureau of Labor Statistics. (2016). 1948–2015 annual averages, Current Population Survey. Retrieved from https://www.bls.gov/cps/.
Voydanoff, P. (1984). *Work and family: Changing roles of men and women.* Mountain View, CA: Mayfield Publishing Company.
Weiner, L. (2003). *From working girl to working mother: The female labor force in the United States, 1820–1880.* North Carolina: University of North Carolina Press.
World Health Organization (WHO). (2017). Mental health in the workplace. Retrieved from http://www.who.int/mental_health/in_the_workplace/en.
Yu, X., Wang, P., Zhai, X., Dai, H., & Yang, Q. (2015). The effect of work stress on job burnout among teachers: The mediating role of self-efficacy. *Social Indicators Research, 122*(3), 701–708. doi 10.1007/s11205-014-0716-5.

Chapter 10

"I Need Collaboration Too!"

Exploring the Nature of Collaboration between a Literacy Coach and University Teacher Collaborator

Grace Kang

ABSTRACT

This study examined a literacy coach's evolving relationships with teachers and a university teacher collaborator (UTC) by focusing on the collaborative culture in an elementary school building. The study highlights how the literacy coach provided effective professional development for teachers by seeking out collaboration with the UTC. Research has shown that a change agent in the school who has relationships with the staff is apt to have a long-lasting impact on a teacher's instruction (Cantrell & Hughes, 2008; Desimone, Porter, Garet, Yoon, & Birman, 2002; Parise & Spillane, 2010), yet the literacy coaches also need their own form of professional development, collaboration, and inquiry (Parise & Spillane, 2010; Rodgers & Rodgers, 2007). Valued tenets of collaboration that arose from the study are also highlighted. A call is made for more job-embedded opportunities for professional development that will lead teachers to inspiration and meaning in the work they do. In this study, a literacy coach's collaborative episodes played a significant role in affecting teacher practice.

KEY WORDS

Collaboration; Literacy Coach; Job-embedded; Professional Development

Heidi and Claire are friends after first establishing a relationship as colleagues. Heidi is a university teacher collaborator (UTC) and Claire is a literacy coach. They have spent numerous hours together in planning sessions for lessons they will do with the teachers at Claire's school. As the literacy coach, Claire provides professional development to the teachers in her school. However, at times literacy coaches also need opportunities to grow and learn in their practice.

LITERACY COACHING AS A FORM OF PROFESSIONAL DEVELOPMENT

Professional development (PD) and teacher learning are not limited to the traditional K-12 skill training workshops, where outside experts come in for a short period of time or where teachers attend a workshop outside of their school for a few days. These forms of PD structures have been criticized for being decontextualized from teachers' instruction and lacking collegiality (Cochran-Smith & Lytle, 1999). Workshops and conferences fail to lead to significant change in practice when teachers return to their classrooms, and teachers' dissatisfaction with traditional "one-shot workshop" approaches may be a reason for a paradigm shift (Applebee & Langer 2009; Hawley & Valli, 1999). The field of PD is moving to more job-embedded forms that are dynamic, meaningful, and contextualized (Borko, 2004; Parise & Spillane, 2010; Wood & McQuarrie, 1999). School-level PD in literacy has become a focus in recent years, as evidenced by the fact that many states, districts, and schools are moving toward the literacy coach position as a model of PD (Dole, 2004).

Literacy coach positions have gained prominence in recent years mainly because of the accessibility to teachers in each building. Literacy coaching has been described as "hot" in recent international reports (Cassidy & Cassidy, 2008) and has had an impact on teacher efficacy (Cantrell & Hughes, 2008). Recent research indicates that literacy coaching is responsible for significant improvements in students' literacy learning (Biancarosa, Byrk, & Dexter, 2010) as well as improvements in teachers' knowledge and quality of their language and literacy practices.

Teachers value collaboration with the coaches, ongoing support, and instructional strategies they learn through coaches' work in their classroom and in study groups (Vanderburg & Stephens, 2010). Yet, coaching can be filled with tensions between teachers' goals and improving literacy instruction (Ippolito, 2010) and result in differences in relationships of power and resistance (Rainville & Jones, 2008) and include various emotional aspects within literacy coaching interactions (Hunt, 2016). In Walpole and Blamey's (2008) two-year study of an intense staff development program created by Walpole, the authors studied principals and literacy coaches in twenty different schools. Coaches identified themselves as having multiple roles including assessor, curriculum manager, formative observer, modeler, teacher, and trainer. The participants typically identified coaches as either directors (i.e., "change coaches") or mentors ("content coaches"). Regardless of how literacy coaches identify themselves, they are seen as leaders in their school buildings who have an opportunity to collaborate with teachers, provide contextualized PD, and improve teacher efficacy.

Walpole and Blamey (2008) assert, "Coaching is evolving. In theory, literacy coaches serve teachers through ongoing, comprehensive PD consistent with a system of theory, demonstration, practice, and feedback" (p. 222). Desimone (2009) expands on this notion by finding that learning occurs in many different aspects of practice. To understand teacher learning, it must be studied within multiple contexts, taking into account both the individual teacher learners and the social systems in which they are participants.

Showers and Joyce (1996) explain that in the early 1980s, teachers were expected to learn new strategies, return to school, and implement their new learning smoothly and appropriately. However, the lack of research on how people learn teaching strategies and how schools successfully disseminate innovations contributed to failures in PD (Hawley & Valli, 1999). In today's practice, attention to social organization (Wenger, 2000) and job-embedded PD (Parise & Spillane, 2010) is extremely important and effective. Showers and Joyce (1996) elaborate that the collaborative work of peer coaching is much broader than observations and conferences. Teachers' collaborations inspire and impact their professional growth and learning as they plan instruction, develop curricular materials, and team-teach.

A SOCIOCULTURAL VIEW OF LITERACY COACHING

As coaches and teachers participate in a shared culture, language becomes a social phenomenon that exists as it is used in dialogue within a community of practice. This study is situated within a sociocultural perspective where I draw from Vygotsky's (1978) social constructivism, Bakhtin's (1986) dialogism, and Wenger's (2000) communities of practice. Working in collaboration with a coach or other colleagues has been meaningful and effective in leading to change in teacher practice. Showers and Joyce (1996) assert that teachers who had a coaching relationship where they planned and taught together, practiced new skills and strategies more frequently, then applied these skills and strategies more appropriately than their counterparts who worked alone.

Wenger (2000) views learning as a social process, where competence is historically and socially defined. Learning is defined "as an interplay between social competence and personal experiences. It is a dynamic, two-way relationship between people and the social learning systems in which they participate" (p. 227). Wenger's conceptual framework is based on social-constructivist theory (Vygotsky, 1978), where learning occurs through interaction and scaffolded support from more knowledgeable others. Vygotskian learning theory, often employed when designing K-6 PD experiences, offers a parallel between the learning of students and teachers.

THE ROLE OF COLLABORATION

Developing interpersonal relationships is highly valued when it comes to learning from interactions with colleagues (Bryk, Camburn, & Louis, 1999; Wenger, 2000). Little (1987) reconceptualizes the role of collaboration and the impact of collegiality, presumably, "Something is gained when teachers work together and something is lost when they do not" (p. 492). She studied the possibilities and limits of collegiality among teachers in three groups: studies of the professional "workplace"; studies of organized teacher teaming; and studies of school improvement, teacher preparation, PD, and the implementation of innovations. Little (1987) found that serious collaboration, where teachers engage in the rigorous mutual examination of teaching and learning, was rare. However, when schools were organized to promote collaboration, teachers' work as colleagues promised greater coherence and integration to teaching. Teachers collaborating together equip individuals, groups, and institutions for steady improvement (Little, 1987).

Taylor, Pearson, Clark, and Walpole (1999) observed seventy 1st- to 3rd-grade teachers from fourteen schools in four states and asked them to keep a weekly time log of instructional activities in reading/language arts for two weeks. The four most effective schools used a collaborative model for reading instruction where the regular education teachers worked regularly with the Title I, reading resource, special education, and ELL teachers to provide small group instruction. This study identifies a critical interaction between strong building communication and the capacity to offer high levels of small group instruction. Hence, when the teachers in a school are able to collaboratively work together toward the goal of raising student achievement, they can realize stronger results.

METHODS

Research Questions

The aim of this study was to unpack the nature of collaboration that took place between the literacy coach and the UTC in turn to provide meaningful

PD to the teachers. This case was part of a larger study exploring the culture of collaboration between the literacy coach, teachers, and UTC in an elementary school building. Kang (2016) has also investigated the nature of the relationships between the literacy coach and the classroom teachers. The research questions revolved around the notion of collaboration and how it was enacted in teacher practice and instruction. In order to examine the coach's collaboration with the UTC the research questions were as follows:

- How were the episodes determined and created?
- How was the collaboration that took place with the coach and teacher collaborator then enacted with the teachers?

Site

The study site is Lincoln Elementary School in a small, urban community in the Midwest. In 2011, Lincoln's demographics were 47.6% white, 26.1% black, 3.3% Hispanic, 22.6% Asian, and 0.5% Native American. Twenty-four percent of the families were classified as low-income, which is significantly lower than both the district and the state averages. The teaching staff was also diverse with 83.7% white, 10.8% black, 2% Hispanic, and 3.6% Asian. Most of the staff is seasoned in their teaching experience, however a handful of newer teachers were seen within the school as well.

Participants

The participants involved were Claire, the literacy coach, and Heidi, a UTC. Claire is a European-American female in her fifties with fifteen plus years of teaching in the classroom; it was Claire's second year as the literacy coach in the building. Claire's position involved working with students part-time as a reading specialist and with teachers part-time as a literacy coach.

As a literacy coach, Claire worked with Heidi for her own professional growth. Heidi, the UTC, is an Asian American in her mid-thirties with a wealth of teaching experience, and teachers in the district highly coveted working with her. In this context, the UTC worked with educators by observing classrooms, sharing research, co-planning, demonstrating lessons, side-by-side teaching, and debriefing.

Data Collection

I employed qualitative methods to tell the story of a literacy coach, UTC, and classroom teachers in a small, urban elementary school in the Midwest. This study was a case study that sought to understand the specific context and highlight the participants' perspectives and lived experiences (Bogdan & Biklen, 2007; Dyson & Genishi, 2005). During the observations, I tried to notice and examine particular behaviors by the ways that participants talked and interacted with each other in this particular building.

Observations

The primary form of data collection was observation of collaborative sessions (e.g., conversations with Claire, planning sessions with Heidi and teachers). Observations were audiotaped and transcriptions were embedded in the field notes. Because this study was part of a larger study, I observed at Lincoln Elementary School for three months at different times of the school day depending on Claire's schedule, ranging from two to three times a week for one to three hour(s) each observation session.

Interviews

Semi-structured interviews were also conducted with the literacy coach and the UTC (Kvale, 1996). I stayed close to Kvale's (1996) notion that "the research interview is based on the conversations of daily life and is a professional conversation" (p. 5). I identified key themes and suggested questions a priori to the interviews, yet I was not bound to them, and I altered the questions depending on the depth and different nuances in the participants' responses. I interviewed Claire to validate many of the notions that I gathered to be her values and beliefs, and to see if her perspective was consistent with the data. My purpose through these interviews was to understand the themes of the lived experience from the participants' world, specifically surrounding the nature of collaboration in the school. Interviews were also audiotaped and transcribed.

Data Analysis

I read and analyzed the data inductively through a sociocultural perspective—emphasizing teachers' collaboration as a social activity where meaning and change in one's practice is made when teachers are able to enact and interpret the recurrent events of everyday life through interactions and collaboration with one another (Vygotsky, 1978; Watson-Gegeo, 1988).

Collaboration is defined from the perspectives of the literacy coach and the UTC. I also draw from the sociocultural view of teaching and learning, which is embedded in the role of interaction in the events and practices that are visible in the relationships established among the literacy coach, teachers, and the UTC (Vygotsky, 1978). The collaborative episodes that I observed between Claire and Heidi were all collaborative sessions housed in Claire's office, either between the two of them or with a few other teachers present. These sessions would range from the UTC sharing materials/ideas, discussing current research trends, brainstorming new ideas, pairing children's literature to lessons, writing and co-planning lessons/units, cocreating booklists, crafting plans for a new course of study with the coach and other teachers, and debriefing on lessons/units with the coach and other teachers.

I looked for recurrent patterns/themes and repeated actions/responses from the different participants involved. Then I created emic terminology from the participants' perspectives. For example, Claire noted, "*I need collaboration too!*" Claire expressed that she didn't have anyone in the building to share ideas and brainstorm with and was constantly bombarded by questions and needed for support. Her relationship with Heidi provided an opportunity to "bounce ideas off of each other" and coplan/coconstruct lessons and units.

During the second phase of data analysis, I took notice of consistent valued tenets of open collaboration between all of the participants in the study (many of which were recurrent themes in the first phase of data analysis), which was meaningful specifically to the nature of collaboration as shown in box 10.1.

BOX 10.1 VALUED TENETS IN OPEN COLLABORATION

1. Relationship Capital: The quality of interpersonal connections and relationships (e.g., Claire and Heidi met for lunch to collaborate over spring break, Heidi was able to offer suggestions and Claire didn't take offense because of the trust and rapport that was established).
2. Reciprocal/Coplanned: Goals and content of sessions were created by all participants that were involved (e.g., both Claire and Heidi brainstormed ideas, they both came with texts and materials to share, and they both suggested PD texts and bounced ideas off of each other. They didn't act as the directors with the teachers, but all equally contributed).
3. Constructed/Organic: Authentic meaning making where appropriate lessons, sessions, and units were created for the situation (e.g., Claire and Heidi created a memoir unit with a teacher that was meaningful to the specific needs of the class, Claire observed in a teacher's room to offer suggestions that were tailored to her classroom needs).
4. Job-embedded/Sustained: On-the-job learning opportunities that are contextualized and apply throughout the school day (e.g., Claire and Heidi coconstructed the conclusion to an autobiography unit and it was taught that same day by Claire in a 3rd-grade classroom; notion of open door policy where Claire conversed with teachers readily and daily in her office or in the hallway).

FINDINGS

Valued Tenets in Open Collaboration

Data analysis revealed consistent valued tenets in the nature of open collaboration across the sessions between the literacy coach and the UTC, and the literacy coach and the teachers (box 10.1). This is by no means a comprehensive list of the essential qualities involved in collaboration. Within these four tenets were significant overlap and similarities, but each tenet was salient and meaningful to collaboration meriting a separate category. Moreover, these were the recurrent ideas and topics that were consistent in the participants involved in this study; they are consistent with the notion of informal on-the-job learning opportunities among teachers that can act as powerful tools and inspirations toward professional growth and learning (Little, 1990; Parise & Spillane, 2010). In addition, it is important to note that the nature of collaboration is dynamic, constantly growing, and embedded in teachers' daily experiences throughout the day.

Relationship Capital

Rainville and Jones (2008) state, "For literacy coaches this [shift] might mean asking about a teacher's sick daughter at one moment and guiding a teacher in conducting running records the next; in other words, it involves enacting varied identities to build personal relationships as well as scaffold teachers' ongoing learning in literacy education" (p. 441).

Interpersonal relationships are valuable and necessary within collaboration (Bryk et al., 1999), however, coaching relationships are not easily established (Ippolito, 2010). Putnam and Borko (2000) reveal that teachers developing relationships with a literacy coach is an integral component for learning and knowledge development. In this study, forming a relationship, friendship, or "getting along" was found to be meaningful as the participants were working together.

Reciprocal/coplanned

Vanderburg and Stephens (2010) reveal that teachers did not focus on a list of particular practices when asked about their beliefs and practices, they focused on how they re-envisioned themselves as teachers. Teachers' notions of teaching began to parallel the ways in which they were being taught by their coaches; teachers began to facilitate rather than to direct. In the same vein, Claire did not lead the sessions with teachers, but she waited to see what the teachers were interested in or what they needed assistance with. The UTC, Claire, and the teachers co-planned during the collaborative sessions and teaching and learning were reciprocal.

Constructed/Organic

This tenet talks back to traditional models of PD including "one-size-fits-all" presentations to teacher audiences in "one-shot workshops" with no follow-up support (Robb, 2000), which have been shown to be ineffective (Guskey, 2000; Hawley & Valli, 1999). In contrast, the collaborative episodes in this study provided an opportunity for tailor-made PD that was constructed and organic for specific and individualized contexts.

Job-embedded/Sustained

Borko (2004) suggests that learning can occur in many different aspects of practice for teachers, including their classrooms, their school communities, and PD courses or workshops. Job-embedded PD is becoming more and more prevalent as the traditional forms of PD are receiving more criticism. Parise and Spillane (2010) investigated the empirical relationship between teachers' learning opportunities and changes in their instructional practice. The authors suggest that "it may be worthwhile for both school leaders and policymakers to pay more attention than they traditionally have to on-the-job learning opportunities by allocating time for teachers to collaborate" (p. 342). Job-embedded/sustained PD was taking place between Claire, the UTC, and the teachers in the unplanned nature of collaboration and in the notion of the "revolving door."

Coach's Collaboration with Teacher Collaborator

"I Need Collaboration Too!"

Claire and Heidi's collaborative relationship embodied all four of the valued tenets in open collaboration (Box 10.1) and served as a model collaborative relationship. They have worked together for two years, and they met weekly in collaboration sessions. I began my observations in the middle of their second year working together, where they were extremely comfortable with brainstorming ideas together, and even at times, disagreeing with each other.

Claire expressed that "I need collaboration too!" and that it was helpful to have someone to plan, brainstorm, and work with at the same level. Claire shared that she had not had the opportunity to collaborate with anyone else in the building, whereas a grade-level teacher had teammates and Claire to seek out collaboration. She found value in the trust and rapport that she had developed with Heidi and believed it was a privilege to have the opportunity to meet with her weekly; the other literacy coaches in the district did not have the wealth of knowledge and plethora of resources that Heidi offered. Claire shared that the relationship she had with Heidi is one she would *aspire* to have with her teachers. Claire truly valued the collaborative sessions with Heidi because "we brainstorm together, we come up with what's in the best interests of kids, we talk about how to look at work."

Claire and Heidi's collaborative relationship was not only valuable in the resources and opportunity to coconstruct lessons, but it was also a model relationship in how Claire hoped to collaborate with the teachers in the building. This was not Claire's intent; but it was apparent that Claire gleaned a lot from her relationship with Heidi. The tenets of valuable open collaboration were consistent between Claire's relationship with Heidi and Claire's relationships with the teachers.

Substantial collegiality among teachers must go beyond "getting along" and "working well together" (Little, 1990, p. 511). Little (1990) revealed that a deeper way that researchers can look at collegiality is to pay attention to the strong and weak ties among teachers, which can be seen by looking at the extent to which teachers affect one another's practice. Claire was taking graduate courses at the local state university and Heidi was also pursuing a degree, so Claire had asked Heidi to look over a project in one of the first sessions I observed. Both of them apologized and assured me that they don't usually use their sessions to discuss graduate school projects, but I was interested in what these sessions looked like at all levels. Heidi made a comment to Claire about the validity of representing culture by focusing on the music and traditions of ethnic holidays in a discussion they had about Claire's project on multiculturalism.

Heidi: I think one criticism that people have about multiculturalism in schools and I think she might have brought it up, is the whole idea of what we mean by multicultural . . . like "Hey, it's International Fest Day or so we're going to have an International Fest and that's how we're going to take care of the fact that people are different." So, I see the "I am" part as a very, much more contextualized, indepth look at differences more than it's Chinese New Year, so we're going to have a Lunar Festival, it's Black History month, so we're going to do a Black History month walk, it's Kwanza, so let's all wear our whatever clothes.
Claire: Right, right. And I had issues with it's Black History month, it's always be whatever literature or . . .
Heidi: And not that it's a bad thing, I just think there is criticism over how schools are going to address things like that, maybe that's the answer to it, you know?
Claire: And maybe I should put it out there that this is one of many things that we do, but there is question out there if that's the way to embrace it.
Heidi: Right, and is it a way to honor it. I think it's interesting to just hear and especially if you've got a whole bunch of different people in your class.
Claire: We have great conversations.
Heidi: So, it would be good to hear . . . like Veronica, what do you think about this?

Claire: Yeah!
Heidi: So, she just went to Chicago to celebrate Chinese New Year. "Do you get offended by this? Do you think this is a good way to actually represent what that actually means to you and your family and to your culture? Like what do you think about the music that we use?" And I think it would be interesting to hear what people have to say about that.
Claire: Interestingly enough we had a celebration that night and 250 people showed up.
Heidi: Wow, at school?
Claire: I know, at school, on a Friday night.
Heidi: So, I would talk about that and see what people have to say. And then your presentation will be like an hour (Laughing).
Claire: I know.
Heidi: But, I think it's interesting because I feel like it's that whole thing we have the best of intentions, and then when you hear someone else's take on it, you're like, wait, that's not what I intended it to be like or how you would think of it. So, I don't know, just something I'm thinking.
Claire: Alright, I appreciate that comment.

Although Heidi made a comment that could have made Claire feel uncomfortable or judged, she was able to say it respectfully, and Claire's notion of multiculturalism was altered. It was also meaningful that they felt safe and comfortable looking at Claire's project during the bulk of this session. They had spent over thirty minutes looking at Claire's PowerPoint presentation, discussing multiculturalism, and working on citing references. As in a friendship, they naturally segued into what the teachers were working on and started planning for next week's session. It was a relaxed and comfortable environment where it was apparent that they had worked together on a weekly basis. Claire and Heidi valued relationship capital, which was built on trust and rapport. They would be described as colleagues who were "developing a friendship" and "working well together," but at the same time they were willing to offer advice and suggestions that could ultimately affect one another's practice.

"This unit sounds really cool." Joseph, a 5th-grade teacher in the building, had collaborated with Claire throughout the course of the year, and it was a relationship that had grown and developed. Claire and Joseph had co-planned organic units and she modeled lessons in Joseph's classroom. She saw a drastic and dynamic change in his instructional planning and teaching. Claire was thrilled to share about Joseph's desire for the learning to be authentic and genuine in a collaboration session with Heidi. Claire and Joseph had talked earlier that day and Joseph shared that he would love to have Claire come in again over 4th quarter. He had mentioned a memoir and poetry unit that he was planning. Following is the conversation that Claire and Heidi had in the initial planning stages:

Claire: The other thing to think about before I dash down there, *Joseph is so excited.*
Heidi: About the photo-memoir?
Claire: And you're going to be excited because you know what he does?
Heidi: What?
Claire: He rolls poetry and memoirs all together.
Heidi: Oh that's good.
Claire: And let's you create.
Heidi: So, you can pick the genre that your memoir's going to be in. That's perfect because I brought—
Claire: I know, isn't he cool?
Heidi: I brought different examples of how people put a memoir together and a couple of them are poetry.
Claire: Oh, that's awesome.
Heidi: I was totally thinking that.
Claire: So then I mentioned that we had sort of brainstormed for him about, you know, the photo. And he was like, "I love it, and the kids could walk around the school and they could be like, my life at Lincoln." And he was like, "Wouldn't that be cool, kids could have cameras hanging around their necks." He was like all over it (almost shouting).
Heidi: Oh good, good.
Claire: So I'm thinking some kids could use the template and I was thinking along the lines of this, but taking this up to that fifth grade level, more of a memoir because he wants them to have a book when they're finished to take home at the end of the year.
Heidi: Mmm hmm.
Claire: Then I said, "Would you care if we kind of play with that?" And he was like, "I would love to have you in fourth quarter again, if you want to do this with me."
Heidi: Yeah, that would be cool.

Due to the unplanned, yet job-embedded, nature of collaboration I was unable to observe the discussion with Joseph, but I was able to observe some sessions that Heidi and Claire had when co-planning this memoir unit. Heidi excitedly commented, "This unit sounds really cool, I almost want to do it with you guys," and this is how she gained entry into not only co-planning and constructing this unit but modeling the lessons with Claire in Joseph's room over the course of this unit. In the span of the three-week spring break, Heidi and Claire had met several times to co-plan and construct this unit outside of school, which was organic and authentic for the needs of Joseph's class.

Later, Claire revealed to me that the unit was progressing well and Joseph even wanted to meet with Heidi as well. She wanted to give Joseph space and autonomy since the idea was his initial idea and it was his classroom.

Heidi→Claire→Krystal

In another collaborative session, Claire sought out Heidi's expertise when faced with difficultly in creating a concluding lesson for an autobiography unit in a 3rd-grade teacher's, Krystal's, classroom. Krystal was at the final stages of an autobiography unit that she coplanned with Claire, which originally Claire had co-planned with Heidi. Since this unit had originally been co-planned with Heidi, Claire came back to brainstorm ideas on how to pull the biographies together for the ending piece. Heidi suggested going back to look at the conclusions in the model texts that were used. Claire wasn't exactly sure what they looked like, so she rushed off to the 2nd-grade classroom to look through the tub of biographies. Claire came back with a tub of books and they dug through them. They noticed that many of the books, instead of having concluding endings, had circular endings. Heidi suggested that it would be a good idea for students to write about where they are intending to go in the future or possibly thinking about what they have learned about themselves or about life through working on this autobiography.

Heidi: Yeah, maybe it would be appropriate for them to talk about their futures- what they hope to do, this coming year, goals.
Claire: Yeah, I don't want it to be, "When I grow up I want to be a fireman," because I think that's like for some kids they can't even, (start to whisper) like I have kids that are taking care of themselves. They don't know where dinner's coming from. They don't know what the heck they want to be when they grow up. I think that's asking a lot of kids.
Heidi: Or maybe something that you learned so far.
Claire: Oh, that's good.
Heidi: Now that I look back at this autobiography that I made, what have I learned about myself? Or what have I learned about life? Maybe you can pose questions and they could choose to answer one of them for a conclusion. And it kind of goes with what you've been doing already with reader's response.
Claire: Yeah, it really does. Cause they've actually said they pull out a line, kind of thing.
Heidi: Because in the questions that we did for reader's response we did what does the author want us to learn.
Claire: I really like that even *better*. See, I *knew* you would brainstorm and come up with some—I trust you, see I have like 40 minutes.
Heidi: (Laughing).

Shortly after the discussion, Claire modeled this lesson in Krystal's 3rd-grade classroom. She started off by rereading the ending of their mentor text, *Once Upon a Time* by Eve Bunting aloud to them. Claire then went through the questions that she co-planned with Heidi on an overhead:

Ask yourself.
What have you learned about yourself?
What have you learned about your life?
What have you learned about your family?
What piece of advice would you give after thinking about your life?
What do you want people to remember about you from this book?

After she shared the suggestions of what they could include in their endings, she modeled three of the questions in her own conclusion. She reiterated that this was just a start and that she would proceed to add more details about each question in her ending.

I learned that I really enjoy having a big family. I would tell people to enjoy their time together. I learned that I always want the best for everyone, especially my students.

In Claire's modeling in Krystal's classroom, Heidi's words reverberated through Claire's words in the classroom (Bakhtin, 1986). Claire's word choice in her modeling supports Bakhtin's theory (1986) that language is a social phenomenon that exists as it is used by people to address each other; that is, it exists in dialogue.

When Krystal was at a standstill about how to end the autobiography unit she immediately ran to Claire; when Claire was in a conundrum, she quickly sought out Heidi for assistance. Claire had complete trust that through dialogue with Heidi about this unit, she would be able to provide the additional support Krystal needed. This collaborative culture is apparent in the similar questions in bold suggested by Heidi and the actual questions that Claire proposed to Krystal's class.

This notion of collaborative culture is a reverberation of ideologies, values, beliefs, and words beginning with Heidi to Claire, then Claire to Krystal, in this instance, and then in turn, to the rest of the school building. Similarly, Dyson and Genishi (2005) assert that Bakhtin's notions of our everyday voices are absorbed into more complex and artful forms of communication, which is true of children and adults alike.

IMPLICATIONS AND SIGNIFICANCE

Literacy coaches serve teachers through ongoing, comprehensive PD consistent with a system of theory, demonstration, practice, and feedback (Joyce &

Showers, 2002). The field of literacy coaching as a form of job-embedded, ongoing, and contextualized PD is a developing and burgeoning field. Many studies look at the roles and responsibilities of coaching (Dole, 2004; L'Allier & Elish-Piper, 2007; L'Allier, Elish-Piper, & Bean, 2010; Walpole & Blamey, 2008), and the impact that coaching has on teachers' beliefs and practices (Biancarosa et al., 2010; Blachowicz, Obrochta, & Fogelberg, 2005; Vanderburg, & Stephens, 2010). However, what is needed is more studies on the development and growth of meaningful collaborative relationships within coaching. This study highlights how collaboration and PD between a literacy coach and UTC was enacted, how it contributed to the teachers' collaborative culture, and how it inspired professional growth and learning.

This case study of a literacy coach and a UTC reveals that a literacy coach's own professional growth and collaboration can improve and strengthen teacher practice. Literacy coaching is a form of PD that is built on social-constructivist theories of learning (Rodgers & Rodgers, 2007). One of Vygotsky's (1978) key components of social constructivism is scaffolding, where a more able peer provides assistance throughout learning in order to advance learning. Scaffolding played an important role as Heidi collaborated with Claire, and Claire worked with the teachers. These collaborative episodes can be considered an instantiation of Vygtosky's zone of proximal development as the UTC collaborated with Claire, and as Claire interacted with the teachers to build independence for new teaching practices and ideas. These opportunities for collaboration provided PD that was contextualized where Claire and the teachers improved their practice and directly applied the work with Heidi. These relationships highlight how job-embedded PD can be dynamic and nuanced, whereas traditional PD from an outside expert may never make it back into the classroom.

Claire talked and interacted with teachers in similar ways to Heidi's interactions with her. Both Claire and Heidi co-planned their collaborative sessions with teachers and allowed teachers to choose the topic of the sessions before they offered suggestions or ideas. Also, the ways in which Claire repeated Heidi's words and the teachers also repeated Claire's words demonstrates the dialogic nature of their appropriations of ways of talking across episodes (Bakhtin, 1986). Moreover, Heidi's words and talk reverberated within all of the participants across various collaborative episodes.

Claire's relationships with the UTC and the teachers embodied strong relationship capital, reciprocal learning, organic construction, and job-embedded work to create a strong culture of collaboration in this building. The valued tenets in the nature of open collaboration across the sessions among all of the participants in this study were consistent. Furthermore, this study suggests that a literacy coach can be a means for more job-embedded PD that can provide opportunities for teachers to be inspired in their practice. The study suggests it is worth allocating time and opportunities for teachers to collaborate during the school day.

A limitation to this study includes the accessibility of teachers that were closed to collaboration. It would be meaningful to understand teachers' perspectives and why teachers were closed to collaboration with a literacy coach. A second limitation was the difficulty when trying to observe teachers who chose to collaborate with Claire due to the sporadic nature of collaboration sessions.

It is also important to note that like all social practices, coaching is situated and each participant carries multiple identities in a specific context. Each teacher in this study approached and interacted with the literacy coach with multiple identities, such as age, race, gender, years of teaching experience, and years of teaching specifically at Lincoln Elementary School. Further research on the nature of how multiple identities play a role in the collaboration with a literacy coach would be dynamic and meaningful.

Rainville and Jones (2008) studied how coaches' verbal and nonverbal language can be used to position themselves, both consciously and unconsciously, in ways that are supportive or detrimental to their work as a coach. They found that power struggles between teachers and coaches were less likely to occur when coaches were able to develop some type of relationship with their teachers. Further research on the relationship between the coach and the teachers is also needed in order to see how trust and rapport with the coaches is developed in order to impact teacher practice. This opens a door for more case studies on literacy coaches to provide a deep analysis of the collaboration that takes place in a specific context.

Although literacy coaching has been criticized as another fad in education, it is continuing to receive more attention as a favorable form of PD. The work of a literacy coach is complex; it's essential to have a strong knowledge base in literacy instruction, a deep understanding of the interplay of relationships, and experiences with the dynamic nature of collaboration. Despite the complexity, the work of a literacy coach can lead to inspiring and impacting teacher practice.

REFERENCES

Applebee, A. N., & Langer, J. A. (2009). What is happening in the teaching of writing? *English Journal, 98*(5), 18–28. Bakhtin, M. (1986). The problem of speech genres. In M. M. Bakhtin (Ed.), *Speech genres and other late essays*. Austin, TX: University of Texas Press.

Biancarosa, G., Bryk, A. S., & Dexter, E. R. (2010). Assessing the value-added effects of literacy collaborative professional development on student learning. *Elementary School Journal, 111*(1), 7–34.

Blachowicz, C. L. Z., Obrochta, C., & Fogelberg, E. (2005). Literacy coaching for change. *Educational Leadership, 62*(6), 55–58.

Bogdan, R. C., & Biklen, S. K. (2007). *Qualitative research for education: An introduction to theories and methods* (5th ed.). Boston, MA: Pearson.

Borko, H. (2004). Professional development and teacher learning: Mapping the terrain. *Educational Researcher, 33*(8), 3–15.

Bryk, A. S., Camburn, E., & Louis, K. S. (1999). Professional community in Chicago elementary schools: Facilitating factors and organizational consequences. *Educational Administration Quarterly, 35*(5), 751–781.

Cantrell, S. C., & Hughes, H. K. (2008). Teacher efficacy and content literacy implementation: An exploration of the effects of extended professional development with coaching. *Journal of Literacy Research, 40*(1), 95–127.

Cassidy, J., & Cassidy, D. (2008). What's hot, what's not for 2008. *Reading Today, 25*(4), 1–11.

Cochran-Smith, M., & Lytle, S. (January 1999). Relationship of knowledge and practice: Teacher learning in communities. In A. Iran-Nejad & C. Pearson (Eds.), *Review of research in education, 24*, 249–306. Washington, DC: American Educational Research Association.

Desimone, L. M. (2009). Improving impact studies of teachers' professional development: Toward better conceptualizations and measures. *Educational Researcher, 38*(3), 181–199.

Desimone, L., Porter, A. C., Garet, M. S., Yoon, K. S., & Birman, B. F. (2002). Effects of professional development on teachers' instruction: Results from a three-year longitudinal study. *Educational Evaluation and Policy Analysis, 24*(2), 81–112.

Dole, J. (2004). The changing role of the reading specialist in school reform. *Reading Teacher, 57*(5), 462–471.

Dyson, A. H., & Genishi, C. (2005). *On the case: Approaches to language and literacy research.* New York, NY: Teachers College Press.

Guskey, T. R. (2000). *Evaluating professional development.* Thousand Oaks, CA: Corwin Press.

Hall, B. (2004). Literacy coaches. An evolving role. *Carnegie Reporter, 3*(1), 10–19.

Hawley, D. W., & Valli, L. (1999). The essentials of effective professional development. In L. Darling-Hammond & G. Sykes (Eds.), *Teaching as the learning profession: Handbook of policy and practice* (pp. 127–150). San Francisco, CA: Jossey-Bass.

Hunt, C. (November 2016). Getting to the heart of the matter: Discursive negotiations of emotions within literacy coaching interactions. *Teaching and Teacher Education, 60*, 331–343.

Ippolito, J. (2010). Three ways that literacy coaches balance responsive and directive relationships with teachers. *Elementary School Journal, 111*(1), 164–190.

Joyce, B., & Showers, B. (2002). *Student achievement through staff development* (3rd ed.). Alexandria, VA: Association of Supervision and Curriculum Development.

Kang, G. (2016). The value of coaching: Collaborative relationships spur professional growth. *Journal of Staff Development, 37*(5), 49–52.

Kvale, S. (1996). *Interviews.* Thousand Oaks, CA: Sage.

Little, J. W. (1987). Teachers as colleagues. In V. Richardson-Koehler (Ed.), *Educators' handbook: A research perspective* (pp. 491–518). White Plains, NY: Longman.

Little, J. W. (1990). The persistence of privacy: Autonomy and initiative in teachers' professional relations. *Teachers College Record, 9*(4), 504–536.

L'Allier, S. K., & Elish-Piper, L. (November 2007). *Does literacy coaching make a difference? The effects of literacy coaching on reading achievement in grades K-3 in a reading first district.* Paper presented at the meeting of the National Reading Conference, Austin, TX.

L'Allier, S., Elish-Piper, L., & Bean, R. M. (2010). What matters for elementary literacy coaching? Guiding principles for instruction improvement and student achievement. *The Reading Teacher, 63*(7), 544–554.

Parise, L. M., & Spillane J. P. (2010). Teaching learning and instructional change: How formal and on-the-job learning opportunities predict change in elementary school teachers' practice. *The Elementary School Journal, 110*(3), 323–346.

Putnam, R. T., & Borko, H. (2000). What do new views of knowledge and thinking have to say about research on teacher learning? *Educational Researcher, 29*(1), 4–15.

Rainville, K. N., & Jones, S. (2008). Situated identities: Power and positioning in the work of a literacy coach. *The Reading Teacher, 61*(6), 440–448.

Robb, L. (2000). *Redefining staff development: A collaborative model for teachers and administrators.* Portsmouth, NH: Heinemann.

Rodgers, A., & Rodgers, E. M. (2007). *The effective literacy coach: Using inquiry to support teaching and learning.* New York, NY: Teachers College Press.

Showers, B., & Joyce, B. (1996). The evolution of peer coaching. *Educational Leadership, 53*(6), 12–16.

Taylor, B. M., Pearson, D. P., Clark, K. F., & Walpole, S. (1999). Effective schools/accomplished teachers. *The Reading Teacher, 53*(2), 156–159.

Vygotsky, L. S. (1978). *Mind and society.* Cambridge, MA: Harvard University Press.

Vanderburg, M., & Stephens, D. (2010). The impact of literacy coaching: What teachers value and how teachers change. *Elementary School Journal, 111*(1), 141–163.

Van Manen, M. (1990). *Researching lived experience.* New York, NY: The State University of New York.

Walpole, S., & Blamey, K. L. (2008). Elementary literacy coaches: The reality of dual roles. *Reading Teacher, 62*(3), 222–231.

Watson-Gegeo, K. (1988). Ethnography in ESL: Defining the essentials. *TESOL Quarterly, 22*(4), 575–592.

Wenger, E. (2000). *Communities of practice: Learning, meaning, and identity.* Cambridge, NY: Cambridge University Press.

Wood, F. H., & McQuarrie, F. (1999). On-the-job-learning. *Journal of Staff Development, 20*(3), 1–5.

Chapter 11

Charter School Special Educators

Expressions of Hope, Courage, and Strength

Sarah Irvine Belson

ABSTRACT

Public charter school legislation came about in the United States in large part because of dissatisfaction with the traditional public school system (Nathan, 1997). Whether or not that dissatisfaction is justified or manufactured by advocates of school choice and privatization, children with disabilities enroll in these schools and therefore qualified special teachers must staff these schools in order meet each student's educational needs. Special education teachers in public charter schools must draw on hope, courage, and strength in order to engage in evidence-based special education practices, even when faced with a lack of resources or willingness to differentiate or modify charter school's curriculum or approach. The work of special education teachers in charter school settings should be examined to uncover how teachers make use of evidence-based practice while also maintaining commitment to social justice and educational equity, as they advocate and provide opportunities for students with disabilities. Just as all special education teachers need mentoring and support as they engage in practices derived from evidence-based practice grounded in hope, courage, and strength, so should charter school teachers given the particular needs of their work in these experimental settings.

KEY WORDS

Special Education; Educational Equity; Hope

INTRODUCTION

The central tenets of special education are grounded in the quest for educational opportunity for all students. Throughout the legislative mandates that authorize special education, an underlying theme of increasing access to education for students with disabilities focuses on a greater purpose. For example, the *Individuals with Disabilities Education Act* (IDEA, 2004), the federal act that requires that states provide special education services, states that the purpose of the law is

> (a) To ensure that all children with disabilities have available to them a free appropriate public education that emphasizes special education and related services designed to meet their unique needs and prepare them for further education, employment, and independent living; (b) To ensure that the rights of children with disabilities and their parents are protected; (c) To assist states, localities, educational service agencies, and federal agencies to provide for the education of all children with disabilities; and (d) To assess and ensure the effectiveness of efforts to educate children with disabilities. (IDEA, 2004, pp. 2653–2654)

These four purposes evoke a mission to provide a broad set of services with the goal of increasing access to a high-quality educational experience. In the first purpose, an individual can easily infer that by meeting each child's "unique needs," schools are entrusted with the responsibility and opportunity to understand and appreciate the diversity of the human experience. Through the process by which school "prepare(s) them for further education, employment, and independent living" (IDEA, 2004, p. 2648) teachers must believe the child is capable of growth and eventual success as an independent individual functioning fully in society.

The second purpose (IDEA, 2004, p. 2657) states specifically that the child's rights must be protected. While a direct interpretation of the law means access to due process and appropriate assessments, the second purpose also suggests that the child with a disability has the same rights afforded to all students. An individual might envision that the "rights" of a child with a disability include those rights dictated by the Bill of Rights or other social doctrines that embody a democratic citizenry. The third and fourth purposes of IDEA (IDEA, 2004, p. 2662) are more procedural. However, the third and fourth purposes convey an overall sense that the purpose of the federal mandate for special education is to engage in a process that allows all individuals to participate in society and in schooling, with the expectation will ultimately result in increased opportunities for every child. The IDEA further states,

> The State must have in effect policies and procedures to demonstrate that the State has established a goal of providing full educational opportunity to all

children with disabilities, aged birth through 21, and a detailed timetable for accomplishing that goal. (IDEA, 2240, sec. 300.109)

This element of the Act suggests that in its very purpose and design, the goal of *IDEA* embodies an underlying expectation that access to education will increase opportunities for children with disabilities.

Context of Special Education in Public Charter Schools

Teachers of special education in public charter schools are particularly challenged in that they often do not have the same level of resources that a state or school district has to meet the needs of students with disabilities (Gawlik, 2016; Gross & Lake, 2014). Public charter schools, by their very nature, often have a specific focus, such as a college preparatory program, arts-integration, or bilingual education (Nathan, 1997). These specific areas of focus may serve as challenge to the requirement to focus on the needs of students with a disability.

While public charter schools represent just 8% of public schools, the number of schools has increased significantly (Waitoller, Maggin, & Trzaska, 2017). Since 1999 the number of students *enrolled in public charter schools increased from 0.3 million students to 2.3 million students* (Kena et al., 2015). The rapid growth and autonomous nature of the public charter school offers an opportunity to study how hope, courage, and strength can support the work of special education teachers and offer a model for classroom teachers in other settings. Students with disabilities are often the most challenging learners in the classroom, and by embracing these students with compassion and creativity, classroom teachers in public charter schools may be in a special position to help these students succeed.

Nationally, the placement of children with disabilities in public charter schools has been an area of concern (Drame, 2011; Miron & Nelson, 2002). While charter schools have autonomy from district authority and room for creativity, charter schools must still meet state and federal mandates regarding the provision of education, including providing a Free and Appropriate Public Education (FAPE) and Individualized Education Programs (IEPs) to students with disabilities as directed by IDEA (2004) (Miron & Nelson, 2002).

Some researchers have observed weaknesses in the provision of special education services in public charter schools and limits in the degree to which public charter schools develop special education personnel and infrastructure to support students with disabilities (Drame, 2010; Rhim, Ahearn, & Lange, 2007; Rhim & McLaughlin, 2001). It has been documented that students with disabilities are less likely to be placed in public charter schools than traditional public schools (Estes, 2004; Howe & Welner, 2002), resulting in fewer educational opportunities and inequity. In addition, researchers have observed greater teacher turnover in some public charter schools (Stuit & Smith, 2010). This turnover has been associated with poor academic performance of charter school students including students with disabilities (Bettini, Cheyney, Wang, & Leko, 2014; Sass, 2006).

For example, in Washington, DC, the Office of the State Superintendent of Education, which oversees the delivery of services for students with special education needs, operates under a corrective action compliance agreement (Aguirre, Maisterra, & Masoodi, 2014). This compliance agreement requires close oversight of timelines, placements, and a range of services for students across the city in all settings. In DC, the majority of students with special education needs are served in the traditional public school system or through nonpublic placements rather than charter schools, which suggests that students with disabilities do not have the same educational opportunities as their non-disabled peers (Associated Press, 2017; Rhim & O'Neill, 2013).

In 2014, approximately 7,000 students in Washington, DC, were identified as students with disabilities. Of those, 85% were enrolled in the traditional public schools or nonpublic placements (Boundy, 2012). While the overall enrollment of students with disabilities in public charters is approaching 50% as compared with the enrollment of students with disabilities in traditional school systems, only 15% of special education students are enrolled in public charters (Rhim & O'Neill, 2013). The District of Columbia Municipal Regulations contains the FAPE requirement that all local education agencies (LEA) "shall ensure, pursuant to the IDEA, that all students with disabilities, ages 3 to 22, who are residents or wards of the District of Columbia, have available to them a FAPE and that the rights of these students and their parents are protected" (DC Monitoring Compliance Manual, 2013–14, p. 6). According to a 2012 Mathematica report on public charter schools in Washington, DC, charter schools were more likely to enroll students eligible for free and reduced price lunch but less likely to enroll special education students or students of limited English proficiency (Wolf, Kisida, Gutmann, Puma, Eissa, & Rizzo, 2013).

Theoretical Framework for Hope, Courage, and Strength in Special Education

In their 2007 book, *Deconstructing Special Education*, Thomas and Loxley suggest that special education should be driven by ideals, namely the ideals of equity, social justice, and equality. After taking time to address some of the major critics of special education that restrict, rather than uplift, the student with a disability, Thomas and Loxley argue that the goals of special education should ultimately be driven by an inclusive education that builds on teachers' knowledge and experiences (2007). Examining special education through the ideals of hope, courage, and strength may help teachers to both articulate and act on their ideals as well as their pedagogical knowledge and skills (Hoy & Spero, 2005).

Each student comes to school with hopes and dreams and it is the hope that special education teachers function to help every student, as well as their colleagues in the school, fulfill these ambitions (Allinder, 1994; Gawlik, 2016). Special education teachers are looking constantly for opportunities to creatively engage students so that they can reach these aspirational goals. Special education teachers also must have a great amount of courage, hope, and determination; they are often the last opportunity for a student with whom no teacher has been successful. Special education teachers must share a desire to work, both behaviorally and academically, with the most challenging students (Castro, Kelly, & Shih, 2010; Moore, 2004). Special education teachers must also engage in hopeful behavior as they look for opportunities to create environments in which they will be able to reach students who have never been able to compete successfully.

Special education teachers' behaviors, particularly those who stay in high-needs urban schools, can be defined by resilience (Hoy & Spero, 2005). These teachers must believe that their students are resilient enough to overcome past failures. In their study of teachers in special education and in rural areas, Castro, Kelly, and Shih (2010) found traits of resiliency as teachers looked for opportunities to adopt approaches that would increase student learning. These researchers found that teachers made use of strategies that demonstrate resilience, such as advocating for resources, seeking out and forming teacher mentors, and worked to create new resources where none previously existed. Additional research indicates that these skills are needed in public charter school special education environments where resources are few and turnover is high (Wolf et al., 2013).

Special education and special education teacher preparation are often understood to be overly technical and focused solely on students' academic and self-actualization needs (Allinder, 1994). However, patience with traditional classroom practice is rarely a defining characteristic of a special education teaching (Cook & Schirmer, 2003). Special education teachers want to push the outer boundary of what is possible in the classroom and tackle the challenges faced by each of their students (Hoy & Spero, 2005). Special education teachers constantly monitor and encourage their students to perform beyond what they thought was possible or what they feel their students are capable of doing (Boardman, Argüelles, Vaughn, Hughes, & Klingner, 2005). In discussions about their students, special education teachers seek not just to help students learn basic skills but rather to develop their self-esteem and self-assurance (Castro, Kelly, & Shih, 2010). Students in special education often have experienced failure over and over. What they must find in their special education teachers is a person who believes in them and pushes and pulls them to perform in the way they never could before.

Special education teachers are idealistic (Brunetti, 2006). In his study of teachers who had work in high-needs schools over twelve years, Brunetti (2006) found that the ideals of hope, courage, and strength are among those characteristics that special education teachers hold closely and act on every time they are in the classroom. Patterson, Collins, and Abbott (2004) found that special education teachers believe that they can serve students who have been unsuccessful in the school environment. This comports with what Burnetti (2006) found about special education teachers—they believe that they can adapt the curriculum, manipulate the environment, and create modifications to the curriculum that allow the student to succeed where he or she has been failed many times before. Special education teachers constitute a special group of teachers also have courage on a day-to-day basis; their students might forget what they learned the day before and their students might lash out at their teachers in frustrations or anxiety. But special education teachers have the courage to go back to the classroom and strive to support these students (Castro, Kelly, & Shih, 2010).

In their book *What's Public about Charter Schools: Lessons Learned about Choice and Accountability*, Miron and Nelson indicated that some teachers reported as if they felt they did not have the support or resources they needed to meet the needs of students with disabilities (p. 85). Special education teachers regularly try to help the students meet the overall goals of the charter school alongside meeting each child's individual needs (Miron & Nelson, 2002). Parents who place their children with special education needs in the public charter school also act with courage, and hope that their children will succeed in a new environment when they haven't succeeded in the traditional school environment (Gawlik, 2016; Hanushek, Kain, Rivkin, & Branch (2007). Charter schools offer an option to be successful in school, given a different perspective and focus. Special education teachers working in public charter schools are critical for students with disabilities.

In her 2009 essay in *Teacher Education Quarterly* entitled "The Disposition of Hope in Teaching," Birmingham frames a definition of hope as "a belief and action in which teachers engage in an orientation toward a goal or object with a passion and motivation experienced through a moral orientation toward goodness" (p. 31). She describes hope as a teacher desire for the well-being of her students and an approach to strengthen her belief in the learning of all students is not just possible, but an achievable goal (p. 35).

By its very nature, special education is grounded in hope. While the mandate to provide a special education is grounded in a legal precedent through a

FAPE (IDEA, 2004), the act of the provision of an education to children with disabilities could be construed as an act of hope. By providing special education services in the United States, society and schools demonstrate the value of each individual to provide opportunities through education. In another essay, Birmingham (2010) discusses the experiences of mothers of children with autism, suggesting that parents hold a belief that their children are intrinsically good. Many special education teachers appear to hold this same belief in the goodness and worthiness of each student (Castro, Kelly, & Shih, 2010; Cook & Schirmer, 2003). In taking on the provision of educational opportunities for student who may not learn through typical methods, special education teachers frequently embody the hope that drives their everyday actions.

In their book *Educational Courage: Resisting the Ambush of Public Education*, Schniedewind and Sapon-Shevin (2012) outline a process by which teachers engage in acts of resistance to market-driven forces in education policy. The authors suggest that through processes that support the creation of spaces for authentic educational experiences for students (as opposed to high-stakes, assessment-driven activities), teachers demonstrate courage to resist policies that cause stress among teachers and students, force competition among children, and narrow the focus of the curriculum (p. 103). This book encourages teachers and parents to protect students from the stressors of school and pushes teachers and administrators to find ways to provide all students with a democratic education and to provide teachers with the support to engage in a more personal level with their students (p. 32). The authors also suggest that through courage to resist, teachers can provide a more equitable education for all students. Relative to special education and students with disabilities, the authors argue that policies such as IEP diplomas and graduation assessments undermine the achievements of students with disabilities (p. 74).

In his book *Courage to Teach*, Palmer (2010) suggests that teachers undertake a process by which they go beyond the intellectual demands of sharing information but expose themselves and their students to the emotional and perhaps spiritual processes that underlie learning. Palmer posits that teaching should involve a personal connection to one's students and that students and teachers should experience some degree of exposure in order to open themselves up to the curriculum and to deep learning (p. 211). The Center for Courage and Renewal, which offers programming based on Dr. Palmer's writings and perspectives, provides teachers with materials and workshops focused on finding the deeper meaning in their roles as teachers and accepting all of their students (Center for Courage and Renewal, 2017). This work also encourages teachers to provide all students (including students with disabilities) with the opportunity to become self-actualized individuals.

Strength, as it applies to special education, can be conceptualized in two dimensions. The first dimension can be conceived of as a measure of the quality of the interventions applied in special education settings (Cook & Schirmer, 2003). From a technical perspective, special education teachers make use of interventions and approaches that have the quality of strength in that they are applied with consistency and fidelity. This quality of strength draws on the premise of using evidence-based practices—that there are certain sets of practices that have been proven to work in experimental or quasi-experimental studies. The use of research-based practice was described in the reauthorization of IDEA, which demands a "focus on applying replicable research and proven methods of teaching and learning for children with disabilities" (IDEA, 2004, Section 1400(c)(5)). The use of evidence-based practices is a major area of focus in special education teacher preparation as scholars and practitioners look to legitimize the field (Odem et al., 2005).

Making use of practices with strong evidence for success is appealing; special education teachers tend to approach their work with the sense of determination and eagerness to find effective and efficient practices that will help students overcome difficulties (Castro, Kelly, & Shih, 2010; Sharma, Forlin, & Loreman, 2008). Making use of the long history of research on practices and interventions in special education settings is logical in that they provide teachers with approaches that have been successful in other settings. Special education teachers need to have the knowledge of strong practices that they can adapt to make use of in their own classrooms. Knowledge of strong practice can come both from preparation and through the teacher's interaction with communities of practice in special education. Clearly, it makes sense to build on prior experiences in special education as the teacher determines which approaches will most benefit the student.

The second dimension of strength can be thought of as the quality by which special education teachers act on the ideals of hope and courage (Curran, 2017). Without strength in their convictions to act in ways that benefit the student, hope and courage can turn into anxiety and distress (Brunsting, Sreckovic, & Lane, 2014). Special education teachers need not only to know about strong practice, they also need to have strength, as they apply their knowledge of those practices. Strength must combine with the ideals of hope and courage as they work with their colleagues and the child's family to help design the best possible setting for the child. With strength and knowledge behind their convictions, the special education teacher can assert the teacher's knowledge of the field and of the student to make decisions on how to progress forward.

Inclusion and Resilience: Embodiments of Hope, Courage, and Strength in Special Education

Inclusion is a common interpretation of the special education mandate that requires that students with disabilities receive a FAPE in the least restrictive environment (LRE) (IDEA, 2004). Inclusion can be described as an approach to increasing the amount of time the student with a disability spends in the mainstream school environment, during academic and nonacademic components of the school day. Efforts to include the student with a disability in the mainstream school environment have been made for a variety of reasons ranging from economic to social. One reason to support inclusion is to incorporate students with disabilities into the mainstream classroom and promote access to the educational opportunities available to all students.

Advocates of mainstreaming the special education student presume that all students should be part of the social fabric of the school, and that the presence of a student with a disability with peers has benefits for all students. Criticisms of inclusion have arisen, particularly when teachers in general education settings do not have the special education knowledge needed to help the child succeed (Hallahan & Kauffman, 1995). Inclusive practices afford the student with a disability greater access to the general education environment and can be successful with the support of special education approaches and teachers in the design and delivery of instruction.

Inclusion, as a practice common to special education, can be considered as a manifestation of hope, courage, and strength by both teachers and students (Burke & Sutherland, 2004). In order to engage in inclusive practices, special education teachers need to work with their colleagues to create receptive environments for different needs across the school environment (Solis, Vaughn, Swanson, & Mcculley, 2012). This approach includes everything from physically accessible buildings to the use of adaptations and modifications within the general education classroom for both student assessment and instructional approaches (Turnbull, 1995).

To successfully include students who have previously failed without special education supports, teachers need to draw on strong practices and have the knowledge, hope, and courage to act in ways that benefit the student (Turnbull, 1995). The very concept of the provision of special education in general education settings can seem daunting; how can the teacher meet the needs of each of the students in the classroom and ensure that each child is able to succeed? Inclusion demands that the general education and special education teacher have faith in the knowledge and practices each brings to the environment, and that they work together to find ways to fulfill the requirements of each student.

In today's assessment-driven accountability systems, teachers are under great pressure to be certain that each child is able to demonstrate progress (Miron & Nelson, 2002). Many teachers believe that having a student with a disability in the classroom can distract from his or her ability to increase test scores and enhance achievement. However, with courage and strength, teachers can find ways that benefit all students that allow every student to engage in a deeper understanding of the content of the curriculum. Inclusion requires that teachers provide students with multiple ways to represent their understandings, which may ultimately result in broader and deeper content knowledge.

In order to succeed in inclusive environments, students themselves must also be able to draw on hope, courage, and strength (Wehmeyer, Agran, & Hughes, 2000). Children with disabilities in the general education setting must know their strengths and weaknesses and be able to articulate and advocate for themselves. Self-advocating requires a great deal of skill and strength, that is, to be able to acknowledge one's weaknesses is significant in itself; to act on that knowledge requires maturity and conviction. Special and general education teachers must know their students well enough to help them understand what to do to advocate for themselves in the classroom. No small feat, this expectation requires the teacher to be knowledgeable about learning new skills, communicating needs, and responding to needs. The teacher of children with disabilities must have the mental and emotional capability to handle the everyday challenges of gaining access to the curriculum and the social aspects of the school. These demands can be supported by a building resilience on a foundation of hope, courage, and strength (Castro, Kelly, & Shih, 2010).

Beyond the legal mandates for special education is an underlying assumption that access to education will allow a student to experience resilience (Gilmore, Campbell, Shochet, Garland, Smyth, Roberts, & West, 2014). Resilience is the use of hope, courage, and strength as tools to overcome adversity (Castro, Kelly, & Shih, 2010). The purpose of special education is to help children develop these tools. A function of special education is to help children develop strength, to encourage them to advocate for themselves, building hope, and ultimately to achieve.

Morrison and Cosden (1997) suggest that one way to conceptualize resilience for students with disabilities is through an ecological and cultural viewpoint, which the authors term the "ecocultural" context (p. 45). A student's ability to overcome resilience may be based on the settings in which they receive their education and the cultural perspectives on the student's ability to overcome adversity (Castro, Kelly, & Shih, 2010). The programs and elements of special education, as well as the home environment, can serve as protective factors against dropping out of school, substance abuse, and juvenile delinquency (Morrison & Cosden, 1997). Charter schools clearly contribute to the ecocultural context for students with disabilities, given characteristics such as a focus on college access, or because of the requirements that charter school might set for parental involvement (Horvat & Baugh, 2015).

In their chapter on resilience in students with learning disabilities in the *Handbook of Resilience and Children*, Mather and Ofiesh (2005) point out that teachers play a major role in the development of the environment for students with disabilities. Teachers create opportunities for success and enhance the self-esteem and competence of the student (Mather & Ofiesh, 2005). The authors suggest that teachers must make use of effective instruction, support, and empathy (p. 17) in the delivery of special education services. Special education in public charter schools affords the opportunity for teachers to create these environments focused on empathy and grounded in hope, courage, and strength by supporting the unique needs of each student.

Just as hope is an underlying assumption of special education, courage and strength are the tools by which children with disabilities overcome adversity. Resilience can serve as a key component of the provision of special education as teachers expect that the experiences that students have once they are in the support of the special education system will help them overcome challenges faced in the general education classroom (Castro, Kelly, & Shih, 2010).

An example of the interrelation between courage and resilience in students with disabilities can be found in the use of the Circle of Courage Model in special education settings (Brendtro, Brokenleg, & Van Bockern, 2014). In her chapter in the *Handbook of Resilience in Children*, Werner describes her longitudinal studies of resilience in students who were at risk for school failure, and how the concept of resilience is underutilized in school environments (p. 93). Along with effective academic practices in special education, Werner argues that students at risk for school failure (including students with disabilities) need to feel attachment and belonging and need to be treated with altruism and generosity (p. 94). These ideals match well to the concepts of hope, courage, and strength.

In order to create classroom environments in which students can overcome adversity, special education teachers need to act with hope that each student can ultimately succeed (Birmingham, 2009). Without hope, the passion and energy that goes into supporting a student with a disability can fade and reduce the teacher's ability to increase effort to find effective approaches. With strength in conviction and courage to try new approaches, teachers create environments in which resilience can be realized.

Teachers Acting on Hope, Courage, and Strength in Public Charter Schools

To illustrate how the ideals of hope, courage, and strength operate in special education in urban, public charter schools, the following vignettes are recorded from observation in public charter schools in Washington, DC, from the fall, 2015. The vignettes each use pseudonyms for both teachers and students.

Scott

Scott works in a bilingual public charter school and has been affiliated with the school for five years. He started out working in afterschool programs and is now one of the special education teachers supporting children with IEPs. His students come from all over the world. Scott earned his teaching license through an alternative route to the classroom, completing a yearlong residency while taking seminars in the evenings. He is now in his third year of teaching, working in several co-teaching settings (where he supports the general education teacher in the delivery of instruction to all students, including those with disabilities) in classrooms for 2nd through 5th graders. Scott's dedication to the students and the school is powerful. Many of the students relocated from Central or South America, and Scott sees the school as a place that honors the students' cultural backgrounds while helping develop their language skills in both English and Spanish.

Scott's 3rd-grade classroom includes students who have recently joined the school community and who are new to the United States. One of his students from Ecuador has never attended formal schooling. This student, Luis, joined the classroom in mid-October. I saw Scott take Luis aside during a math lesson. He was helping Luis, not with the math lesson, but with his understanding of the classroom and U.S. school culture. Through this act, Scott was making a place of belonging for Luis, encouraging him to engage with him as the teacher, and inviting him into the community. Scott wasn't focused on developing Luis's language skills or making sure he understood conceptual division; Scott was treating him like a human who shouldn't be shunned or ignored. In this act of courage and humanity, Scott was making the decision that Luis's engagement in school should be one of love and caring.

Scott's reflection on his practice illustrates the depth of courage and strength he holds relative to his work as a teacher. He was able to easily rationalize that the most important experience for Luis was that he learns that he can be part of the school environment. Scott felt that his main job during the lesson was not to engage the Luis in his pathway to becoming part of the classroom community.

Gwen

Gwen works in a college preparatory public charter school and teaches 12th graders. The recently completed building would have most college faculty drooling with large classrooms, plentiful laboratory materials, and an airy and open space architecture. Gwen is in her second year as a special education teacher, and, like Scott and the other teachers in this chapter, entered the teaching profession through an alternative certification route. She teaches environmental science and biology to students with disabilities ranging from health disorders to intellectual disabilities to behavior problems.

Gwen exemplifies hope with her determination that all of her students will go on to college. After her first year, she learned to pull back a little; while she doesn't expect all her students to go on to four-year universities right out of high school, she helps them each build pathways to higher education that makes sense and are aspirational. The parents at this school are also determined and hopeful.

One student in Gwen's classroom, Kayla, has already started taking courses at a local trade school and plans to be a hair stylist. However, her parents insist that she earn a high school diploma. Kayla comes to school tired and can be found napping in Gwen's classroom from time to time. While some, more seasoned teachers might see this as disrespectful, Gwen allows her to slump over on her desk and close her eyes. As long as Kayla gives Gwen a thumbs-up when she is asked, she is allowed to look as though she is sleeping through environmental science class. This act of strength and trust in her students allows Gwen to continue to manage her classroom while providing the needed compassion that Kayla so desperately needs. These few moments of exposure, where she can simply close her eyes, give Kayla the sense that she is loved and understood by her teacher.

Gwen reflected on her approach with Kayla as one of mutual respect. She feels that Kayla trusts her to push her when needed while still allowing her the space to relax and recover from the challenges of her life. Gwen's attitude reflects her sensitivity and the depth of her knowledge of her students' needs. She appreciates that in order to create positive outcomes for Kayla, she needs to focus on both her emotional and intellectual needs. Within this relationship built on mutual respect, Gwen can push Kayla to rise above her current situation and aspire to postsecondary education.

Jordan

Jordan is a middle school special education teacher at a public charter, which is among the highest performing public schools in terms of students' test scores on the city's annual standardized tests. After completing his bachelor's degree at an Ivy League university, Jordan joined the school through an alternative route to teaching. The majority of students who attend Jordan's school live right across the street in a housing project, which serves families well below the poverty line. In order to enroll in the school, a student's guardian must commit to strict enrollment, behavioral, and participation policies, which mandate that the student follow specific procedures related to attendance, dress code, and behavior guidelines and consequences. In addition, the guardian must maintain regular communication with the school administrator or risk the student's dismissal from the school. These cornerstone elements of the schools' policies and charter mission are central to the themes of the school, along with a focus on college preparation. Each class group takes the name of various college and universities, and each student is expected to attend and graduate from postsecondary education.

Jordan's role is that of a special education teacher in English and Language Arts. He teaches large classes that include students with and without disabilities. His curriculum is focused on developing students' appreciation of literature, as well as their abilities to write and express their ideas. Jordan looks to engage his students through literature that he feels is meaningful and relatable. He begins each class by reading to students from books such as *One Crazy Summer* by Williams-Garcia (2011); he clearly focuses on students' abilities to analyze the books and look for evidence-based statements.

Jordan also has the courage to have students talk about their own experiences and relate those narratives to the experiences of the characters in the books. For example, he can pick up the book *The Crossover* by Kwame Alexander (2014) to help students find examples of literary devices and Common Core State Standards skills. Jordan's depth of knowledge of his content and his students is demonstrated by the ease with which he draws students into literature and into reflections on what they are learning.

The strength of the urban public charter school special education teacher can be seen in the teacher's capacity to engage with colleagues, to help educate the school's administration, and to work with students who may seem resistant to making changes. The latter, working with students who seem to demonstrate learned helplessness, may be the clearest example requiring strength. Teachers must rely on their commitment to persist when the potential beneficiary of their efforts may be rejected. Students with disabilities in Jordan's classes often have tough outer skins, having felt failure and frustration over their entire educational experience. These outcomes occur when added to the struggles of adolescence along with antagonism, apathy, and the potential for dropping out of school. Middle school is the age when many students make the decision to continue to persevere or begin the process of dropping out (Wang & Fredricks, 2014).

Jordan has to muster all the strength he has to engage the large classroom and address the needs of students with and without disabilities. He draws on his knowledge of the content and his experience with his students in order to navigate the challenges of the middle school years' desires for both belonging and individuality. Jordan's everyday practices embody his hope, courage, and strength that translate into a command of his classroom and strong relationships with his students.

CONCLUSION

Special education teachers who work in public charter schools must draw on hope, courage, and strength in order to meet the demands of the classroom given limited resources and stressful environments (Burnetti, 2006; Birmingham, 2009; Castro, Kelly, & Shih, 2010). Because students with disabilities may not come to school with the skills needed to be successful in the classroom, students with disabilities need teachers who are brave and optimistic enough to work with them (Miron & Nelson, 2002). While some charter schools may offer an opportunity for students with disabilities, educators and families should assess whether these settings can offer alternative environment and focus on approaches that can and should complement parents' desires for their childrens' educational experiences.

School choice and market-driven initiatives in education have led to the growth of the charter schools across the United States (Miron & Nelson, 2002). Teacher educators have an opportunity to support classroom teachers and teacher candidates in all schools including public charter school settings given this knowledge. The challenges and opportunities for students with disabilities in public charter schools are not all that different than the challenges and opportunities for students in traditional schools; however, in a public charter school setting, the child may be afforded a new start and new perspective based on a particular mission and environment.

Hope, courage, and strength are ideals that ground the work of special education teachers in all types of environments, particularly environments that provide inclusive practices (Birmingham, 2009; Brendtro, Brokenleg, & Van Bockern, 2014). By including the student with a disability in the general education curriculum, school systems are acting on hope and courage, as well as strong, evidence-based practices that demonstrate that all students can benefit from a diversity of instructional practices in order to develop deeper and more diverse sets of understandings and approaches to content (Turnbull, 1997; Werts, Carpenter, & Fewell, 2014). Further, hope, courage, and strength are also necessary ingredients to the creation of environments of resilience, where students can overcome adversity and break out of the cycle of poverty. The hope for resilience cannot be realized unless teachers act with the courage and strength of their convictions and knowledge. Special education teachers in public charter schools need to be aware of evidence-based practice as well as acceptance and determination for the success of their students in order to create opportunities for resilience.

In the provision of special education, the ideals of hope, courage, and strength are embodied both the in the underlying assumptions of the field and also in the legislation that makes special education possible. IDEA provides the legislative guidance for states in the mission of creating educational opportunities for students with disabilities. However, it is the responsibility of teachers who enact these policies to translate them into practices that respect the dignity of the child and the hopes and dreams of their parents. With hope embedded in the general premise that students with disabilities are deserving of educational opportunities, teachers act with courage and strength to design educational environments that help them succeed.

REFERENCES

Alexander, K. (2014). *The crossover*. Boston, MA: Houghton Mifflin Harcourt HMH Books for Young Readers.

Allinder, R. M. (1994). The relationship between efficacy and the instructional practices of special education teachers and consultants. *Teacher Education and Special Education, 17*(2), 86–95.

Aguirre, J., Maisterra, A., & Masoodi, J. (2014). *Special education monitoring and compliance manual (IDEA Part B)*. Washington, DC: DC Office of the State Superintendent of Education.

Associated Press. (May 22, 2017). Do charter schools serve special needs kids? The jury is out|WTOP. Retrieved from https://wtop.com/education/2017/05/do-charter-schools-serve-special-needs-kids-the-jury-is-out.

Bettini, E. A., Cheyney, K., Wang, J., & Leko, C. (2015). Job design: An administrator's guide to supporting and retaining special educators. *Intervention in School & Clinic, 50*(4), 221.

Birmingham, C. (2009). The disposition of hope in teaching. *Teacher Education Quarterly, 36*(4), 27–39.

Birmingham, C. (2010). Romance and irony, personal and academic: How mothers of children with autism defend goodness and express hope. *Narrative Inquiry, 20*(2), 225–245. http://doi.org/10.1075/ni.20.2.01bir.

Boardman, A. G., Argüelles, M. E., Vaughn, S., Hughes, M. T., & Klingner, J. (2005). Special education teachers' views of research-based practices. *The Journal of Special Education, 39*(3), 168–180.

Brendtro, L. K., Brokenleg, M., & Van Bockern, S. (2014). Environments where children thrive: The circle of courage model. *Reclaiming Children and Youth, 23*(3), 10.

Brunetti, G. J. (2006). Resilience under fire: Perspectives on the work of experienced, inner city high school teachers in the United States. *Teaching and Teacher Education, 22*(7), 812–825.

Brunsting, N. C., Sreckovic, M. A., & Lane, K. L. (2014). Special education teacher burnout: A synthesis of research from 1979 to 2013. *Education and Treatment of Children, 37*(4), 681–711.

Burke, K., & Sutherland, C. (2004). Attitudes toward inclusion: Knowledge vs experience. *Education, 125*(2).

Castro, A. J., Kelly, J., & Shih, M. (2010). Resilience strategies for new teachers in high-needs areas. *Teaching and Teacher Education, 26*(3), 622–629.

Center for Courage and Renewal: Our mission & values. (n.d.). Retrieved from http://www.couragerenewal.org/about/mission/.

Cook, B., & Schirmer, B. R. (2003). What is special about special education? Overview and analysis. *Journal of Special Education, 37*(3), 200–205.

Curran, A. (2017). *Burnout: Special education teachers experiences with career demands.* Doctoral dissertation, Northeastern University.

Drame, E. R. (2011). An analysis of the capacity of charter schools to address the needs of students with disabilities in Wisconsin. *Remedial and Special Education, 32*(1), 55–63. https://doi.org/10.1177/0741932510361259.

Estes, M. B. (2009). Charter schools and students with disabilities: How far have we come? *Remedial and Special Education, 30*(4), 216–224.

Gawlik, M. (2016). The US charter school landscape: Extant literature, gaps in research, and implications for the US educational system. *Global Education Review, 3*(2), 50–83.

Gilmore, L., Campbell, M., Shochet, I., Garland, R., Smyth, T., Roberts, C., & West, D. (2014). Promoting resilience in children with intellectual disability: A randomized controlled trial in Australian schools. In S. Prince-Embury & D. H. Saklofske (Eds.), *Resilience interventions for youth in diverse populations* (pp. 353–373). New York, NY: Springer.

Gross, B., & Lake, R. (2014). *Special education in charter schools: What we've learned and still need to know.* Seattle, WA: Center for Reinventing Public Education.

Hallahan, D. P., & Kauffman, J. M. (1995). From mainstreaming to collaborative consultation. In D. P. Hallahan & J. M. Kauffman (Eds.), *The illusion of full inclusion: A comprehensive critique of a current special education bandwagon* (pp. 5–17). Austin, TX: PRO-ED.

Hanushek, E. A., Kain, J. F., Rivkin, S. G., & Branch, G. F. (2007). Charter school quality and parental decision making with school choice. *Journal of Public Economics, 91*(5), 823–848.

Horvat, E. M., & Baugh, D. E. (2015). Not all parents make the grade in today's schools. *Phi Delta Kappan, 96*(7), 8–13.

Howe, K. R., & Welner, K. G. (2002). School choice and the pressure to perform déjà vu for children with disabilities? *Remedial and Special Education, 23*(4), 212–221.

Hoy, A. W., & Spero, R. B. (2005). Changes in teacher efficacy during the early years of teaching: A comparison of four measures. *Teaching and Teacher Education, 21*(4), 343–356.

Individuals with Disabilities Education Act (IDEA), 20 U.S.C. § 1400 (2004). Retrieved from http://uscode.house.gov/view.xhtml?path=%2Fprelim%40title20%2Fchapter33%2Fsubchapter1&req=granuleid%3AUSC-prelim-title20-chapter33-subchapter1&f=&fq=&num=0&hl=false&edition=prelim.

Kena, G., Musu-Gillette, L., Robinson, J., Wang, X., Rathbun, A., Zhang, J., . . . Dunlop Velez, E. (2015). *The condition of education 2015* (No. NCES 2015144). Retrieved from http://nces.ed.gov/pubsearch/pubsinfo.asp?pubid=2015144.

Mather, N., & Ofiesh, N. (2005). Resilience and the child with learning disabilities. In S. Goldstein & R. B. Brooks (Eds.), *Handbook of resilience in children* (pp. 239–255). Boston, MA: Springer. Retrieved from http://link.springer.com.proxyau.wrlc.org/chapter/10.1007/0-306-48572-9_15.

Miron, G., & Nelson, C. (2002). *What's public about charter schools? Lessons learned about choice and accountability*. Thousand Oaks, CA: Corwin Press.

Moore, A. (2004). *The good teacher: Dominant discourses in teaching and teacher education*. East Sussex, UK: Psychology Press.

Morrison, G. M., & Cosden, M. A. (1997). Risk, resilience, and adjustment of individuals with learning disabilities. *Learning Disability Quarterly, 20*(1), 43–60. http://doi.org/10.2307/1511092.

Nathan, J. (1997). *Charter schools: Creating hope and opportunity for American education. The Jossey-Bass Education Series*. San Francisco, CA: Jossey-Bass.

Palmer, P. J. (2010). *The courage to teach: Exploring the inner landscape of a teacher's life*. San Francisco, CA: John Wiley & Sons.

Patterson, J. H., Collins, L., & Abbott, G. (2004). A study of teacher resilience in urban schools. *Journal of Instructional Psychology, 31*(1), 3–11.

Rhim, L. M., Ahearn, E. M., & Lange, C. M. (2007). Charter school statutes and special education: Policy answers or policy ambiguity? *The Journal of Special Education, 41*(1), 50–63.

Rhim, L. M., & McLaughlin, M. J. (2001). Special education in American charter schools: State level policy, practices and tensions. *Cambridge Journal of Education, 31*(3), 373–383.

Rhim, L. M., & O'Neill, P. (2013). *Improving access and creating exceptional opportunities for students with disabilities in public charter schools*. Washington, DC/USA: The National Alliance for Public Charter Schools.

Sapon-Shevin, M., & Schniedewind, N. (2012). *Educational courage: Resisting the ambush of public education*. Boston, MA: Beacon Press.

Sass, T. R. (2006). Charter schools and student achievement in Florida. *Education, 1*(1), 91–122.

Sharma, U., Forlin, C., & Loreman, T. (2008). Impact of training on pre-service teachers' attitudes and concerns about inclusive education and sentiments about persons with disabilities. *Disability & Society, 23*(7), 773–785.

Solis, M., Vaughn, S., Swanson, E., & Mcculley, L. (2012). Collaborative models of instruction: The empirical foundations of inclusion and co-teaching. *Psychology in the Schools, 49*(5), 498–510.

Stuit, D., & Smith, T. M. (2010). *Teacher turnover in charter schools. Research brief*. National Center on School Choice, Vanderbilt University (NJ1).

Thomas, G., & Loxley, A. (2007). *Deconstructing special education*. London, UK: McGraw-Hill Education.

Turnbull, A. P. (1995). *Exceptional lives: Special education in today's schools*. Old Tappan, NJ: Merrill/Prentice Hall.

Waitoller, F. R., Maggin, D. M., & Trzaska, A. (2017). A longitudinal comparison of enrollment patterns of students receiving special education in urban neighborhood and charter schools. *Journal of Disability Policy Studies, 28*(1), 3–12.

Wang, M. T., & Fredricks, J. A. (2014). The reciprocal links between school engagement, youth problem behaviors, and school dropout during adolescence. *Child Development, 85*(2), 722–737.

Wehmeyer, M. L., Agran, M., & Hughes, C. (2000). A national survey of teachers' promotion of self-determination and student-directed learning. *The Journal of Special Education, 34*(2), 58–68.

Werner, E. E. (2013). What can we learn about resilience from large-scale longitudinal studies? In S. Prince-Embury & D. H. Saklofske (Eds.), *Handbook of resilience in children* (pp. 87–102). New York, NY: Springer.

Werts, M. G., Carpenter, E. S., & Fewell, C. (2014). Barriers and benefits to response to intervention: Perceptions of special education teachers. *Rural Special Education Quarterly, 33*(2), 3–11.

Wolf, P. J., Kisida, B., Gutmann, B., Puma, M., Eissa, N., & Rizzo, L. (2013). School vouchers and student outcomes: Experimental evidence from Washington, DC. *Journal of Policy Analysis and Management, 32*(2), 246–270.

Chapter 12

Preparing Elementary School Mathematics Specialists

Aspirations for a University Endorsement Program

Susan Swars Auslander,
Stephanie Z. Smith, and Marvin E. Smith

ABSTRACT

For the last several years our aspirations have focused on preparing Elementary Mathematics Specialists (EMSs) with the needed expertise to facilitate and support critical changes in elementary schools. Our university is located in one of the limited number of states in the United States offering advanced elementary teacher certification in mathematics, specifically a K-5 Mathematics Endorsement (K-5 ME). Within the constraints of elementary school teachers too often having negative affects or dispositions toward mathematics and needing more developed content knowledge, we designed and implemented a K-5 ME program with course experiences grounded in the current literature on ways to best prepare elementary school teachers mathematically, with the hopes of prompting motivation, learning, and change. The focus of this paper is twofold: (a) to provide a rich description of the K-5 ME program, including example course assignments with rationales and (b) to report research outcomes on the effectiveness of this program in accomplishing our aspirations for it.

KEY WORDS

Mathematics Specialists; Teacher Education Programs; Teacher Beliefs; Cognitively Guided Instruction

As mathematics educators we are committed to the goal of improving mathematics teaching and learning in elementary schools. For that reason, for the last several years our aspirations have focused on preparing Elementary Mathematics Specialists (EMSs) who possess the necessary mathematical expertise to support needed, critical changes in schools—changes such as those found in the *Common Core State Standards for Mathematics* (CCSS-M) (National Governors Association Center for Best Practices & Council of Chief State School Officers (NGACBP & CCSSO), 2010). The CCSS-M have been adopted by most states in the United States, and they require increased rigor and depth in mathematical understandings, problem solving, and other mathematical practices. Specifically, we aim to provide meaningful program and course experiences grounded in the current research on elementary school teacher mathematical development that would prompt EMSs' motivation, learning, and change.

Many professionals in the field of mathematics education are proponents of EMS certification, and the critical roles these professionals play by supporting effective elementary school mathematics instruction and student learning. For example, the National Mathematics Advisory Panel (2009, p. 14) asserted: "The use of teachers who have specialized in elementary mathematics teaching could be a practical alternative to increasing all elementary teachers' content knowledge (a problem of huge scale) by focusing the need for expertise on fewer teachers." Accordingly, the recent collective stance of several prominent mathematics education organizations, including the Association of Mathematics Teacher Educators (AMTE, 2010, 2013), posits that every elementary school in the United States have access to EMSs, and that advanced specialist certification be offered via rigorous preparation programs.

The state where our university is located is one of a limited number of states in the United States offering advanced elementary school teacher certification in mathematics. In the early 2000s, our university's state governing agency mandated all public institutions of higher education with undergraduate elementary school teacher preparation programs include twelve hours of elementary school mathematics, resulting in all of our undergraduate teacher candidates qualifying for the state's elementary school mathematics endorsement. The negative effects of the additional mathematics courses offered by the mathematics department on student progression through our teacher preparation program were substantial; many students failed or withdrew from the courses, thus delaying student teaching and graduation. Generally, over time, there was increasing recognition that a mathematics endorsement is better suited for practicing teachers who can draw from classroom experiences and have immediate applications. Consequently, a new K-5 Mathematics Endorsement (K-5 ME) was introduced at the graduate level for certified teachers who have completed at least one year of teaching experience. Completers of the K-5 ME receive an annual stipend from the state of $1,000 for each of the five years following completion of the endorsement, as long as certain criteria are met (e.g., currently teaching elementary school mathematics, etc.). After five years, continuation of the stipend is dependent upon satisfaction of student achievement criteria established by the state Office of Student Achievement. This opportunity to support transformation of mathematics education in elementary schools via the preparation of EMSs was extremely attractive to teachers with aspirations for acquiring additional specialized knowledge for teaching, for earning certification to work as EMSs, or for becoming teacher leaders in mathematics education at their schools.

The first group of elementary school teachers was admitted to our K-5 ME Program in 2010. However, this new program had to address the considerable challenges known to exist specific to the mathematical preparation of elementary school teachers. For example, many elementary school teachers tend to have negative affect (e.g., emotions, attitudes, and beliefs) toward mathematics, such as a dislike and an avoidance of the subject (Bekdemir, 2010; Philipp, 2007) as well as a propensity to espouse traditional, procedural beliefs informing their meanings of mathematical knowledge and the ways it is learned (Conference Board for Mathematical Sciences, 2012). These difficulties are compounded by the perspective of some elementary school teachers who think they do not need to learn more mathematics, as their experiences thus far have provided them sufficient content knowledge needed for teaching in the elementary school classroom. In addition, as elementary school teachers are typically prepared as generalists for teaching all subjects in the elementary school classroom, this multipurpose education has led to a corpus of elementary school teachers needing improved content knowledge for effectively teaching the increased mathematical expectations of the CCSS-M (NGACBP & CCSSO, 2010).

The significance of teacher mathematical affect and knowledge is noteworthy, as these constructs have been linked to teachers' instructional practices and student learning. Providing program and course learning experiences that positively shift mathematical affect and develop the mathematical knowledge needed for teaching in the elementary school classroom are crucial. Our hopes have been to create and implement a graduate-level K-5 ME Program that addresses these challenges, grounded in the current literature on the best ways to prepare elementary school teachers for teaching mathematics with and for understanding. Within the context of our K-5 ME Program, the focus of this paper is twofold: (a) to provide a rich description of the program, including example course assignments with rationales and (b) to report research outcomes on the effectiveness of this program in accomplishing our aspirations for it.

RELATED RESEARCH AND THEORETICAL PERSPECTIVES

Elementary School Mathematics Specialists

The roles of EMSs have largely been considered over time from two perspectives including EMSs who primarily work with students or EMSs who primarily work with teachers (AMTE, 2010; Reys & Fennell, 2003). Alternatively, EMSs may work with both students and teachers. In general, the specific roles and responsibilities of EMSs vary according to the contextual needs and plans of schools, school systems, and states. The research related to EMSs is somewhat limited but increasing over time. Generally, the studies have focused on improving instructional practices, designing coaching programs, and improving student achievement, with overall results showing positive impacts of EMSs on teacher development and student learning (Brosnan & Erchick, 2010; Campbell & Malkus, 2011; Gerretson, Bosnick, & Schofield, 2008; Kessel, 2009; McGee, Polly, & Wang, 2013; Meyers & Harris, 2008).

When considering the states offering pathways for advanced elementary school certification in mathematics, variability related to the number of course hours, course foci, and practicum experiences for program completion is noted (Mason & Bitto, 2012). The AMTE (2010, 2013) proposes an EMS preparation model with three program areas: (a) content knowledge for teaching, including deep understanding of mathematics for grades K-8 and further specialized knowledge for teaching; (b) pedagogical knowledge for teaching, including learners and learning, teaching, and curriculum and assessment; and (c) leadership knowledge and skills. Further, programs intended to prepare EMSs should include a supervised mathematics teaching practicum in which teachers acquire experience working with a range of student and adult learners.

Teacher Knowledge, Beliefs, and Classroom Teaching Practices in Mathematics

Teachers require deep and broad knowledge of mathematics to be effective in their teaching (Hill, 2010), especially to create Standards Based Learning Environments (Tarr et al., 2008) that promote classroom discourse and foster conceptual understandings of mathematics. Multiple efforts have attempted to define the exact mathematical knowledge needed for teaching, and several researchers (Ball & Forzani, 2010; Ball, Thames, & Phelps, 2008; Hill, 2010) have emphasized a *specialized content knowledge* (SCK) that includes teachers' abilities to (a) analyze and interpret students' mathematical thinking and ideas, (b) use multiple representations of mathematical concepts, and (c) define terms in mathematically correct and accessible ways (Hill, 2010; Thames & Ball, 2010).

Another salient factor influencing teacher effectiveness is teacher beliefs. Over time, research has established a robust relationship between teachers' beliefs and teaching by showing that beliefs influence teacher thinking and behaviors including instructional decision-making and use of curriculum materials (Clark & Peterson, 1986; Philipp, 2007; Romberg & Carpenter, 1986; Thompson, 1992; Wilson & Cooney, 2002). Beliefs are considered to be the cognitive set of psychological understandings, premises, or propositions through which interpretations are made of the surrounding world (Philipp, 2007). Teachers have deep-rooted mathematical beliefs formed during their seminal years as students in K-12 classrooms (Lortie, 1975); teachers tend to resist changing these beliefs during teacher education (Bird, Anderson, Sullivan, & Swidler, 1992; Handal & Herrington, 2003; Philipp, 2007). Two relevant belief constructs include pedagogical beliefs (i.e., beliefs about teaching and learning) and teaching efficacy beliefs (i.e., beliefs about capabilities to teach effectively and influence student learning). The authors of this study have previously published research on changes in these important beliefs and knowledge in the context of various other teacher education experiences (Smith, Swars, Smith, Hart, & Haardoerfer, 2012; Swars, Hart, Smith, Smith, & Tolar, 2007; Swars, Smith, Smith, & Hart, 2009; Swars, Smith, Smith, Hart, & Carothers, 2013).

The *Principles and Standards for School Mathematics* (National Council of Teachers of Mathematics (NCTM), 2000) and the CCSS-M (NGACBP & CCSSO, 2010) recommend the intersection of mathematical content and process standards requiring a pedagogical approach different from the traditional direct instruction in computational skills still found in many U.S. classrooms. Research by Tarr et al. (2008) indicates this change in pedagogy is more important for improving student achievement than the use of particular curriculum materials. Many of the suggested changes in teaching practices are grounded in social-constructivist methods of teaching in which teachers engage students in authentic, nonroutine problem-solving tasks and discourse intended to develop students' understandings of concepts and mathematical practices in ways that foster their abilities to solve problems and to reason and communicate mathematically. Specifically, teachers are being asked to create Standards Based Learning Environments (SBLEs) where students are encouraged to explain their problem-solving strategies and reasoning and to make conjectures and other generalizations about mathematical ideas based on their specific problem-solving experiences and contextualized understanding. Student statements are used to build discussion or work toward a shared understanding for the class. Moreover, multiple perspectives are encouraged and valued, and enacted lessons foster the development of deep, well-connected conceptual understanding. According to the Tarr et al. (2008) study, the improved student achievement was linked to the extent of enactment of such a SBLE.

Features of Effective Elementary School Teacher Education in Mathematics

Several features of effective elementary school mathematics teacher education programs have been previously identified (Conference Board of the Mathematical Sciences, 2012; Philipp, 2007; Smith et al., 2012; Sowder, 2007; Swars et al., 2007, 2009). In particular, courses should examine in depth, and from a prospective teacher's viewpoint, the vast majority of K-5 mathematics and its connections to PreK and middle school mathematics. Further, coursework should provide time and opportunities for students to think about, discuss, and explain mathematical ideas, while developing mathematical habits of mind and furthering mathematics as a sense-making enterprise. In addition, program design should include a seamless blend of study of the mathematical content and teaching methods, and departments of education and mathematics should collaborate in the education of elementary school teachers. Specific methods for engaging teacher learning in mathematics include studying children's thinking, using reform-oriented curricula and cognitively demanding instructional tasks, emphasizing problem solving and other mathematical processes, examining case studies of teaching and learning, and relating coursework to K-12 classrooms (Lannin & Chval, 2013; Philipp, 2008; Philipp et al., 2007; Sowder, 2007).

K-5 MATHEMATICS ENDORSEMENT PROGRAM

Program Overview

The K-5 ME Program is two semesters in duration and includes four three-semester-hour mathematics content courses that integrate pedagogy, plus one three-semester-hour practicum course providing an authentic residency. All courses are taught by mathematics educators in the Early Childhood and Elementary Education Department. Students can complete the courses leading to the endorsement only, or they can complete the courses while simultaneously pursuing the endorsement and a graduate degree. The four content/pedagogy courses include Number & Operations in the Elementary Classroom, Algebra in the Elementary Classroom, Data Analysis & Probability in the Elementary Classroom, and Geometry & Measurement in the

Elementary Classroom. The Number & Operation and Algebra courses are offered in the fall semester with the Data Analysis & Probability and Geometry & Measurement courses offered in the spring semester. Each course is offered for 7 weeks, meeting one evening per week for 5.5 hours (for a total of 37.5 contact hours per course).

The teachers also complete a three-semester-hour practicum course during the second semester of the endorsement program that provides an authentic residency enacting the synthesis of content knowledge and problem-based pedagogy emphasized in the program. Practicum assignments include the creation of a portfolio demonstrating expertise in teaching elementary school mathematics, analyzing impact on diverse student learning and technology integration. This expertise is documented across grade levels and age groups through a minimum of ten lessons, aligned with the topics of the four courses, and various required reflections and analyses from those contexts. A university supervisor observes the teaching of two of these lessons, prompting reflection and providing support, feedback, and evaluation. The teacher and supervisor consider the extent to which classroom practices foster a SBLE. Successful completion of the practicum and all four of the content/pedagogy courses lead to recommendation for the K-5 ME.

A foremost goal of the program is the development of a deep and broad understanding of elementary school mathematical content, including the *SCK* for teaching elementary school mathematics. The program also focuses on high-leverage teaching capabilities in the elementary school classroom including (a) selection and implementation of mathematical tasks with high levels of cognitive demand, (b) use of multiple mathematical representations, (c) use of mathematical tools, (d) promotion of mathematical dialogic discourse, explanation and justification, problem solving, and connections and applications typical of a SBLE (NCTM, 2000), and (e) use of children's thinking and understandings to guide instruction. Learning during course sessions occurs via (a) active inquiry and analysis of the mathematics in the elementary curriculum, (b) study of children's thinking and learning via video clips and teaching cases, (c) examination of examples of classroom practice via video clips and teaching cases, and (d) examination and analysis of the research base related to mathematics teaching and learning in the elementary school grades.

In addition to assigned readings of various articles, texts used during the courses include Schifter, Bastable, and Russell's *Developing Mathematical Ideas* series (2008), *Children's Mathematics: Cognitively Guided Instruction* (Carpenter, Fennema, Franke, Levi, & Empson, 1999, 2014), *Extending Children's Mathematics: Fractions and Decimals* (Empson & Levi, 2011), *Thinking Mathematically: Integrating Arithmetic and Algebra in Elementary School* (Carpenter, Franke, & Levi, 2003), *Connecting Arithmetic to Algebra: Strategies for Building Algebraic Thinking in the Elementary*

Grades (Russell, Schifter, & Bastable, 2011), and *Implementing Standards-based Mathematics Instruction* (Stein, Smith, Henningsen, & Silver, 2009). Key learning assignments and performance assessments across the courses, two of which are described in detail below, include clinical-style interviews of children's understandings of mathematical concepts; selection, adaptation, or generation and analyses of worthwhile mathematical tasks; an in-depth data design, collection, and analysis project; and examination, synthesis, and analysis of extant research in the field of mathematics education.

Study of Children's Thinking and Related Assignments

Studying children's thinking is an important component threaded across all of the K-5 ME courses. The aims of these experiences are producing positive shifts in beliefs about mathematics (Lannin & Chval, 2013; Philipp, 2008; Philipp et al., 2007) while concurrently building *SCK* that includes teachers' abilities to analyze and interpret students' mathematical thinking and ideas (Hill, 2010; Thames & Ball, 2010). Rather than trying to interest elementary school teachers in mathematics for the sake of mathematics itself, teacher education should provide connections to children's thinking—in which teachers are fundamentally concerned—to effectively prompt motivation, learning, and change (Lannin & Chval, 2013; Philipp, 2008; Philipp et al., 2007). Studying children's thinking is expected to also lead elementary school teachers to the recognition that their own mathematical understandings need enrichment for teaching elementary school mathematics with understanding and an increased awareness of the need for additional SCK.

One means of studying children's thinking during the courses is the professional development materials from the Cognitively Guided Instruction (CGI) Project (Carpenter et al., 1999, 2014). CGI is an approach to teaching and learning mathematics focusing on teachers using knowledge of children's mathematical thinking to make instructional decisions (Carpenter & Fennema, 1991). CGI includes research-based knowledge about children's mathematical thinking and well-defined frameworks of problem types and children's strategies for mathematical operations. The problem types summarized in box 12.1 of the CCSS-M (NGACBP & CCSSO, 2010) are well aligned with those in CGI. The use of CGI in university courses and professional development shows that participating elementary school teachers change their mathematical beliefs (Fennema et al., 1996; Fennema, Franke, Carpenter, & Carey, 1993; Peterson, Fennema, Carpenter, & Loef, 1989; Swars et al., 2009; Vacc & Bright, 1999).

The taxonomy of problem types within the CGI framework includes four basic classes of addition/subtraction problems, dependent upon the types of action or relationship described in the problems: Join, Separate, Part-Part-Whole, and Compare (Carpenter et al., 1999, 2014). Within each class are several distinct problems based upon which quantity is the unknown. For example, a Separate-Start Unknown problem is: "Betty had some pebbles. She gave 6 to Juan. Now she has 9 pebbles left. How many pebbles did Betty have to start with?" In this Separate-Start Unknown problem, elements are removed from a given set, with the unknown being the initial or starting quantity. When considering children's solution strategies, the structure of each problem is unique and is related to the ways that children solve the problems. The three broad categories for children's solution strategies are direct modeling, counting, and number facts, which over time become more abstract and efficient. That is, direct modeling strategies are replaced with more abstract counting strategies, which in turn are replaced with number facts.

The CGI materials available include video clips, cases, and descriptions of teachers, children, and classroom pedagogy in a CGI text that focuses on children's thinking (Carpenter et al., 1999; 2014). With the support of these materials, assignments in the Number & Operations course require the teachers to conduct interviews using the frameworks of problem types and children's solution strategies provided in CGI. An example interview assignment focusing on children's understandings of addition and subtraction is provided in box 12.1. Similar assignments involve interviews focusing on the multiplication and division framework, with another integrating base-ten understanding. Additional interview assignments in other courses focus on equality, specifically the meaning of the equal sign and relational thinking, and a performance assessment in geometry or measurement. The purpose of such assignments is to provide integrated learning activities/performance assessments focused on the important SCK developed in course sessions and readings through authentic instructional interactions with children.

BOX 12.1 EXAMPLE CGI ADDITION AND SUBTRACTION INTERVIEW ASSIGNMENT

1. Prepare a script of eleven addition and subtraction word problems to pose to a child. Include one of each type of problem identified in the CGI framework of addition and subtraction problem types. Vary the names of participants, objects, and numbers used in the collection of problems. Provide for your selection of alternative number sizes during the interview, depending on the as yet unknown needs of the child. The problems must make sense with all of the alternate number sizes. Use realistic contexts for all problems, but make the problems as simple in context and syntax as possible. The goal is for the problems to be engaging yet easily understandable. Further, the problems should be sequenced from least to greatest difficulty as identified by the CGI framework.

2. Interview one child with the purpose of coming to know what that child understands about solving addition and subtraction word problems. Provide a collection of appropriate physical materials as well as paper and pencil for the child to use in solving the problems. Begin by asking one of the easier problems from your script and record in as much detail as possible what the child does and says in trying to solve the problem. On the basis of the child's strategy and success in solving the first problem, sequence additional problems that will explore the extent of the child's strategies and understanding while continuing to encourage and support the child's success in solving the problems you pose.
3. Write a report that lists the problem you posed, identifies the problem type from the CGI framework (e.g., JRU for Join Result Unknown), describes the child's response as completely as possible, and analyzes the child's response on the basis of the CGI framework for solution strategies. Repeat this process (problem as posed, CGI problem type, child's response, and CGI analysis) for each of the problems that you posed. At the end of this report, write one paragraph that summarizes what you learned about the child's understanding of addition and subtraction, the types of problems the child successfully solved and struggled with, the range of numbers with which the child was familiar, and the types of strategies the child demonstrated. Also include a good next problem for this student, identifying the problem type, and justifying the decision with evidence from the report.

Use of Conceptually Oriented Curricula/Cognitively Demanding Tasks and Related Assignments

In addition to studying children's thinking, the use of conceptually oriented curricula materials and cognitively demanding tasks can also be effective as a means of changing elementary school teachers' beliefs and building SCK (Lannin & Chval, 2013; Philipp, 2007; Spielman & Lloyd, 2004). In the courses, example elementary school curricular materials and instructional tasks are drawn from *Investigations in Numbers, Data, and Space*; the National Council of Teachers of Mathematics' *Navigations* and *Curriculum Focal Points* series; *Contexts for Learning Mathematics;* and *Everyday Mathematics*. Examination of mathematical tasks, including analysis of these tasks based on level of cognitive demand during selection, set-up, and implementation use the framework by Stein et al. (2009) in *Implementing Standards Based Mathematics Instruction.* They encourage the analysis of mathematics instructional tasks by teachers for "the level and kind of thinking in which students engage" (p. 1) in order to successfully solve the task. Their analysis of *cognitive demands* divides mathematical tasks into two general categories, each of which is divided further into two subcategories: *Lower-Level Demands* (including *Memorization Tasks* and *Procedures without Connections Tasks*) and *Higher-Level Demands* (including *Procedures with Connections Tasks* and *Doing Mathematics Tasks*). Cognitively demanding tasks offer the potential to engage students in complex forms of thinking with the goal of increasing students' abilities to reason and solve problems. Specifically, some characteristics of *Doing Mathematics Tasks* are that they require complex and non-algorithmic thinking with no suggested solution pathway; exploration of the nature of mathematical concepts, processes, or relationships; significant effort and persistence (e.g., productive struggle); student self-monitoring; and careful analysis of the task, including potential constraints that limit solutions and solution strategies.

Elementary school tasks that require higher levels of cognitive demand are used as an instructional tool in all of the courses. These tasks challenge the teachers' perceptions that elementary school mathematics is "easy" and also provide perceived relevance of the mathematics in the courses by connecting to the elementary school classroom. Further, given the prevalence of mathematics anxiety among elementary school teachers, the tasks provide an avenue to see themselves as competent mathematical reasoners, as well as develop SCK (e.g., the use of multiple representations of mathematical concepts). Not only are such tasks an instructional tool in the context of the class sessions, a course assignment across all four courses involves selecting, adapting, or generating a collection of tasks with higher levels of cognitive demand, with solving the tasks and explaining solutions as a component of the assignment. An example of this assignment is in box 12.2.

BOX 12.2 EXAMPLE WORTHWHILE MATHEMATICAL TASK COLLECTION AND RATIONALES ASSIGNMENT

The NCTM *Professional Standards for Teaching Mathematics* (1991) emphasizes the posing of learning activities it calls *worthwhile mathematical tasks*. These tasks are to be based on—
- Sound and significant mathematics;
- Knowledge of students' understandings, interests, and experiences;
- Knowledge of the range of ways that diverse students learn mathematics;

These tasks are intended to—
- Engage students' intellect;

- Develop students' mathematical understandings and skills; stimulate students to make connections and develop a coherent framework for mathematical ideas;
- Call for problem formulation, problem solving, and mathematical reasoning;
- Promote communication about mathematics;
- Represent mathematics as an ongoing human activity;
- Display sensitivity to, and draw on, students' diverse background experiences and dispositions;
- Promote the development of all students' dispositions to do mathematics (p. 25).

Stein, Smith, Henningsen, and Silver (2009) encourage the analysis of mathematics instructional tasks for "the level and kind of thinking in which students engage" (p. 1) in order to successfully solve the task. Their analysis of *cognitive demands* divides mathematical tasks into two general categories, each of which are divided further into two subcategories: *Lower-Level Demands* (including *Memorization Tasks* and *Procedures without Connections Tasks*) and *Higher-Level Demands* (including *Procedures with Connections Tasks* and *Doing Mathematics Tasks*). Worthwhile mathematical tasks align with those characterized as *Procedures with Connections Tasks* and *Doing Mathematics Tasks*.

For this assignment, select, adapt, or generate (and organize) ten (10) worthwhile mathematical tasks across grades P-5 focusing on developing understanding of the major concepts of number and operations. For each of the tasks in the collection, provide a complete solution strategy of your own work. Following your solution, explain in writing your thinking used to complete the task. For each task collected, provide a rationale/cover page that identifies the following (refer to Stein, Smith, Henningsen, & Silver, 2009):
- Anticipated students (age, grade level, and prior knowledge/experience);
- Goals for student learning (from CCSS-Mathematics or NCTM Standards);
- Mathematical features of the task, including what students are asked to do, in what context, with what tools (including the impact of the use of calculators or other technology), and so on;
- Level of cognitive demands (kinds of thinking required by the task);
- Rationale for the categorization of cognitive demands.

Attach the worthwhile mathematical task immediately following the cover page. Then, attach your evidence of solving the worthwhile mathematical task and your explanation of mathematical thinking to complete the task.

RELATED RESEARCH OUTCOMES AND DISCUSSION

Our aspirations of providing a K-5 ME Program with course experiences leading to well-prepared EMSs were examined via a mixed methods study of mathematical beliefs, SCK, and the extent to which the teachers implement a SBLE (Swars, Smith, Smith, Carothers, & Myers, 2016). Data (n=32) were collected over the two-semester program via belief surveys, a content knowledge assessment, observations of teaching practices, and individual interviews from elementary school teachers participating in the program. It is evident in the results that teachers' pedagogical beliefs experienced significant positive shifts toward cognitive orientation during the program, coupled with significant increases in their teaching efficacy beliefs (i.e., beliefs in their capabilities to teach mathematics effectively and influence student learning). The timing and extent of changes of the mathematical belief constructs varied across the program. The findings show that the learning experiences of these teachers can quickly change self-reported beliefs about the ways that children learn mathematics and the cognitively guided pedagogy needed to implement a SBLE. However, similar changes in self-reported teaching efficacy beliefs take more time and continued support, similar to other findings in our undergraduate teacher education program (Smith et al., 2012; Swars et al., 2009).

Other changes were evident related to teacher content knowledge and instructional practices. The program emphasis on deepening teacher content knowledge needed for teaching elementary school mathematics for understanding resulted in significant improvements in SCK. Also of note are the important pedagogical shifts that the teachers made, including expecting children to explain their mental reasoning, problem-solving strategies, and understanding of important mathematical concepts. By the end of the program, the teachers learned to enact lessons that fostered development of conceptual understanding through worthwhile mathematical tasks, and encouraged and valued multiple strategies and perspectives in classroom discourse.

The interview data corroborated and illuminated the findings of the quantitative data. At the conclusion of the program, all of the teachers described effective mathematics instruction as inquiry-based, reflecting the pedagogical model emphasized in the program, including (a) posing a worthwhile mathematical task, (b) circulating around the classroom as children work in order to learn about children thinking and to question them about their work, and (c) orchestrating classroom discourse as children explain their thinking and solutions to the task. Example expressions of the primary roles of a teacher included being a "facilitator" which included "posing problems," "asking questions," and "allowing [children] to explore their own thinking." One teacher stated her role was "guiding [children], asking them more questions to help them discover things, not showing them how to do things exactly, but helping them [to] use their ideas and challenge each other." Further, all of the teachers stated they were confident in their ability to fulfill these roles, with a strong sense of mathematics teaching efficacy and a professed confidence in their knowledge of elementary school mathematics. Coupled with a described shift away from traditional instructional practices, they also described their advocacy among peers for the problem-based pedagogical approach emphasized in the program.

The teachers also noted benefits for students' learning as they indicated that several changes in their students' learning and thinking were evident as they applied the knowledge, skills, and dispositions they had learned during the program. They mentioned improvements in student achievement as measured by standardized tests and that they believed they were reaching all learners during instruction, including those who otherwise might struggle to learn mathematics, not just high achievers. Frequent references to their students engaging in more "problem solving," "critical thinking," "discussion," "questioning each other," "reasoning," and "logic," resulting in students "retaining" and "understanding" mathematics were evident. The teachers spoke of their students' increasing confidence or self-efficacy as problem-solvers and in approaching mathematics in general. Said one participant, "I noticed I can give them a lot more complex, multistep problems, and they wouldn't shy away from them." One participant noted changes:

> In the way my students are thinking and the way they approach things. A lot of it is more problem solving. They're not [just] sitting there; now they are saying, "Okay, tell me what to do." They're taking initiative on their own to find different ways to make stuff work or investigate things.

The teachers attributed their changes to key components of the K-5 ME Program experiences, with frequent references to notions of applicability and immediacy. Multiple references made to the assignments involved making collections of worthwhile mathematical tasks in each of the four mathematical content areas. The teachers spoke of about being required to engage in worthwhile mathematical tasks themselves increased their own knowledge of elementary school mathematics content and the ways to use worthwhile tasks in their classroom practice across elementary school grade levels and consistent with expectations of the NCTM *Principles and Standards* (2000) and CCSS-M. The teachers also described the benefits of studying children's mathematical thinking, with frequent references to the research-based frameworks from CGI (Carpenter, Fennema, Franke, Empson, & Levi, 1999, 2014), as well as case studies of teaching episodes and children's thinking in other readings in the program. The participants also mentioned the instructors were important to their learning in the courses, including comments that the instructors modeled SBLE instructional practices such as problem posing and cultivating discourse through questioning. Further, the participants spoke of the supportive learning environment of the courses in the program.

In sum, the preparation experiences designed to develop EMSs seem to have had the desired effects. The teachers in the program connected their learning of theory and methods in the program courses to their enacted practices in classrooms. It seems the program learning experiences buoyed this very difficult translation, supporting the crucial goal of pedagogical shifts, in addition to the goals of positive changes in mathematical beliefs and development of SCK. Given the considerable challenges associated with the mathematical education of elementary school teachers, such as negative affect and a need for more developed content knowledge, we are encouraged that the created and implemented program and course experiences seem to produce our anticipated outcomes. The content and sequence of the courses in the program, as well as an intensive and thorough focus on study and analysis of children's thinking, engagement in cognitively demanding tasks and conceptually oriented curricula for the elementary school classroom, examination and analysis of the relevant research base, and other embedded experiences and assignments produced the aspired for results related to elementary school teacher development. With these learning experiences grounded in the current literature on ways to best prepare elementary school teachers mathematically, we hope our EMSs have the needed expertise to facilitate and support crucial changes in mathematics education for elementary school classrooms.

REFERENCES

Association of Mathematics Teacher Educators (AMTE). (2010, 2013). *Standards for elementary mathematics specialists: A reference for teacher credentialing and degree programs.* San Diego, CA. Retrieved from http://www.amte.net/sites/all/themes/amte/resources/EMSStandards_Final_Mar2010.pdf.

Ball, D. L., & Forzani, F. M. (2010). What does it take to make a teacher? *Phi Delta Kappan, 92*(2), 8–12.

Ball, D. L., Hoover Thames, M., & Phelps, G. (2008). Content knowledge for teaching: What makes it special? *Journal of Teacher Education, 59*(5), 389–407.

Bird, T., Anderson, L. M., Sullivan, B. A., & Swidler, S. A. (1992). *Pedagogical balancing acts: A teacher educator encounters problems in an attempt to influence prospective teachers' beliefs.* (Research Report 92-8). East Lansing, MI: Michigan State University, National Center for Research on Teacher Learning.

Bekdemir, M. (2010). The pre-service teachers' mathematics anxiety related to depth of negative experiences in mathematics classroom while they were students. *Educational Studies in Mathematics, 75*(3), 311–328.

Brosnan, P., & Erchick, D. (2010). Mathematics coaching and its impact on student achievement. In P. Brosnan, A. Manochehri, & D. Owens (Eds.), *Proceedings of the psychology of mathematics education North America*. Columbus, OH: PME-NA. Retrieved from https://s3.amazonaws.com/conference-handouts/2016-nctm-sf-research/pdfs/Harbour,%20Karp,%20%26%20Adelson_MCSs_NCTM%20Research%202016-2.pdf.

Campbell, P., & Malkus, N. (2011). The impact of elementary mathematics coaches on student achievement. *The Elementary School Journal, 111*(3), 430–454.

Carpenter, T. P., & Fennema, E. (1991). *Integrating research on teaching and learning mathematics*. Albany, NY: State University of New York Press.

Carpenter, T. P., Fennema, E., Franke, M. L., Levi, L., & Empson, S. B. (1999, 2014). *Children's mathematics: Cognitively guided instruction*. Portsmouth, NH: Heinemann.

Carpenter, T. P., Franke, M. L., & Levi, L. (2003). *Thinking mathematically: Integrating arithmetic & algebra in elementary school*. Portsmouth, NH: Heinemann.

Clark, C. M., & Peterson, P. L. (1986). Teachers' thought processes. In M. C. Wittrock (Ed.), *Handbook of research on teaching* (3rd ed., pp. 255–296). New York, NY: Macmillan.

Conference Board of the Mathematical Sciences (CBMS). (2012). *The mathematical education of teachers II*. Providence, RI: American Mathematical Society.

Empson, S. B., & Levi, L. (2011). *Extending children's mathematics: Fractions and decimals*. Portsmouth, NH: Heinemann and the National Council of Teachers of Mathematics.

Fennema, E., Carpenter, T. P., Franke, M. L., Levi, L., Jacobs, V. R., & Empson, S. B. (1996). A longitudinal study of learning to use children's thinking in mathematics instruction. *Journal for Research in Mathematics Education, 27*(4), 404–434.

Fennema, E., Franke, M. L., Carpenter, T. P., & Carey, D. A. (1993). Using children's knowledge in instruction. *American Educational Research Journal, 30*(3), 403–434.

Gerretson, H., Bosnick, J., & Schofield, K. (2008). A case for content specialists as the elementary classroom teacher. *The Teacher Educator, 43*(2008), 302–314.

Handal, B., & Herrington, A. (2003). Mathematics teachers' beliefs and curriculum reform. *Mathematics Education Research Journal, 15*(1), 59–69.

Hill, H. C. (2010). The nature and predictors of elementary teachers' mathematical knowledge for teaching. *Journal for Research in Mathematics Education, 41*(5), 513–545.

Kessel, C. (Ed.). (2009). *Teaching teachers mathematics: Research, ideas, projects, evaluation*. Retrieved from http://www.msri.org/calendar/attachments/workshops/430/TTM_EdSeries3MSRI.pdf.

Lannin, J. K., & Chval, K. B. (2013). Challenge beginning teacher beliefs. *Teaching Children Mathematics, 19*(8), 508–515.

Lortie, D. (1975). *Schoolteacher: A sociological study*. Chicago: University of Chicago Press.

Mason, M. M., & Bitto, L. E. (February 2012). *How should we prepare elementary mathematics specialists? An examination of one successful program*. Paper presented at the meeting of Association of Mathematics Teacher Educators, Irvine, CA.

McGee, J. R., Polly, D., & Wang, C. (2013). Guiding teachers in the use of a standards-based mathematics curriculum: Teacher perceptions and subsequent instructional practices after an intensive professional development program. *School Science and Mathematics, 113*(1), 16–28.

Meyers, H., & Harris, D. (April 2008). *Evaluation of the VMI through 2008*. Retrieved from http://www.uvm.edu/~vmi/index_files/2008%20VMI%20Evaluation.pdf.

National Council of Teachers of Mathematics (NCTM). (2000). *Principles and standards for school mathematics*. Reston, VA: Author.

National Governors Association Center for Best Practices & Council of Chief State School Officers (NGACBP & CCSSO). (2010). *Common core state standards for mathematics*. Washington, DC: Authors.

National Mathematics Advisory Panel. (2008). *Foundations for success: Final report of the National Mathematics Advisory Panel*. Washington, DC: U.S. Department of Education.

Peterson, P. L., Fennema, E., Carpenter, T., & Loef, M. (1989). Teachers' pedagogical content beliefs in mathematics. *Cognition and Instruction, 6*(1), 1–40.

Philipp, R. A. (2007). Mathematics teachers' beliefs and affect. In F. K. Lester (Ed.), *Second handbook of research on mathematics teaching and learning* (pp. 257–315). Charlotte, NC: Information Age Publishing.

Philipp, R. A. (2008). Motivating prospective elementary school teachers to learn mathematics by focusing on children's thinking. *Issues in Teacher Education, 17*(2), 7–16.

Philipp, R. A., Ambrose, R., Lamb, L., Sowder, J. L., Schappelle, B. P., & Sowder, L. (2007). Effects of early field experiences on the mathematics content knowledge and beliefs of prospective elementary teachers: An experimental study. *Journal for Research on Mathematics Education, 38*(5), 438–476.

Reys, B. J., & Fennell, F. (2003). Who should lead mathematics instruction at the elementary school level? A case for mathematics specialists. *Teaching Children Mathematics, 9*(5), 277–282.

Romberg, T., & Carpenter, T. (1986). Research on teaching and learning mathematics: Two disciplines of scientific inquiry. In M. C. Wittrock (Ed.), *Handbook of research on teaching* (3rd ed., pp. 850–873). New York, NY: Macmillan.

Russell, S. J., Schifter, D., & Bastable, V. (2011). *Connecting arithmetic to algebra: Strategies for building algebraic thinking in the elementary grades*. Portsmouth, NH: Heinemann.

Schifter, D., Bastable, V., & Russell, S. J. (2008). *Developing mathematical ideas: Casebooks*. Parsippany, NJ: Dale Seymour/Pearson Education.

Smith, M. E., Swars, S. L., Smith, S. Z., Hart, L. C., & Haardoerfer, R. (2012). Effects of an additional mathematics content courses on elementary teachers' mathematical beliefs and knowledge for teaching. *Action in Teacher Education, 34*(4), 336–348.

Sowder, J. T. (2007). The mathematical education and development of teachers. In F. K. Lester (Ed.), *Second handbook of research on mathematics teaching and learning* (pp. 157–223). Charlotte, NC: Information Age.

Spielman, L. J., & Lloyd, G. M. (2004). The impact of enacted mathematics curriculum models on prospective elementary teachers' course perceptions and beliefs. *School Science and Mathematics, 104*(1), 32–42.

Stein, M. K., Smith, M. S., Henningsen, M. A., & Silver, E. A. (2009). *Implementing standards-based mathematics instruction.* New York, NY: Teachers College Press and the National Council of Teachers of Mathematics.

Swars, S. L., Hart, L., Smith, S. Z., Smith, M., & Tolar, T. (2007). A longitudinal study of elementary pre-service teachers' mathematics beliefs and content knowledge. *School Science and Mathematics, 107*(9), 325–335.

Swars, S. L., Smith, S. Z., Smith, M. E., Carothers, J., & Myers, K. (2016). The preparation experiences of Elementary Mathematics Specialists: Examining influences on beliefs, content knowledge, and teaching practices. *Journal of Mathematics Teacher Education.* Advance online publication. doi: 10.1007/s10857-016-9354-y.

Swars, S. L., Smith, S. Z., Smith, M. E., & Hart, L. C. (2009). A longitudinal study of effects of a developmental teacher preparation program on elementary prospective teachers' mathematics beliefs. *Journal of Mathematics Teacher Education, 12*(1), 47–66.

Swars, S. L., Smith, S. Z., Smith, M. E., Hart, L. C., & Carothers, J. (2013). Providing space for elementary prospective teachers' viewpoints on mathematics content courses: A two-dimensional model of learning. *Action in Teacher Education, 35*(5–6), 372–386.

Tarr, J. E., Reys, R. E., Reys, B. J., Chavez, O., Shih, J., & Osterlind, S. J. (2008). The impact of middle-grades mathematics curricula and the classroom learning environment on student achievement. *Journal for Research in Mathematics Education, 39*(3), 247–280.

Thames, M. H., & Ball, D. L. (2010). What mathematical knowledge does teaching require? Knowing mathematics in and for teaching. *Teaching Children Mathematics, 17*(4), 220–225.

Thompson, A. G. (1992). Teachers' beliefs and conceptions: A synthesis of the research. In D. A. Grouws (Ed.), *Handbook of research on mathematics teaching and learning* (pp. 127–146). New York; London: Macmillan Library Reference USA; Simon & Schuster and Prentice Hall International.

Vacc, N. N., & Bright, G. W. (1999). Elementary preservice teachers' changing beliefs and instructional use of children's mathematical thinking. *Journal for Research in Mathematics Education, 30*(1), 89–110.

Wilson, M., & Cooney, T. (2002). Mathematics teacher change and development: The role of beliefs. In G. Leder, E. Pehkonen, & G. Toerner (Eds.), *Beliefs: A hidden variable in mathematics education?* (pp. 127–148). Dordrecht, The Netherlands: Kluwer Academic Press.

Chapter 13

Fighting for Hope and Inspiration[*]
Developing Reflective Spaces for Leaders in Elementary School Mathematics

Ryan Flessner, Courtney Flessner,
Katherine Reed, and Susan Adamson

ABSTRACT

In these politicized times, teachers are under attack. Within this heated educational environment, teachers need spaces of support and reflection in order to stay true to their closest held beliefs about teaching and learning. This chapter highlights the reflective work occurring within the Math leadership group sponsored by the Indiana Partnership for Young Writers. The chapter begins with an historical examination of math teaching and learning in the United States. We then introduce readers to the Indiana Partnership for Young Writers and its Math leadership group. After describing activities in which leadership group members participated, we use vignettes from one of the participants as a way to document what mathematical leadership can look like in our current educational landscape.

KEY WORDS

Educational Leadership; Teacher Leadership; Math Leadership; Elementary School Mathematics; Vignettes

---

[*] The authors would like to thank the Indiana Partnership for Young Writers, the members of the Math leadership group (past and current), and its funders—the Indiana Commission for Higher Education and the Nina Mason Pulliam Charitable Trust—for their continued efforts to support, encourage, and promote the work of educators and students across the state of Indiana.

Within the current political context, many educators feel like they are in a boxing ring. Punches are taken from policy makers, the media, and the general public who are inundated with reasons the public schools are failing (Campbell, 2015; McInerny, 2015; Perry, 2015). Policies approved by legislators far removed from classroom life often breed confusion, tension, and the need for educators to compromise what they know is best for children. It is astounding that we don't hear more than we already do about mass retirements, low enrollment in teacher education programs, and teacher shortages (Beck, 2015; FitzGerald, 2013; Westervelt, 2015).

Given the bare-knuckled tendencies of the current political landscape in education, it is imperative that educators continue to acknowledge the good in our field. That is, educators—alongside parents, community organizations, business leaders, elected officials, and others who consider themselves allies of public education—must celebrate what we know *is* working in our public schools.

The goal is to provide insight into one group of educators' efforts to inspire, collaborate with, and provide hope for one another, even in these trying times. In order to achieve this goal, we examine ways in which several teachers in the state of Indiana are gathering to reflect, partner, and support one another in the area of elementary school mathematics. The group of Math Leaders discussed here is a prime example of educators taking action in an effort to get out of the boxing ring, dodge the punches leveled at them from a variety of sources, and avoid the tendency to punch back when we know that tendency only extends the bout.

CONTEXT

The following sections detail the history of the political fisticuffs in the field of mathematics education. The historical roots of mathematics teaching have left teachers wanting for spaces where they can engage proactively with colleagues. In this space outside the ring, teachers develop strength and strategies for the good fight filled with hope and inspiration. To this end, we highlight an organization that hosts a Math leaders group, describe the selection process for these Math Leaders, and examine the ways in which these educators collaborate as they study, enact, and reflect upon promising practices in the field of elementary school mathematics.

The Politics of Mathematics Education—A Historical Perspective

For more than a century, conversations about the content that should be taught in mathematics, as well as the ways it should be taught, have been quite contentious. Throughout the 20th century and into the 21st century, educators attempting to teach for understanding have constantly battled a faction of reformers from outside of education who advocate for the rote memorization of mathematical procedures. In February of 1920, the National Council of Teachers of Mathematics (NCTM) convened for the first time. At that gathering, 127 mathematics teachers from 20 different states came together to create a "unified voice to defend against educational interlopers" (Donoghue, 2003, p. 186). C. M. Austin, the first president of NCTM, stated, "Instead of continual criticism at educational meetings, we intend to present constructive programs.... We prefer that curriculum studies and reforms and adjustments come from the teachers of mathematics rather than from educational reformers" (Austin as cited by Donoghue, 2003, p. 187).

Urgency to overhaul American mathematics education peaked with Russia's launching of Sputnik in 1957. Finally, the American public was convinced that the norm in American schools was not enough. Mathematics educators celebrated this turn in public opinion hoping that the time had finally come to move from rote procedures to conceptual understandings in the teaching and learning of mathematics. By 1970, the National Science Foundation (NSF) had provided more than $28.5 million to major math projects. Teacher preparation was an obvious need; however, the majority of teacher preparation was only for high school teachers. "NSF made a deliberate decision not to fund institutes for elementary school teachers on a widespread basis because there were too many teachers and not enough resources to do this job" (Payne, 2003, p. 579). At the same time, attendance to NCTM grew to over 75,000 attendees. Yet, most professional development was offered in small sessions and failed to manifest itself in classroom practice. According to Payne (2003):

> The intended change in the mathematics curriculum was so profound and involved so much content new to elementary school that it was difficult to convey the information in short sessions for teachers and the general public. It was just not realistic to expect the public, or even elementary school teachers, to know enough mathematics and to have a feeling for the spirit in which it was to be taught. (p. 276)

Funding issues and political battles surrounding the teaching of mathematics returned in the 1980s. Mathematics reforms from the post-Sputnik era faltered due to lack of teacher preparation and complaints from the general public, fueled by concerns from parents who struggled to comprehend the new math their children were bringing home (Fey & Graeber, 2003). Soon, the political machine of the back-to-basics movement seized hold of the conversation surrounding mathematics education. Reports commissioned by the Reagan administration such as *A Nation at Risk* (National Commission on Excellence in Education, 1983) and *Educating Americans for a 21st Century* (National Science Board Commission on Precollege Education in Mathematics, Science, and Technology, 1983) reiterated the need for changes to the way American schools were approaching the teaching of mathematics. In 1986, NCTM's Board of Directors elected to begin the writing of the standards document, *Curriculum and Evaluation Standards for School Mathematics* (NCTM, 1989). This document and a second publication, *Professional Teaching Standards* (NCTM, 1991), were adopted by states as part of their reform efforts in developing new state standards for instruction.

More recently, the movement toward a national standards-based system in mathematics education has culminated with the publication of the *Common Core State Standards* (National Governors Association Center for Best Practices & Council of Chief State School Officers, 2010). Rather than assisting educators in becoming better at their craft, the creation of these standards has caused upheaval on both sides of the political spectrum. The political sparring surrounding the *Common Core State Standards* has added to the need for spaces where teachers can find hope and inspiration related to the teaching of mathematics. Interestingly, the Indiana Partnership for Young Writers (IPYW), a seemingly odd place to find hope and inspiration for mathematics teaching, stepped up to meet this challenge. Before introducing the proactive actions IPYW is making, we introduce readers to the organization itself.

Indiana Partnership for Young Writers

The IPYW began as a short-term pilot project in 1999 when policy makers began turning away from urban public schools, advocating standardized instruction, focusing language arts instruction solely on reading, and defining professional development—where it existed—as a trip to a large conference to learn a single curriculum tool.

Under the guidance of Randy Bomer, former co-director with Lucy Calkins of the Teachers College Reading and Writing Project at Teachers College Columbia University, and with funds awarded by the Nina Mason Pulliam Charitable Trust, the IPYW forged a very different path. They invested the majority of their resources into the Indianapolis Public Schools, helping teachers tailor instruction for individual students in writing workshops. They focused on instruction in the writing process (a subject that had never before existed in Indiana as a stand-alone content area in elementary or middle schools) while continuing to uphold the importance of publication rituals and written products. IPYW supported teachers inside of their classrooms, demonstrating excellent teaching, connecting teachers to nationally renowned scholars and mentors, and challenging teachers to continually read, contemplate, debate, and synthesize research published by leading scholars in literacy education.

As a pilot project, IPYW engaged just a small cohort of teachers in three schools but have demonstrated a need and demand for more far-reaching impact serving more than 1,700 teachers and 150 undergraduate teacher-interns from 177 schools since its inception in 1999. Importantly, the work of IPYW is more than simply offering professional development opportunities to educators. Leadership groups have been gathered to provide feedback to the organization and to generate new knowledge about teaching and learning. The Young Leaders in Urban Education group was formed to support early career African American teachers as they transitioned into the teaching profession. In addition, IPYW provides a network of teachers who can collaborate inside and across schools, districts, the state of Indiana, and beyond. Due, in large part, to these efforts to connect with and offer continued support to educators across the state, IPYW has been able to publish a series of books highlighting the writing of students from the classrooms of IPYW-trained teachers (Adamson, 2005, 2007, 2009, 2011, 2015). These books show the power of working with teachers to continually reflect on their craft and their profession while offering children authentic opportunities to express themselves, their ideas, and the knowledge they bring into schools from their lives lived outside of schools.

IPYW and Mathematics

At the demand of teachers and administrators, IPYW expanded their professional development model recognizing that pedagogical beliefs can be supported consistently across content areas, whether teaching writing workshop, reading workshop, math workshop, or early childhood education. Due to the contentious conversations surrounding mathematics teaching and learning mentioned earlier in this chapter, educators were looking for ways to supplement or replace textbooks and traditional practices. IPYW began by offering a workshop entitled, "What About Math Workshop?" The workshop was well attended, and subsequent workshops were planned. These offerings also filled quickly. Clearly, the role of IPYW was extending beyond instruction in the area of elementary school literacy. During the 2014–2015 academic year, a large portion of IPYW's offerings were related to math. Teachers from across the state of Indiana[1] attended these offerings, and plans are in the works for continued efforts in the area of elementary school mathematics.

IPYW Math Leaders

During the 2014–2015 academic year, IPYW offered Indiana educators an opportunity to join a Math leaders group. The intent of the group was to gather educators who were passionate about the teaching and learning of mathematics in an effort to share and produce knowledge that would impact practice in Indiana schools. Educators were asked to apply in teams of two. Each team was expected to be site- or district-based so that each participant in the Math leaders group would have a like-minded confidante close by with whom the participant could connect between meetings.

Agendas for the meetings of the leadership group contained a balance of ideas that educators could take back to their schools and/or districts for immediate use and time to generate new knowledge about the teaching and learning of elementary school mathematics. Protocols for reflection (School Reform Initiative, 2010) were often used to guide discussion, and a host of mathematical activities was presented from a variety of resources (e.g., Madison Metropolitan School District, 2006, 2007; Petersen, 2013; Wheatley & Reynolds, 1999). Educators also self-selected into book clubs to read one of three texts (Hiebert et al., 1997; Hoffer, 2012; Wedekind, 2011) related to mathematics teaching and learning. Book club groups set their own reading schedules and created homework assignments for participating members. The group also began work on a Problem Solving Continuum similar to a Running Record (Clay, 2000) in reading that could assist teachers in finding the strengths their students possess as well as the needs of individual students.[2]

One final element of the monthly meetings was the construction of vignettes about leadership in the area of elementary school mathematics. The remainder of the chapter explores the ways that vignettes were used to guide the work of the Math leaders group while also uncovering themes that were prevalent throughout our time together.

VIGNETTES

Knowing the power of reflective practice (Dana & Yendol-Hoppey, 2014; Schön, 1983; Zeichner & Liston, 2013) and the importance of capturing that reflection for other educators to examine (Barth, 2001; Hatch et al., 2005; Shulman, 2004), we needed a mechanism to acquire the reflective work in which the Math Leaders were engaging. Vignettes were used to help the Math Leaders reflect on their roles as teacher leaders in the area of mathematics, capture moments of significance (whether the experience was positive or negative) and explore areas for future growth. First, we examine vignettes as a form of research and discuss the ways that Math Leaders were engaged in this process. Then we examine excerpts from the written pieces of one of the Math Leaders, Katherine Reed.

Vignettes as a Form of Research

Closely tied to the work of Ann Lieberman, her colleagues, and the teacher leaders with whom she works (e.g., Lieberman & Friedrich, 2010; Lieberman & Miller, 2004), vignette research assists educators in exploring their practice over time. Perhaps the most essential aspect of vignette research is the public sharing of the vignettes written by participants. Lieberman and Miller (2004) note, "Authorship and audience involve participants in the process of generating an idea, revising it, and making it public to an audience" (p. 35). In order to accomplish these outcomes, significant moments, also known as critical incidents (Flanagan, 1954; Gremler, 2004; Woolsey, 1986), are captured in the writings of those who utilize vignettes as a form of research (Miles, Saxl, & Lieberman, 1988). In capturing these critical incidents, a collection of vignettes can be examined for themes that appear across the writing of several educators or within a collection of pieces from one educator. In the words of Lieberman and Friedrich (2010):

> When a number of people write vignettes in response to a common set of questions, their writing reveals dynamic practices because we can see common elements that emerge across several stories as well as the complexities and specificity of each individual's story. (p. 1)

The common questions to which the authors refer typically engage educators in focusing their writing on specific aspects of their practice. For instance, researchers and professional developers could assist teachers in exploring the effects of a new curriculum on student engagement, the ways in which collaboration improves school culture, or the impact of an educational policy on teachers' relationships with their students. In our case, we asked teachers to explore their roles as leaders in the area of elementary school mathematics. The following section describes our efforts.

Vignettes with the Math Leaders

To begin our year together, each member of the Math leadership group read the book *How Teachers Become Leaders: Learning from Practice and Research* (Lieberman & Friedrich, 2010). Though the focus of this book is not on mathematics education, it introduced the Math Leaders to the concept of vignette research and provided the group with specific examples of vignettes from practicing teachers.

Over the course of our first year together, each member of the group was asked to capture three different critical incidents from the member's work inside schools. Group members focused on the events during their critical incidents, the ways that these incidents related to their roles as Math Leaders, and the reasons these moments were turning points in their thinking about mathematics. At our meetings, members of the group exchanged their written pieces, provided feedback to their peers, and discussed themes they were noticing across their pieces. Not surprisingly, themes such as isolation, lack of support, and feelings of insufficiency were often noted; however, themes related to collaboration, forward progress, and excitement for mathematics also arose.

As group members read the work of their colleagues, they provided feedback on the writing, ideas for further reflection, and possibilities for future action. In addition, the group leaders provided feedback on each of the vignettes. This feedback ranged from assistance with grammar and punctuation to suggestions for exploring an idea more deeply or tying a critical incident to a theme that the group had identified as essential to the role of a Math Leader. The expectation was that Math Leaders would take the feedback from their peers and the group leaders and use it to revise the vignette that had been shared and/or to inform their next vignette. At our final meeting, each Math Leader brought a polished revision of one of the vignettes she had written over the course of our year together.

In the following section we highlight the work of one of the Math Leaders, Katherine Reed. During our first year together, Katherine was serving as a district-level administrator charged with providing professional development and support to the Instructional Specialists from each of the nine elementary school buildings across her district. Prior to this role, Katherine served as a classroom teacher, a building level Instructional Coach, and a district-wide Teacher Development Specialist. She is now an assistant principal at an elementary school.

Katherine's Vignettes

Portions of Katherine's vignettes capture several of the ideas expressed by other Math Leaders throughout the first year of our work together. While an exhaustive exploration of the themes found across the Math Leaders' vignettes is beyond the scope of this chapter, excerpts from Katherine's vignettes will provide the reader with glimpses into the types of reflective work completed by members of the Math leaders group. Ideas explored below include being purposeful, the importance of quality over quantity, and careful collaboration.

Being Purposeful

Much of discussion during the Math leaders group focused on the importance of being purposeful: making well-reasoned decisions, decisions we could justify mathematically and educationally. The following vignette captures a moment inside a classroom in one of the elementary schools where Katherine supported teachers:

> Several weeks ago, I was able to visit a third grade classroom during a math lesson that focused on geometry. At the start of the lesson, the teacher demonstrated how to cut and then fold a cube from a blackline master. The students then spent 48 minutes cutting, gluing and taping their cubes together. The teacher scrambled from student to student, helping with scissor skills. Some students couldn't find glue sticks. Other students resorted to playing catch with their completed cubes.
>
> With two minutes to spare before departing for their special area class, the teacher called for attention and gave the class these final instructions: *Ok class. Put these cubes into your backpacks. Show them to your mom and dad tonight and tell them what you learned about cubes. Tomorrow we will learn about rectangular prisms!*
>
> What did this teacher want the students to learn about cubes? What did this teacher want the students to be able to do with this learning? How did this teacher know if the students learned anything about cubes while constructing them? (Katherine, Vignette #3)

All of us have seen lessons like this lesson. Many of us have *taught* lessons like this lesson. However, most of us have not captured the lessons in written form so we, and other educators, can examine these critical incidents. In order to truly learn from experiences such as this lesson, we need to capture these moments. However, simply writing about these critical incidents isn't enough. We have to dig into the issues. We must use purposeful reflection to examine the situation and decide the next steps. What roles can we, as Math Leaders, play in addressing the situation? What do we know about good teaching and learning that can help this teacher? In what ways have our own actions contributed to situations such as this? Katherine addresses these questions later in her vignette:

> Leaders, Coaches, Specialists: We all have to focus on assisting teachers in designing purposeful experiences that focus on student learning and outcomes. (How do we know when students understand?) Just as we think aloud for our students so they can actually see our thinking, processing, decision-making and intentionality, we need to do the same with teachers. I'm beginning to realize that, unless I support teachers at the planning level, chances are good that I'm just putting Band-Aids over more serious concerns. (Katherine, Vignette #3)

Rather than placing all of the blame for this lesson on the teacher, Katherine realizes that she, too, may be complicit in its failure. She discusses the importance of teachers being purposeful in their planning, but she does not stop at that time. She calls herself to task while reminding others in positions such as hers to "focus on assisting teachers in designing purposeful experiences that focus on student learning and outcomes." Here, Katherine notes the importance of educators working together to improve teaching practices. Instead of bemoaning the ineffectiveness of a teacher after one observation, she imagines ways that she, herself, can be purposeful with this teacher and with other educators. In addition, she alerts other educators to the importance of this work. This process is the power of the vignette: capturing learning moments that have something from which we all can benefit.

Quality over Quantity

Standards for the teaching of mathematics have changed significantly in recent years. Because of this change, teachers are being asked to employ new pedagogies they may have never experienced, themselves, as learners. Because of this change, we need to give teachers experiences similar to the experiences we hope they will provide for their students. After providing one such experience for teachers, Katherine reflected on one of the participants' responses:

> My favorite comment from the teachers' exit slips that morning was, "One problem with lots of student thinking and discussion is much more powerful than many problems trying to be solved." We can get to deeper understanding and transfer when I am working with smaller quantities. We lose focus, purpose, and intentionality when there are too many things to be purposeful about. In order for new learning to become a habit of mind, we need time. As leaders, we would do well to spend time on fewer problems and going deeper with those fewer problems. (Katherine, Vignette #4)

Through the use of a vignette, Katherine was able to layer her understandings. As she solidified her thinking about the need for teachers to do more with less in their instruction, she came to understand that Math Leaders need to do the same for the teachers with whom they work. Whether working at the classroom, school, or district level, deeper understandings build more sustainably. As Math Leaders, we need to provide professional development that will assist educators in becoming better practitioners in the area of mathematics. In order for this transformation to happen, we need to preserve our colleagues' sanity by working to introduce one idea at a time. In subsequent professional development sessions, we can build upon this single idea. We provide spaces where teachers can become more comfortable with previous ideas while learning new concepts. By carefully crafting cumulative experiences for teachers, we model the approaches we want them to show their students. As Katherine reflected on the concept of quality over quantity, she connected her work to a parallel situation in teachers' classrooms. Katherine reminds us that, as Math Leaders, the relationships we forge with teachers are very similar to teachers' relationships with students. Reflecting on these many layers of relationships can assist us all in empathizing with one another as educators.

Careful Collaboration

Many of the Math Leaders discussed ideas related to collaboration in their vignettes. Some discussed the power of collaboration, and some examined the barriers to, or risks necessary for, purposeful collaboration. One of Katherine's vignettes helps to elucidate the ways in which members of the group were examining their roles as Math Leaders:

> After watching his colleague's lesson, one teacher responded, "Well, what I got was that I suck." The third grade teachers sat down . . . dropping papers and pencils on the tabletop while glancing at their colleagues' faces. We had just spent 75 minutes visiting a teammates' math block. The teacher's response, "Well, what I got was that I suck" was not the intended outcome after spending time in another teacher's classroom. There wasn't really a wrong answer . . . except for that one. (Katherine, Vignette #2)

It is not difficult to see the reasons Katherine chose this particular moment as a critical incident. The reaction from one teacher after observing a colleague is rife with emotion—negative emotion. As Math Leaders, Katherine and her colleagues had to ensure that they were able to lead in their schools and/or districts, but they also needed to tread lightly. Many of the Math Leaders were, themselves, still mastering their own understandings of teaching and learning mathematics with understanding (Hiebert et al., 1997). Trying to lead collaborative efforts with teachers who had not had sufficient time to read and think about this type of instruction was a messy business. Katherine used her vignette to continue to explore this issue:

> When teachers spend time watching other teachers, powerful learning and reflection can take place. Yet, as a facilitator, I have to be . . . careful [with the] words and actions that frame the experience—before, during, and after. When we choose or invite teachers to open their classroom doors to their colleagues, we have to consider who and when we invite. It's also important to frame the experience with agreements—like how to sit, where to sit, whether to engage with students or not, etc. . . . Facilitating classroom visits is powerful and complicated. We're dealing with teacher identity—we're invading their worlds—and the more often that we do so, the more comfortable and productive I think it will become. (Katherine, Vignette #2)

Katherine's words remind us that collaboration, in its most basic form, is not enough. We must collaborate with care. We must honor the strengths that each educator brings to the table and use these strengths to address any needs they (or we) identify. We know this asset-based (Cramer, 2006) approach is powerful with students; yet, we often forget to use such care with our colleagues. Katherine's vignette was a powerful learning moment for her, and, because she captured the moment, we can all benefit from this critical incident.

Synthesis

Katherine's example of students spending forty-eight minutes constructing cubes with little instruction on the characteristics of a cube reminds us we must be purposeful in the work we do with students. Katherine ties this to her own work with teachers noting the ways she could model a think aloud to demonstrate the process of planning purposeful instruction. When we consider Katherine's thoughts around quality over quantity, we realize that the current political environment of schools and schooling often causes teachers to cover too much at one time. Katherine notes that she must think about the ways she is developing deeper understandings with her teachers, just as she wants them to do with their students. Finally, our hearts break when we read that a teacher's only discovery from a classroom visit is that he believes he "sucks" at teaching. In her vignette, Katherine notes that powerful learning can occur when teachers open their doors to other educators; however, without careful collaboration—supported by effective facilitation—this time may not be as productive as we may hope.

Katherine's vignettes remind us of the difficulties as well as the celebrations of working toward change in elementary school mathematics. Through her reflections, we gain insight into the spaces needed for educators to make meaning of their work. Without a network of other Math Leaders with whom to interact, would Katherine have polished her ideas in a way that would allow her to communicate with others in the profession? Without monthly meetings, would she have even taken the time to reflect on the events happening in her daily practice? Knowing Katherine, we are sure she would have reflected, but the ways she could others benefit from the opening of these spaces?

CONCLUSION

We began our description using a boxing metaphor to describe the environment in which educators are situated. We discussed the punches that teachers have taken historically and the bouts that teachers currently face.

Additionally, we acknowledged the political sparring among stakeholders as they continue to argue over the content and the ways that students, especially children, should learn mathematics. Today's environment of increasing antagonism has caused a surfeit of teachers to give up, burn out, and/or leave the profession. Whether finding an organization like the IPYW, gathering like-minded educators into a school-based book club, or taking the time to write vignettes about our experiences for others to read and dissect, we must find ways to inspire one another, learn from other educators' experiences, and construct networks of professionals attempting to change the dialogue surrounding education.

The story of Cassius Clay provides inspiration:

> The ring was crowded with has-beens and would-bes, liege men and pugs. Clay ignored them. He began bouncing on the balls of his feet, shuffling joylessly at first, like a marathon dancer at ten to midnight, but then with more speed, more pleasure. After a few minutes, Sonny Liston, the heavyweight champion of the world, stepped through the ropes and onto the canvas, gingerly, like a man easing himself into a canoe. He wore a hooded robe. His eyes were unworried, and they were blank, the dead eyes of a man who'd never got a favor out of life and never given one out. He was not likely to give one to Cassius Clay. (Remnick, 1998, para. 1)

In the current educational environment, educators are unlikely to be given such a favor. Instead, we must work together within the profession to engage, motivate, and challenge one another. We must avoid the temptation to bow to the demands of policymakers and big business in order to provide our students with the educations they deserve. We all know the next events as Cassius Clay emerged as Mohammed Ali and, ultimately, one of the most "original and magnetic athletes" (Remnick, 1998, para. 1) of the 20th century. We also know that he stood for something bigger than himself and his boxing titles.

> As Cassius Clay, he entered the world of professional boxing at a time when the expectation was that a Black fighter would defer to White sensibilities, that he would accede to the same mobsters who ran Liston, that he would play the noble and grateful warrior in the world of the Southern Jim Crow and the Northern hypocrisy. As an athlete, he was supposed to remain aloof from the racial and political upheaval going on around him: the student sit-ins in Nashville, the Freedom Rides, the March on Washington, the student protests in Albany, Georgia, and at Ole Miss. (Remnick, 1998, para. 6)

Like Mohammed Ali, educators must see something bigger, something beyond the ring. We must know, deep in our hearts, who we are and what we stand for. We must understand our students' needs and the ways we will ensure that those needs are fulfilled. We must advocate for our profession in proactive ways. If we're going to fight, let's fight for the hope and inspiration to do what's right for ourselves, for our students and for our profession.

NOTES

1. In addition, two educators from Nashville, TN, attended professional development offerings in the area of elementary school mathematics.
2. The 2015–2016 Math leaders group has continued to work on this Problem Solving Continuum.

REFERENCES

Adamson, S. (Ed.). (2005). *Touching water*. Indianapolis, IN: Indiana Partnership for Young Writers.
Adamson, S. (Ed.). (2007). *Coming to light*. Indianapolis, IN: Indiana Partnership for Young Writers.
Adamson, S. (Ed.). (2009). *Moving earth*. Indianapolis, IN: Indiana Partnership for Young Writers.
Adamson, S. (Ed.). (2011). *Blazing the real*. Indianapolis, IN: Indiana Partnership for Young Writers.
Adamson, S. (Ed.). (2015). *Listening still*. Indianapolis, IN: Indiana Partnership for Young Writers.
Barth, R. S. (2001). *Learning by heart*. San Francisco, CA: Jossey-Bass.
Beck, E. (2015). State faces teacher shortage, decreased enrollment in teacher education programs. *Indiana Daily Student*. Retrieved from http://www.idsnews.com/article/2015/08/teacher-shortage.
Campbell, J. (2015). Some N.Y. schools could face takeover. *Elmira Star Gazette*. Retrieved from http://www.stargazette.com/story/news/politics/2015/04/06/new-york-schools-takeover/25382549/.
Clay, M. (2000). *Running records for classroom teachers*. Portsmouth, NH: Heinemann.
Cramer, K. D. (2006). *Change the way you see everything through asset-based thinking*. Philadelphia, PA: Running Press.
Dana, N. F., & Yendol-Hoppey, D. (2014). *The reflective educator's guide to classroom research: Learning to teach and teaching to learn through practitioner inquiry* (3rd ed.). Thousand Oaks, CA: Corwin Press.
Donoghue, E. F. (2003). The emergence of a profession: Mathematics education in the United States 1890–1920. In G. M. A. Stanic & J. Kilpatrick (Eds.), *A history of school mathematics* (pp. 159–194). Reston, VA: National Council of Teachers of Mathematics.
Fey, J. T., & Graeber, A. O. (2003). From the new math to the agenda for action. In G. M. A. Stanic & J. Kilpatrick (Eds.), *A history of school mathematics* (pp. 521–558). Reston, VA: National Council of Teachers of Mathematics.

FitzGerald, E. (2013). Teachers retiring this year in high numbers. *Danbury News-Times*. Retrieved from http://www.newstimes.com/local/article/Teachers-retiring-this-year-in-high-numbers-4628502.php.

Flanagan, J. C. (1954). The critical incident technique. *Psychological Bulletin, 51*(4), 327–358.

Gremler, D. D. (2004). The critical incident technique in service research. *Journal of Service Research, 7*(1), 65–89.

Hatch, T., Ahmed, D., Lieberman, A., Faigenbaum, D., White, M. E., & Pointer Mace, D. H. (Eds.). (2005). *Going public with our teaching: An anthology of practice*. New York, NY: Teachers College Press.

Hiebert, J., Carpenter, T. P., Fennema, E., Fuson, K. C., Wearne, D., Murray, H., Olivier, A., & Human, P. (1997). *Making sense: Teaching and learning mathematics with understanding*. Portsmouth, NH: Heinemann.

Hoffer, W. W. (2012). *Minds on mathematics: Using math workshop to develop deep understanding in grades 4–8*. Portsmouth, NH: Heinemann.

Lieberman, A., & Friedrich, L. D. (2010). *How teachers become leaders: Learning from practice and research*. New York, NY: Teachers College Press.

Lieberman, A., & Miller, L. (2004). *Teacher leadership*. San Francisco, CA: Jossey-Bass.

Madison Metropolitan School District. (2006). *Learning mathematics in the primary grades*. Madison, WI: Author. Retrieved from https://mathweb.madison.k12.wi.us/files/math/LMPGcomplete.pdf.

Madison Metropolitan School District. (2007). *Learning mathematics in the intermediate grades*. Madison, WI: Author. Retrieved from https://mathweb.madison.k12.wi.us/files/math/LMIGcomplete.pdf.

McInerny, C. (2015). Preliminary A-F data show huge increase in failing schools. *State Impact Indiana*. Retrieved from https://www.wfyi.org/news/articles/preliminary-a-f-data-shows-huge-increase-in-failing-schools.

Miles, M. B., Saxl, E. R., & Lieberman, A. (1988). What skills do educational "change agents" need?: An empirical view. *Curriculum Inquiry, 18*(2), 157–193.

National Commission on Excellence in Education (NCEE). (1983). *A nation at risk: The imperative for educational reform*. Washington, DC: U.S. Government Printing Office.

National Council of Teachers of Mathematics (NCTM). (1989). *Curriculum and evaluation standards for school mathematics*. Reston, VA: Author.

National Council of Teachers of Mathematics (NCTM). (1991). *Professional teaching standards*. Reston, VA: Author.

National Governors Association Center for Best Practices & Council of Chief State School Officers (NGACBP & CCSSO). (2010). *Common core state standards for mathematics*. Washington, DC: Authors.

National Science Board Commission on Precollege Education in Mathematics, Science and Technology. (1983). *Educating Americans for the twenty-first century*. Washington, DC: National Science Foundation.

Payne, J. N. (2003). The new math and its aftermath, grades k-8. In G. M. A. Stanic & J. Kilpatrick (Eds.), *A history of school mathematics* (pp. 559–598). Reston, VA: National Council of Teachers of Mathematics.

Perry, M. J. (2015). Detroit public schools are failing academically and financially, but their teachers and administrators get high marks. *American Enterprise Ideas*. Retrieved from https://www.aei.org/publication/detroit-public-schools-are-failing-academically-and-financially-but-their-teachers-and-administrators-get-high-marks/.

Petersen, J. (2013). *Math games for independent practice: Games to support math workshop and more*. Sausalito, CA: Math Solutions.

Remnick, D. (1998). American hunger. *The New Yorker*. Retrieved from http://www.newyorker.com/magazine/1998/10/12/american-hunger.

Schön, D. A. (1983). *The reflective practitioner: How professionals think in action*. New York, NY: Basic Books.

School Reform Initiative. (2010). *The School Reform Initiative resource book*. Bloomington, IN: Author.

Shulman, L. S. (2004). *The wisdom of practice: Essays on teaching, learning, and learning to teach*. San Francisco, CA: Jossey-Bass.

Wedekind, K. O. (2011). *Math exchange: Guiding young mathematicians in small-group meetings*. Portland, ME: Stenhouse.

Westervelt, E. (2015). Where have all the teachers gone? *National Public Radio*. Retrieved from http://www.npr.org/sections/ed/2015/03/03/389282733/where-have-all-the-teachers-gone.

Wheatley, G. H., & Reynolds, M. (1999). *Coming to know number: A mathematics activity resource for elementary school teachers* (2nd ed). Tallahassee, FL: Mathematics Learning.

Woolsey, L. K. (1986). The critical incident technique: An innovative qualitative method of research. *Canadian Journal of Counseling, 20*(4), 242–254.

Zeichner, K. M., & Liston, D. P. (2013). *Reflective teaching: An introduction* (2nd ed.). Mahwah, NJ: Lawrence Erlbaum Associates.

Chapter 14

The Impact of Privatized Funding in Education and a Proposal for Reform

Todd Cherner and Catherine M. Scott

ABSTRACT

With the *Every Student Succeeds Act* (*ESSA*) (2015), once again hope is renewed that education will serve the needs of all students. One area that has gone unaddressed, however, is the power that edu-philanthropists, that is, affluent citizens and organizations, have in funding educational initiatives that align to their agendas. The danger in not addressing the influence of edu-philanthropists is that initiatives they have funded can potentially harm education and not support it, with the charter school and national standards movements being preeminent examples (Layton, 2008; Scott, 2009). These movements have been financially supported by edu-philanthropists in the form of top-down competitive grants, which push the agendas of the funding groups and not necessarily those of public education. These examples are discussed and an alternative, grassroots model for applying for grants funded by edu-philanthropists is offered.

KEY WORDS

Educational Initiatives; Philanthropy; Educational Funding

The funding for education provided by philanthropic groups is an issue that lurks in the shadows of education, though its impact is widespread. Unlike the attention given to political funding and super pacs, that is, political action committees (*Citizens United v. Federal Elections Commission*, 2010), grant-based funding for educational initiatives continues to fly under the radar. The result of its invisibility is that affluent citizens and groups are allocating enough funding in the form of grants to directly and indirectly influence how students are prepared and then assessed to ensure their college and career readiness.

The implications of this funding directly affect the type of schools students attend, the focus of education they receive while attending school, and the methods used to assess teacher effectiveness (Dillon, 2011; Layton, 2008). These three forces are so tightly intertwined that they are a driving force behind public education in the United States. Directly stated, the problem presented with private groups and affluent citizens funding education is that they are able to purchase the political capital needed via lobbyists, media, campaign donations, educational materials, and instructional technology to make their politicized agendas and initiatives reality in public schools using nondemocratic processes. With the election of a new president, the public, especially educators, now see a renewed opportunity to address this situation.

The purpose of this research is first to provide an overview of educational funding since the Great Recession of 2009 and second to demonstrate how edu-philanthropists have used their political capital to realize their own educational agendas and initiatives. This research will use the charter school and national standards movements to exemplify the actions of edu-philanthropists before proposing a strategy for educational funding reform rooted in existing policy.

FUNDING EDUCATION

Education is not mentioned in the U.S. Constitution, which results in local- and state-level governmental agencies being the authorities for education. Educational funding falls into that purview, and it includes funding from local and state taxes, federal monies, and private funding. The U.S. Department of Education (2005) reported that in 2005 an average of 45.6% of every dollar spent for education was funded by states and 37.1% was funded by local governments. These funds were collected through a variety of state and local taxes. In that same year, the federal government provided 8.3% of the funding, and private sources provided the remaining 8.9%. These 2005 numbers are significant. First, they represent pre-recession funding levels. Since then, a significant change has occurred in the edu-philanthropists who have provided educational funding in recent years.

When the Great Recession of 2009 hit, funding for education, like so many other budgets, was cut. Evans, Schwab, and Wagner (2014) found that the cuts in education budgets from across the nation were severe and "nearly 300,000 teachers and other school personnel" (p. 2) lost their jobs. In response to these cuts and the firing of teachers to balance budgets, the Obama administration launched the *Race To The Top* (RTTT) initiative, which was a competitive grant program initiated by the federal government to reform education (US Department of Education, 2014). The program provided over four billion dollars' worth of funding, and it allocated those monies especially to states that were willing to adopt the Common Core State Standards (CCSS) (National Governors Association Center for Best Practices and the Council of Chief State School Officers [NGACBP] [CCSSO], 2010), support school choice models, and rework teacher accountability models.

Over a three-phase reward system lasting from June 2010 through December 2011, nineteen states received *RTTT* funds (US Department of Education, 2015). As Ravitch (2014) explains, *RTTT* provided the Obama administration a means to emphasize its educational priorities (e.g., the CCSS and charter schools) by offering states large sums of money when they were in dire need. According to the terms of *RTTT*, states had a four-year period to spend their funds (US Department of Education, 2011). As this time limit has now expired, the need for new sources of funding has opened the door to edu-philanthropists.

Money is not free and political agendas come with a cost. Edu-philanthropists know this adage, and they are willing to invest. To be clear, the term edu-philanthropists was chosen for this research because it is commonly used to describe the individuals and groups that donate large sums of money to education in the form of grants to push educational agendas. Two prominent examples of edu-philanthropists are the Bill and Melinda Gates Foundation and the Walton Family Foundation. Both groups, among several other foundations, have given large sums of money to educational causes but not necessarily to public education.

As reports indicate, both groups have given extensively, over two billion dollars collectively, to support the opening of new charter schools by funding lobbyists, legislation, and the schools themselves (Clawson, 2015; Sawchuk, McNeil, Morones, & Peele, 2013). The underlying challenge to edu-philanthropists and programs like *RTTT* is that they are designed to fund educational initiatives and programs that do not necessarily support public education (Lipman, 2013). Rather, these initiatives and programs are pouring billions of dollars into other areas that have limited research bases and are implemented using nondemocratic processes (Ayers, 2015; Dora, 2015; Reich, 2012; Weiss, 2013).

When a policy or initiative is adopted without a public vote or a time period is not provided for citizens and stakeholders to provide feedback, democracy is not being practiced. By excluding these practices, deals are made in the backroom and agendas are forced. When 50.1 million children attend public school in the United States (National Center for Education Statistics, 2015a), major initiatives that directly impact the education these children receive should be put to a vote at the state level. Regardless of the quality of the initiatives, it is essential the initiatives are adopted through a democratic process lest they risk public backlash and scrutiny that waste money and end worthy causes.

Initiative #1: Charter Schools and Implications for Public Education

Since the early 2000s, charter schools have been rising in popularity and they are packaged as something new, different, and innovative. Albert Shanker, past president of the American Federation of Teachers, first proposed charter schools in 1988 as a way to "allow teachers to experiment with innovative approaches to educating students. Publicly funded but independently managed, these schools would be given a charter to try their fresh approaches for a set period of time and be renewed only if they succeeded" (Kahlenberg & Potter, 2014, p. 4). Essentially, Shanker envisioned charter schools as being educational laboratories for teachers to experiment using innovative strategies and methods to increase student learning (Shanker, 1988).

The National Center for Education Statistics (NCES) (2015b) explains that each charter school must have a charter, that is, a stated agreement that explains the school's mission and includes specifics about its budget, curriculum, and accountability policies for achieving its mission. For a charter school to open, an authorizer must approve the initial charter and then revisit it every three-to-five years to recommend whether its charter is renewed or denied. If renewed, the school stays open; if denied, the school closes. Depending on state law, authorizers may include school districts, nonprofits, municipalities, and colleges of education (for a complete discussion of charter school authorizers, please see Shen, 2011). Since the first charter schools opened, they have experienced enormous growth (NCES, 2015b).

According to NCES (2015b), 1,500 charter schools were operating when the 1999–2000 school year opened. By the 2012–2013 school year, the number of operating charter schools had grown to 6,100 schools. As of 2017, the National Alliance for Public Charter Schools (2017) estimated that 3.1 million students were attending charter schools, and the NCES (2015b) reports that charter school demographics reflect some demographic trends experienced by public schools. For example, both charter and public schools are seeing a decrease in the numbers of Caucasian students enrolled and an increase in Hispanic, Asian/Pacific Islander, and American Indians/Native Alaskan students (Badger, 2014). However, public schools are also expecting an increase in the numbers of African American students while charter schools are seeing a decrease in the number of African American students.

From the 1999–2000 school year to the 2012–2013 school year, the numbers of African American students enrolled in charter schools decreased from

34% to 28%. During that same timeframe, the population of African American students in public schools rose from 39% to 49%. The implications of these demographics shift are significant. As Ravitch (2014) explains, charter schools are essentially choosing the students they will educate while leaving the students they do not select to public schools. As early as 2004, Dee and Fu saw this selection of students happening in Arizona's charter schools, and they used the term skimming students to describe it.

Although charter schools' policies must allow all students to apply, Dee and Fu (2004) found that there could be financial and bureaucratic barriers for sending students to charter schools, which precluded all students having equal access to charter schools. Additionally, West, Ingram, and Hind (2006) found evidence that some charter schools admit students who will support the interest of the school. For example, admitting students who have the potential to pass high-stakes tests limits students with special needs from being admitted. Because all students are guaranteed a public education according to state's constitution, students who are not admitted to charter schools have a place in public schools. The result is public schools may serve as a catchall for students unable to attend charter schools regardless of the quality of education charter schools may provide.

According to the Center for Education Policy (CEP) (2012), it is challenging to conclusively state the effectiveness of charter schools as a whole because the studies that analyzed their effectiveness only offer snapshots of student achievement and not long-term data. The CEP (2012) explained that these challenges were caused by the studies that analyzed only charter schools within a specific state, centering solely on one charter school provided, focusing on charter school policy, or describing qualitative characteristics of a school. Comparing different types of charter schools across states in the same region illustrates the complications. To explain, charter schools can be grouped into one of two categories: Startups or Conversion.

Startup Charter Schools

Startup charter schools can be created by a group of individuals, a for-profit group, or a nonprofit group. (In this context, the term group refers to organizations or companies.) The group drafts their school plan that evolves into the school's charter and budget, and then the group presents those documents to an authorizer for approval. Once approved, work to open the school begins. (For a complete discussion of beginning a startup charter school, please see Cannata, Thomas, and Thombre [n.d.].)

Conversion Charter Schools

Conversion charters, in general, are traditional public schools that are either low performing or have identified a way to provide students with an alternative style of education that cannot be implemented in a traditional public school setting. Because each state has different guidelines for conversion charter schools, providing definitive procedures and descriptions for different charter school types is not possible. Table 14.1 illustrates the challenges in comparing types of charter schools from two states.

TABLE 14.1 COMPARING THE CLASSIFICATION OF CHARTER SCHOOLS

Georgia School Type	Description	Louisiana School Type	Description
Startup	"A charter school that did not exist prior to becoming a charter school"	Type 1 Charters	A new charter school operated by a nonprofit group and is authorized by the local school board
Conversion Charter	"A traditional public school entered into a charter to gain additional flexibility for greater accountability"	Type 2 Charters	A conversation or startup charter operated by a nonprofit group authorized by the Board of Elementary and Secondary Education
State Charter Commission School	"A school that has been approved by the State Board of Education after having been denied by a local school district"	Type 3 Charters	A conversion charter school operated by a nonprofit authorized by a local school board
Charter Career Academy	"A specialized charter school established by a partnership between business, instruction, and community stakeholders to advance workforce development"	Type 4 Charters	A conversion or startup charter school operated by a for-profit group and authorized between the local school board and the Board of Elementary and Secondary Education

Georgia School Type	Description	Louisiana School Type	Description
		Type 5 Charters	A conversion charter school operated by a nonprofit group and is authorized by the Board of Elementary and Secondary Education

Georgia Charter Schools Association (2015). Types of charters. Retrieved from http://www.gacharters.org/schools/types-of-charters/

The multiple types of charter schools described in table 14.1 represent schools with a variety of purposes and are authorized by different groups. These differences make it challenging to compare the effectiveness of different types of charter schools and to compare charter schools' effectiveness to the effectiveness of traditional public schools. Nonetheless, researchers have made some general comparisons.

When analyzing student learning at charter schools compared to public schools, Hull (2015) found that on average 17% of charter school students performed better than students in public schools, while "students in 37% of charter schools performed significantly worse, and students in the remaining 46% of charter schools did not perform significantly better or worse than if they had attended their neighborhood traditional public school" (para. 3).

An earlier study conducted by Lubienski and Lubienski (2006) compared 4th- and 8th-grade student test scores on the 2003 National Assessment of Educational Progress (NAEP) for math. According to their analysis, without controlling for student demographic or school location, charter school students scored lower as compared to public and religious school students. When compared to private schools, charter school students scored about two grade levels lower. "After demographic differences had been controlled, no charter or private schools' [test score] means were higher than public school means . . . moreover, particularly at Grade 4, public schools actually scored significantly higher than did private and charter schools" (pp. 679–80).

Though this research points to lower student achievement for students attending charter schools, some research suggests that charter schools do produce some increase in student achievement (Scott & Villavicencio, 2009; Winters, 2012). Though the results are mixed at best, the lack of conclusive evidence does not warrant the current amounts of funding and legislation that supports charter schools, whose growth are projected to increase as a result of the new administration's push for "school choice" among students.

Specifically, it can be argued that the pending maybe harming traditional public schools.

Schools are funded on a cost per pupil model that provides schools with money based on their enrollment. Although cost per pupil varies state-by-state, the national average spent per pupil during the 2015 fiscal year was $11,392, with New York providing the most funding at $21,206 per pupil and Utah providing the least at $6,575 per pupil (U.S. Census Bureau, 2015). Therefore, when a charter school is opened, students apply to it, and students who are accepted transfer from their current school into the charter school. As they transfer, a large portion of money they brought with them to their original school is then shifted to the charter school, but not 100% of it. As the National Alliance for Public Charter Schools (2014) reports, charter schools receive on average 30% less funding than public schools. Nevertheless, as the charter school movement gains momentum regarding the numbers of schools and percentage of students who attend them, the movement, in turn, defunds public schools. In 2017 this movement was exacerbated by the current administration's cuts to the education budget, while at the same time increasing charter school funding by $168 million (Zinshteyn, 2017). This defunding puts public schools in an economic siege (Giroux, 2011) in that corporate reformers, in the name of education, have exploited Shanker's original idea for charter schools and turned it into a system that is bankrupting public schools (Ravitch, 2014). To disguise this practice as palatable, edu-philanthropists have invested in the marketing of charter schools.

Though charter school legislation is voted by states, not the federal government, the individuals funding the campaigns for this legislation are largely wealthy business people. For example, Washington's charter school law was passed in 2012 before being found unconstitutional by the state's Supreme Court because the charter schools were not considered common and open to all students. This legislation was funded by Bill Gates (3 million dollars); Alice Walton (1.7 million dollars); Nicholas Hanauer (1 million dollars); and Jackie and Mike Bezos (750 thousand dollars) (Strauss, 2015). These numbers account only for the funds that were spent on developing and promoting the legislation; the numbers do not include the multimillion dollars spent to fund research, to open charter schools, and to market them (Dora, 2015).

As Baral (2012) explains, once a group, whether it is a for-profit or nonprofit, is approved to operate a charter school and has received funds, the charter school has the authority to hire outside groups to provide support services, similar to public schools. These services may include professional development for teachers, tutoring for students, supplemental educational materials, technology assistance, and more. Consequently, the group operating the school is using public funds to hire private companies, and, if funds are left over, the funds become profit. However, charter schools may not be outperforming traditional public schools, but they are taking money away from them and using that money to earn a profit. In this regard, Miron and Applegate (2007) found that early career teachers working in charter schools located in Connecticut, Delaware, Illinois, and Ohio are leaving the profession at higher rates than their more experienced colleagues, which reflects an ineffectiveness in connection to the professional development being offered to support and retain them. Yet, as Giroux (2011) and Ravitch (2014) explain, charter schools are working to earn profit that overrides the sanctity of education, and public schools along with their students are the ones who are paying the price.

Initiative #2: New National Standards and Federal Accountability Measures

The CCSS were initiated in 2009 by the Council of Chief State School Officers (CCSSO) and the National Governors Association (NGA) as a means to create college- and career-ready students (NGACBP, CCSSO, 2010). Under the direction of David Coleman, current president of the College Board and former director of Student Achievement Partners (SAP), a leading goal of these groups was curriculum coherence on a national level (Resmovits, 2013). Prior to the CCSS, states were responsible for developing their own learning goals and objectives for grade K-12. The development of the CCSS came at a time when the United States was in dire need of educational support, particularly in the wake of Bush's *No Child Left Behind* Act (*NCLB*) (2002).

While CCSS developers and advocates promoted the actual standards as created by teachers and state departments of education, many people questioned the rapid rate and secrecy under which standards were developed and shared around the nation (Bidwell, 2014). The individuals who began promoting the need for a common set of standards were not teachers; rather, they included politicians, corporation owners, and other people who had both high financial status and clout. Coleman's organization, SAP (a nonprofit dedicated to helping educators and administrators improve student performance), led the development process of the CCSS, with a team of over twenty individuals (from SAP, the NGA, CCSO, and Achieve) and with a $147.9 million budget provided by the Bill and Melinda Gates Foundation (Conley, 2014). After the CCSS were developed, then the Foundation funded the organizations charged with evaluating the CCSS in addition to soliciting the American Federation of Teachers (FTE) and National Education Association (NEA) for their support. Only after the standards were written, teachers were asked for feedback, serving on Work and Feedback groups for the standards and providing input during the public comment periods (NGACBP, 2010).

While introduced as voluntary standards for each state to adopt, the CCSS were linked to a critical funding source for schools: *RTTT* funds.

RTTT provided states with additional educational funding if they committed to a set of criteria for evaluating school performance. These criteria included a teacher evaluation system, adoption of college- and career-ready standards, and turning around failing schools (Office of the State Superintendent of Education [OSSE], n.d.). With the need for funding, many states quickly agreed to adopt the CCSS the following year, noting that these standards were marked as preparing students for college and beyond. Interestingly, some states were willing to adopt the CCSS before the first draft was even released in March 2010, with Kentucky committing to the standards the month prior to the release of the standards. By the end of 2010, thirty-five states had committed to the CCSS, and ten additional states had endorsed them (Association of Supervision and Curriculum Development [ASCD], 2015).

With the majority of states adopting the CCSS, states scrambled to adjust curricular materials to align with them. Fittingly, the Bill and Melinda Gates Foundation provided funding for over 200 grants that focused on curriculum development and that reached across the country. In September of 2010, the U.S. Department of Education awarded *RTTT* grants to the Partnership for Assessment of Readiness for College and Careers (PARCC) and the Smarter Balanced Assessment Consortium to develop assessments aligned to the CCSS. Both companies developed computer-implemented standardized tests for students, which then linked student performance on these tests to teacher and school performance accountability measures (Partnership for Assessment Readiness for College and Careers [PARCC], 2010). The implementation of these new assessments was a boon for the technology industry, given the need to provide schools with the proper software and hardware needed to administer them to all of their students. Furthermore, the Pearson testing preparation company used this opportunity to develop their own versions of curricula and test prep materials (and eventual testing alternatives for state adoption).

However, the adoption of the CCSS was not without issues. Upon use of the new standardized assessments aligned with the CCSS, many states saw a significant impact in their student performance data. Coupled with the realization that these data would be used to evaluate teacher performance, many states withdrew their adoption of the CCSS and/or the assessments aligned with them. In 2010, twenty-six states were using PARCC assessments; by 2015, less than twelve states remained (Strauss, 2014). Of the forty-five states (including the District of Columbia and the Department of Defense) that adopted the standards, more than ten states introduced legislation to repeal the CCSS, and Indiana, Oklahoma, and South Carolina have withdrawn their use (Markell & Perdue, 2014; Ujifusa, 2015). These changes have required states to develop their own standards and assessments, which have provided companies further revenue-producing opportunities in terms of creating standardized assessments and supporting materials.

Currently, states are left in troubling waters. Many states have chosen to create their own state standards but are using CCSS-esque standards under the guise of another name (Chiaramonte, 2014). For example, Alaska, Arizona, and South Carolina all have adopted standards very similar to the CCSS, and their standards essentially use revised wording and new titles to differentiate them from the CCSS. These states are again using money to develop new materials, new tests, and new standards, essentially throwing away the millions of dollars invested by the Bill and Melinda Gates Foundation and other edu-philanthropists when the CCSS was created and implemented. At this juncture, community of educational stakeholders must offer solutions to the current administration in order to better this situation and improve the status of education for all students, public, charter, and private alike.

Implications

The implementation of the *NCLB* of 2002 reauthorized the *Elementary and Secondary Education Act* (ESEA) (1965). More than ten years later, the *ESSA* (2015) was proposed as the newest reauthorization of the *Elementary and Secondary Education Act*. In this new version, states are regaining power to create their own academic standards, accountability tests, and education plans, which significantly reduce the federal government's role in education. Alexander (n.d.) states that ESSA prohibits the federal government from "influencing, incentivizing, or coercing states or school districts to adopt any specific academic standards, including the Common Core State Standards . . . [or] endorsing, approving, or sanctioning the alignment of any assessment, instructional content, or curriculum to any specific academic standards" (para. 3). In turn, states are empowered to create their own academic standards and tests. The rub, however, is that *ESSA* Section 1201(b) (2015) permits grants to be used for the development and implementation of both academic standards and accountability tests, if approved by the individual state. This opportunity to use grants to fund the development and implementation of both standards and assessments leaves the door open for edu-philanthropists to continue influencing education. In addition, *ESSA* continues to support the expansion of school choice via charter schools.

When the *NCLB Act* (2002) was adopted, charter schools were used to promote school choice and to support school restructuring. With *ESSA*'s empowerment of states and purposeful lack of prescriptive strategies for improving low-performing schools, *ESSA* uses a variety of grants to support charter schools (Senate Committee on Health Education, Labor, and Pensions, n.d.). Specifically, *ESSA* combined two grant-funding programs to create the Charter Schools Program, which uses grants to support high-quality charter schools, facilitates assistance for charter schools, and replicates and expands effective charter management organizations. In this way, section 4303 of *ESSA* is written so that it continues using grant funding coupled with private funds to support multiple educational reforms that have roots in initiatives that pre-date *ESSA* (2015). These initiatives may include educational management organizations, merit pay, teachers accepting additional instructional roles in schools, and migrating teachers to hard-to-staff schools. In these ways, ESSA leaves opportunities for groups to use funding that promote specific educational initiatives that are yet to be proven successful on a large scale, which puts *ESSA* in contestable waters.

As teacher educators, supporters of effective charters schools, and proponents of academic standards that support students' content area literacy and STEM development, our research concerns *ESSA*'s implementation. For example, although the researchers of this chapter value charter schools (one of the researchers sends children to a charter school and sits on its board and the other researcher wrote a plan for a charter school as part of the researcher's doctoral studies), the researchers share concerns about the widespread implementation of charter schools without quality assurances. In addition, the researchers are deeply invested in preparing teacher candidates with the best practices for developing their future students' content area literacy and STEM skills alike; however, the researchers also believe that the standards used to reinforce these practices must be adopted, implemented, and evaluated using democratic processes. From these perspectives the researchers propose a bottom-up process for schools to apply for funding provided by edu-philanthropists.

A PROPOSAL FOR REFORMING EDUCATIONAL PHILANTHROPIST FUNDING

Despite the concerns regarding funding for schools, many educators still support the education of students and schools using monies from a variety of sources. However, the research presented in this chapter calls for stronger regulatory systems to be put in place for ensuring the funds are used appropriately and that democratic principles are being followed when implementing initiatives. As a basis for structuring these types of reforms, "For Each and Every Child (EEC)" (2011), a report presented to the U.S. Secretary of Education by the Equity and Excellence Commission, can be used as a guide.

The EEC report expresses the need for multiple national reform movements regarding funding and schooling that include (a) the allocation of funds based on student needs, (b) the value of including teachers' voices and input in educational reform, (c) the inclusion of early childhood education initiatives, and (d) the need to include parental involvement in schooling and school decision-making. The commission noted that with the development of the CCSS, both state and federal agencies had an opportunity to examine their own systemic issues and to develop ways to address those issues, which included the allocation of funds and the monitoring of both public and charter school efforts to further ensure student success.

The commission also noted that charter schools hold promise because they promote innovation, provide parents with educational options for their children, offer public schools incentive for improving the education they provide, and have potential to reform education for underserved populations. The report contends that, with these opportunities provided by the current educational climate, "the time has come for bold action by the states—and the federal government—to redesign and reform the funding of our nation's public schools" (p. 17). The report's missing piece, however, was the role that teachers, parents, and community members could play in assisting with funding allocations. Given that the report's focus was on federal funding rather than donations from edu-philanthropists, this outcome was not unexpected. Now, with the transition to *ESSA*, educational policymakers are once again provided an opportunity to examine educational funding practices and put in place procedures that will ensure democratic processes are followed.

Edu-philanthropy is not the sole cause of dysfunction in schooling today; however, it has contributed to funding initiatives that impact education. The ways in which schools, districts, and states have been allocated funding has come from a top-down system, with edu-philanthropists and politicians often dictating who receives additional funding, how those monies shall be spent, and when the funds should be exhausted. When *ESSA* was implemented, states and school districts became more empowered in funding initiatives, which gives promise for reforming the influence of edu-philanthropists.

In the current funding system used, edu-philanthropists and other funding agencies provide money in the form of competitive grants. A competitive grant is usually announced when the funding agency releases its requests for proposals that outline the guidelines for how the grant funding can be used. Applicants have a time period to compose their applications and submit them for review, and the grant agency uses a process to accept or deny applications. Though different agencies have variations of this process, this process is top-down in that the funding agency holds the powers regarding which applicants receive funding and which applicants do not. In addition, no requirement is put on the funding agency for explaining to the denied applicants why their proposal went unfunded. This dynamic empowers the funding agency to drive educational initiatives; it does not support local educational initiatives.

Considering the recommendations of the *EEC*'s report, which include the input of community, families, and teachers in decision-making processes, the value of examining funding from a grassroots perspective must be considered. Starting the bottom-up process, school funding reform must start locally so the voices of teachers, administrators, parents, students, and community members are heard. Given the broad diversity that cuts across schools, the researchers of this chapter recommend that each school and school district conduct a needs assessment that identifies and analyzes current school-wide and district-wide initiatives and makes recommendations regarding if these initiatives should be continued and how best to ensure their success. Table 14.2 identifies initiatives by grade levels that were suggested in the *EEC*'s report.

TABLE 14.2 IDEAS FOR FUNDING INITIATIVES BY GRADE LEVEL, BASED ON EEC REPORTS

Grade Level	Suggested Starting Points
Elementary School (PK-5)	• Providing a comprehensive PK program in all schools • Funding for long-term, sustainable PD is targeted subject areas (to be determined by school) • Funding for basic educational equipment/classroom/supplies • Funding to provide exposure to the arts, STEM, and instructional support in the classroom (additional teachers, materials, field trips) • Developing programs that increase educational opportunities for parents and connections to the community
Middle School (6–8)	• Funding for long-term, sustainable PD is targeted subject areas (to be determined by school) • Funding for basic educational equipment/classroom/supplies • Developing programs that increase educational opportunities for parents and connections to the community
High School (9–12)	• Funding for long-term, sustainable PD is targeted subject areas (to be determined by school) • Funding for basic educational equipment/classroom/supplies • Developing programs that increase educational opportunities for parents and connections to the community • Providing students with resources to prepare them for college or career readiness (e.g., college visits, bridge support in the transition to college)

Once schools have conducted their needs assessment and identified the initiatives they wish to continue, the schools would submit the needs assessment to the school district. In turn, the school district would honor the individual school's work by acting as a liaison between the school and the edu-philanthropist. Essentially, this process is put in place so that schools can only apply for grants that align to the initiatives identified in their needs assessment. School districts would follow a similar structure in that they would conduct a needs assessment based on the needs assessments received from schools and report their findings to the state. The state would ensure that any grants sought align to the districts' needs assessments. Furthermore, states can also communicate with edu-philanthropists to convey the needs of their constituents and to encourage them to broaden or modify their request for proposal so they align to the initiatives identified in the various needs assessments. By enabling individual schools, school districts, and states to first identify their needs and then apply only for grants that align to their needs, reversing the ways edu-philanthropists fund schools would begin by making it more of a bottom-up process.

CONCLUSION

With the passing of *ESSA*, hope has been renewed to reform public education in the United States in the preparation of students to be successful in postsecondary opportunities, the workforce, and as democratic citizens. Part of this renewal, however, needs to include reforming the power edu-philanthropists have in deciding which educational initiatives are funded and which initiatives are not funded. Based on past experiences, research shows that unnecessary fallout, wasteful spending, and political unease have occurred in response to the initiatives funded by edu-philanthropists.

As *ESSA* proposes to return the decision-making power to states and school districts over the education of their students, the influence of edu-philanthropists cannot be excluded. Enabling affluent organizations to fund educational initiatives that they deem important goes against democratic principles; rather, it exemplifies top-down reform efforts that have historically been problematic. In response, educators should consider a proposal for an organic, bottom-up process for identifying initiatives that are localized and reflect the voices of teachers, parents, students, administrators, and community members.

If the state of public education in the United States is going to be improved for all students, the role edu-philanthropists play cannot continue to be hidden in the shadows. A change in how educational initiatives are identified must be made and the groups that fund those initiatives cannot continue to drive education reforms. This proposal is intended to start that conversation by offering a method for empowering schools and school districts when seeking funding from edu-philanthropists.

REFERENCES

Alexander, L. (n.d.). The every student succeeds act and "Common Core state standards." Retrieved from https://www.help.senate.gov/imo/media/doc/ESSA%20-%20Ends%20federal%20Common%20Core%20mandate.pdf.

Association of Supervision and Curriculum Development [ASCD]. (2015). *ASCD and the Common Core policy timeline.* Retrieved from http://www.ascd.org/common-core-state-standards/cc-policy-timeline.aspx.

Ayers, R. (November 10, 2015). *The revolution will not be funded: Testing and the problem with grant-driven educational products.* Retrieved from http://www.kzoo.edu/praxis/the-revolution-will-not-be-funded/.

Badger, E. (August 2014). The rapid demographic shift of American public schools. *Washington Post.* Retrieved from http://www.washingtonpost.com/blogs/wonkblog/wp/2014/08/18/the-rapid-demographic-shift-of-american-public-schools.

Baral, A. (July 5, 2012). Education for profit: The darker side of charter schools. *The Roosevelt Institute.* Retrieved from http://www.nextnewdeal.net/new-guard/education-profit-darker-side-charter-schools.

Bidwell, A. (February 27, 2014). The history of the Common Core Standards. *U.S. News.* Retrieved from http://www.usnews.com/news/special-reports/articles/2014/02/27/the-history-of-common-core-state-standards.

Cannata, M., Thomas, G., & Thombre, Z. (n.d.). Starting strong: Best practices in starting a charter school. *Vanderbilt Peabody College of Education.* Retrieved from https://my.vanderbilt.edu/marisacannata/files/2013/10/Starting_Strong_final.pdf.

Center for Education Policy (CEP). (2012). *Charter schools: finding out the facts.* Retrieved from http://www.centerforpubliceducation.org/Main-Menu/Organizing-a-school/Charter-schools-Finding-out-the-facts-At-a-glance/default.aspx.

Chiaramonte, P. (February 22, 2014). Name game: Amid opposition, states change title of Common Core. *Fox News.* Retrieved from http://www.foxnews.com/us/2014/02/22/name-game-amid-opposition-states-change-title-common-core/.

Citizens United v. Federal Elections Commission. (2010). *558 US 1. Supreme Court of the United States.*

Clawson, L. (June 27, 2015). Walton family spends big to make American education more like Walmart. *Daily Kos Labor.* Retrieved from http://www.dailykos.com/story/2015/06/27/1395883/-Walton-family-spends-big-to-make-American-education-more-like-Walmart.

Conley, D. T. (2014). The Common Core State Standards: Insight into their development and purpose. Retrieved from http://www.ccsso.org/Resources/Publications/The_Common_Core_State_Standards_Insight_into_Their_Development_and_Purpose.html.

Dee, S. T., & Fu, H. (2004). Do charter schools skim students or drain resources? *Economics of Education Review, 23,* 259–271.

Dillon S. (2011). Behind grass-roots school advocacy, Bill Gates. *New York Times,* May 21. http://www.nytimes.com/2011/05/22/education/22gates.html.

Dora, T. (September 7, 2015). Bill Gates has spent $440M to push charter schools: Here is the list of recipients. *Seattle Education.* Retrieved from https://seattleducation2010.wordpress.com/2015/09/07/15765/.

The Equity and Excellence Commission. (2011). *For each and every child: A strategy for education equity and excellence.* Retrieved from http://www2.ed.gov/about/bdscomm/list/eec/equity-excellence-commission-report.pdf.

Evans, W. N., Schwab, R. M., & Wagner, K. L. (2014). *The Great Recession and public education.* Retrieved from https://www3.nd.edu/~wevans1/working_papers/Russell%20Sage%20Paper%20final.pdf.

Freedberg, L. (June 29, 2017). Trump's proposed cuts to education funding create friction in charter school community. Retrieved from https://edsource.org/2017/trumps-proposed-cuts-to-education-funding-creates-friction-in-charter-school-community/583796.

Georgia Charter Schools Association. (2015). *Types of charters.* Retrieved from http://www.gacharters.org/schools/types-of-charters/.

Giroux, H. A. (2011). *Education and the crisis of public values: Challenging the attack on teachers, students, and public education.* New York, NY: Peter Lang.

Hull, J. (2015). How do charter schools compare to traditional public schools in student performance? *Center for Public Education.* Retrieved from http://www.data-first.org/questions/how-do-charter-schools-compare-to-regular-public-schools-in-student-performance/

Kahlenberg, R. D., & Potter, H. (2014). Restoring Shanker's vision for charter schools. *American Educator, 38*(4), 4–13.

Layton, L. (2008). How Bill Gates pulled off the swift Common Core revolution. *The Washington Post,* June 7, 2014. Online: http://www.washingtonpost.com/politics/how-bill-gates-pulled-off-the-swiftcommon-core-revolution/2014/06/07/a830e32e-ec34-11e3-9f5c-9075d5508f0a_story.html.

Lipman, P. (2013). *The new political economy of urban education: Neoliberalism, race, and the right to the city.* New York, NY: Taylor & Francis.

Lubienski, S., & Lubienski, C. (2006). School sector and academic achievement at a multilevel analysis of NAEP mathematics data. *American Educational Research Journal, 43*(4), 651–698.

Markell, J., & Purdue, S. (February 10, 2014). Stop the politics and adopt the Common Core. *Newsday.* Retrieved from http://www.newsday.com/opinion/oped/stop-the-politics-and-adopt-the-common-core-jack-markell-and-sonny-perdue-1.7013345.

Miron, G., & Applegate, B. (2007). *Teacher attrition in charter schools.* Tempe, AZ: Education Policy Research Unit and Boulder, CO: Education and the Public Interest Center. Retrieved from http://epsl.asu.edu/epru/documents/EPSL-0705-234-EPRU.pdf.

National Alliance for Public Charter Schools. (2014). *A growing movement: America's largest charter school communities.* Retrieved from http://www.publiccharters.org/wp-content/uploads/2014/12/2014_Enrollment_Share_FINAL.pdf.

National Alliance for Public Charter Schools. (2017). *Estimated charter public school enrollment.* Retrieved from http://www.publiccharters.org/sites/default/files/migrated/wp-content/uploads/2017/01/EER_Report_V5.pdf.

National Center for Education Statistics. (2015a). *Back to school statistics.* Retrieved from http://nces.ed.gov/fastfacts/display.asp?id=372.

National Center for Education Statistics. (2015b). *The condition of education 2015* (NCES 2015–144). Charter School Enrollment. Retrieved from https://nces.ed.gov/fastfacts/display.asp?id=30.

National Governors Association Center for Best Practices and the Council of Chief State School Officers (NGACBP) (CCSSO). (2010). *About the standards.* Retrieved from http://www.corestandards.org/about-the-standards/.

Office of the State Superintendent of Education. (n.d.). *Race To The Top (RTTT).* Retrieved from http://osse.dc.gov.

Partnership for Assessment of Readiness for College and Careers (PARCC). (2010). *PARCC major milestones.* Retrieved from http://www.parcconline.org/assessments/test-design/test-development/milestones.

Ravitch, D. (2014). *Reign of error: The hoax of the privatization movement and the danger to America's public schools.* New York, NY: Vintage Books.

Reich, R. (2012). A failure of philanthropy: American charity shortchanges the poor, and public policy is partly to blame. *Civic Investment in Public Education.* Retrieved from http://wwww.achievempls.org/sites/default/files/downloads/civic_investment_in_public_education.pdf#page=44.

Resmovits, J. (August 30, 2013). David Coleman, Common Core writer, gears up for SAT rewrite. *Huffington Post.* Retrieved from http://www.huffingtonpost.com/2013/08/30/david-coleman-common-core-sat_n_3818107.html.

Sawchuk, S., McNeil, M., Morones, A., & Peele, H. (November 5, 2013). Follow the money: Gates giving for its teacher agenda. *Education Week.* Retrieved from http://www.edweek.org/ew/section/multimedia/gates-education-spending.html.

Scott, J. (2009). The politics of venture philanthropy in charter school policy and advocacy. *Educational Policy, 23*(1), 106–136.

Scott, J., & Villavicencio, A. (2009). School context and charter school achievement: A framework for understanding the performance "Black Box." *Peabody Journal of Education, 84*(2), 227–243.

Senate Committee on Health Education, Labor, and Pensions. (2015). *The every child achieves act of 2015.* Retrieved from http://www.help.senate.gov/imo/media/The_Every_Child_Achieves_Act_of_2015--summary.pdf.

Shanker, A. (1988). Restructuring our schools. *Peabody Journal of Education, 65*(3), 88–100.

Shen, Y. (2011). Authorizing charter schools. *National Conference of State Legislatures.* Retrieved from http://www.ncsl.org/documents/educ/AuthorizingCharterSchools.pdf.

Strauss, V. (September 6, 2015). Charter school law funded by Bill Gates in Washington state ruled unconstitutional. *The Washington Post.* Retrieved from https://www.washingtonpost.com/blogs/answer-sheet/wp/2015/09/06/charter-school-law-funded-by-bill-gates-in-washington-state-ruled-unconstitutional/.

Strauss, V. (October 23, 2014). Just when things were looking bad for PARCC, they got worse. *Washington Post.* Retrieved from https://www.washingtonpost.com/news/answer-sheet/wp/2014/10/23/just-when-things-were-looking-bad-for-parcc-they-got-worse/.

Ujifusa, A. (June 30, 2015). A 'Common-Core math' problem: How many states have adopted the standards? Retrieved from http://blogs.edweek.org/edweek/state_edwatch/2015/06/a_common_core_math_problem_how_many_states_have_adopted_the_standards.html.

U.S. Census Bureau. (2015). *2015 annual survey of school system finances.* Retrieved from http://www.governing.com/gov-data/education-data/state-education-spending-per-pupil-data.html.

U.S. Department of Education. (2005). *10 facts about K-12 education funding, Washington, DC.* Retrieved from http://www2.ed.gov/about/overview/fed/10facts/index.html?exp.

U.S. Department of Education. (2011). *Race To The Top grantee frequently asked questions.* Washington, D.C. Retrieved from https://www2.ed.gov/programs/racetothetop/faq-grantee.pdf.

U.S. Department of Education. (2014). *Race to the top fund: Purpose.* Retrieved from http://www2.ed.gov/programs/racetothetop/index.html.

U.S. Department of Education. (2015). *Race to the top fund: Amendments/Decision letters.* Retrieved from http://www2.ed.gov/programs/racetothetop/amendments/index.html.

Weiss, E. (September 12, 2013). *Mismatches in race to the top limit educational improvement.* Retrieved from http://www.epi.org/publication/race-to-the-top-goals/.

West, A., Ingram, D., & Hind, A. (2006). "Skimming the cream" admissions to charter schools in the United States and to autonomous schools in England. *Educational Policy, 20*(4), 615–639.

Winters, M. A. (2012). Measuring the effect of charter schools on public school student achievement in an urban environment: Evidence from New York City. *Economics of Education Review, 31*(2), 293–301.

Zinshteyn, M. (March 21, 2017). Charter schools in line to receive extra help despite Trump plan to slash education funding. *EduSource: Highlighting strategies for student success.* Retrieved from https://edsource.org/2017/despite-attempts-to-slash-federal-education-budget-charter-schools-in-line-to-get-additional-funds/578995.

Chapter 15

Urban Teacher Collective Efficacy through Facilitative Leadership

An Illustrative Dialogue

Shelley Nordick, Suzanne H. Jones,
LeAnn G. Putney, and Connie L. Malin

ABSTRACT

Collective efficacy refers to beliefs of a group acting as an effective organization. Educational research has focused on teacher collective efficacy (TCE), primarily through studying teacher perspectives regarding school-wide efficacy. Less examined is the role of the school administrator in developing TCE. Building on an earlier study that examined principals' practice of promoting efficacy among classroom teachers, this dialogue sheds light on the actual practice of a principal who seeks to promote school-wide collective efficacy among faculty and staff. Using findings from the original study, which provided a glimpse of what teachers believed the principal's role to be in building TCE, we engaged the principal in conversation about her role as a facilitative leader. Her insights into actions that promote school-wide efficacy are illustrative and potentially transferable to other administrators and in other school settings.

KEY WORDS

Teacher Efficacy; Facilitative Leadership; Collective Classroom Efficacy

PURPOSE

The structure of this chapter will veer from the research study format due to the way in which it percolated over time. The relationships of the authors are of some import in the development of the ideas presented here. Two of the authors are university professors (LeAnn Putney, UNLV, and Suzanne, aka Suzie Jones, USU), and the other two authors were initially graduate students on whose committees the university professors served (Connie Malin, UNLV, and Shelley Nordick at USU). In each case, the former graduate students have earned their doctorates and now are working in their own respective school settings. Shelley is a former elementary school principal and currently serves as an administrator at the district level in professional development. Shelley completed her dissertation examining facilitative leadership as a means of promoting TCE. Connie is a former elementary school teacher, who is cofounder and principal (CEO) of Innovations International Charter School of Nevada. She completed her doctorate in special education and received her principal certification as well. Their perspectives considering educational theory being played out in practice in their respective educational settings is what makes this dialogue unique.

The purpose of this dialogue was to examine the construct of facilitative leadership enhancing teacher collective efficacy (TCE) as enacted by a principal in an actual public school setting. Shelley, Suzie, and LeAnn had presented together a poster relating the perspectives of teachers about principal actions that promote TCE. It occurred to us then that speaking to a school principal about her actions related to implementing school improvement plans may help us further understand how the findings from the prior study may be played out in practice.

The conversation that took place with Connie was initiated by the knowledge that LeAnn possessed regarding Connie's work in the public charter school. LeAnn is cofounder with Connie and the Governing Body President; they often work in tandem over governance and administrative functioning of the school. The K-12 public charter has a highly diverse school population (70% Latino, 19% African American, the remainder Caucasian, Asian, Native American, and Pacific Islander) and with close to 90% of the students receiving free or reduced lunch. In the past two years, they have been especially diligent about moving the school forward to achieve academic success. This past year, the charter was renewed with a contract through the local school district, and the conversation on leadership hit home with some of the measures Connie has taken care to initiate with the faculty, staff, and families of the school. We took this opportunity as one that could offer valuable information for other principals who wanted to offer such opportunities for building collective efficacy. In the following section are discussion points related to the educational theories undergirding efficacy, hope, learning, and development, leadership, and professional learning communities (PLCs).

THEORETICAL FRAMEWORK

In what follows we explain how we came to initiate the theoretical framework that we developed over time regarding the principal's role in promoting TCE. LeAnn and Suzie first developed the construct of collective classroom efficacy (CCE) by examining Bandura's work through a developmental Vygotskian lens to understand how efficacy is developed among classroom participants over time. The construct of CCE was particular to students developing individual and collective efficacy with the teacher in the role of classroom community organizer. We then discuss how CCE further relates to TCE and the construct of Hope and why those constructs are consequential to life in classrooms.

LeAnn

Suzie and I initially pooled our ideas together in the construct of CCE. My work with a 5th-grade classroom teacher, Ms. Falls, had convinced me that her work with students pulled them together in such a way that they built an efficacious community, while the students also assisted each other in building confidence in their academics. At the time, Suzie and I were working together on data from Ms. Falls and I asked the question, "So what do you call it when the entire classroom collective demonstrates this personal and academic cohesion?"

Suzie

I had been doing some literature reviews on efficacy and kept reading about collective efficacy but primarily at a school-wide level and from the perspective of classroom teachers feeling efficacious about their school as a whole. Could this experience be translated to a teacher and her classroom community? I think so and suggested that we look at those elements in the literature to see if it applied to Ms. Falls's classroom data.

LeAnn & Suzie

We returned to Bandura (1997) and worked forward, drawing upon the researchers who extended their work on collective and teacher efficacy. For example, Goddard, Hoy, and Hoy (2004) explain that perceived collective efficacy consists of the beliefs of individual group members in relationship to the performance capabilities of the group as a whole. This translates at a school level to the individual teacher's judgments concerning whether the faculty can effectively plan and implement lessons and activities that will result in positive student achievement (Goddard, 2001). Schools with faculty members who collectively judge themselves as capable of fostering student achievement create positive learning environments. Likewise, schools with low collective efficacy judge themselves as powerless in promoting academic success (Bandura, 1993; 1997).

In addition, we found that school-wide collective efficacy also involves agency, or the ability to choose to work together to pursue a goal (Goddard, Hoy, & Hoy, 2004). A school may choose to focus on improving reading abilities among their students, while another school may choose to emphasize integrating science throughout the curriculum. Goddard (2001) found that school-wide collective efficacy beliefs have a stronger impact on student achievement than students' past performance, socioeconomic status, race, or culture. An important finding within the literature on school-wide collective efficacy is that student achievement is positively related to a school's collective efficacy (Goddard, 2001). Indeed, Goddard, Hoy, and Hoy (2004) assert, "Collective efficacy beliefs, in turn, foster commitment to school goals and gains in student achievement" (p. 10).

LeAnn

We came to a better understanding about what had been researched at the school-wide level. However, we also realized that, indeed, we could examine the classroom as a collective, and bring collective efficacy to a classroom level through our analysis of field notes and discourse using the 5th-grade classroom data.

Suzie

I also noted similarities between the description of the collective and what I had accomplished as a former 6th-grade teacher with my students. I truly saw my students assisting each other and building that commitment to the goals we set together in our classroom. So, the notion of examining collective efficacy at a classroom level became feasible using data from different classrooms, and different teachers.

LeAnn & Suzie

We came to this "Aha" and began to write about CCE, but LeAnn's Vygotskian background kept edging in to ask, "How is efficacy developed?

It doesn't just come to be one day, and how can the teacher facilitate the development of efficacy both individually and across the classroom collective?" We decided to explore further to find out what a developmental outlook could bring to the construct of efficacy. This resulted in our work on CCE (see Putney & Broughton, 2011).

In combining a Vygotskian approach of individual and collective development (Souza-Lima, 1995), as a means of examining efficacy, we illustrated how a classroom teacher, acting as community organizer (Bandura, 1997), could construct among the individual classroom members a collective sense of relatedness. Through the classroom activities, the students combined that sense of relatedness, with a focus on goal setting and attainment. In the case of the 5th graders, as a collective they established "a social community that shapes its efforts to achieve its common academic and personal goals" (Putney & Broughton, 2011, p. 96).

Furthermore, the students became "local leaders . . . who took on the role of uniting the collective for a common cause of encouraging autonomy, respect, and academic accountability" (Putney & Broughton, 2011, p. 103). The perspective of teacher as community organizer at the micro-level of the classroom provided an avenue through which Shelley could explore the principal as community organizer at the macro-level of the school.

Principal's Role in TCE

Shelley

I began teaching 5th grade in a newly built school with one other 5th-grade teacher. We worked well together, almost as one class. Within four years there were seven 5th-grade teachers. Despite the rapid growth, we continued to grow as a very strong team. We worked hard together and believed in one another. We planned as a team and often taught in tandem or shared one another's students. I knew my students well, but also knew the students in the other six classes. The experience was empowering, with a synergy that was motivating to me as a teacher. There was a power within the team, but I didn't have a label for it at that time.

Moving forward twelve years, I was assigned as an elementary school principal. I wanted nothing more than to replicate the feeling with the staff that I had as a 5th-grade teacher. I was certain it could be done. I tried to be positive and encourage the staff to work as a team. It was a positive environment, and we established strong relationships; however, I always felt like something was missing. I left the school short of my goal to recreate within the staff that sense of "something" for which I still had no label.

As I transitioned from a school to the district office, the opportunity came to begin a doctoral program. Suzie was my instructor and we began learning about Bandura's social cognitive theory and discussed self-efficacy, teacher efficacy and TCE. Everything fell into place when I read that Goddard, Hoy and Hoy (2004) described school staffs with high TCE as those that accept challenging goals, demonstrate strong effort, accept personal responsibility for student learning, believe they can teach students despite negative external forces, and display persistence and resiliency when working with students. I was able then to put the label of TCE on the synergy we had as a 5th-grade team and what I hoped to achieve as an elementary school principal. So, after years of trying to achieve a concept I had no label for, I quickly settled that my doctoral work would focus on TCE.

I was intrigued by LeAnn and Suzie's research on classroom collective efficacy, where they examined the notion of collective efficacy from a classroom perspective, with the role of teacher as fostering the development of CCE (Putney & Broughton, 2011). In that study, LeAnn and Suzie purposefully examined the role of teacher as community organizer. The role of community organizer is "an individual with the major task of constructing a self-directing community that is motivated and unified" (Bandura, 1997, p. 501).

After reading their research, I became interested in the role the principal played as the community organizer. Bandura (1997) suggested that all members of the community should be mindful that their individual problems are "shared social problems that can be alleviated only by working together" (p. 501). He continued, "None of the factions are likely to achieve what they want on their own, but by supporting one another's aspirations, they can realize those of special personal concern" (p. 501).

The importance of school community had been emphasized throughout my work as an administrator. I was familiar with the research of Marzano, Waters, and McNulty (2005), who conducted meta-analysis on sixty-nine studies exploring school leadership and discussed the importance of a school leader creating a culture of cohesiveness, well-being, purpose, and shared goals. This tied directly to Bandura's (1995) assertion that principals who excel in establishing a sense of purpose and getting their staff to work together and who advocate on behalf of teachers enhance collective teacher efficacy (Bandura, 1995).

In their work together, LeAnn and Suzie asked the question, "How can the teacher facilitate the development of efficacy across the classroom collective?" I chose to ask a similar question, "How can the principal facilitate the development of efficacy across a staff collective?" I was grateful to have Suzie's expertise through this process.

Suzie & Shelley

We discussed often how principals were in a position to utilize skills and behaviors to establish school cultures where educators believed that the staff's collective efforts could overcome outside influences and positively impact student achievement. Our search of the literature found correlation studies between TCE and leadership styles, but missing from the current literature was qualitative information related to characteristics of principals that fostered school-wide TCE.

In one study, we set out to examine the characteristics and practice that high-quality principals employed as they fostered TCE in their respective schools (Nordick, Jones, & Putney, 2015). Findings from that study suggested that the characteristics and practice of principals as community organizers included facilitative leadership, collaborative opportunities, professional expectations, and increased capacity. This current conversation allowed us to examine these constructs in more detail in an actual urban public school setting.

Dialogue with Principal Connie—A Situated Case of Facilitative Leadership

Shelley

Teachers in the study described that an environment with TCE felt safe and validating among and between faculty as well as between faculty and principal. Literature relating to adult learning suggests that adults work more effectively when placed in social, collaborative environments (Wenger, 2006). This becomes important as leaders determine where to exert their effort. Leithwood, Seashore, Anderson, and Wahlstrom (2004) suggested that leadership studies provide evidence that educational leaders should pay the most attention to teachers and the professional community that teachers form with colleagues. Moolenaar, Sleegers, and Daly (2012) found that faculties that build a network of collaboration and exchanges of expertise and guidance are more likely to build stronger collective efficacy beliefs. These researchers recommended that school leaders "invest in advice relationships" in order to support collective efficacy (p. 258).

In the initial study (Nordick et al., 2015) we found that principals built stronger collective efficacy beliefs through what we called facilitative leadership. The components of facilitative leadership included communication, trust, and optimism. Participants spoke of the importance of the principal building trust by validating teachers through communication. One participant described the importance of talking to staff members about reducing fear in order to increase trust. Principals used formal and informal collaboration opportunities to build teacher trust and to promote unity. One principal described the staff as a family and expressed how the staff met regularly as a family as well as meeting regularly as departments. One teacher explained the value of providing opportunities for teachers to get to know one another within and across grade levels and/or disciplines. Bandura (1997) discussed the power of models to provide "hopeful determination" and "confidence in the face of difficulties" (p. 88).

To further illustrate facilitative leadership in an urban school, we began a dialogue with Connie, principal of an urban public K-12 charter school here called *Innovations*, to understand how she enacted the tenets of leadership in that setting. Shelley noted to Connie that one of the tenets of facilitative leadership is to find ways to promote communication, trust, and positive attitude among your faculty and staff. Shelley then asked Connie, how have you been able to do that?

Connie

Let me explain first that at Innovations we have licensed teachers, and also licensed staff (here referred to as faculty) who are not in the classroom on a routine basis, such as Special Education facilitators and assistants, school counselors, and Literacy and Learning Specialists. We also involve the support staff such as office personnel, school nurse, security officers, and kitchen staff as part of the PLCs since they interact with the students on an ongoing basis outside of the classroom. Our goal is for everyone to work in concert for the benefit of the students. Students may need to leave the classroom for a time for discipline, health, or emotional issues, and while we accommodate them, our collective job is to get them back into the classroom for the sake of learning.

We first began this process of promoting communication among teachers through the use of mentors and grade-level chairs. Once we started with PLCs, we began shifting responsibilities to other faculty members as well such as the PLC strategists' positions, the PLC grade-level leaders' positions, the special education facilitator, and the Leaning Strategist. We have always had our counselors work alongside administration and teachers and enabled them to work with small groups, large groups, and among PLC teams. Trust is something that has become an earned commodity as we have enabled teachers and other staff members to pilot their ideas, present them to other staff members, and then rewarded a job well done. We have always worked from the glass half full attitude at the school.

Anything that happens in the classrooms for discipline, parent communication, student feedback, and so on is set with a positive wording. An example would be: Traditional schools use *Required Parent Conference*, while at Innovations we use *Parent Advisory Meeting*. The wording shifts the intention from referring a student to the parent to bringing the parent into discussion about their child so that we can be effective educational partners. I also believe that a positive nature comes from the top. While I may get discouraged at times, I do not show this to staff. I keep things honest, but I use a positive spin and work for problem solving rather than complaining. Staff members also know that if they have a problem, they need to have a suggested solution that will benefit the students before approaching me with the problem. This gives them time to speak with each other and brainstorm before I have to give an answer.

LeAnn

In working with Connie, I have noticed that anybody who comes to her with a request to initiate change in the school is met with the question, "How will this solution benefit the kids in the school?" This stance is proactive and causes everyone to think through issues and potential unintended consequences before jumping to a quick fix. Suzie, how do you see this approach in terms of your work in generating hope?

Suzie

The idea of staff members discussing issues in terms of student benefit actually becomes an avenue for nurturing hope among the faculty and staff. By asking the teachers to come up with different solutions related to student progress, Connie keeps in the forefront the objective of improving student learning, while also encouraging teachers to explore different pathways of teaching. Nurturing hope is all about sustaining willpower and providing waypower (Snyder, 2002). Willpower is enhanced when Connie lets teachers know that they have the agency and expertise to come up with ways to address a challenge. At the same time, the solutions have to be student oriented and student centered so as to maintain the school-wide improvement. Bringing together teacher expertise to enhance student learning illustrates a reciprocal relationship between Hope and TCE.

Shelley

In our earlier work we noted that principals emphasized the importance of common goals when establishing a collaborative culture. Principals viewed creating and accomplishing common goals as helping to build unity. An illustrative example of collaborating on a school-wide goal was shared by a principal who explained that a strong sense of cohesiveness was experienced by the principal and faculty as they implemented a school-wide student leadership program.

Some of the more fine-grained findings of the study helped explain the nuances of being a community organizer. For example, having common goals is not a new concept, but reaching collective agreements relative to the goals is a more specific concept that moves beyond goal setting. Finding a collective solution to a school's issues ensures greater buy-in from the entire staff. Kurz and Knight (2003) found goal consensus or vision to be a significant predictor of collective teacher efficacy.

In reflecting on the role of goal generating as an important component of facilitative leadership, Shelly asked Connie the question, "How do you generate common goals? What are some examples of common goals in your school setting?"

Connie

Common goals are built around our school performance plan, which are built to ensure student achievement. We began the school's process among the teachers with grade-level chairs. These chairs met with me monthly as we talked about the school's mission and goals. As we became more in tune with collecting, analyzing, and letting student data drive us, we moved to PLCs. We sent twenty-two staff members to the PLC Training set by the DuFours (DuFour, 2003), and Solution Tree (Buffum, Mattos, Weber, & Hierck 2015). During this training, we were introduced to a new way of working collaboratively and given the opportunity to structure ourselves in the way that we could work together in our own setting.

Once the training was completed, we came back to the school for a week during the summer break to work extra time in setting our school's goals, our alignment of intervention times with student needs, and in setting norms for the school. Because last year was our first year of doing this, I hired three PLC strategists to oversee the kickoff of the program, to ensure work was accomplished, to facilitate communication and collaboration, and to help mentor teachers who had not had the training. From the first twenty-two members—our Guiding Coalition—we then picked grade-level PLC leaders and school-level PLC leaders to meet and discuss our continued movement toward meeting goals and determining where we still needed assistance.

This year, we will continue the process by using three of our own strong leaders as the PLC strategists. We are beginning to grow our program from within, thus empowering more teachers in the process and continuing until all members, over an approximate three-year period, have the same level of competency, professional development, and ability to coordinate groups of people. We are using a type of Train the Trainer model to empower all staff members.

We have rearranged our teaching PLC groups to incorporate licensed, nonteaching faculty, and our support staff as well. This enables all staff members at the school to see that their views of where we are and where we are going are valued as well. This variety of perspectives can only be acquired from considering all points of view. Some examples of common goals we generated are (a) increasing the proficiency levels of all students in reading and language arts, (b) increasing the proficiency levels of all students in mathematics, (c) increasing the communication and parent engagement with our families, (d) increasing the collaboration between and among grade levels and disciplines, and (e) fostering our mission of the school by everyone knowing, facilitating, and living the mission set forth.

LeAnn

As you can see, Connie was building a PLC collective with the original twenty-two members who went through the professional development program. These members became the "more experienced others" who then could mentor the other teachers and staff members, and especially those new to the school. This experience of the more experienced taking responsibility to bring the knowledge to the other teachers and staff members is an example of the Vygotskian Zone of Proximal Development in action. What the teachers do together with the PLC leaders today, they can implement in their classrooms tomorrow. We hoped that the teachers would apply these same principles in the classroom—as they learn more about the strategies to improve instruction, they could see their students working together in a similar way in their own classroom settings.

Suzie

To bring in the work on teacher efficacy, as the teachers and staff members become more comfortable with the PLC work, they will continue to use the strategies and build their own efficacy. As they all become more involved in attaining the common/collective goals, they will see a stronger collective efficacy across the grade levels. Ideally we would see a similar striving for common goal attainment in their classrooms, resulting in higher CCE.

In addition to CCE, it is likely that teachers will experience an increased sense of hope. Hope, as defined by Snyder (2002), has three facets—*waypower*, *willpower*, and *agency*. As we noted earlier, waypower means that the individual, or in this case the collective, have multiple pathways to help them attain their goals. Willpower is the driving force, or determination to succeed regardless of how difficult the pathway to achieving the goal may become. Agency is at play as individuals within the collective choose whether they will initiate and pursue the goal, and to what extent they choose to participate. Lopez (2013) recognizes that applying hope now for the future helps us to behave differently today. More specifically, he states, "How we think about the future—how we hope—determines how well we live our lives" (Lopez, 2013, p. 9).

Principal's Role in Offering Leadership Opportunities to Staff Members

Shelley

Principals in our 2015 study held attitudes that motivated them to act intentionally with confidence that they could make an impact, and they believed it was their responsibility to help teachers do the same. Offering leadership opportunities for teachers was a frequently used strategy to help teachers grow their own confidence while building capacity among the staff.

Derrington and Angelle (2013) found a "clear and strong relationship between collective efficacy and teacher leadership in a school" (p. 6). Goddard and colleagues (2004) reported links between teachers' opportunities to influence school decisions and teachers' perceived collective efficacy and suggested that when teachers are given the opportunity to influence school decisions, they tend to have stronger beliefs in the school's capability. In addition, Nordick, Jones, and Putney (2015) found that the faculty of a participating school experienced a strong sense of cohesiveness when the principal empowered teachers to lead department collaboration meetings.

While reflecting on the ways in which principals offered leadership opportunities for teachers, Shelley asked Connie to explain how she managed to build capacity among teachers and staff members.

Connie

We begin with those teachers, licensed noninstructional faculty, and support staff members who volunteer or who have shown the ability to take a leadership capacity. They are given tasks or select tasks they would like to work on with groups. We celebrate accomplishments and acknowledge the acts of leadership. We rotate leadership roles and invite other team members to join the leadership team in order to allow others to have the empowerment to understand what needs to be done, how to do it, how to rally the others in their grade levels to do it, and then how to mentor others.

I believe that leadership is only as good as the team you have working on something, so I always seek others' opinions, work from a team model, and empower others to try something new. My thought process is to give everyone a chance to try the PLC team leader role and to know how to orchestrate collaboration, give feedback, and share strategies that help others. If the only leadership given is from the top, the teachers are unable to get behind what you ask them to do. I work alongside my entire staff, attend meetings with them, provide multiple instances of professional development, and work with the PLC teams to move us forward. I am big on sharing information that is critical to the welfare of the school in a positive manner that allows teachers to grasp responsibility and to put their own spin onto something in order to ensure all have the opportunity for inclusion.

Let me give you a great example of teacher responsibility that presented itself at one of our grade-level PLC meetings. Teachers were discussing their formative assessment data as it pertained to instructional objectives as they collaborated in a weekly scheduled grade-level meeting. As the PLC strategist asked probing questions, one of the teachers related to the response given by a colleague to a student. She was having difficulty with this student's behavior in her homeroom class in spite of trying numerous classroom management techniques. Other teachers began to share strategies with her, as this was her first year of teaching, and they wanted to support her endeavors with this student.

The PLC strategist noted that through her interventions with the student in question, she observed that this child craved closeness and kindness more than rigidity and goal setting. She gave multiple examples to illustrate how this young boy interacted in her intervention group. One of the grade-level teachers gasped and noted that while she was new to this grade level and still struggling with the grade-level content, that people skills and compassion were her forte—something this child needed. The homeroom teacher responded that while she was entirely new to teaching, the content was her forte, and building strong relationships and people skills was not yet within her comfort zone. Her teaching style was more aligned with goal setting and rewarding student choices.

Simultaneously both teachers asked the PLC strategist if it would be possible to ask for a student exchange to help this boy. In the discussion that ensued, it was noted that the second teacher (not goal-oriented) had a boy who needed goals and physical rewards that she was uncomfortable keeping track of daily. The grade-level team asked the PLC strategist to approach administrative team with the possibility of exchanging classrooms for these two students to pilot test a re-matching of student learning needs with instructional styles. Their common goal was to benefit not only the grade level, but also the students and teachers in each of the classrooms.

The PLC strategist approached our administrative team with the conversation and the suggestions made by the teachers. In order to fully evaluate what the intended and unintended consequences of the movement might be, our administrative team consisting of the Learning Strategist, Director of Security, special education facilitator, and myself, the principal, met to discuss the proposal made by the teachers. We discussed the potential impact of the requested classroom exchange on the social, emotional, and academic outcomes for the boys. We agreed that making this change would most likely enhance the classroom cultures, improve the grade-level academic achievement, and meet the needs of the teachers, and all students involved. They contacted the parents of the students, and discussed the classroom exchange, suggesting that it would prove beneficial to the learning, emotional, and social development for both boys. The parents were supportive and anxious to see their children succeed.

As of the writing of this chapter, the classroom exchange had just been accomplished. We are waiting to see the outcomes, but the teachers and administrative team were hopeful and optimistic that they had found, not only the willpower, but also the waypower to assist the teachers and students involved in this educational issue.

Principal's Role in Offering Support and Mentoring to Teachers

Shelley

In the TCE study (Nordick et al., 2015), principals and teachers spoke of the importance of support. Teachers appreciated the efforts of a principal in providing the materials and time needed to plan instruction and implement new programs. Principals also discussed the importance of providing professional support to teachers. This support could come in the form of providing professional development or supporting teachers with classroom management, instructional strategies, and innovation.

Bandura (1997) stated, "Evidence of progressive improvement sustains a sense of personal efficacy and provides a continuing source of self-satisfaction" (p. 92). A principal focus on continuous professional improvement creates an expectation that school and personal improvement is an ongoing process. Ware and Kitsantas (2007) indicated that efficacy was reinforced when teachers believed they could obtain support from principals to have control over the teaching-learning process.

One area of support that may be overlooked is in the mentorship of new teachers. Shelley posed this question to Connie, "In terms of mentoring new teachers, Connie, how do you bring into the fold the new teachers who join the current faculty and staff?"

Connie

We initiate mentoring in our new teacher orientation and continue it through our PLC meetings. I begin the year with a one-week new member orientation (to include support staff), in which we discuss critical aspects of our charter and school procedures. Since they come from a variety of backgrounds, it is easier to coach them all together without the returning teachers and staff in attendance. The Learning Strategist and the special education facilitator take part in the coaching as well. This allows new members the chance to hear from their expertise and also to have a friendly face they recognize once school starts. Mentor teachers are assigned prior to the school year in an effort to have assistance immediately ready for the new staff.

While we understand that mentoring allows for physical communication and action between teachers, we also understand that the instructional day is filled with obligations and duties to the students and the school. To allow for teachers to have the chance to process and reprocess information, the school has developed an inner school video library. Here, the teachers may view, as frequently as they need, a series of short video sessions informing them on a variety of measures needed for proficiency in the school.

An example of this video coaching is the use of the monthly data generated by our formative assessments in reading and mathematics. The video sessions walk the teachers step by step through accessing the data, aligning the data with the reports generated by the formative assessment, using the data to drive instruction in the classroom, and using the data to individualize and align lessons with the Depth Of Knowledge (DOK) levels of instruction (Webb, 2009).

Each of the videos are developed and formulated on a teacher-to-teacher level. In other words, teachers with specific expertise are enlisted to make the videos for their colleagues in "teacher talk" and examples. This becomes a less threatening delivery of information from their colleagues, rather than being a perceived top-down demand. Lessons are short, specific, and modeled so new teachers can see and emulate what is expected in an accepting manner. This allows new teachers to seek additional help if needed from their peers without having to admit their lack of understanding to administration. The PLC strategists and PLC grade-level leaders facilitate these suggestions and lessons for their colleagues based on questioning and feedback gathered from weekly meetings.

Principal's Role in Offering Support and Mentoring to Staff

Taken together, we have seen the role of the principal as critical to engendering hope among teachers, as well as in the classroom with the students. Relative to this point, Shelley asked Connie to give some specific ideas of what strategies have worked with her Innovations support staff members so that they can engender hope that translates to the students and teachers as well.

Connie

We have attended two training sessions with the DuFours (2003) over the last year and I have found that their philosophy is one that empowers others.

In looking at the Tiers of Instruction, many of the grants and federal programs have narrowed in on Tier I instruction (instruction for all students) in the classroom as a critical element for student achievement. In traditional schools, especially in the past, if a child is unable to succeed in the classroom, a referral is made to get the child additional assistance outside of the classroom.

Since we are an inclusive school, we bring the resources to the teachers. For example, we may have a student who has the capability to complete the work in class, but refuses to do so. This refusal to accomplish the work is what Buffum, Mattos, Weber, and Hierck, (2015) call a *lack of will*. In this case, the counselor is called into the classroom to conduct a series of interventions while the classroom teacher takes notes, works alongside the counselor, and then takes the strategies covered back to his/her peers for further use in the grade level.

If we have a student who *lacks a particular skill* related to the classroom curriculum (Buffum et al., 2015), we bring the special education staff in to work with the students and classroom teacher on a series of instructional interventions showing teachers how to work with students having difficulties with the materials. Again, the classroom teacher takes notes, works alongside the special education staff, and then takes the strategies covered back to his/her peers for further use in the grade level.

This inclusive practice allows for general education teachers, counselors, and special education staff to work alongside each other in an effort to share expertise. In each case, we need to consider whether the student is exhibiting a lack of will, a lack of skill, or a combination of the two. This type of assessment assists the team in determining what type of intervention will benefit the student the most.

Finally, we send our second language teachers and professional developers into the classrooms as well to show second language instructional strategies to the teachers, watch them use the strategies, and provide feedback for how to correct errors made. At the same time, they are assisting students in small groups to master the English language and achieve academic proficiency.

Shelley

As Connie aptly illustrated for us, education can no longer be an isolated endeavor. According to Bandura (1997), efficacy beliefs are increased as colleagues support each other and model coping strategies. Inviting the counselor and/or special education staff to work in the classroom with a struggling student as the teacher observes, illustrates the power of models to provide what Bandura (1997) calls "hopeful determination" (p. 88).

Principal's Role in Facilitating Teacher Implementation of Will and Skill Strategies

Connie

The division of students into the will, skill, and will/skill groups (Buffum et al., 2015) has been a new concept for the teachers as a differentiated instructional strategy rather than the prior rating of students on low, average, and high academic performance. They were curious as to how the counselor and facilitators could model strategies for them from this mindset of will and skill that would be beneficial for meeting the social, emotional, behavioral, and academic needs of their students.

While counselors are more trained to deal with the social and emotional areas of learning (will), they also needed to see how their expounding of character education traits played out in the classroom as transferrable/generalizable tools to support student learning. Special education staff members are trained to work with small groups of students having specific diagnosed needs (skill). They also needed to see that their specialized learning strategies served as useful instructional accommodations for all students whether or not they had a documented label.

The PLC strategists and administration remained adamant about modeling this new thinking process for the teachers in spite of their initial apprehension. The first groupings of students were conducted with the PLC strategists and administration modeling the thought process for making the group assignments by looking at classroom performance, behavior interventions, and academic achievement.

Teachers actively began to have input into the group separations and took notes on how the characteristics of the students as learners influenced weekly which group suited their needs. Within a four- to six-week period of time, the identification of students for the intervention groups became a more fluid discussion for the teachers using the will and skill terms. While teachers have now actively embraced these terms, discussion of Tier I, II, and III instructional needs has become pertinent to the placement of students based on formative data collected weekly and presented in the PLC team meetings.

The teachers have decided for themselves by collecting and analyzing data that these groups are fluid and more pertinent to academic achievement as they address underlying issues that keep a student from becoming motivated to extend their own learning process. Mixing the expertise of the will, skill, and will/skill strategies has become very powerful in the process of utilizing peer mentoring and student engagement through the use of learning stations.

For two hours each day, a team consisting of administration, counselors, the learning strategist, and the special education facilitator work with the will and will/skill groups on phonetics, vocabulary development, reading comprehension, and character education using a selected novel as the basis for learning. Planning is done within the team aligned with the needed state standards for literacy and language development. Students rotate through the four learning stations on the blended standards needed for literacy mastery.

Questioning within the groups is deliberately aimed for DOK levels 3 and 4 (Webb, 2009) in order to encourage active thinking on the part of the students. This type of questioning moves students beyond recall (Level 1) and skills and concepts (Level 2) to facilitate strategic thinking, both short term (Level 3) and extended (Level 4). For example, students have been asked to find evidence in the novel to support their answers to probing questions, thus allowing them to produce higher-level thinking and problem-solving skills than they may receive within their classroom work. Feedback from the teachers, students, and parents has been amazing. All have noted an increase in reading fluency, sentence writing, spelling, listening, and participation skills within the classroom practices. Students themselves are excited to join the groups, complete the work asked of them, and actively discuss concepts with their peers and the learning station teachers. This is evidenced by their willingness to read aloud to each other, help each other with words they struggle to decode, discussing illustrations, characters, plot, settings, and story line conflicts that some would have believed to be too difficult for these students to comprehend.

We use these during our regularly scheduled mandated daily intervention times. Teachers determine the groups during their weekly PLC meetings. While they do the differentiated instruction during their own work with their classrooms, the groups for interventions are built around the needs that students have to succeed while working with people who have expertise. We have also set a Wall of Fame celebrating students as they move through our monthly Evaluate testing. This testing is done in language arts and mathematics to achieve formative and summative data on achievement levels. This is one method we use for documenting student growth as needed for reporting to our sponsor.

Shelley

I'd like to speak to Connie's use of a Wall of Fame to celebrate student progress. Bandura (1993) introduced four sources of self-efficacy, which were shown by Goddard et al. (2004) to apply to collective efficacy as well. Mastery experience is considered the most "powerful" source of efficacy (Goddard et al., 2004, p. 5). I believe the Wall of Fame, which places "mastery" on display, may illustrate a reciprocal relationship between student self-efficacy and teacher self-efficacy. A school that includes students who have efficacy most likely includes teachers who have efficacy. Involving many staff members in the process of helping students succeed could turn the Wall of Fame into a mastery experience that builds collective teacher efficacy and potential for CCE as well.

RESULTS AND CONCLUSIONS

Our intention with this chapter was to examine theoretical perspectives related to TCE being enacted through the principal's practice as community organizer in a public school setting. Indeed, three of the four TCE themes identified in Nordick and colleagues (2015) were further illustrated in this study: Facilitative Leadership, Collaborative Opportunities, and Building Capacity. This work contributes to the discussion of TCE by illustrating the relationship of TCE and Hope, thus extending the TCE construct beyond a belief system and moving the teachers into positive action relative to their collective efficacy.

As far as the illustrations of TCE in relation to facilitative leadership, this principal enacted facilitative leadership as a continual process of working with classroom teachers and staff members through progressive professional development. The introduction of the PLC models (DuFour, 2003) as a professional development program for this school was a vehicle for implementing the facilitative leadership model. These PLC meetings afforded the teachers and support staff both the willpower and the waypower to facilitate building hope among the teachers that adds depth to their belief in their abilities to empower students.

Second, TCE was promoted through open communication between and among the principal, faculty, and support staff specifically by collaborating and developing strategies for addressing challenges related to student learning. One outcome of the collaborative opportunities was the generating of school-wide common goals built around the school performance plan. The school performance plan was utilized as a pathway to school improvement with specific hope-based learning strategies for teachers to use in the classroom setting. The leadership team initiated a teacher-led series of video clips of strategy use so that other teachers and staff could use these clips for their own self-improvement.

Third, building capacity was accomplished by inviting teachers to join the leadership team and empower them with an understanding of school improvement goals, skills needed to accomplish those goals, and to rally their peers to employ those skills with their students. Faculty members were rotated into the leadership team so they could learn how to orchestrate collaboration, provide feedback, and share strategies among their peers. In addition, support staff members were encouraged to work closely with classroom teachers, as peers to model specific will, skill, or will/skill type interventions with particular students. The interactions among teachers and support staff were a way of sharing expertise in a highly collaborative and peer-to-peer effort. Using this relational model was a way of combining hope and efficacy through active classroom practice, thus moving teachers and support staff beyond beliefs and into productive action. This type productive action is a key outcome of hope-based pedagogy.

IMPLICATIONS

A central tenet of collective efficacy "relates to how well group members respond and relate to one another as they work toward common goals" (Putney & Broughton, 2011). As noted in the review of literature, a strong sense of collective efficacy among teachers can result in higher expectations for student achievement, thus increasing opportunities for improving student learning outcomes. The additional construct of hope brings to the forefront the need for positive and constructive action to fulfill the promise of efficacious beliefs.

To better understand how principals can foster high levels of collective efficacy, while enacting collective hope, we examined a telling case (Mitchell, 1984) of one principal, her administrative team, and her PLC strategists who viewed themselves as community organizers (Bandura, 1993). From this perspective, the principal and instructional strategists were responsible for establishing and sustaining the common goals and practices that result in a sense of school-wide community accomplishment. They sustained these common goals through their hope-based actions and collaborations.

This telling case further confirmed findings related to the principal's role, and illustrated that role in actual practice within an urban public school. These findings may guide principals to enhance their current methods of leadership or may be used by district administrators and educational leadership faculty responsible for educating new principals.

REFERENCES

Bandura, A. (1993). Perceived self-efficacy in cognitive development and functioning. *Educational Psychologist, 28*(2), 117–148.
Bandura, A. (Ed.). (1995). *Self-efficacy in changing societies.* Cambridge, UK: Cambridge University Press.
Bandura, A. (1997). Self-efficacy. *Harvard Mental Health Letter, 13*(9), 4–7.
Bandura, A. (1997). *Self-efficacy: The exercise of control.* New York, NY: Freeman.
Buffum, A., Mattos, M., Weber, C., & Hierck, T. (2015). *Uniting academic and behavior interventions: Solving the skill or will dilemma.* Bloomington, IN: Solution Tree Press.

Derrington, M. L., & Angelle, P. S. (2013). Teacher leadership and collective efficacy: Connections and links. *International Journal of Teacher Leadership, 4*(1), 1–13.

DuFour, R. (2003). Building a professional learning community. *The School Administrator, 60*(5), 13–18.

Goddard, R. D. (2001). Collective efficacy: A neglected construct in the study of schools and student achievement. *Journal of Educational Psychology, 93*(3), 467–476.

Goddard, R. D. (2002). A theoretical and empirical analysis of the measurement of collective efficacy: The development of a short form. *Educational and Psychological Measurement, 62*(1), 97–110.

Goddard, R. D., Hoy, W. K., & Hoy, A. W. (2004). Collective efficacy beliefs: Theoretical developments, empirical evidence, and future directions. *Educational Researcher, 33*(3), 3–13.

Kurz, T. B., & Knight, S. L. (2004). An exploration of the relationship among teacher efficacy, collective teacher efficacy, and goal consensus. *Learning Environments Research, 7*(2), 111–128.

Leithwood, K., Seashore, K., Anderson, S., & Wahlstrom, K. (2004). *Executive summary: Review of research: How leadership influences student learning*. Retrieved from http://hdl.handle.net/11299/2102.

Lopez, S. J. (2013). *Making hope happen: Create the future you want for yourself and others*. NY: Atria Paperback.

Marzano, R. J., Waters, T., & McNulty, B. A. (2005). *School leadership that works: From research to results*. Alexandria, VA: Association for Supervision and Curriculum Development (ASCD).

Moolenaar, N. M., Sleegers, P. J. C., & Daly, A. J. (2012). Teaming up: Linking collaboration networks, collective efficacy, and student achievement. *Teaching and Teacher Education, 28*(2), 251–262.

Mitchell, J. C. (1984). Case studies. In R. F. Ellen (Ed.), *Ethnographic research: A guide to general conduct* (pp. 237–241). San Diego, CA: Academic Press.

Nordick, S., Jones, S. H., & Putney, L. G. (February 2015). *Developing teacher collective efficacy: Case studies of principals as community organizers*. Poster presented at Ethnographic and Qualitative Research Conference, Las Vegas, NV.

Putney, L. G., & Broughton, S. H. (2011). Developing collective classroom efficacy: The teacher's role as community organizer. *Journal of Teacher Education, 62*(1), 93–105.

Snyder, C. R. (2002). Hope theory: Rainbows in the mind. *Psychology Inquiry, 13*(4), 249–275.

Souza-Lima, E. (1995). Culture revisited: Vygotsky's ideas in Brazil. *Anthropology and Education Quarterly, 26*(4), 443–457.

Ware, H., & Kitsantas, A. (2007). Teacher and collective efficacy beliefs as predictors of professional commitment. *The Journal of Educational Research, 100*(5), 303–310.

Webb, N. (2009). *Webb's depth of knowledge guide: Career and technical education definitions*. http://www.mde.k12.ms.us; http://redesign.rcu.msstate.edu.

Wenger, E. (2006). *Communities of practice: A brief introduction*. Retrieved from http://www.ewenger.com/theory/.

Chapter 16

Are You a Hope Buster or a Hope Muster?

Angela Webster

ABSTRACT

For educational spaces that seem desperate, despondent, and disheartened, this chapter offers hope. The author discusses the notion of hope, parallel conceptions of hope, and variances of hope. In this chapter, preK-12 educators and teacher educators become more conversant with the cognitive processes of hope (goals thinking, pathways thinking, and agency thinking), the legitimacy of the affective states of hope (persistence, endurance, and action) as well as some beliefs and habits of mind of hope such as growth mindset and grit. In addition, this chapter extends hope to educators who, in turn, can help students cultivate hope, and thereby, maximize hope in schools. This exposition of hope aspires to convene a cadre of hope musters and alleviate the stronghold of hope busters in education.

KEY WORDS

Hope; Growth Mindset; Agency

My childhood was a story of hope. Although I lived in a depleted and dreary government-housing complex in the urban landscapes of Memphis, Tennessee, I had a relationship with the future. Assignments to low-achieving schools did not dim my view of my potential, my possibilities, or my promise. Even through the years when I could not gauge my personal value, I maintained positive beliefs about my tomorrows. During times when I unknowingly surrendered my personal power, I had faith that I possessed the inner capacity to create a brighter outlook for myself.

Did my teachers know I had hope? My recollection is most probably did not. Unfortunately, many educators at my school did not extend their souls to us. They, in large measure, honored their contractual duty. The interpretation for contractual duty is that they offered unrelated and unimaginative content in a sterile, uninspiring, and controlling school culture. Whenever our achievement or behavior disappointed, they were quick to remind us of their mantra that was delivered in a snarky tone, "I have my education; you need to get yours."

Much like the working-class schools described in Finn's (2009) *Literacy with an Attitude*, teachers were not inclined to explain the nature, reasons, or connectedness of assignments. Low-ordered worksheets were a mainstay. Students did not construct their own knowledge. Procedures and processes were important to the adults on campus. Students had few choices or decision-making power and authorities closely watched and controlled our movement and sadly, it was commonplace for students to hear derogatory comments made about them. These educators were hope busters. They could not see us beyond our circumstances and they viewed our economic situations as permanent and even diminishing.

Of all of my K-12 principals and teachers, the minority who dispensed hope are indelibly marked in my heart because they talked to us about their world and life beyond our bleak environment. They even made pronouncements of their belief in us. During their moments of frustration and displeasure, they remained hopeful for us. When we let them down, they reminded us "You're going to be somebody." Without our pleading, they were willing to see beyond our zip code, our Ebonics native language pattern, our basement-bargain clothing, and our need to accept the free breakfast and lunch that the school provided. They did not necessarily understand the texture of our hair but they did not eschew us because of it. They realized that even when we groomed our hair in the morning it might not be kempt by the time we made it to school; it was less likely to survive recess or gym class, intact.

My memory of these treasured educators is that they noticed the light in my eyes and my easy smile. They observed my love for learning even though this passion did not always parallel school subjects. Even though I was loquacious, the great teachers accepted it as part of my interpersonal intelligence. They recognized my penchant for details and my need for order, orderliness, and organization as a burgeoning leadership spirit to be cultivated not squelched. They created a space for me to dream, think, and do. For instance, when I had learned all the tenets of the basic 6th-grade curriculum, which was very early in the academic year, my teacher allowed me to visit the school library for hours on-end to explore and imagine a better life for myself.

Similarly, one of my freshman high school teachers allowed me to devote her class period in the library after telling me that she had nothing left to teach me. During my sophomore year of high school, one of my teachers, whose full story I share in another publication (Webster-Smith, 2017), singlehandedly placed me on the college track in the middle of the academic year. Even though I was in a racially isolated (all Black), 100% free- and reduced-meal school, this first year, Caucasian teacher noticed and acknowledged my potential then summoned the courage to advocate for my participation in the school's more rigorous curriculum. I designate these latter educators as hope musters. They beckon hope from within themselves while they also help students rally all possible courage to advance the notion of hope.

Regrettably, many of America's students then and today experience fragile familial circumstances, unengaging classrooms, unsupervised time after school, and a lack of community resources. America allows children to remain trapped in schools with an unacceptable range of teaching talent, less than rigorous course offerings, and insufficient resources. We know that children in low-performing schools receive a substandard education that perpetuates the well-documented underachievement of historically underrepresented students, economically disadvantaged students, children with disabilities, and English learners (National Center for Educational Statistics [NCES], 2014). We also know that opportunity gaps, excellence gaps, and achievement gaps stem largely from societal ills, not individual or group deficiencies (Banks, 2008; Gay, 2002).

Generational and societal factors persist through academically poor schools with uninviting educational climates. Enrollment in an ineffective school can be a lifelong sentence to second-class citizenry and economic poverty in that low academic achievement equates to decreased matriculation, retention, and graduation from high school and college (NCES, 2014). Intellectual underachievement unequivocally leads to underemployment, unemployment, and disempowerment. The well-crafted sequence is thus. Education determines income, which determines where we can afford to live. Where we live determines where we can go to school because enrollment maps link funding formulas to income/tax base. This vicious cycle has its way of slowly eroding all signs of hopefulness from many of America's at-risk youth. This hopelessness includes general hope and academic hope.

Even now, I wonder how much better my journey and that of my classmates might have been had we experienced mostly educators and schools that distributed hope. More importantly, I am concerned about the outcomes of children today who are considered to be among the least, the lost, the last, the looked over, and the left out. I continue to believe that all educators and schools can abandon their roles as hope busters and become hope musters. To that end, this chapter puts forth working descriptors for hope, how schools can become transformative bastions of hope, and even maximize hope on behalf of America's future. All are important in that "embedded in the self-image of children is the hope for all our futures" (Kuykendall, 1991, p. 19).

CONCEPTUAL FRAMEWORK

What is hope? *Research captures various images of the idea of hope. C.R. Snyder is the father of the theory of hope. According to Snyder (1994, 2000a, 2000b), hope is a human strength manifested in the three cognitive capacities of goals, pathways, and agency.* Goals-directed thinking includes goals that are short- and long-term, abstract and concrete, as well as general and specific. Goals thinking is aspirational *and allows one to initiate purposeful behavior.* Pathways thinking includes belief in one's capacity to generate the cognitive routes and plans to attain goals. Agency thinking pertains to belief in one's capacity to begin focused action and continue along selected, yet flexible pathways to attain goals. To a great extent, *hopeful thinking is the linchpin for the successful completion of goals (Feldman & Snyder, 2005) that includes what to do; how to do; and I can do.*

Now it is instructive to point out the differences between similar notions and variances in hope. *Optimism is a positive anticipatory state in with a positive expectancy for the future and the likelihood of a realized outcome* (Scheier & Carver, 1985). Snyder, Harris, Anderson, Holleran, Irving, Sigmon, Oshinobu, Gibb, Langelle, and Harney (1991) *are committed to the bilateral expectancies of efficacy (agency) and outcome expectancies (pathways), rather than the unilateral outcome expectancies of focused behavior (goals).*

The primary difference between hope and optimism is that hope is an emotion while optimism is a cognitive process (Averill, Catlin, & Chon, 1990; Bruininks & Malle, 2006). *Wanting and desire are states that come about for favorable and easily attainable goals whereas hope remains secure even through difficult circumstances and is reserved for more controllable goals than is wishful thinking* (Malle & Knobe, 2001). *Just as we note a link between joy, happiness, and contentment* (Bruininks & Malle, 2006), *hope is associated with less materialistic, socially acceptable, more intangible, and more enduring goals* (Roseman, Spindle, & Jose, 1990).

All the same, variance exists within the construct of hope. For instance, those individuals with active hope not only dream, they plan and do. The adage, *if it is to be, it is up to me* rings true. When they hope something will occur, they are willing to make it happen. Those individuals with passive hope are fine to wish for things, but are not willing to exert the effort, or they believe their desire is out of their control to pursue (Miceli & Castelfranchi, 2010). Hopeful thinkers turn wish lists into to-do lists (Lopez, 2010).

In essence, hope is a form of personal capital that reflects one's orientation toward the future while it inspires goal-directed behavior. Hope can be a transformative experience in that it has the capacity to shape action (Robb, O'Leary, Mackinnon, & Bishop, 2010). *Helping students to cultivate hope is advisable yet helping them to reach the status of high hope is even better. A high-hope adolescent is one who is almost certain of attending college and living to age 35* (Bennett, Wood, Butterfield, Kraemer, & Goldhagen, 2014). High-hope students also have social capital that includes general connectedness with their family, neighborhood, and school. *These researchers identified several school factors that influence a student's high-hope status to include (a) students believe the school is not prejudiced; (b) teachers treat students fairly; (c) students are happy to be at their school; (d) students feel close to people at school; (e) students feel a part of their schools; (f) students feel safe at school; and (g) students feel teachers care about them.*

According to Bennett et al. (2014), hope enables positive development in youth. *For instance, an adolescent's expectation of educational attainment and self-reported life expectancy can predict risk-taking behaviors as well as actual educational achievement and health outcomes.* In fact, *several critical success measures of students relate to hope, according to Gallup (2009a; 2009b; 2009c). Hope positively correlates to attendance, credits earned, and academic achievement. Hopeful middle school students earn better grades in core subjects and score higher on achievement tests. Hopeful high school students earn higher grade point averages. The significant predictive power of hope remains even when controlling for intelligence, prior grades, and self-esteem. Hope does not correlate to native intelligence or family income. All of the aforementioned findings demonstrate that the student-school relationship is important and that schools should aspire to become conveyors of hope.*

HOPE-BASED SCHOOLS

The hallmarks of hope-based schools are a culture of collaboration, positive interactions, home-school synchronicity, and personal empowerment (Webster-Smith, 2010). Systemic and systematic teamwork between administrators, teachers as well as other school personnel, parents, and community stakeholders is the norm because that is what it takes to address the myriad school- and societal-based challenges. Positive interactions ensure that educators focus on both the capital that children bring (glows) and illuminate improvement (grows) to promote a strengths-based climate where students make progress. Besides, it is critical that all stakeholders contribute to the surety of a physically and emotionally safe place for children to learn and play.

Further, a school that builds bridges (i.e., home-school synchronicity) through cultural understanding, cultural relevance, culturally responsive pedagogy, and engagement of familial and community assets, enlivens its curriculum as well as its teaching and learning while it also alleviates the marginalization and disenfranchisement of the families it serves. When schools approach teaching and learning through the prism of students' natural talents, gifts, and abilities, students become educated for personal empowerment to serve humanity through community. Overall, when educators lift the children behind the test scores, the scores themselves will be lifted.

In hope-based schools, every administrator, every teacher, and all other school personnel are early adapters of this notion of hope. To be certain, cafeteria workers, bus drivers, the service/maintenance team as well as all volunteers are educators, by virtue of their role. The school is ensconced in helping children strengthen their hopeful thinking. This belief is important because regardless of a student's current level of hope, it can grow to a level of hopeful thinking that yields a fruitful difference in the life of the student (Lopez, Rose, Robinson, Marques, & Pais-Ribeiro, 2009) even for youth with "histories of family breakdown, neglect, abuse, poverty, addition, and violence" (Bryant & Ellard, 2015, p. 497). The culture of teaching and learning then includes the three cognitive proficiencies of hope—goals thinking, pathways thinking, and agency thinking.

Help Students Establish Goals Thinking

While educators introduce goals thinking based on the student's age, developmental stage, and specific circumstances, goal setting remains the foundation stone of hope construction (Lopez et al., 2009) and having a variety of goals allows students to turn to another goal if one goal seemingly comes to a standstill. Educators use past success, in any arena of life, to jumpstart the process of hope development. Reflecting upon meaningful and pleasurable recent goal attainment helps to engender attainable future goals (Lopez et al., 2009).

It is also imperative to consider the student's values, interests, and inherent genius when setting goals. Students are more apt to attain internal, energizing goals that are within their wheelhouse than those students grounded in someone else's vision for them as the latter undermines intrinsic motivation and performance (Conti, 2000). Likewise, students learn that specific goals are easier to reach than vague goals (Emmons, 1992). Students who are particularly low in hope learn to prioritize goals, as they tend to have the maladaptive practice of impulsively attempting to pursue all goals that come to mind, without success of course (Feldman & Snyder, 2005).

Moreover, students learn to set goal markers that help them track progress (Pennebaker, 1989). Another essential lesson in goal setting is that approach goals (i.e., moving toward a target) are typically more reinforcing than avoidance goals (i.e., trying to prevent something from happening) based on the research of Snyder, Feldman, Taylor, Schroeder, and Adams, III, 2000). Finally, "we" goals in addition to "me" goals have advantages (Snyder, Cheavens, & Sympson, 1997). For example, educators encourage children to work together to solve academic challenges as well as authentic matters within their school and community. Since educators in hope-based schools model collaboration, students can readily practice the success strategies of individual and group hopeful thinking in general, and goals thinking, in particular (Robitschek, 1996).

Help Students Develop Pathways Thinking

Effective pathways thinking involves the inclusion of micro goals that offer successes that eventually lead to the macro or ultimate goal. Stepping is especially important for low-hope students, as they wrongly believe in instant goal attainment. Stepping offers a more realistic picture as well as confidence and motivation (Snyder et al., 1997). Sometimes such students have difficulty in charting more than one path to their desired goals.

Helping students with alternative routes is important because some roads are blocked and detours are necessary; again, this strategy is especially helpful for low-hope students as they are likely to see the obstacle as a lack of talent, ability, or confirmation that a goal is unattainable (Snyder et al., 2002). Pathways thinking is akin to reframing failure in that students can formulate obstacles as information that leads to a better passageway.

Help Students Improve Their Agency Thinking

Agency is the belief in one's power to make conscious and deliberate decisions and actions (Moje & Lewis, 2009), while efficacy speaks to the belief that one is responsible for enough variables to make positive change in one's outcomes (Bandura, 1977). To be sure, students require agency and efficacy as well as positive internal dialogue and stretch goals. Low-hope students are particularly critical of themselves and need to master the art of encouraging self-talk. Students learn to identify negative and unproductive personal narratives and replace it with agentic thinking and affirmations (Snyder et al., 2002). Schools make available hope-related stories, books, and community members that represent triumphing hardship, harsh conditions, and hard times as overcoming adversity helps to develop a sense of agency (Snyder, 1994; Snyder et al., 2002). Stretch goals enhance agency in terms of considering previous performance of students and establishing goals that are more complex, thereby, inspiring hope (Lopez et al., 2009).

MAXIMIZING HOPE IN SCHOOLS

In order to maximize hope in schools, educators do not pride themselves on being hope busters but see themselves as hope musters. Hopeful educators ignite excitement about the future. They inspire rather than exhaust students. Messengers of hope create hope games that teach problem-solving strategies, sing hope songs, engage in hope projects, and keep visuals of hope present whether they are photos, collages, or videos.

Hope musters understand that their relationship with students calls for consistency, firmness, and fairness, yet trust and hope. Champions of hope have high expectations for students and provide clear directions on how to master course objectives, fashion solutions, and earn good grades. Nonetheless, hope musters create an environment where students chase the learning, not the grade (Lopez et al., 2009). These couriers of hope also make it clear that hope does not always translate into one's specific goal. Considering factors such as time, energy, and resources, one may need to re-goal in alignment with initial values and desires (Lopez, 2010).

In order to maximize hope in schools, educators also help students decode, decrypt, and demystify the psychology of learning. In that work, educators teach beyond their curriculum or their regularly assigned duties by giving students psychological tools. Kirp (2016) purported that students who only learn about good study habits perform less well than those students whose educators also taught psychological tools. Some of the indispensable instruments of hope include growth mindset and grit.

Growth Mindset and Goals

According to Carol Dweck (2016), growth mindset is a testament to the learner's beliefs about how their actions determine their future and inform their theories of intelligence. As an example, Dweck (1986) has expounded upon motivation as it pertains to goal orientation. Her study of achievement motivation asserts that learning goals, where students seek to increase their competence by understanding, learning, or mastering something new is more constructive than performance goals because such goals merely seek favorable judgment of others and avoid negative evaluations by others.

Performance goals align with the entity theory in that intelligence is fixed and persistence is low in the face of challenges. To the contrary, learning goals align with the incremental theory in that intelligences are malleable with the tendency to seek appropriate challenges with persistence and high energy. Children who pursue performance goals are proud and relieved when school does not stretch their intelligences. For them, effort in the face of challenge is aversive, as anxiety about performance tends to overwhelm. Children who embrace learning goals report school as boring and disappointing when they are under-challenged intellectually. Interest and enjoyment of effort are easy to access for them. In fact, the brain experiences positive change when learning and moving through challenge. These two systems of self-concept and their attending goals produce two distinct sources of self-esteem, one positive and the other negative, one fatalistic and the other, hopeful (Dweck, 1986; 2016).

The types of goals students employ create their motivational patterns. Dweck's (2016) investigation of motivational patterns maintain that adaptive motivational patterns promote personally challenging and personally valued achievement goals while maladaptive motivational patterns are associated with the inability to take on reasonable, esteemed goals and the failure to make consistent progress toward goals. The former mastery-oriented pattern serves students better than the latter hopeless-oriented pattern. A case in point is that children who perceive themselves as helpless attribute their failure to a lack of ability and see that inability as insurmountable; however, children who perceive themselves as hopeful view failure as surmountable (Diener & Dweck, 1980). In essence, motivation influences how a child learns and uses knowledge and the child's motivational patterns determine whether they pursue success and how they respond to failure. Thankfully, schools can intervene to modify the less constructive patterns.

Encouraging students to practice intrinsic motivation and to surrender their destructive motivational patterns is important because even when the intelligence of two students is equivalent, counterproductive patterns have a profoundly negative effect on cognitive performance. Besides, where native abilities are different, schools can help students put into operation positive motivational factors that grow their abilities (Dweck, 2016). They might be reminded of the words of Linda Ellerbee (n.d.), "What I like most about change is that it can be a synonym for hope. If you are taking a risk, what you are really saying is, 'I believe in tomorrow, and I will be part of it.'"

Successful schools offer children an environment of helpfulness. This refuge is important because asking for and receiving help allows individuals to hold on to hope (Dweck, 2016). Educators can help by vizualizing their work as an endeavor of helping students with their intellectual blooming and human flourishing. With that, educators teach higher-ordered thinking and high-level skills. Brown, Palincsar, and Purcell (1984) argued that low performance is the prevailing outcome of low expectations, undemanding curricular offerings, and substandard, dismissive instructional methods.

Hopeful educators encourage students' belief in their ability to invest the requisite time, effort, and strategies to attain their goals rather than singling out and relying upon their raw intelligence. Hope-filled educators promote the use of single-minded, intensified attention to the pursuit of their goals. They inspire students to channel their emotions into tasks that lead to goal pursuit. They also help students nurture their intrinsic motivation to sustain them when challenges surface and when called upon to deliver high effort (Dweck, 2016). Since students move through the world with positive and negative core assumptions, the optimal goal for educators is to use a social-cognitive approach to motivation and personality to help students make the best possible cognitive, affective, and behavioral choices as they all can be developed (Dweck & Leggett, 1988).

Grit Development vis-à-vis Pathways and Agency

Angela Duckworth (2016) in her research on grit development provides insight into the cognitive competences of pathways and agency in ways that require and cultivate grit. Duckworth (2016) defines grit as the ability to stick to one's most valued goals. Activities that are challenging, fun, and within the child's control facilitate grit, hopefulness, and happiness to rise above obstacles,

Duckworth (2016) also conveyed that children need love, latitude, and limits. As a result, psychologically wise educators provide a spectrum of professional practices that fosters educational environments that balance nurturance and high expectations. Such educators do not take less than the best from students. Additionally, educators who aspire to develop grit and agency in students offer specific feedback. For instance, when students are not giving their best, the educator reaches out to them because they know the students can offer more. They give students specific and short-term reasons for failures (i.e., you did not study enough) and positive and pervasive reasoning for success (i.e., you are a good student). Psychologically wise educators care for students, are empathic, and notice the intellectual and affective changes in students (Duckworth, 2016).

Any school, according to Duckworth (2016), can adopt a gritty culture. For example, the school can apply the "hard thing" rule (Duckworth, 2016), which helps to develop grit and agency. The school, as a principle, insists that all students do something that is hard for them. Better still, they do not allow students to quit until a natural break occurs such as the end of a semester, season, or year, or they have received the benefits of a paid experience. Those students who learn to do hard tasks demonstrate more rigor and endurance for hard tasks and cultivate learned industriousness rather than learned helplessness (Eisenberger, 1992). Duckworth (2016) described skill as talent time effort and achievement as skill time effort. As students are developing grit, they are also forging various pathways to get to the finish line with adeptness and perseverance. Some of the long-term outcomes of developing grit as a child includes faring better in almost every metric (i.e., better grades, higher self-esteem, higher college graduation rates, greater community involvement rates, and greater follow-up on the tasks of life).

Duckworth (2016) affirms that schools are an ecosystem of educators that supports the dreams of students. A meta-analysis of grit determined that grit moderately correlates with performance and retention (Credé, Tynan, & Harms, 2016) and that grit is a very strong correlate of conscientiousness. With that confirmation, the following grit acronym offers additional tips for educators to help students develop an assiduous form of hope.

Growth: Successful educators encourage students to believe in their ability to learn and grow whether they are at the top of the class or the bottom of the class. High-achieving students do not rest on their laurels and underachieving students persist, knowing that their efforts will pay off. Rehearse: Educators insist that all students exercise the discipline of practice. Educators expect all students to expend effort generously, commit to becoming better, and to improve. Interest: Educators deliver a curriculum of interest and meaning to students. In order for this outcome to occur, educators get to know students, that is, what they love, what they hate, what grieves them, the population they are passionate about serving, and the geographical location in which they want to serve (Murdock, 2007). They help students to understand that their life's work will call for a season of preparation, which may require an obsession-like focus (Murdock, 2007). Tenacity: Educators hearten students to commit to their most treasured goals, to keep going, never give up, and remain hopeful. As Aristotle (n.d.) once said, "Excellence is never an accident. It is always the result of high intention, sincere effort, and intelligent execution. It represents the wise choice of many alternatives. Choice, not chance, determines your destiny."

CONCLUSION

This examination of literature demonstrates that hope is necessary. Hopeful thinking students are energetic and excited about life. They are resourceful in that they are able to establish goals, plan a course of action, and change such plans when faced with unforeseen events. They view obstacles as opportunities unlike hopeless students faced with blocks who become discouraged and stuck (Snyder, 1994).

What is more, hope is a contagion; hence, I am inclined to agree with the words of Robert F. Kennedy (1966),

It is from numberless diverse acts of courage and belief that human history is shaped. Each time a man [person] stands up for an ideal, or acts to improve the lot of others, or strikes out against injustice, he [she] sends forth a tiny ripple of hope, and crossing each other from a million different centers of energy and daring, those ripples build a current which can sweep down the mightiest walls of oppression and resistance.

This statesman possessed the foresight to understand that producing citizens who are prepared to move beyond America's intractable issues of race, gender, and class, necessitates educational institutions that are citadels of hope. Besides, just as hope can be cultivated in students, so it is with educators. Guiding students with strategies such as goals thinking, pathways thinking, and agency thinking also transforms educators from the status of hope busters to hope musters, creating hope-based schools that inculcate students with the requisite mindset and actions for success. This belief is especially important for high-needs children (Ohio Board Certified Teachers, 2006): children who experience physical or intellectual impairment, reside in families that have a low-income, speak a language other than English, have difficult social and economic conditions, substandard housing, family and/or neighborhood instability, and/or are located in urban or rural settings. Such a campaign for America's future keeps hope alive for generations to come.

REFERENCES

Aristotle. (n.d.). AZQuotes.com. Retrieved from http://www.azquotes.com/quote/365116.

Averill, J. R., Catlin, G., & Chon, K. K. (1990). *Rules of hope.* New York, NY: Springer-Verlag.

Bandura, A. (1977). Self-efficacy: Toward a unifying theory of behavior change. *Psychological Review, 84*, 191–215.

Banks, J. (2008). *An introduction to multicultural education* (4th ed.). Boston, MA: Pearson Education.

Bennett, A., Wood, D., Butterfield, R., Kraemer, D., & Goldhagen, J. (2014). Finding hope in hopeless environments. *International Journal of Child Health and Human Development, 7*(3), 313–324.

Brown, A. L., Palincsar, A. S., & Purcell, L. (1984). Poor readers: Teach don't label. In U. Neisser (Ed.), *The academic performance of minority children: A new perspective* (pp. 105–143). Hillsdale, NJ: Erlbaum.

Bruininks, P., & Malle, B. F. (2006). Distinguishing hope from optimism and other affective states. *Motivation and Emotion, 29*(4), 327–355.

Bryant, J., & Ellard, J. (2015). Hope as a form of agency in the future thinking of disenfranchised young people. *Journal of Youth Studies, 18*(4), 485–499.

Conti, R. (2000). College goals: Do self-determined and carefully considered goals predict intrinsic motivation, academic performance, and adjustment during the first semester? *Social Psychology of Education, 4*(2), 189–211.

Credé, M., Tynan, M. C., & Harms, P. D. (June 16, 2016). Much ado about grit: A meta-analytic synthesis of the grit literature. *Journal of Personality and Social Psychology*. Advance online publication. Retrieved from http://dx.doi.org/10.1037/pspp0000102.

Diener, C. I., & Dweck, C. S. (1980). An analysis of learned helplessness: II. The processing of success. *Journal of Personality and Social Psychology, 39*(5), 940–952.

Duckworth, A. (2016). *Grit: The power of passion and perseverance*. New York, NY: Simon & Schuster, Inc.

Dweck, C. S. (1986). Motivational processes affecting learning. *American Psychologist, 41*(10), 1040–1048.

Dweck, C. S. (2016). *Mindset: The new psychology of success*. New York, NY: Ballantine Books.

Dweck, C. S., & Leggett, E. L. (1988). A social-cognitive approach to motivation and personality. *Psychological Review, 95*(2), 256–273.

Eisenberger, R. (1992). Learned industriousness. *Psychological Review, 99*(2), 248–267.

Ellerbee, L. (n.d.). AZQuotes.com. Retrieved from http://www.azquotes.com/quote/521363.

Emmons, R. A. (1992). Abstract versus concrete goals: Personal striving level, physical illness, and psychological well-being. *Journal of Personality and Social Psychology, 62*(2), 292–300.

Feldman, D. B., & Snyder, C. R. (2005). Hope and the meaningful life: Theoretical and empirical associations between goal-directed thinking and life meaning. *Journal of Social and Clinical Psychology, 24*(3), 401–424.

Finn, P. (2009). *Literacy with an attitude: Educating working-class children in their own self-interest*. Albany, NY: State University of New York Press.

Gallup. (2009a, March). Relationships between hope, income, and teacher-student ratio. *Gallup Student Poll*. Omaha, NE. Unpublished raw data.

Gallup. (2009b). Hope as an outcome of strengths development in freshmen in high school. *Gallup Student Poll*. Omaha, NE. Unpublished raw data.

Gallup. (2009c). Hope, engagement, and well-being as predictors of attendance, credits earned, and GPA in high school freshmen. *Gallup Student Poll*. Omaha, NE. Unpublished raw data.

Gay, G. (2002). Preparing for culturally responsive teaching. *Journal of Teacher Education, 53*(2), 106–116.

Kennedy, R. (June 6, 1966). *Robert F. Kennedy, Speech at the University of Capetown, South Africa, Day of Affirmation*. Retrieved from https://www.mtholyoke.edu/acad/intrel/speech/rfksa.htm.

Kirp, D. L. (October 30, 2016). Nudges that help struggling students succeed. *The New York Times*. Page SR2. Retrieved from https://nyti.ms/2dRnebu.

Kuykendall, C. (1991). *From rage to hope: Strategies for reclaiming Black and Hispanic students*. Bloomingdale, IN: National Educational Service.

Lopez, S. (2010). Making ripples: How principals and teachers can spread hope throughout our schools. *Phi Delta Kappan, 92*(2), 40–44.

Lopez, S. J., Rose, S., Robinson, C., Marques, S. C., & Pais-Rubeiro, J. (2009). Measuring and promoting hope in schoolchildren. In R. Gilman, E. S. Huebner, & M. J. Furlong (Eds.), *Handbook of positive psychology in the schools* (pp. 37–51). New York, NY: Routledge.

Malle, B. F., & Knobe, J. (2001). The distinction between desire and intention: A folk-conceptual analysis. In B. F. Malle, L. J. Moses, & D. A. Baldwin (Eds.), *Intentions and intersectionality: Foundations of social cognition* (pp. 45–67). Cambridge, MA: MIT Press.

Miceli, M., & Castelfranchi, C. (2010). Hope: The power of wish and possibility. *Theory & Psychology, 20*(2), 251–276.

Moje, E. B., & Lewis, C. (2009). Examining the opportunity to learn literacy: The role of critical sociocultural literacy research. In C. Lewis, P. Enisco, & E. B. Moje (Eds.), *Reframing sociocultural research on literacy: Identity, agency, and power* (pp. 15–48). New York, NY: Routledge.

Murdock, M. (2007). *Signposts to your assignment*. Fort Worth, TX: The Wisdom Center.

National Center for Education Statistics (NCES). (2014). The condition of education. *U.S. Department of Education*. Washington, DC. Retrieved from https://nces.ed.gov/pubs2014/2014083.pdf.

Ohio Board Certified Teachers. (2006). *Meeting all students' needs: What will it take for all educators to be able to meet the needs of all students?* Retrieved from http://www.ohionbctsummit.org/documents/Meeting%20All%20Students%20Needs_10-25-06.pdf.

Pennebaker, J. W. (1989). Stream of consciousness and stress: Levels of thinking. In J. S. Uleman & J. A. Bargh (Eds.), *Unintended thought* (pp. 327–349). New York, NY: Guilford.

Robb, S., O'Leary, P., Mackinnon, A., & Bishop, P. (2010). *Hope: The everyday and imaginary life of young people on the margins*. Kent Town, MA: Wakefield Press.

Robitschek, C. (1996). At-risk youth and hope: Incorporating a ropes course into a summer jobs program. *The Career Development Quarterly, 45*(2), 163–169.

Roseman, I. J., Spindle, M. S., & Jose, P. E. (1990). Appraisals of emotion-eliciting events: Testing a theory of discrete emotions. *Journal of Personality and Social Psychology, 59*(5), 899–915.

Scheier, M. F., & Carver, C. S. (1985). Optimism, coping, and health: Assessment and implications of generalized outcome expectancies. *Health Psychology, 4*(3), 219–247.

Snyder, C. R. (1994). *The psychology of hope: You can get there from here*. New York, NY: Free Press.

Snyder, C. R. (Ed.). (2000a). *Handbook of hope: Theory, measures, and applications*. San Diego, CA: Academic Press.

Snyder, C. R. (2000b). The past and possible futures of hope. *Journal of Social and Clinical Psychology, 19*(1), 11–18.

Snyder, C. R., Cheavens, J., & Sympson, S. C. (1997). Hope: An individual motive for social commerce. *Group Dynamic: Theory, Research, and Practice, 1*(2), 107–118.

Snyder, C. R., Feldman, D. B., Taylor, J. D., Schroeder, L .L., & Adams III, V. H. (2000). The roles of hopeful thinking in preventing problems and promoting strengths. *Applied & Preventive Psychology: Current Scientific Perspectives, 15,* 262–295.

Snyder, C. R., Harris, C., Anderson, J. R., Holleran, S. A., Irving, L. M., Sigmon, S. T., Oshinobu, L., Gibb, J., Langelle, C., & Harney, P. (1991). The will and the ways: Development and validation of an individual-differences measure of hope. *Journal of Personality and Social Psychology, 60*(4), 570–585.

Snyder, C. R., Shorey, H. S., Cheavens, J., Pulvers, K. M., Adams III, V. H., & Wiklund, C. (2002). Hope and academic success in college. *Journal of Educational Psychology, 94*(4), 820–826.

Webster-Smith, A. (2010). Hope-based schooling that advances democracy: The mission of 21st century leaders. *Learning for Democracy, 3(*3), 144–152.

Webster-Smith, A. (2017). Enhancing efficacy with the disposition of CARE. In Freddie A. Bowles & Cathy J. Pearman (Eds.), *Self-efficacy in action: Tales from the classroom for teaching, learning, and professional development* (pp. 13–25). Lanham, MD: Rowman & Littlefield.

Extension Questions for Reflection and Conversation

LeAnn G. Putney and Nancy P. Gallavan

The eight chapters selected for Section II share authors' research findings associated with inspirations and aspirations for teachers and school leaders exhibiting effective leadership. The coeditors of ATE Yearbook XXVI have provided extension questions to prompt reflection and conversation for each of the chapters.

Chapter 9, authored by Denise Demers of the University of Central Arkansas, titled "Preparing the Leaders/Teachers of Tomorrow by Improving the Well-Being of Teachers Today," reveals important information related to understanding how to assist teachers in coping with additional work-related stress in the ever-changing world of educational achievement and goal attainment.

Extension Questions for Reflection and Conversation:

1. What are the top five sources of stress for teachers reported in this study?
2. In what ways might we reduce demoralization of teachers related to administrative decision-making?
3. Why does the level of stress increase for achievement goal-oriented teachers when bureaucratic issues prevail?
4. How might we increase the level of social support for classroom teachers?
5. How might we incorporate mindfulness training in our schools?

Chapter 10 is titled "'I Need Collaboration Too!' Exploring the Nature of Collaboration between a Literacy Coach and University Teacher Collaborator" and is authored by Grace Kang of Illinois State University. In this qualitative study, Kang examines the collaborations between a literacy coach, classroom teachers, and a university teacher collaborator.

Extension Questions for Reflection and Conversation:

1. What are the four valued tenets of collaboration?
2. What are the different roles identified that literacy coaches can employ?
3. In what ways can literacy coaches help to improve student learning?
4. What role did scaffolding play in bolstering the relationships Claire developed with the teachers?
5. How did Claire and Heidi's collaborative relationship result in improved coaching on the part of Claire with the classroom teachers?

In chapter 11 we encounter Sarah Irvine Belson from American University with her study titled "Charter School Special Educators: Expressions of Hope, Courage, and Strength." This study is an examination of the work of special educators in public charter schools and how they work to serve students with disabilities in spite of encountering funding and curricular issues.

Extension Questions for Reflection and Conversation:

1. What ideals should drive special education teachers to work for student success?
2. What strategies might special education teachers use that demonstrate resilience?
3. What do students with special needs need aside from assistance with academics?
4. What are some of the characteristics of the teachers of focus in the study?
5. What are some strategies the teachers of focus make special connections with their students?

Chapter 12 titled, "Preparing Elementary School Mathematics Specialists: Aspirations for a University Endorsement Program" was authored by Susan Swars Auslander and Stephanie Z. Smith from Georgia State University along with Marvin E. Smith from Kennesaw State University.

Extension Questions for Reflection and Conversation:

1. What are the challenges in preparing elementary school teachers for mathematics?
2. What are the critical program areas that would be addressed by a math specialist preparation model?
3. What are some specific methods for engaging teacher learning in mathematics?
4. How did the K-5 ME Program promote learning during course sessions?
5. How does the Cognitively Guided Instruction (CGI) approach differ from other approaches in terms of focusing teacher's knowledge?
6. What improvements did teachers recognize in student learning through this program?

In chapter 13, "Fighting for Hope and Inspiration: Developing Reflective Spaces for Leaders in Elementary School Mathematics," is prepared by collaborating authors Ryan Flessner from Butler University, Courtney Flessner from Indiana University, Katherine Reed, from the Hinkle Creek Elementary School, and Susan Adamson, also from Butler University. Their study documents what mathematical leadership can look like in our current educational landscape.

Extension Questions for Reflection and Conversation:

1. What have been the results of the implementation of the Common Core State Standards in the teaching of mathematics in this chapter?
2. How were vignettes used in this study for reflective practice?
3. What were the themes discussed that teachers found in common across their classroom experiences?
4. What did Katherine learn about collaboration from her vignette study?
5. In what ways might vignettes be used to inspire teachers in their respective classroom settings?

Chapter 14, brings us "The Impact of Privatized Funding in Education and a Proposal for Reform," authored by Todd Cherner of Portland State University and Catherine M. Scott of Coastal Carolina University. The authors offer an alternative, grassroots model for applying for grants to help in further initiatives that align with public education issues.

Extension Questions for Reflection and Conversation:

1. What are the three driving forces of public education identified in this chapter?
2. Why is it an issue for private groups to fund public education?
3. What was the original rationale for charter schools?
4. What is different about the newest version Every Student Succeeds Act (ESSA)?
5. Why would a bottom-up approach to external grants improve reform efforts?

Chapter 15, "Urban Teacher Collective Efficacy through Facilitative Leadership: An Illustrative Dialogue" is co-authored by Shelley Nordick from Jordan School District, Suzanne H. Jones from Utah State University, LeAnn G. Putney from the University of Nevada, Las Vegas, and Connie L. Malin from Innovations International Charter School of Nevada. This chapter offers insights into actions of a facilitative leader who promotes school-wide efficacy.

Extension Questions for Reflection and Conversation:

1. How does the role of community organizer shift when applied to school principal rather than classroom teacher?
2. How was the video library of successful teacher practice beneficial to other teachers in the school?
3. Given the example of "hopeful determination," in the chapter, what example can you think of from your experience that would illustrate this construct?
4. How have the teachers benefitted from the PLC team meetings?
5. How did the principle work to build capacity of the teachers?
6. Why does building teacher capacity improve school and classroom efficacy?

Chapter 16 completes the Yearbook with Angela Webster of the University of Central Arkansas in her study titled, "Are You a Hope Buster or Hope Muster?" Webster provides an examination of hope-based schools to shed light on what educators can do to introduce goals, pathways, and agency to maximize hope in schools.

Extension Questions for Reflection and Conversation:

1. What are some differences between hope and optimism?
2. What school factors influence a student's high hope status?
3. What type of culture is the hallmarks of hope-based schools?
4. What are the components of grit development?
5. How do hope-based strategies help students overcome perceived inabilities?

The eight chapters of Section Two, associated with the factors of hope, strength, and courage that impact the inspirations and aspirations of leaders and leading, include studies from the field as well as concept pieces about school reform efforts. In all these chapters make visible the need for promoting a hope-based effort in schools and classrooms, to ensure efficacy of teachers and students throughout our educational system. These efforts are crucial for all students, but particularly for our schools with highly vulnerable students with special needs and from linguistically and economically diverse backgrounds. Even the suggestions about approaching school reform and external funding were grounded in hope-based strategies.

Written by authors from various types of institutions, and multiple perspectives, along with theoretically grounded practitioners, Section Two makes visible the importance and benefits of conducting research and reporting findings for educational professionals and teacher educators in all capacities to extend their knowledge base relative to engendering hope and efficacy in our schools.

Afterword

Napoleon Hill (n.d.), a U.S. novelist (1883–1970), wrote, "Patience, persistence, and perspiration make an unbeatable combination for success." And Albert Bandura (n.d.), a U.S. psychologist (1925–), wrote, "In order to succeed, people need a sense of self-efficacy, to struggle together with resilience to meet the inevitable obstacles and inequities of life." These insightful quotes embody the influence of two powerful forces, persistence and resilience, which help us balance our daily encounters and existence.

Each of us relies on our individual preserves of persistence to remain calmly focused, to exert determined tenacity, and to generate seemingly endless energy. Through persistence, educators, specifically, establish their goals personally, professionally, and pedagogically; start their journeys; and invest themselves into their advancement toward achievement. Educators' paths of persistence integrate hope, courage, and strength as inspirations of optimism, boldness, and vitality to stay the course and, usually, enjoy the journey.

Feelings of success and satisfaction contribute to the development of self-efficacy: understanding and accepting one's capacity to produce desirable outcomes in ways that demonstrate responsibility to everyone affected and ownership for attitudes and actions. Educators, especially teacher candidates, benefit from opportunities for investigation, disaggregation, reflection, and articulation related to their understanding and development of self-efficacy in relationship to guiding and supporting their students. Educators of all ages and in all stages of education must reach deep inside themselves to be aware of and accountable for their educational commitments.

Likewise, each of us also relies upon our individual reserves of resilience to draw upon our spirited resolute to remain flexible, to sustain our open readiness, to analyze situations from multiple perspectives as we encounter inevitable obstacles, and to judiciously resolve them in ways that promote peace and understanding. Furthermore, we must both recognize and reconcile the inequities of life by providing comprehensive information, access, and opportunities for everyone to promote cultural competence in ourselves, for others, and across society in ways that are honest, natural, authentic, and holistic. Partnered with persistence, educators' reservoirs of resilience incorporate hope, courage, and strength as aspirations of enthusiasm, confidence, and stamina to guide, guard, and support educators' journeys.

Recently a novice classroom teacher reflected, "I always wanted to be a teacher; I visualized my life-long career enriched by learning all I could, reaching every child, and becoming the best teacher possible. I am well-parented, well-educated, well-read, well-traveled, well-prepared, and well-experienced for the classroom, students, and parents; plus I am 'rarin' to go' (as my father would say to me). I have earned a master's degree and worked with children in various capacities. I bought a home and I'm active in the community. I have so much to offer any student, classroom, and school . . . and I was sure that I would love it. But, now that I'm here in the classroom, I'm afraid of the future. I believe I have the determination, but I'm not sure I have the hardiness that being an effective teacher seems to require. Can I really fulfill all the expectations (that seem to increase daily), maintain my well-being, and enjoy life?"

This revealing narrative encapsulates the desire and need for inspiration (vision) and aspiration (vigor) synchronized with persistence (endurance) and resilience (elasticity) voiced by many contemporary classroom teachers. Most likely, you know novice teachers expressing these concerns; perhaps as a classroom teacher, school administrator, or teacher educator, you have expressed or find yourself stating similar concerns. Articulation of the dynamics impacting today's educators must be accompanied with positive and productive attitudes and actions to advance self-efficacy and professionalism.

From her research with novice classroom teachers, Tait (2013) suggests seven strategies for reinforcing resilience that may benefit each of us. The seven strategies include (1) Demonstrating Social Competence—establishing a network of family, friends, mentors, and so on to listen attentively and to offer feedback supportively. (2) Accessing Available Opportunities and Developing Self-Efficacy—seeking colleagues to conduct classroom observations to build upon effectiveness and to identify areas needing attention. (3) Using Problem-Solving Strategies—reflecting on challenges objectively, asking colleagues for recommendations and resources, and projecting possible solutions. (4) Rebounding from Difficulties—identifying difficulties, prioritizing energies, and rallying to start anew. (5) Learning from Experience and Setting Future Goals—gaining insights from effective and ineffective teaching and learning experiences to advance new goals and outcomes.

(6) Taking Care of Oneself—reflecting realistically on one's well-being and striving for balance to stay healthy: physically, mentally, socially, and emotionally. (7) Maintaining a Sense of Optimism—creating a metaphor of effective teaching and learning (and perhaps placing an artifact or photograph of the artifact) in the classroom to highlight hope, courage, and strength.

All educators profit with increased awareness of their own inspirations and aspirations synchronized with their persistence and resilience, especially resilience. Resilience must be nurtured both internally by the individual and externally by family, friends, colleagues, mentors, and so on. As novice teachers (and novice teacher educators) grow and develop into master teachers (and master teacher educators), they become the sources and supporters of novice teachers (and teacher educators) through their attitudes and actions to advance hope, courage, and strength.

REFERENCES

Bandura, A. (n.d.). BrainyQuote. Retrieved from https://www.brainyquote.com/authors/albert_bandura.

Hill, N. (n.d.). BrainyQuote. Retrieved from https://www.brainyquote.com/authors/napoleon_hill.

Tait, M. (2008). Resilience as a contributor to novice teacher success, commitment, and retention. *Teacher Education Quarterly, 35*(4), 57–75.

References

Association of Teacher Educators (ATE). (2014). ATE Yearbook XXV and XXVI call for proposals. Retrieved from http://www.ate1.org/pubs/Call_for_Yearbook__1.cfm.

Bandura, A. (n.d.). BrainyQuote. Retrieved from https://www.brainyquote.com/authors/albert_bandura.

Cochran-Smith, M. (2017). *Democratic accountability in teacher education: Now more than ever*. Keynote address presented at the 42nd annual meeting of the Association of Teacher Educators Europe. Dubrovnik, Croatia, October 25–27.

Dewey, J. (1916). *Democracy and education: An introduction to the philosophy of education*. NY: Macmillan Company.

Embry-Jenlink, K. (2017). *Preparing the next generation of educators for democracy*. Keynote address presented to the Southeastern Regional Association of Teacher Educators (SRATE) 42nd annual meeting in Rogers, AR, October 5–7.

Forsyth, P. B., Adams, C. R., & Hoy, W. K. (2011). *Foundations of collective trust in schools*. New York, NY: Teachers College Press.

Goodard, R. D., Hoy, W. K., & Hoy, A. (2004). Collective efficacy beliefs: Theoretical developments, empirical evidence, and future directions. *Educational Researcher, 33*(3), 3–13.

Goddard, R. D., Tschannen-Moran, M., & Hoy, W. K. (2001). Teacher trust in students and parents: A multilevel examination of the distribution and effects of teacher trust in urban elementary schools. *Elementary School Journal, 102*(1), 3–17.

Hill, N. (n.d.). BrainyQuote. Retrieved from https://www.brainyquote.com/authors/napoleon_hill.

Hoy, W. K., & Tarter, C. J. (2011). Positive psychology and educational administration: An optimistic research agenda. *Educational Administration Quarterly, 47*(3), 427–445.

Johnson, S. M., & Birkeland, S. E. (2003). Pursuing a "sense of success": New teachers explain their career decisions. *American Educational Research Journal, 40*(3), 581–617.

Ladd, H. F. (2011). Teachers' perceptions of their working conditions: How predictive of planned and actual teacher movement? *Educational Evaluation and Policy Analysis, 33*(2), 235–261.

Leech, N. L., & Haug, C. A. (2015). Teacher workforce: Understanding the relationship among teacher demographics, preparation programs, performance, and persistence. *Research in the Schools, 22*(1), 15–26.

Mezirow, J. (1994). Understanding transformation theory. *Adult Education Quarterly, 44*(4), 222–232.

Patterson, A. D., McGeoch, D. M., & Olsen, H. C. (1990). *A brief history of the association of teacher educators, 1920–1990*. Retrieved from https://www.ate1.org/history.

Putney, L. G., & Broughton, S. (2011). Developing classroom collective efficacy: The teacher's role as community organizer. *Journal of Teacher Education, 62*(1), 93–105.

Seligman, M. E. P., & Csikszentmihalyi, M. (2000). Positive psychology: An introduction. *American Psychologist, 55*(1), 5–14.

Shirrell, M., & Reininger, M. (2017). School working conditions and changes in student teachers' planned persistence in teaching. *Teacher Education Quarterly, 44*(2), 49–78.

Smith, P. A., Hoy, W. K., & Sweetland, S. R. (2001). Organizational health of high schools and dimensions of faculty trust. *Journal of School Leadership, 11*(2), 135–151.

Sutcliffe, K. M., & Vogus, T. J. (2003). Organizing for resilience. In Cameron, K., Dutton, J. E., & Quinn, R. E. (Eds.), *Positive Organizational Scholarship* (pp: 94–110). San Francisco: Berrett-Koehler. Chapter 7.

Tait, M. (2008). Resilience as a contributor to novice teacher success, commitment, and retention. *Teacher Education Quarterly, 35*(4), 57–75.

Tschannen-Moran, M., Woolfolk Hoy, A., & Hoy, W. K. (1998). Teacher efficacy: Its meaning and measure. *Review of Educational Research, 68*(2), 202–248.

Wheatley, K. F. (2002, Sept). Teacher persistence: A crucial disposition, with implications for teacher education. *Essays in Education, 3*. Retrieved from https://www.researchgate.net/publication/268441017_Teacher_Persistence_A_Crucial_Disposition_with_Implications_for_Teacher_Education.

About the Contributors

Susan Adamson, PhD, is an assistant professor of teacher education at Butler University and director of the Indiana Partnership for Young Writers, and believes in the power of publishing to celebrate and illuminate the craft and process of writing. She works to support pre-service/in-service teachers in developing multicultural learning communities through workshop teaching.

Glenda L. Black is an associate professor at Nipissing University. As a member of the Schulich School of Education, she teaches in the Bachelor of Education and Graduate Studies programs. Dr. Black is a faculty facilitator for the Biidaaban Community Service-Learning program. Her research interests are in curriculum development and assessment, international teaching practicums, and indigenous education.

Angela Malone Cartwright, PhD, is an assistant professor at Midwestern State University, Wichita Falls, Texas. She received a BA in Integrated Social Studies 7–12 from Mount Vernon Nazarene University; an MA in Drama, Literacy, Language Arts, and Reading; and a PhD in Multicultural and Equity Studies in Education, both from Ohio State University. Her research interests include multicultural and social justice education with a focus on cultural competency in teacher education.

Nancy Caukin is an assistant professor in the College of Education at Middle Tennessee State University. Her research interests began with science writing heuristics, scientific epistemological view, and science self-efficacy. Dr. Caukin's research interests have turned to impacts of Residency I on teacher candidate beliefs, self-efficacy, and teaching philosophy statement.

Todd Cherner, PhD, is an assistant professor of education in Portland State University's Graduate School of Education. Cherner specializes in using instructional technology to develop students' literacy abilities across the content areas, and he is committed to the purposeful use of technology to promote students' reading and writing in the classroom. His past research has offered tools, strategies, rubrics, and frameworks that teachers can blend into their instruction. Cherner works to bridge the research-to-practice gap via App Ed Review, a website he co-founded that shares practical advice for edtech-using teachers.

Daphney L. Curry, PhD, is an assistant professor and interim chair of the Curriculum and Learning Department in the West College of Education at Midwestern State University. She received a BSIS and an MEd in Reading from Midwestern State University and a PhD in Language and Literacy Studies with a minor in Early Childhood Studies from the University of North Texas. She entered the teaching profession as a special education and early childhood teacher. She continued her professional career at the university level and currently works with pre-service and classroom teachers in professional development schools. Her research interests focus on new literacies, professional learning communities, and professional development schools.

Denise Demers, PhD, CHES, is an assistant professor at the University of Central Arkansas. Her research is centered on the mental health of women and women and/or mother-students. Particularly, she is interested in how they take care of their health amid the demands of school and family. Additionally, she is part of motherscholar research, adding to the literature of the work-family balance. Women, particularly mothers, in academia (from elementary school to higher education) find themselves overwhelmed with the load. Denise wants to find ways to ease the ubiquitous struggles.

Heather K. Dillard is an assistant professor in the Department of Educational Leadership at Middle Tennessee State University and specializes in professional learning communities, self-efficacy, and new teacher attrition. Previously, Dr. Dillard taught middle and high school social studies for sixteen years.

Kim Dockery is the former principal of Westlawn Elementary in Fairfax County Public Schools. She led the design of the Teacher Leadership Institute that extended teachers contracts to buy teacher more time to collaborate and for professional development. She was hired as the superintendent of instructional services and since then has retired and serves as an educational consultant on the topic of strengthening professional learning communities in schools.

Karen Embry-Jenlink, ATE President (2017–2018), is a professor of doctoral studies in educational leadership at Stephen F. Austin State University in Nacogdoches, TX. Throughout her thirty-year career in education, Dr. Embry-Jenlink has worked to promote equity, democracy, and creativity in P-12 schools and in higher education. She has published over sixty scholarly, peer-refereed articles and book chapters and authored three books. For her innovation and service to education, she has received numerous awards, including Outstanding College of Education Alumnae (TAMU, 2005), and she was awarded honorary lifetime member of the TXPTA for her service to public education in Texas (2014). She currently serves on the ATE Board of Directors and the Board of Directors of the World Federation of the Association of Teacher Educators.

Courtney Flessner is a PhD candidate double majoring in Educational Policy & Leadership and Mathematics Education at Indiana University. At various points in her career, Courtney has served as a teacher, instructional coach, and school administrator. Courtney is passionate about how school cultures shape the teaching and learning of mathematics.

Ryan Flessner, PhD, is an associate professor of teacher education at Butler University. His teaching and research interests include elementary education, mathematics education, practitioner inquiry, and issues of diversity, equity, and social justice. Prior to working in higher education, Ryan taught elementary school students in Indianapolis, New York City, and Madison, Wisconsin.

Nancy P. Gallavan, PhD, is professor of teacher education in the Department of Teaching and Learning at the University of Central Arkansas, and specializes in classroom assessments, cultural competence, social studies education, and internship supervision in their nationally recognized MAT Program. With 20 years of experience in K-12 education, 25 years of experience in higher education, and 180+ peer-reviewed publications across her areas of expertise, Nancy has received awards for teaching, service, and scholarship. Notably, Nancy served as the 2013–2014 ATE President and was honored as a 2013 KDP Eleanor Roosevelt Legacy Chapter inaugural member and a 2016 ATE Distinguished Member.

Mair Greenfield is the Indigenous Education Lead at the Rumie Initiative. Greenfield works with Indigenous communities and partners to support community-voiced projects by pinpointing and collecting resources that are already found on the Internet. Projects include language preservation, culturally relevant teaching resources, self-care, reconciliation, and curriculum support for learners and teachers. Greenfield is a member of Kebaowek First Nation.

Sarah Irvine Belson, PhD, researches educational opportunities for children with disabilities and teacher education policy. Her focus is on applied interventions for children at risk in technology and teacher preparation. His work includes books and articles on special education interventions including reducing cognitive load in children with specific learning disabilities.

Leona M. Johnson, PhD, is assistant dean and associate professor in the Department of Psychology at Hampton University, and specializes in teaching and learning styles, cultural competence, and pedagogical methodology. Leona has fifteen years of experience in higher education with many peer-reviewed journals, a book, and a book chapter across her area of expertise in educational psychology. Johnson serves as a member of the ATE Nominations Committee and is a member of the 2018 ATE Summer Conference Planning Committee.

Suzanne H. Jones, PhD, is an associate professor in the School of Teacher Education and Leadership at Utah State University. She is a former elementary school teacher. Suzanne's research primarily focuses on the role of emotions in learning, including topic emotions for fostering conceptual change. She recently began investigating hope as a motivational factor with learning. In addition, Suzanne's research examines collective classroom efficacy as well as teacher collective efficacy. She received her doctorate in educational psychology from the University of Nevada, Las Vegas.

Grace Kang, PhD, is an assistant professor in the School of Teaching and Learning at Illinois State University. She teaches various literacy courses and conducts research surrounding professional development, collaboration, literacy practices, digital literacies, and teaching in diverse racial and linguistic contexts.

Jayne M. Leh, PhD, is an assistant professor of special education at Pennsylvania State University Berks, and investigates methods to prepare teacher candidates for diverse classrooms through field experiences with students in diverse settings. Her interest areas include childhood trauma resulting from school violence, problem behavior, and mathematics word problem solving for low-performing students.

Connie L. Malin, PhD, serves as co-founder and CEO at Innovations International Charter School of NV (IICSN), a K-12 public community charter school serving highly diverse families in Las Vegas. She earned a master's in elementary education with literacy specialization, a second master's in special education with learning disabilities and gifted education as a specialization, a doctorate in special education from UNLV, and an administrative credential at UNLV. Along with twenty-five years of educational experience in district elementary schools, Connie has over fifteen years of experience in charter schools in Nevada.

Jennifer P. Merritt is a former middle school and high school art teacher in Arkansas who taught art for six years both in classrooms and online for rural schools sharing art teachers. Jennifer earned her undergraduate degree at Ouachita Baptist University and her master of art in teaching (MAT) at the University of Central Arkansas, where she serves as an adjunct instructor supervising MAT interns primarily in K-12 art classrooms. Additionally she teaches individual art classes for all ages in the community and for large groups in a popular painting store.

Shelley Nordick, PhD, is an educator with 30 years of experience in Jordan School District, a K-12 Utah district serving over 53,000 students. Shelley began her career as a classroom teacher in the district and has served as a technology teacher specialist, a middle school assistant principal, an elementary school principal, a district consultant, and currently serves as staff assistant in curriculum and staff development. Shelley earned a bachelor's degree in elementary education from Utah State University, a master's in curriculum with a specialization in instructional technology from the University of Texas in Austin, and a doctorate in educational leadership from Utah State University.

LeAnn G. Putney, PhD, is a full professor in educational psychology at UNLV. Her ethnographic and action research projects have focused on how teachers and students construct responsible communities for academic success in K-12 schools. She has examined teacher and collective classroom efficacy from a Vygotskian perspective to illustrate how efficacy can be developed and enhanced. She also coauthored *A Vision of Vygotsky*, a book on Vygotskian theories related to pedagogical principles for teachers. LeAnn co-founded Innovations International Charter School of NV (IICSN) and serves as director of Research and Governing Body President.

Katherine Reed is an assistant principal at Hinkle Creek Elementary in Noblesville, Indiana. She is passionate about providing spaces in which teachers and students alike can engage in "real" learning through practices that promote reflective inquiry. And above all, she pledges to Choose Kind.

Emily Reeves, PhD, is an assistant professor at Midwestern State University, Wichita Falls, Texas. She received a BSIS in interdisciplinary studies and an

MEd in education administration from Lubbock Christian University and a PhD in curriculum and instruction focusing on language and literacy from Texas Tech University. Her research interest include culturally responsive pedagogy supporting literacy with a focus on developing culturally responsive teachers.

Catherine M. Scott, PhD, earned her PhD in elementary science and Math education from the University of North Carolina at Greensboro and her master's degree in K-6 Science Education from the University of North Carolina at Greensboro. Dr. Scott spent five years teaching elementary school at the 4th, 5th, and K-5 Science levels. Her scholarship is in the area of outdoor and environmental education.

Marvin E. Smith, PhD, is an associate professor in the Elementary and Early Childhood Education Department at Kennesaw State University. His interests include learning and teaching elementary mathematics, classroom assessment, and teacher education and development.

Stephanie Z. Smith, PhD, is an associate professor in the Early Childhood and Elementary Education Department at Georgia State University. Her scholarly interests include learning and teaching elementary mathematics, conceptions of mathematics, and teacher education and development.

Jennifer M. Suh, PhD, is an associate professor in the Graduate School of Education, George Mason University. Dr. Suh teaches mathematics courses in the Mathematics Education Leadership and Elementary Education programs. Dr. Suh is also the PDS University Facilitator at Westlawn Elementary School in Falls Church, Virginia. Her research focuses on professional development schools as site for teacher learning and lesson study.

Susan Swars Auslander, PhD, is an associate professor in the Early Childhood and Elementary Education Department at Georgia State University. Her scholarly interest is elementary teacher development within university mathematics courses having varying contexts, features, and experiences, with a focus on the outcomes of beliefs and content knowledge.

Angela Webster, PhD, serves as associate vice president for Institutional Diversity and associate professor of Leadership Studies at the University of Central Arkansas. She specializes in K-16 inclusive leadership. Webster authored *In the Presence of a King* about her childhood experience of hearing the final speech of Dr. Martin Luther King, Jr. She is an American Council on Education Fellow, received a 2016 National Role Model Administrator Award, and a 2014 President's Service Award from ATE.

www.ingramcontent.com/pod-product-compliance
Lightning Source LLC
Chambersburg PA
CBHW071759300426
44116CB00009B/1143